NATIONAL GEOGRAPHIC

Science

INQUIRY • CONTENT • LITERACY

TEACHER'S EDITION

Rocks and Soil

Earth Science

PROGRAM AUTHORS

Kathy Cabe Trundle, Ph.D.

Randy Bell, Ph.D.

Malcolm B. Butler, Ph.D.

Nell K. Duke, Ed.D.

Judith S. Lederman, Ph.D.

David W. Moore, Ph.D.

Built to target your standards, *National Geographic Science* is a research-based program that brings science learning to life through the lens of National Geographic.

Promote Science success as you share

The National Geographic Experience . . .

- **Immerse Students in the Nature of Science and Inquiry**
- **Unlock the Big Ideas in Science for All Learners**
- **Build Scientific and Content Literacy**

Earth

Physical

Immerse Students in: The Nature of Science

In *National Geographic Science* process skills build at each grade level to ensure a complete understanding of the Nature of Science. This chart shows how process skills and the Nature of Science work together to help students think and act like scientists.

	Grade K	Grades 1 & 2
PROCESS SKILLS	**OBSERVE**	**OBSERVE & INFER**
Nature of Science	• Science knowledge is based on evidence. • Science knowledge can change based on new evidence.	• Science conclusions are based on observation and inference. • Science theories are based partly on things that cannot be observed.

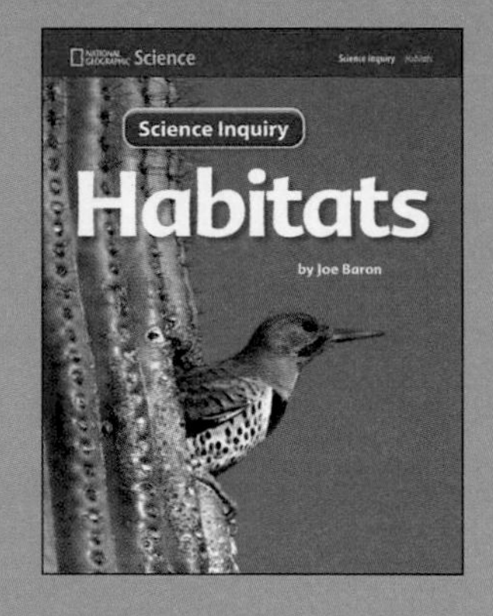

Immerse Students in: Leveled, Hands-on Inquiry

National Geographic Science provides students with abundant and relevant hands-on explorations to facilitate a thorough understanding of key Science concepts. The four levels of inquiry in *National Geographic Science* are designed to help students build confidence and competence in scientific thought and inquiry.

Explore Activity

The *Explore Activity* builds background for the unit. This activity *Engages* students as they *Explore*.

Explore Activity

Investigate Habitats

Question: Which plants and animals live on land and which live in water?

Science Process Vocabulary

observe verb

When you **observe**, you use your senses to learn about an object or event.

Materials: two sorting circles, blue and green cards, marker, plant picture cards, animal pi[cture] cards

What to Do

1. Unfold your sorting circles.

Directed Inquiry

In *Directed Inquiry,* the teacher gives direct instruction throughout the activity. Students are given opportunities to *Explain* what they have done, *Elaborate* by asking further questions, and *Evaluate* by using a self-reflection rubric.

Directed Inquiry

Investigate How Desert Plants Survive

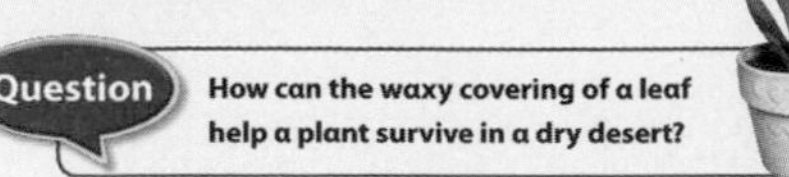

Question: How can the waxy covering of a leaf help a plant survive in a dry desert?

Science Process Vocabulary

model noun

You can make a **model** to show how something works.

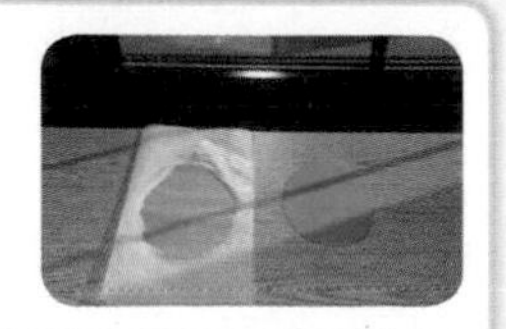

predict verb

Materials: green construction paper, scissors, spray bottle with water, waxed paper

What to Do

1. Draw two leaf shapes. Cut out the leaf shapes. These are **models** of leaves.
2. Spray both leaf models with the same amount of water.

Grade 3

CLASSIFY

- There is often no single "right" answer in science.

Grade 4

PREDICT/HYPOTHESIZE

- Scientific theories provide the base upon which predictions and hypotheses are built.

Grade 5

DESIGN EXPERIMENTS

- There is no single scientific method that all scientists follow.
- There are a number of ways to do science.

Also Includes

Science in a Snap!

Offers quick investigations to activate understanding of science concepts.

Guided Inquiry

In *Guided Inquiry*, students become independent learners with guidance from the teacher. Students manipulate variables, provide *Explanations, Elaborate* by asking further questions, and *Evaluate* by using a self-reflection rubric.

Guided Inquiry

Investigate a Mealworm Habitat

Question What happens if mealworms are given more than one type of food?

Science Process Vocabulary

predict verb

When you tell how you

Materials

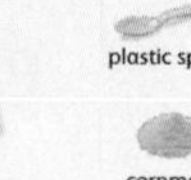
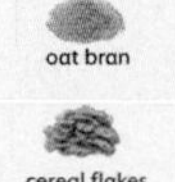

Do a Fair Test

Write your plan in your science notebook.

Make a Prediction

Mealworms eat food that comes from plants. In this investigation, you will give cornmeal to mealworms. You will choose a second food for the mealworms. Will more mealworms move to one of the foods? Write your **prediction.**

19

Open Inquiry

In *Open Inquiry,* students choose their own questions, create their own plans, carry out their plans, collect and record their own data, look for patterns, and share that data. Students *Explain* their results, *Elaborate* by asking further questions, and *Evaluate* by using a self-reflection rubric.

Open Inquiry

Do Your Own Investigation

Question Choose a question or make up one of your own to do your investigation.

- What happens if you plant a water plant on dry land?
- What happens if some bean seeds get water and others do not?
- What happens if you give mealworms a choice of dark or light habitats?

Science Process Vocabulary

data noun

You collect **data** when you gather information in an investigation.

Open Inquiry Checklist

Here is a checklist you can use when you investigate.

- ☐ Choose a **question** or make up one of your own.
- ☐ Gather the materials you will use.
- ☐ Tell what you **predict.**
- ☐ Plan a **fair test.**
- ☐ Make a **plan** for your investigation.
- ☐ Carry out your **plan.**
- ☐ Collect and record **data.** Look for **patterns** in your data.
- ☐ Explain and **share** your results.

The Big Ideas in Science Unlocked and In Depth

The Big Ideas in Science should be targeted and focused for the teacher and the student. Therefore, *National Geographic Science* was created to be targeted and focused on these Big Ideas in Science as well.

Big Idea Questions

1. Where do plants and animals live?

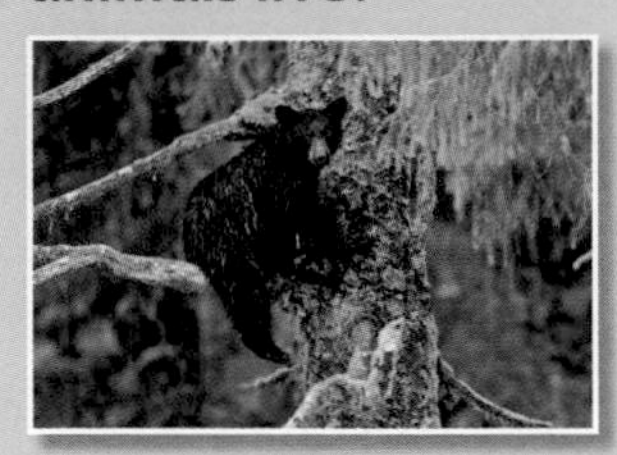

2. What do plants and animals need to survive?

3. How do plants and animals depend on each other?

Each chapter in each unit centers on one Big Idea that focuses instruction on your science standards.

Science Vocabulary

Earth (page 5)
Earth is the planet on which we live.

energy (page 28)
Energy is the ability to do active things.

habitat (page 7)
A **habitat** is a place where living things can get what they need to stay alive.

nutrients (page 26)
Nutrients are parts of food and soil. They help living things stay healthy and grow.

oxygen (page 30)
Oxygen is a gas in air and water.

shelter (page 18)
A **shelter** is a safe place where a living thing can make its home and grow.

survive (page 17)
When living things **survive,** they get what they need to stay alive.

Academic vocabulary is a key to student success in understanding science concepts. Academic vocabulary is pictured, defined in context, and taught to ensure understanding and success for ALL students.

Chapter 1

Big Idea Question

Where Do Plants and Animals Live?

Plants and animals live almost every place on Earth. These places can be wet or dry or hot or cold.

A place where plants and animals get what they need to stay alive is a **habitat**. What are Earth's habitats like? What kinds of plants and animals live in these habitats? Let's find out.

Chapter 2

Big Idea Question

What Do Plants and Animals Need to Survive?

A habitat is important. It provides plants and animals with air, water, food, and space—all the things they need to stay alive, or **survive**.

But a habitat has to be the right match for each animal. For example, a squirrel could not survive in the ocean. And a whale could not survive in a forest.

17

Chapter 3

Big Idea Question

How Do Plants and Animals Depend on Each Other?

Can you imagine a world without plants? Animals could not survive without plants. But plants could survive without animals.

Access Science through Literacy

Students move through multiple leveled experiences to ensure that content understanding is deep and lasting.

Proven Reading Comprehension Strategies to Improve Reading Informational Text Success

Preview and Predict

Monitor and Fix Up

Make Inferences

Sum Up

Guide Application of Multiple Strategies

Leveled Books

Become an Expert books tie directly to the Big Ideas and are presented at three reading levels. This enables you to effectively differentiate instruction for ALL students.

Independent Application of Multiple Strategies

Explore On Your Own books

Build Scientific Literacy for Your Future Scientists

Students will build scientific literacy and gain an understanding of the Nature of Science from real-life National Geographic Explorers. Your students will learn that Science is:

- A way of knowing
- Empirically based and consistent with evidence
- Subject to change when new evidence presents itself
- A creative process

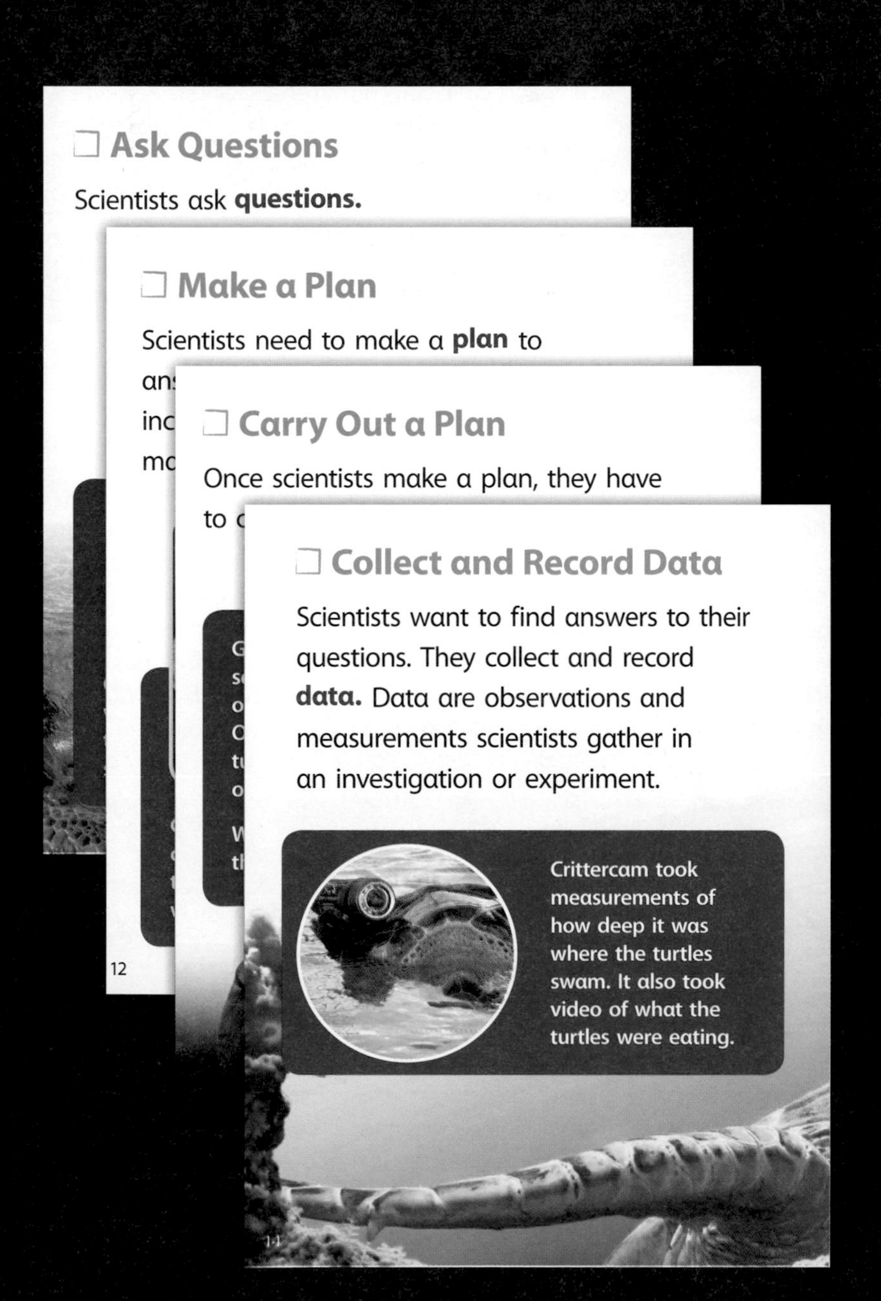

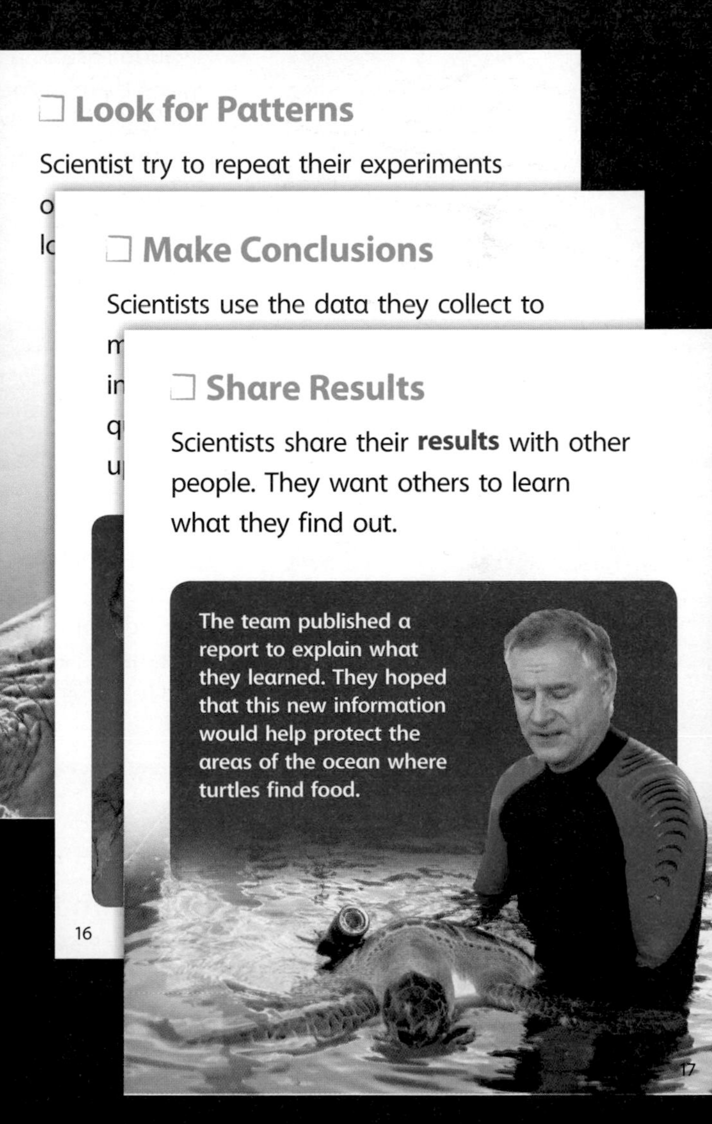

NATIONAL GEOGRAPHIC Science

Program Authors

Kathy Cabe Trundle, Ph.D. **SCIENCE**

Associate Professor of Early Childhood Science Education,
The School of Teaching and Learning,
The Ohio State University, Columbus, Ohio

Dr. Kathy Cabe Trundle has enjoyed her work in science education programs for more than 25 years, including 10 years as a public school teacher. Her research focuses on children and adults' understandings of Earth and space science concepts, including misconceptions and instructional interventions that promote scientific ideas and understandings. Her publications include research reports, professional articles, and curriculum materials. She is also very active in the development of science teacher education and professional development programs. Dr. Cabe Trundle was the recipient of the 2008 Outstanding Teacher Educator of the Year, presented by the Association for Science Teacher Education, an international organization.

Randy Bell, Ph.D. **SCIENCE**

Associate Professor of Science Education,
University of Virginia, Charlottesville, Virginia

Dr. Randy Bell began his career as a forest researcher in the Pacific Northwest. His interest in sharing science with others led him to pursue a teaching license, and he taught science for six years in rural eastern Oregon. Currently, Dr. Bell teaches pre-service teachers, provides professional development for practicing teachers, and researches and develops curricular materials. He has received numerous teaching awards as well as the Early Career Research Award from the National Association for Research in Science Teaching. Dr. Bell has authored dozens of research articles and books, and his two primary areas of research focus on teaching and learning about the nature of science and assessing the impact of educational technology.

Malcolm B. Butler, Ph.D. **SCIENCE**

Associate Professor of Science Education,
University of South Florida, St. Petersburg, Florida

Dr. Malcolm B. Butler's teaching and research address multicultural issues in the classroom. With a specialization in physics, he has worked to support typically underserved student populations and has interests in the areas of writing to learn in science, science content for elementary teachers, and coastal and environmental education professional development for teachers. He has written and contributed to several academic journals, including *The Journal of Research in Science Teaching, The Journal of Science Teacher Education, The Journal of Multicultural Education,* and *Science Activities.*

Nell K. Duke, Ed.D. **LITERACY**

Co-Director of the Literacy Achievement Research Center,
Professor of Teacher Education and Educational Psychology,
Michigan State University, East Lansing, Michigan

Dr. Nell K. Duke's research and teaching focuses primarily on young children—pre-kindergarten through grade two. She is particularly interested in how young children learn to comprehend informational text and what teachers can do to facilitate that process. Dr. Duke has received awards for her research from the International Reading Association, the National Council of Teachers of English, the National Reading Conference, and the American Educational Research Association. She is author and co-author of numerous journal articles, book chapters, and books, including *Reading and Writing Informational Text in the Primary Grades: Research-Based Practices* and *Literacy and the Youngest Learner: Best Practices for Educators of Children from Birth to Five*.

Judith Sweeney Lederman, Ph.D. **SCIENCE**

Director of Teacher Education, Associate Professor of Science Education,
Department of Mathematics and Science Education,
Illinois Institute of Technology, Chicago, Illinois

Dr. Judith S. Lederman's teaching experiences include pre-K to 12th grade science, masters and doctoral level science education courses, and post-graduate professional development for in-service teachers. She is known nationally and internationally for her work in the teaching and learning of Scientific Inquiry and Nature of Science in both formal and informal settings. In 2008 she was awarded a Fulbright Fellowship to work with South African university and museum educators and K–12 science teachers. Dr. Lederman served on the Board of Directors of the National Science Teachers Association (NSTA) and as President of the Council for Elementary Science International (CESI).

David W. Moore, Ph.D. **LITERACY**

Professor of Education, College of Teacher Education and Leadership,
Arizona State University, Tempe, Arizona

Dr. David W. Moore taught reading in Arizona public schools before entering college teaching. He currently is in the Division of Educational Leadership and Innovation at Arizona State University where he researches and teaches courses in literacy across the content areas. He is actively involved with several professional associations. His thirty-year publication record balances research reports, professional articles, book chapters, and books. Noteworthy publications include a history of content area literacy instruction and a quantitative and qualitative review of graphic organizer research. He currently is preparing the sixth edition of *Developing Readers and Writers in the Content Areas: K–12*.

NATIONAL GEOGRAPHIC Science

Program Reviewers

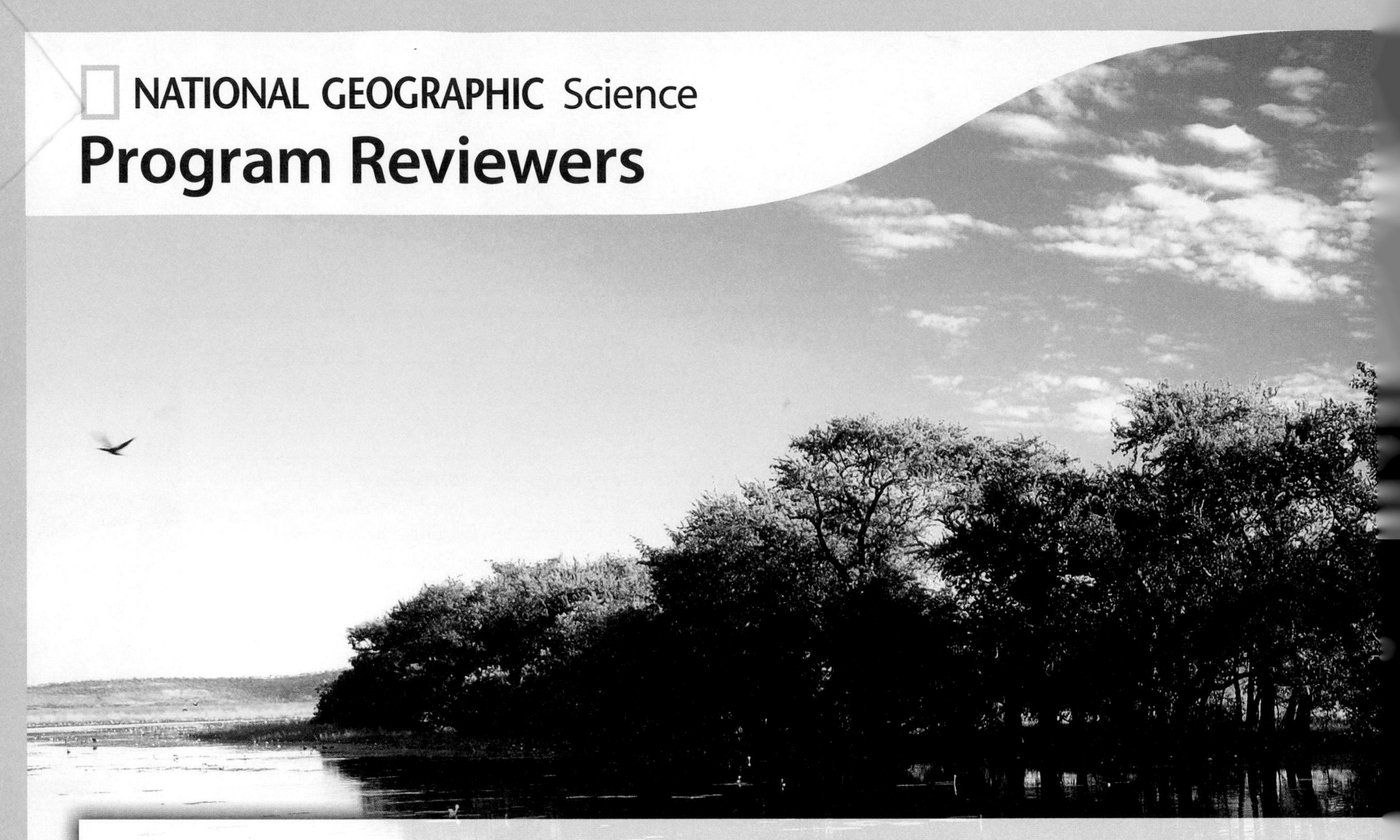

Amani Abuhabsah
Teacher, Dawes Elementary
Chicago, IL

Dr. Maria Aida Alanis
Science Coordinator, Austin Independent School District
Austin, TX

Shernett Alexander
K–12 Science Specialist, St. Lucie County Public Schools
Ft. Pierce, FL

Jamillah Bakr
Science Mentor Teacher, Cambridge Public Schools
Cambridge, MA

Gwendolyn Battle-Lavert
Assistant Professor of Education, Indiana Wesleyan University
Marion, IN

Carmen Beadles
Retired Science Instructional Coach, Dallas Independent School District
Dallas, TX

Andrea Blake-Garrett, Ed.D
Science Educational Consultant,
Newark, NJ

Lori Bowen
Science Specialist, Fayette County Schools
Lexington, KY

Pamela Breitberg
Lead Science Teacher, Zapata Academy
Chicago, IL

Carol Brueggeman
K–5 Science/Math Resource Teacher, District 11
Colorado Springs, CO

Polly Burkhart
Science Coach, Oscar Pope Elementary
Lakeland, FL

Miranda Carpenter
Teacher, MS Academy Leader, Imagine School
Bradenton, FL

Samuel Carpenter
Teacher, Coonley Elementary
Chicago, IL

Diane E. Comstock
Science Resource Teacher, Cheyenne Mountain School District
Colorado Springs, CO

Kelly Culbert
K–5 Science Lab Teacher, Princeton Elementary
Orange County, FL

Karri Dawes
K–5 Science Instructional Support Teacher, Garland Independent School District
Garland, TX

Richard Day
Science Curriculum Specialist, Union Public Schools
Tulsa, OK

Michele DeMuro
Teacher/Educational Consultant,
Monroe, NY

Richard Ellenburg
Science Lab Teacher, Camelot Elementary
Orlando, FL

Beth Faulkner
Brevard Public Schools Elementary Training Cadre, Science Point of Contact, Teacher, NBCT, Apollo Elementary
Titusville, FL

Kim Feltre
Science Supervisor, Hillsborough School District
Newark, NJ

Judy Fisher
Elementary Curriculum Coordinator, Virginia Beach Schools
Virginia Beach, VA

Anne Z. Fleming
Teacher, Coonley Elementary
Chicago, IL

Becky Gill, Ed.D
Principal/Elementary Science Coordinator, Hough Street Elementary
Barrington, IL

Rebecca Gorinac
Elementary Curriculum Director, Port Huron Area Schools
Port Huron, MI

Anne Grall Reichel Ed.D
Educational Leadership/ Curriculum and Instruction Consultant,
Barrington, IL

Mary Haskins, Ph.D.
Professor of Biology, Rockhurst University
Kansas City, MO

Arlene Hayman
Teacher, Paradise Public School District
Las Vegas, NV

DeLene Hoffner
Science Specialist, Science Methods Professor, Regis University, Academy 20 School District
Colorado Springs, CO

Cindy Holman
District Science Resource Teacher, Jefferson County Public Schools
Louisville, KY

Sarah E. Jesse
Instructional Specialist for Hands-on Science, Rutherford County Schools
Murfreeboro, TN

Dianne Johnson
Science Curriculum Specialist, Buffalo City School District
Buffalo, NY

Kathleen Jordan
Teacher, Wolf Lake Elementary
Orlando, FL

Renee Kumiega
Teacher, Frontier Central School District
Hamburg, NY

Edel Maeder
K–12 Science Curriculum Coordinator, Greece Central School District
North Greece, NY

Trish Meegan
Lead Teacher, Coonley Elementary
Chicago, IL

Donna Melpolder
Science Resource Teacher, Chatham County Schools
Chatham, NC

Melissa Mishovsky
Science Lab Teacher, Palmetto Elementary
Orlando, FL

Nancy Moore
Educational Consultant,
Port Stanley, Ontario, Canada

Melissa Ray
Teacher, Tyler Run Elementary
Powell, OH

Shelley Reinacher
Science Coach, Auburndale Central Elementary
Auburndale, FL

Flavia Reyes
Teacher, Oak Hammock Elementary
Port St. Lucie, FL

Kevin J. Richard
Science Education Consultant, Office of School Improvement, Michigan Department of Education
Lansing, MI

Cathe Ritz
Teacher, Louis Agassiz Elementary
Cleveland, OH

Rose Sedely
Science Teacher, Eustis Heights Elementary
Eustis, FL

Robert Sotak, Ed.D.
Science Program Director, Curriculum and Instruction, Everett Public Schools
Everett, WA

Karen Steele
Teacher, Salt Lake City School District
Salt Lake City, UT

Deborah S. Teuscher
Science Coach and Planetarium Director, Metropolitan School District of Pike Township
Indianapolis, IN

Michelle Thrift
Science Instructor, Durrance Elementary
Orlando, FL

Cathy Trent
Teacher, Ft. Myers Beach Elementary
Ft. Myers Beach, FL

Jennifer Turner
Teacher, PS 146
New York, NY

Deborah Vannatter
District Coach, Science Specialist, Evansville Vanderburgh School Corporation
Evansville, IN

Katherine Vazquez
Science Coordinator, Milton Hershey School
Hershey, PA

Sandy Yellenberg
Science Coordinator, Santa Clara County Office of Education
Santa Clara, CA

Hillary Zeune de Soto
Science Strategist, Lunt Elementary
Las Vegas, NV

NATIONAL GEOGRAPHIC Science

Explorers and Scientists

These explorers and scientists help students understand real-world science, the nature of science, and science inquiry.

CONSTANCE ADAMS

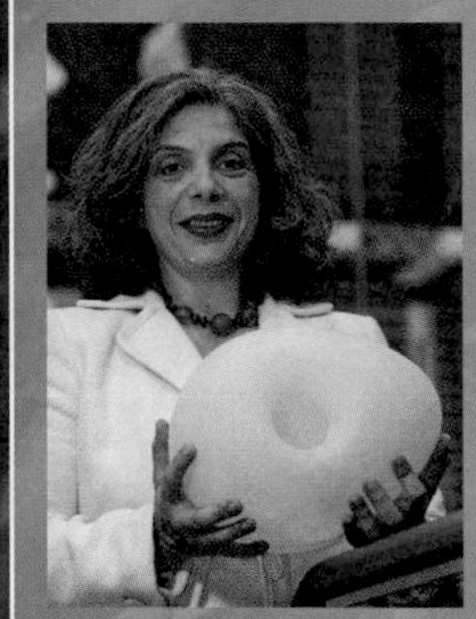

National Geographic Emerging Explorer
Space Architect

"When you have a brand new problem, you need as many tools as you can get. Who knows? An approach from a very different field might give you the insight you need. For example, I'm working to forge communication between advanced engineering and consumer product design to bring more user-centered designs to aerospace."

STEPHON ALEXANDER, Ph.D.

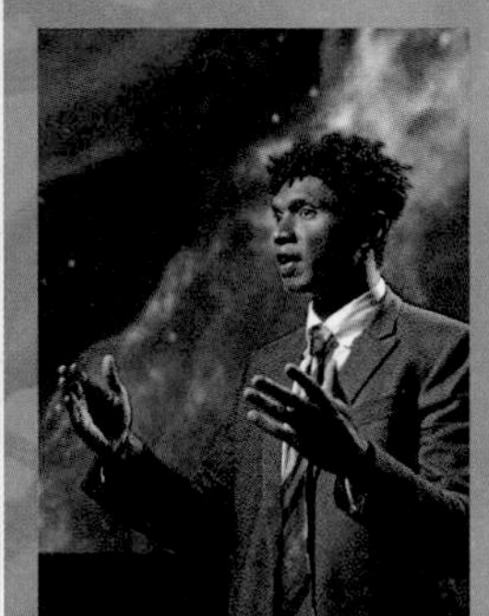

National Geographic Emerging Explorer
Theoretical Physicist

"My childhood was full of surprises. It taught me the idea of embracing the unknown. I cope with unexpected events by making up theories about why they may be happening."

THOMAS TAHA RASSAM "T.H." CULHANE

National Geographic Emerging Explorer
Urban Planner

"During rain forest ecology fieldwork with the Dayak of Borneo and the Maya Itza of Guatemala's jungle villages, I witnessed a culture that used every part of the environment to survive and thrive. This inspired me to rethink urban living along those same ecological principles. Now I want to bring that message to the rest of the world."

LUKE DOLLAR, Ph.D.

National Geographic Emerging Explorer
Conservation Scientist

"When you're in the field, it's muddy, sweaty, stinky, gritty—there's no glamour to it at all. But it's great fun. I wake up every morning knowing I'm one of the luckiest guys on Earth because I'm doing exactly what I want to do, and it's going to make a difference."

MARIANNE DYSON

Science Writer and Former NASA
Flight Controller

"Children who learn to observe, describe, and predict forces in the world will develop the skills to tackle the challenges of a future increasingly dependent on technology."

MARIA FADIMAN, Ph.D.

National Geographic Emerging Explorer
Ethnobotanist

"I was born with a passion for conservation and a fascination with indigenous cultures. Ethnobotany lets me bring it all together. On my first trip to the rain forest, I met a woman who was in terrible pain because no one in her village could remember which plant would cure her. I saw that knowledge was truly being lost, and in that moment, I knew this was what I wanted to do with my life."

BEVERLY GOODMAN, Ph.D.

National Geographic Emerging Explorer
Geo-Archaeologist

"We can learn about our past, present, and future by studying the sea. Coastal regions present a major challenge. I hope the clues I am collecting help avert future catastrophe."

MADHULIKA GUHATHAKURTA, Ph.D.

NASA Astrophysicist

"Earth is inside the atmosphere of the sun. The sun is so big that if you dropped the entire Earth onto the sun's surface, it would barely make a decent sunspot."

ALBERT YU-MIN LIN, Ph.D.

National Geographic Grantee
Archaeologist

"I spent much of my young adulthood dreaming of exploration and have realized that goals can only be reached by many different approaches."

GREG MARSHALL

National Geographic Filmmaker
Marine Biologist, Conservationist, Inventor

"Science is a great adventure in exploration, discovery, and learning new things. We want to expand our knowledge and inspire others to help conserve and protect animals and their habitats."

MIREYA MAYOR, Ph.D.

National Geographic Emerging Explorer
Primatologist, Conservationist

"The more questions I asked, the more it became clear to me that much about our natural world still remained a mystery."

AINISSA RAMIREZ, Ph.D.

Physicist

"In a technologically-driven society, we need citizens who can comprehend science. Knowledge of science is necessary in order to fully appreciate the world's beauty."

TIM SAMARAS

National Geographic Emerging Explorer
Severe-Storms Researcher

"I started to love science when I was a young child. Now I am studying tornadoes to help unlock their secrets for a better understanding of how and why they form."

TIERNEY THYS, Ph.D.

National Geographic Emerging Explorer
Marine Biologist, Filmmaker

"I think what it takes to be an explorer is simply to never lose your curiosity, never lose your desire to learn more, to ask questions, and to keep pushing deeper and deeper into what you're studying. It's a vital time to be an explorer; there's never been a better, more important time."

KATEY WALTER, Ph.D.

National Geographic Emerging Explorer
Aquatic Ecologist, Biogeochemist

"We are researching the greenhouse gas that could have the most powerful effect of all on global warming. It's a worldwide responsibility to reduce our carbon footprint and its effects on the atmosphere."

NATIONAL GEOGRAPHIC

Science K-5

Take your students from the classroom to the world!

Grade K

Life Science
- Plants
- Animals

Earth Science
- Day and Night
- Weather and Seasons

Physical Science
- Observing Objects
- How Things Move

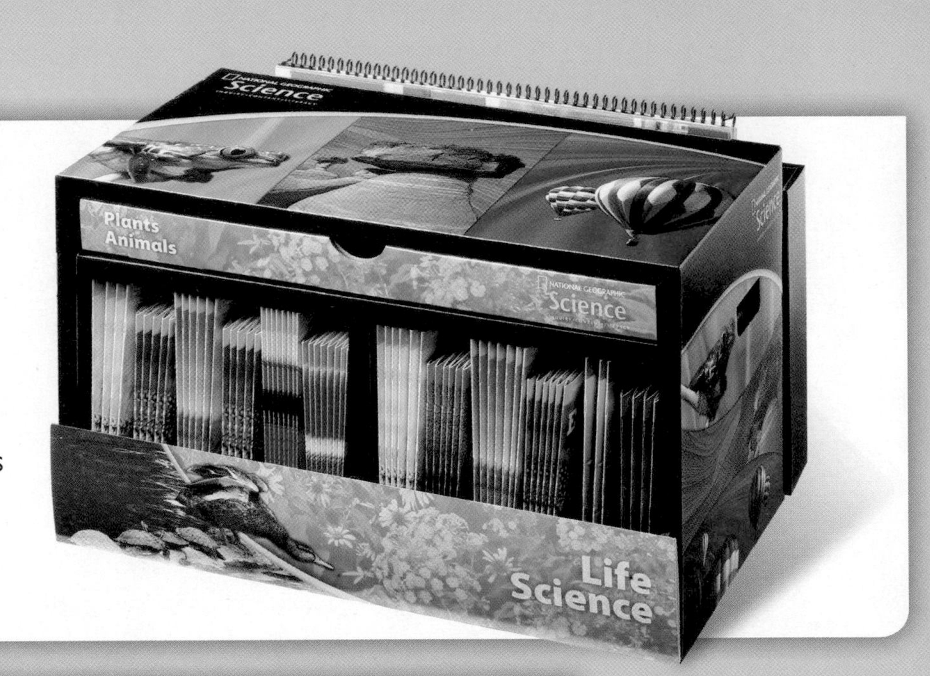

Grades 1-2

- Living Things
- Plants and Animals
- Sun, Moon, and Stars
- Land and Water
- Pushes and Pulls
- Properties
- Habitats
- Life Cycles
- Weather
- Rocks and Soil
- Solids, Liquids, and Gases
- Forces and Motion

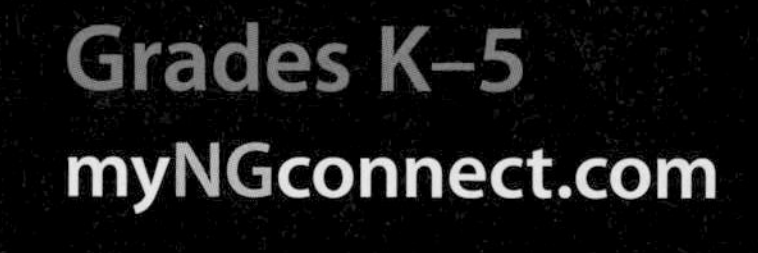

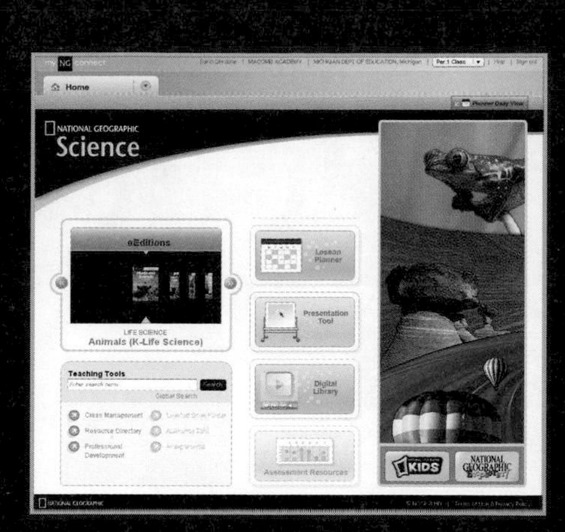

Grade 3

Big Ideas Books

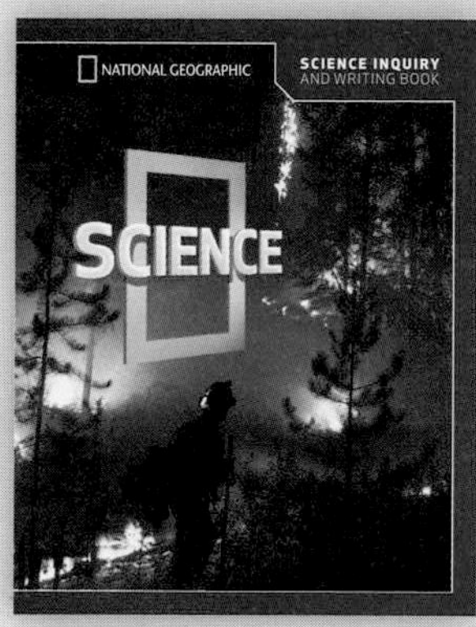

Science Inquiry and Writing Book

Explore on Your Own Books

Grade 4

Big Ideas Books

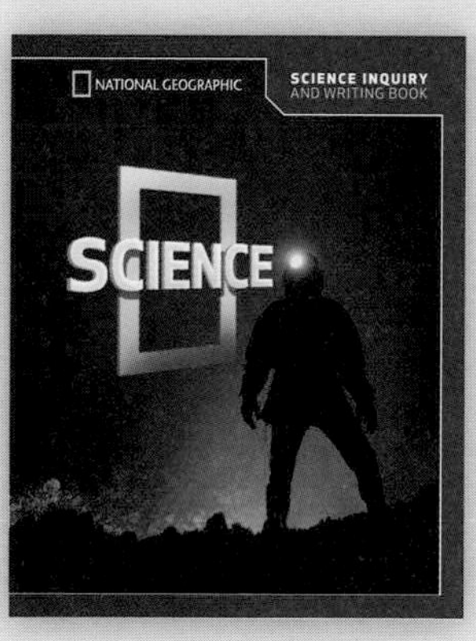

Science Inquiry and Writing Book

Explore on Your Own Books

Grade 5

Big Ideas Books

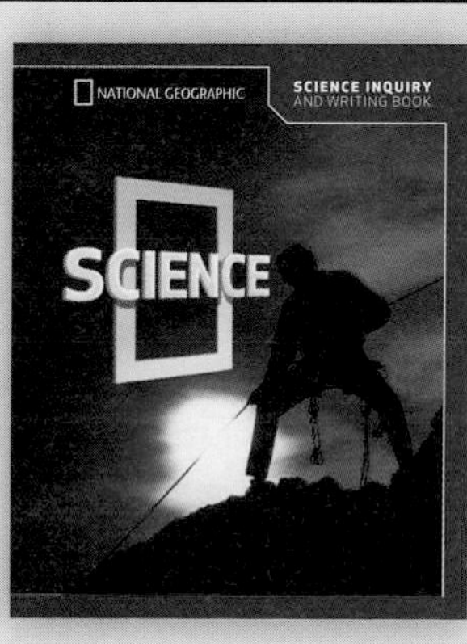

Science Inquiry and Writing Book

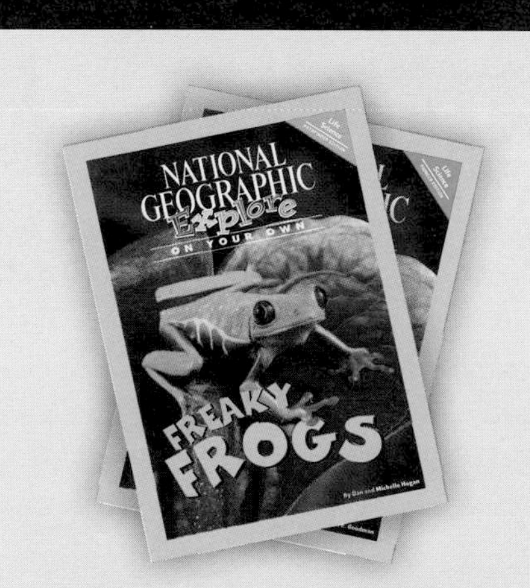

Explore on Your Own Books

NATIONAL GEOGRAPHIC
Science

STUDENT
Unit Components

Become an Expert Books

Big Ideas Book

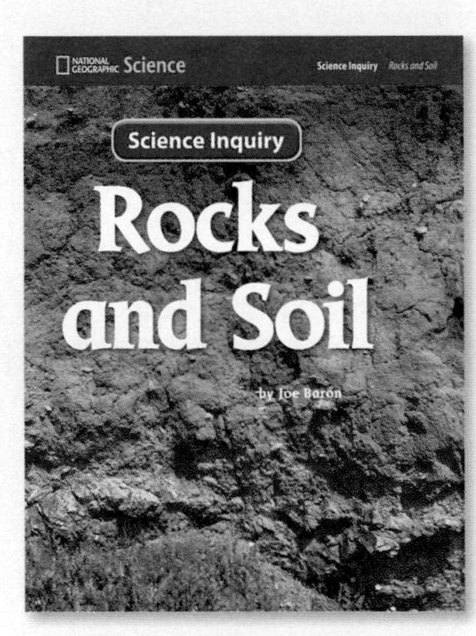

Science Inquiry Book

Unit Launch Videos

Explore on Your Own Books

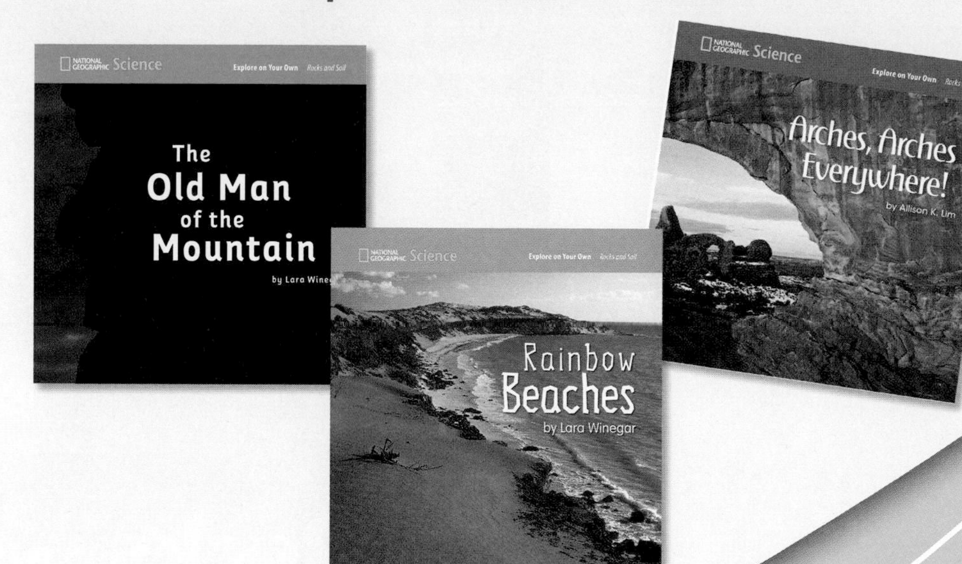

National Geographic Digital Library

Enrichment Activities

Vocabulary Games

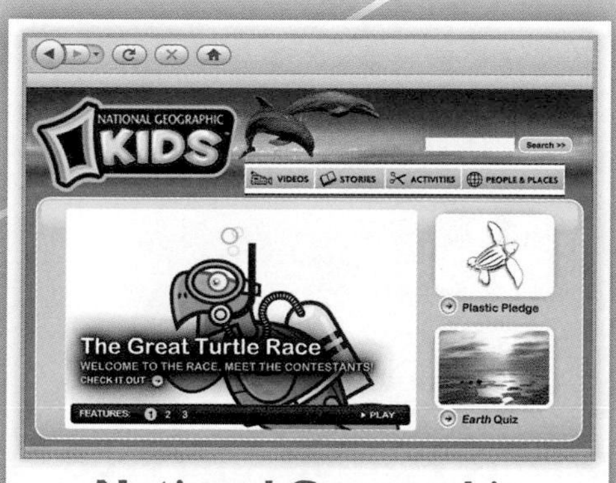

National Geographic Kids Web Site

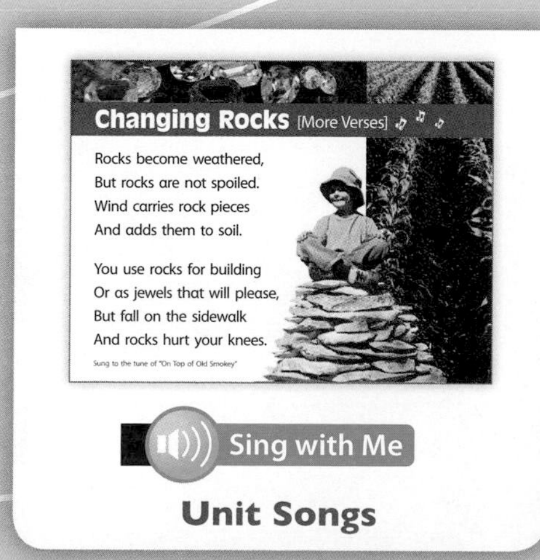

Sing with Me

Unit Songs

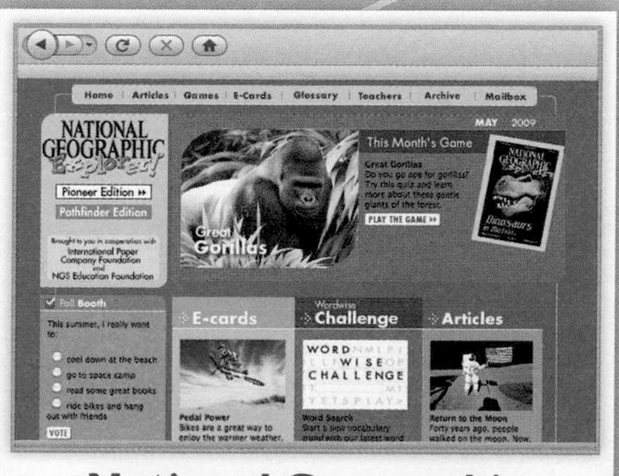

National Geographic Explorer! Web Site

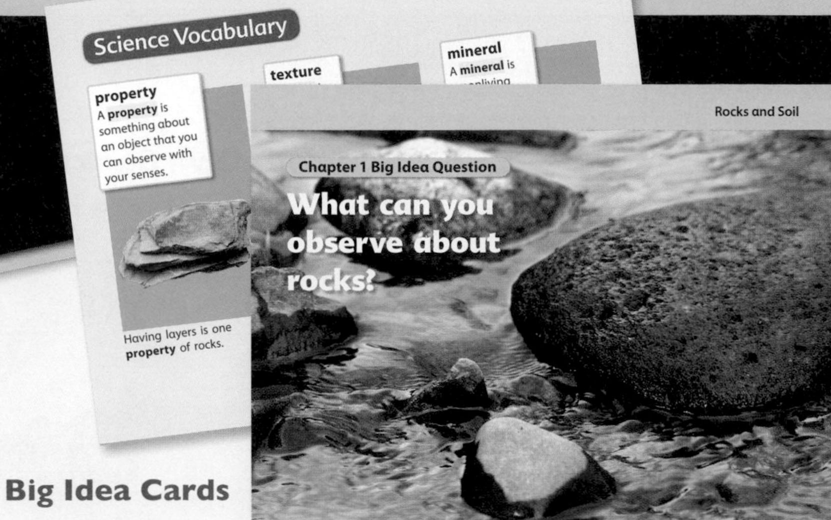

Big Idea Cards

TEACHER
Unit Components

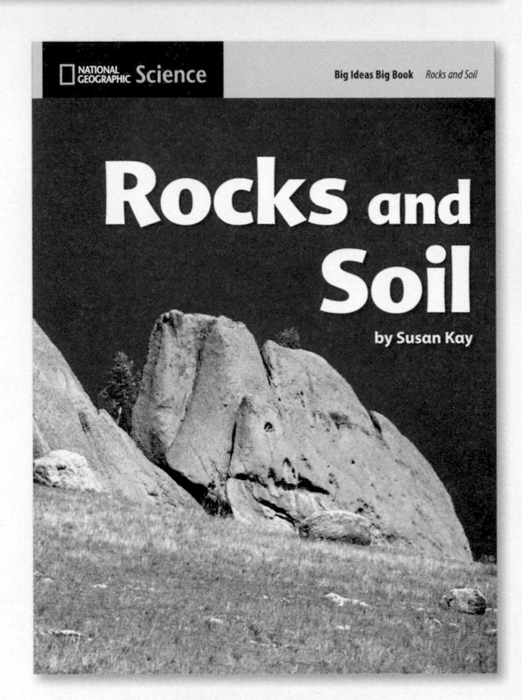

Big Ideas Big Book

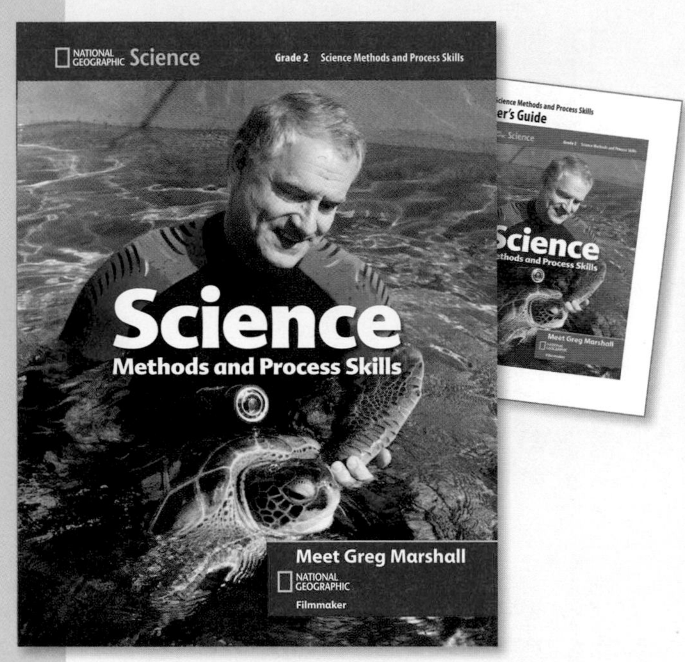

Science Methods and Process Skills Big Book / Teacher's Guide

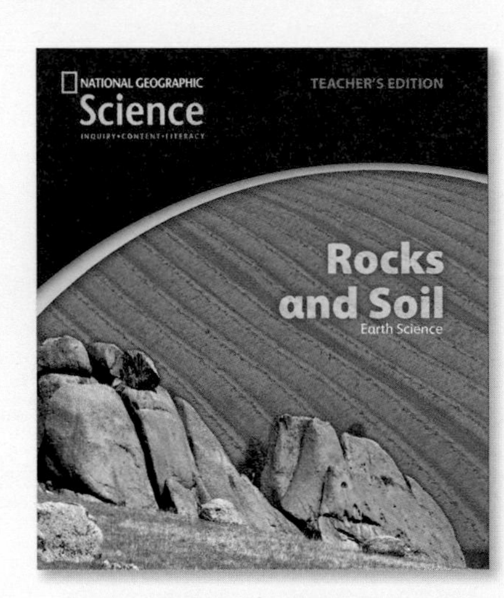

Teacher's Edition

Integrated Online System

Learning Masters

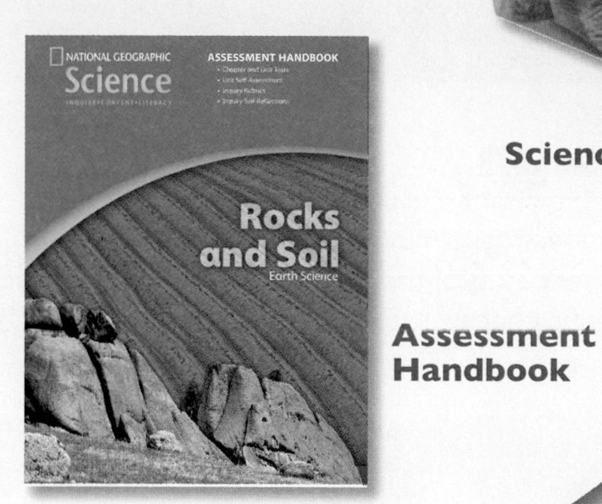

Science Inquiry Kit

Assessment Handbook

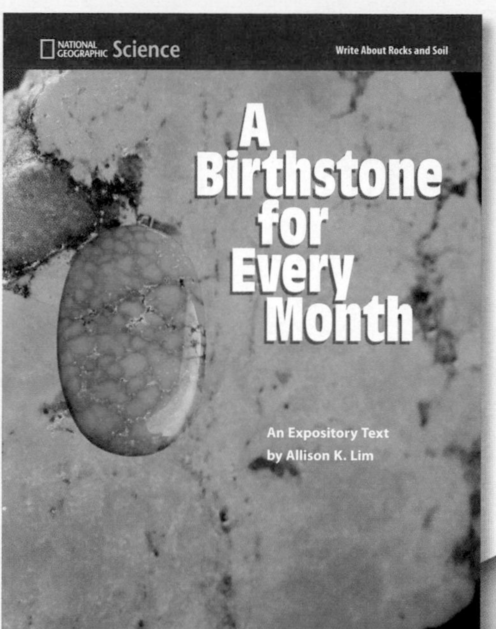

Write About Rocks and Soil Big Book

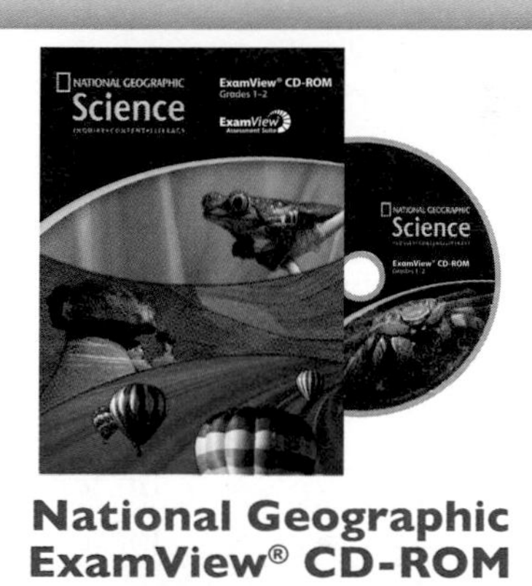

National Geographic ExamView® CD-ROM

Online Lesson Planner

eEdition

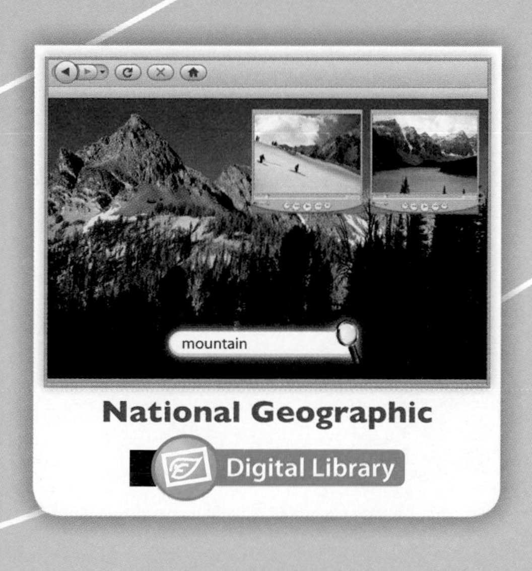

National Geographic Digital Library

National Geographic Presentation Tool

Assessment

Assessment Design

National Geographic Science assessments have been designed so that frequent, varied assessment informs instruction every step of the way. Chapter and Unit Tests provide a window into student thinking about scientific concepts throughout the instructional cycle.

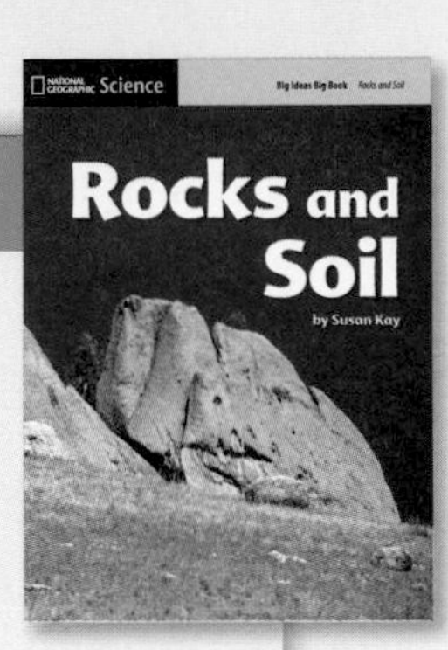

Instruct

Develop an understanding of and provide explicit and systematic instruction in:

- The Big Ideas in Science
- Scientific Inquiry
- Science Academic Vocabulary
- Content Literacy

Assess to Monitor Progress

Chapter Tests provide opportunities for students to apply their understanding of key concepts. Use **Chapter Tests** for timely information about student progress as you deliver instruction.

Show Success!

The **Unit Test** measures a student's overall progress in understanding the unit's Big Ideas.

Assessment Tools

National Geographic Science offers an array of assessments in a variety of formats.

ASSESSMENT TOOLS	Assessment Handbook	PDFs myNGConnect.com	Exam*View*®
CHAPTER TESTS • Chapter Tests provide immediate feedback on students' understanding of standards-based scientific concepts. • The tests are administered at the end of each chapter to provide an early indicator of the students' progress.	✓	✓	✓
UNIT TEST • The Unit Test measures students' progress toward understanding the unit's Big Ideas. • The test is administered at the end of the unit to measure the students' understanding of the science standards taught in the unit.	✓	✓	✓
UNIT SELF-ASSESSMENT • The Unit Self-Assessment empowers students to rate their own understanding of the unit concepts and share their opinions about future interests. • The self-assessment is completed by students before they take the Unit Test.	✓	✓	
INQUIRY RUBRICS • Inquiry Rubrics assess students' performance of skills in Inquiry activities. • The rubrics are completed after students have finished each Inquiry activity.	✓	✓	
INQUIRY SELF-REFLECTIONS • Inquiry Self-Reflections engage students in evaluating their own performance of inquiry skills and in sharing their opinions about the activity process. • The self-reflections are completed by students after they have finished each Inquiry activity.	✓	✓	

NATIONAL GEOGRAPHIC

Unit Overview and Pacing Guide

Nature of Science / Science Notebook

	DAY 1	20 minutes	**Setting Up a Science Notebook**	*page SN3*

Rocks and Soil Big Ideas Book and Inquiry

eEdition

Unit Launch	DAY 1	10 minutes	**Launch Video**	*page T1a*
Chapter 1	DAY 2	20 minutes	**Explore Activity** *Investigate Properties of Rocks* • *Science Inquiry Book, page 6*	*page T1e*
	DAYS 3–7	20–40 minutes each day	**What Can You Observe About Rocks?** • *Big Ideas Big Book*	*page T6*
			Directed Inquiry *Investigate More Properties of Rocks* • *Science Inquiry Book, page 10*	*page T15a*
Chapter 2	DAY 8	20 minutes	**Directed Inquiry** *Investigate How Rocks Wear Away* • *Science Inquiry Book, page 14*	*page T15g*
	DAYS 9–13	20–40 minutes each day	**How Do Rocks Change?** • *Big Ideas Big Book*	*page T16*
			Think Like a Scientist Math in Science: *Measuring Liquids* • *Science Inquiry Book, page 18*	*page T25a*
			Guided Inquiry *Investigate How Water Affects Soil* • *Science Inquiry Book, page 22*	*page T25e*
Chapter 3	DAY 14	30 minutes	**Guided Inquiry** *Investigate Soil Properties* • *Science Inquiry Book, page 26*	*page T25k*
	DAYS 15–20	20–40 minutes each day	**What Can You Observe About Soil?** • *Big Ideas Big Book*	*page T26*
			Open Inquiry *Do Your Own Investigation* • *Science Inquiry Book, page 30*	*page T37a*
			Think Like a Scientist How Scientists Work: *Using Tools to Observe* • *Science Inquiry Book, page 32*	*page T37g*

Read Informational Text

Component	Day	Time	Lesson	Page
Comprehension Strategies WHOLE CLASS	DAY 21	30 minutes (Select one or two mini-lessons.)	Preview and Predict Mini-Lesson	page T42
			Monitor and Fix Up Mini-Lesson	page T43
			Make Inferences Mini-Lesson	page T44
			Sum Up Mini-Lesson	page T45
Become an Expert Books SMALL GROUP eEdition	DAY 22	30 minutes each	*Rocks and Soil in the Rocky Mountains*	page T47
			Rocks and Soil in the High Desert	page T61
			Rocks and Soil Near the Great Lakes	page T75
	DAY 23	45 minutes	Share and Compare	page T89
			Science Career	page T90
Explore on Your Own Books INDEPENDENT eEdition			*The Old Man of the Mountain*	page T92
			Arches, Arches Everywhere!	page T93
			Rainbow Beaches	page T94

Write and Wrap Up

Component	Day	Time	Lesson	Page
Read: Expository Text	DAY 24	40 minutes	*A Birthstone for Every Month*	page T96
Write: Informational Text	DAY 25	40 minutes	Writing Projects	page T101
Wrap Up: *Rocks and Soil* Unit	DAY 26	40 minutes	Build a Rock Collection	page T103

NATIONAL GEOGRAPHIC

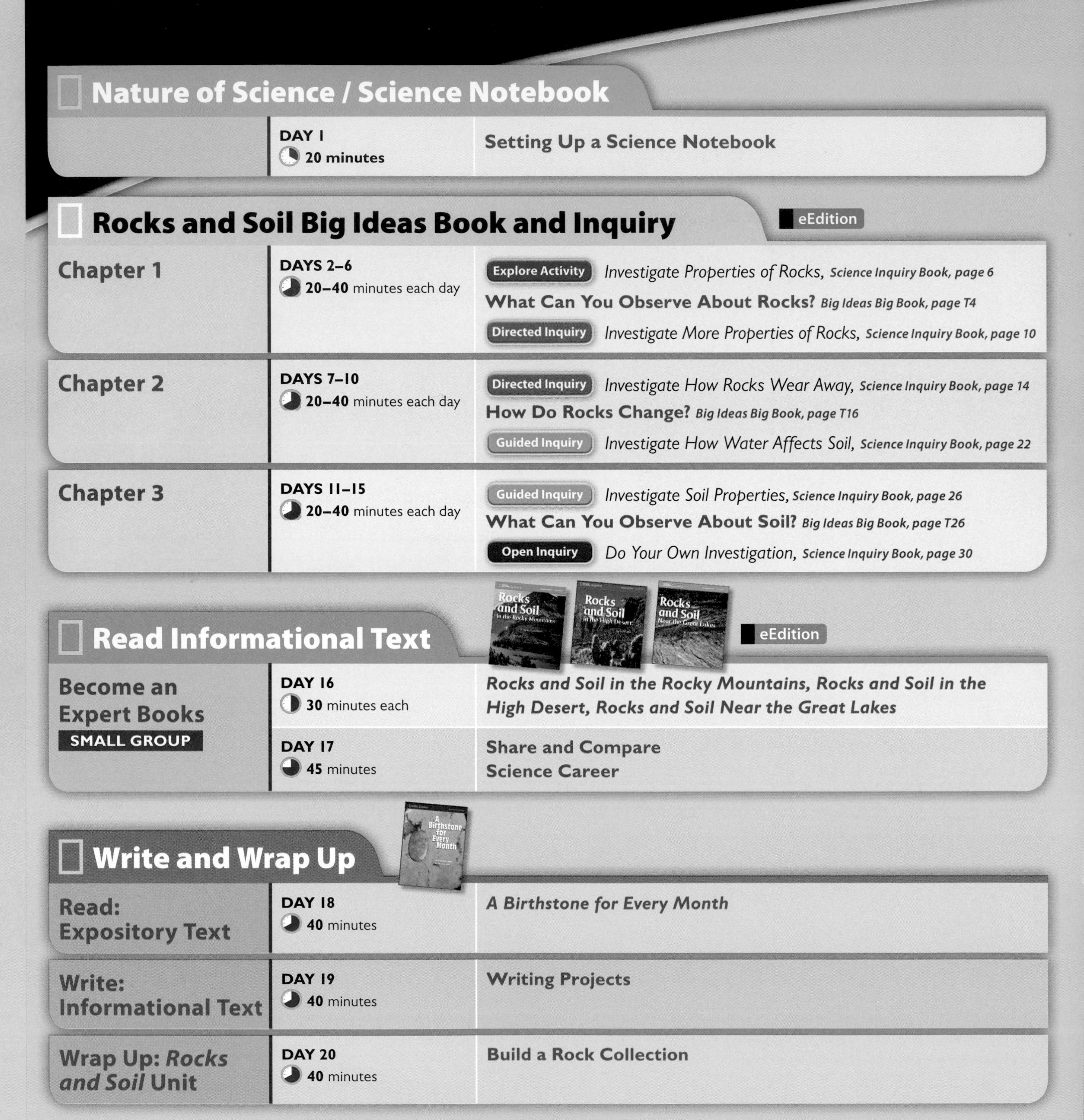

Fast Forward Accelerated Pacing Guide

Nature of Science / Science Notebook

	DAY 1 20 minutes	**Setting Up a Science Notebook**

Rocks and Soil Big Ideas Book and Inquiry

eEdition

Chapter 1	**DAYS 2–6** **20–40** minutes each day	Explore Activity *Investigate Properties of Rocks, Science Inquiry Book, page 6* **What Can You Observe About Rocks?** *Big Ideas Big Book, page T4* Directed Inquiry *Investigate More Properties of Rocks, Science Inquiry Book, page 10*
Chapter 2	**DAYS 7–10** **20–40** minutes each day	Directed Inquiry *Investigate How Rocks Wear Away, Science Inquiry Book, page 14* **How Do Rocks Change?** *Big Ideas Big Book, page T16* Guided Inquiry *Investigate How Water Affects Soil, Science Inquiry Book, page 22*
Chapter 3	**DAYS 11–15** **20–40** minutes each day	Guided Inquiry *Investigate Soil Properties, Science Inquiry Book, page 26* **What Can You Observe About Soil?** *Big Ideas Big Book, page T26* Open Inquiry *Do Your Own Investigation, Science Inquiry Book, page 30*

Read Informational Text

eEdition

Become an Expert Books SMALL GROUP	**DAY 16** **30** minutes each	***Rocks and Soil in the Rocky Mountains, Rocks and Soil in the High Desert, Rocks and Soil Near the Great Lakes***
	DAY 17 **45** minutes	**Share and Compare** **Science Career**

Write and Wrap Up

Read: Expository Text	**DAY 18** **40** minutes	***A Birthstone for Every Month***
Write: Informational Text	**DAY 19** **40** minutes	**Writing Projects**
Wrap Up: *Rocks and Soil* Unit	**DAY 20** **40** minutes	**Build a Rock Collection**

Nature of Science/ Science Notebook

Understanding the Nature of Science

In *National Geographic Science* process skills build at each grade level to ensure a complete understanding of the Nature of Science. This chart shows how process skills and the Nature of Science work together to help students think and act like a scientist. The Nature of Science is embedded in all parts of the program. The Science Notebook is the perfect vehicle for helping students put their thoughts (Nature of Science) and actions (Inquiry) down on paper.

	Grade K	Grades 1 & 2
PROCESS SKILLS	**OBSERVE**	**OBSERVE & INFER**
Nature of Science	• Science knowledge is based on evidence. • Science knowledge can change based on new evidence.	• Science conclusions are based on observation and inference. • Science theories are based partly on things that cannot be observed.

Contents

Grade 3

CLASSIFY

- There is often no single "right" answer in science.

Grade 4

PREDICT/HYPOTHESIZE

- Scientific theories provide the base upon which predictions and hypotheses are built.

Grade 5

DESIGN EXPERIMENTS

- There is no single scientific method that all scientists follow.
- There are a number of ways to do science.

Why Use a Science Notebook?

RECORD OBSERVATIONAL DATA AND INFERENCES

A science notebook is a place for students to record observational data, much like scientists record their observational data. Science notebooks make science more meaningful for students because they are able to observe, record, and reflect on their work. A science notebook is also the place for students to record any inferences that they have made after analyzing their observational data. It is these inferences that help students come to meaningful conclusions. Students will learn through making inferences that not everything in science is directly observable, an important tenet of the Nature of Science.

DEVELOP INQUIRY SKILLS

Using a science notebook can help students develop inquiry skills and practice science process skills, such as observe, sort, infer, predict, collect data, and conclude. Observe and infer are two key process skills that will help students understand the Nature of Science in *National Geographic Science.*

ENHANCE UNDERSTANDING OF SCIENCE CONTENT

A science notebook can help students understand science content. Writing about what they learn helps students understand science concepts and improves organizational skills. Encourage students to use science notebooks to present findings to share with others.

DIFFERENTIATE INSTRUCTION

A science notebook provides a way to support differentiated instruction. You can design science notebook use in the classroom so that students move at their own pace. This may include flexible time frames for completing work or small groups to support student learning.

EVALUATE

You can use the science notebooks for evaluation. Review the notebooks and see what understandings students have reached and what material you need to teach again. You may have students use their notebooks for self-reflection by marking places where they think they have successfully thought about and accomplished a section.

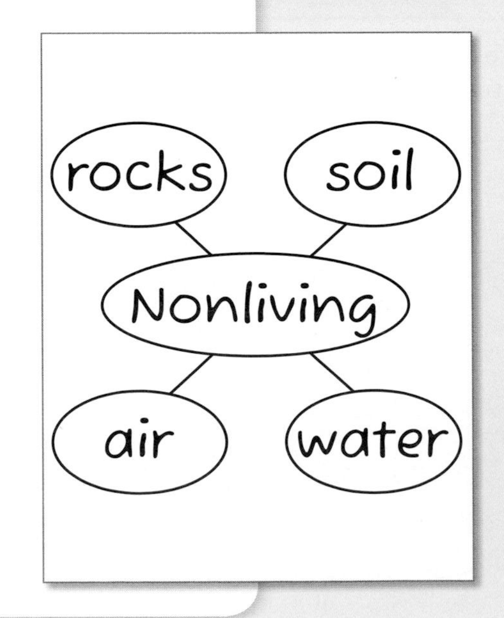

Setting Up a Science Notebook

Guide students to set up a structure that will support their learning and your evaluation of science understanding.

1. **Introduce the science notebook to students.**

   Say: **Like scientists, you will use this science notebook for your science work. It's your own notebook to use every time you do science. Like a real scientist, you will write notes in it, draw pictures, write about experiments, and write vocabulary words.**

2. **Have students choose an organization style.**

   DAILY RECORD: Students can make entries, in order, as they move through the unit. They can take notes about the Nature of Science, content lessons, and inquiry activities.

   SEPARATE SECTIONS: Students can create separate sections for observations, inferences, inquiry activities, vocabulary, notetaking, questions, reflections, and so on.

3. **Have students choose the notebook.**

   Some students may want to put looseleaf paper in a binder.

   Other students may choose a spiral notebook, a two-pocket folder, or a composition book. Still other students might choose a combination of these.

4. **Have students make and/or decorate the cover.**

   Instruct students to include their name and grade on the cover.

5. **Have students write "Contents" on the first right-hand page.**

   Suggest that students save several pages for the Table of Contents and fill in the information as they continue through the unit.

6. **Tell students that they should number the pages as they go along.**

   Tell students to add the appropriate page numbers to the Table of Contents as they proceed through the unit.

TEACHING TIPS

- Have students use the science notebook daily or on a regular basis. Assign a student to pass them out at the beginning of each science period. Collecting the notebooks each day and keeping them in a central place may help them last longer.
- Students may want to tape or staple a ribbon into the notebook and use it to mark their place.
- Tell students to use labels and/or captions for all drawings.
- Students can include graphic organizers to help them understand and organize information. A variety of graphic organizer options are found in the *Rocks and Soil* Learning Masters Book.
- You may want to use sticky notes to indicate corrections or additions that students need to make in their science notebooks.

What's In a Science Notebook?

Science notebook references are included throughout the Teacher's Edition. A science notebook is a place to record observational data and inferences. Students can record their observational data and inferences in a variety of ways.

Soil

STUDENT DRAWINGS

- Have students draw pictures to illustrate the Nature of Science (science is based on observations and inferences) and their understanding of science concepts.

TABLES, CHARTS, AND GRAPHS

- Have students draw tables, charts, and graphs to record information or data.

Type of Soil	Texture and Color	Does it Hold Water?	For Growing Things
Sand soil	like sugar, light brown	very little	poor
Clay soil	soft and sticky, reddish	too much	poor
Humus soil	soft and crumbly, dark brown	average	very good

NOTES

- Encourage students to jot down notes from each lesson in their science notebook. They can include graphic organizers, charts, lists, questions, and sketches. Suggestions for notetaking appear in the Teacher's Edition at point of use.

Uses of Soil
bricks
pottery
concrete

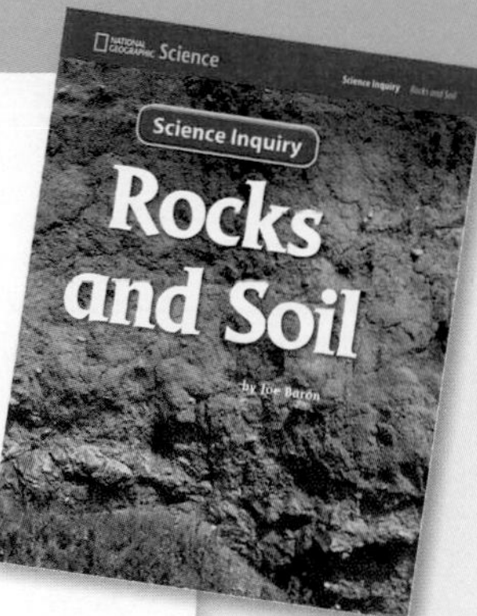

My Collections

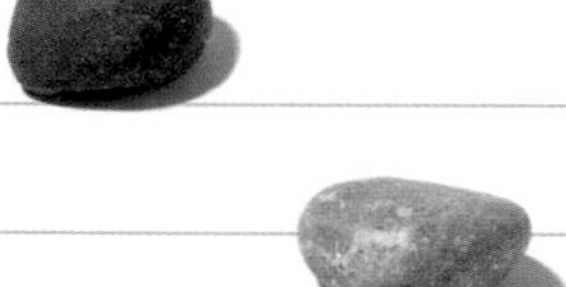

Rocks

Soil

Thoughts
I was surprised to learn that ice can split a large rock.

What other properties can different rocks have?

COLLECTED OBJECTS

- small rocks
- bits of humus and sand
- pictures of rock uses

REFLECTIVE AND ANALYTICAL ENTRIES

- You might want to give students prompts or frames to guide them as they write in their science notebook. For example:

  I want to find out __________.

  If __________, then __________.

  What would happen if I change __________?

  I think __________ because __________.

  The most important thing I learned in this chapter was __________.

  I was surprised to learn __________.

OTHER QUESTIONS STUDENTS HAVE

- Students may have a variety of questions. Have them record questions and help them research the answers.

Integrated Technology

- **Digital Camera** Suggest that students use digital cameras to take photos. The photos can be included in their science notebook.
- **Computer Presentation** Encourage students to share their ideas. They can share their notebooks with each other, present their ideas to the class, or talk about their ideas in small groups. They can also make computer presentations as appropriate.

What's In a Science Notebook?, continued

Weathering

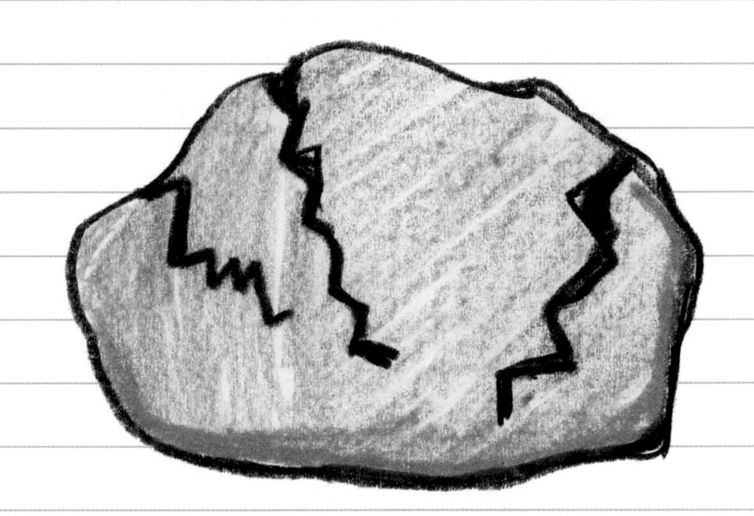

This chapter is about how rocks change. Water, wind, and ice help break rocks apart. I can observe that weathering happens every day. I can infer that rocks are slowly changing all the time.

STUDENT REPORTS

- Students can answer one or two reflective questions at the end of each chapter. Or you can assign special projects or reports for them to write in their notebook.

Name ______________________ Date ______________

My Science Notebook

Chapter 1 Science Vocabulary

Write the word that completes each sentence.
Use the words in the box.

property
texture
mineral

1. A __mineral__ is a nonliving material found in nature.

2. A __property__ is something about a mineral that you observe with your senses.

3. I can tell a rock's __texture__ by feeling the rock.

4. A rock's __texture__ might be rough or smooth.

In the space below, draw a picture of two minerals with different textures. Write a sentence telling how the textures are different.

Students might draw a picture of a mineral with a smooth texture and a picture of a mineral with a rough texture. Sentences should explain how the textures differ.

____

____

SCIENCE ACADEMIC VOCABULARY

- You can have students include the Vocabulary Learning Masters in their science notebook. See page SN11 for other suggestions for using the science notebook with Science Academic Vocabulary.

Name ______________________ Date ______________

My Science Notebook

Directed Inquiry

Investigate More Properties of Rocks

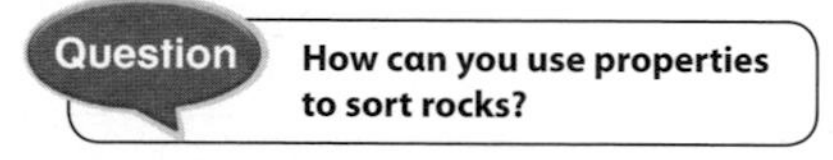

Record

Write or draw in the table.

Rocks' Properties

Drawing of the Rock	Properties of the Rock
Rock 1	Answers will vary depending on the rocks used. Observed properties may include presence of fossils, feel of the rock surface, presence of layers, presence of air holes.
Rock 2	
Rock 3	

INQUIRY ACTIVITIES

- Use Learning Masters or have students write notes about the activities in their notebook. See pages SN8–SN10 for suggestions for using a science notebook with inquiry activities.

Using a Science Notebook for Inquiry Activities

The inquiry activities in *National Geographic Science* provide an opportunity for students to ask questions and do investigations much like scientists do. Writing what they learn will help students understand why they are doing the activity and what it teaches them.

ASK A QUESTION

- Every inquiry activity begins with a question that shows the purpose of the activity. Have students write the question in their science notebook.

What are some properties of rocks you can observe?

BUILD VOCABULARY

- Have students write the **Science Process Vocabulary** words and their definitions in their science notebook.

Observe:
When you observe something, you use your senses to learn about it.

MAKE A PREDICTION

- Have students write a statement predicting what will happen in the activity. Encourage students to use their prior knowledge and experience to make the prediction.
- Please note that in this context it is acceptable to use shape and size, but remember to point out that these properties are not usually very useful for scientists.

I predict that rocks will be many different colors and sizes.

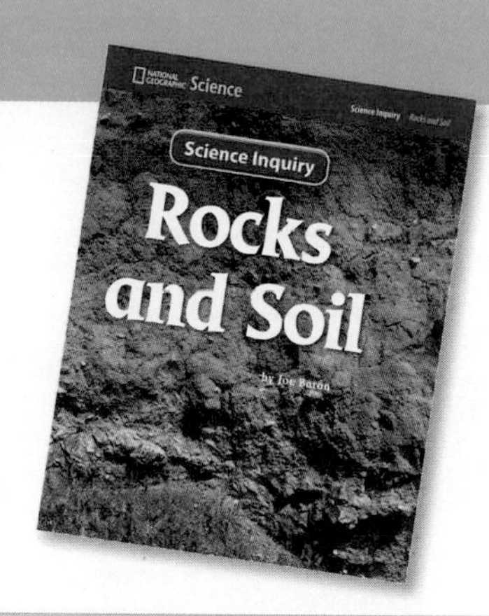

Explore Activity

Guided Inquiry

Directed Inquiry

Open Inquiry

1. Observe 3 rocks.
2. Trace around the rocks and color the drawings.
3. Measure the rocks.
4. Look for fossils.
5. Share observations and inferences with others.

WHAT TO DO

- Have students write or draw the steps of the activity in their notebook.

MAKE AND RECORD OBSERVATIONS AND INFERENCES

- Have students record their observations and inferences in the table on the Learning Master or have them draw and fill in their own table or graph. Students can write or make drawings to record their observations and inferences.

Using a Science Notebook for Inquiry Activities, continued

EXPLAIN AND CONCLUDE

- Have students examine data, or evidence, and use this evidence to make inferences, develop explanations, and draw conclusions about their observations and results. This is what the Nature of Science is all about. Students make observations and then support and extend observations with inferences. Both observations and inferences are then used to draw meaningful conclusions. Students learn that Science conclusions must include *both* observations *and* inferences.

Color and having layers are two properties of rocks that I can observe. I can infer that a mineral gives this rock its color. I can infer that the layers were formed at different times.

THINK OF ANOTHER QUESTION

- Have students reflect about what they have learned. Then have them use their observations to think of other questions that they could study through an investigation. Have them write their questions in their science notebook.

I learned that different rocks can be alike in some ways. They can be the same color, for example. I wonder how people use different kinds of rocks.

Science Academic Vocabulary

Students can use their science notebook as their own vocabulary resource.

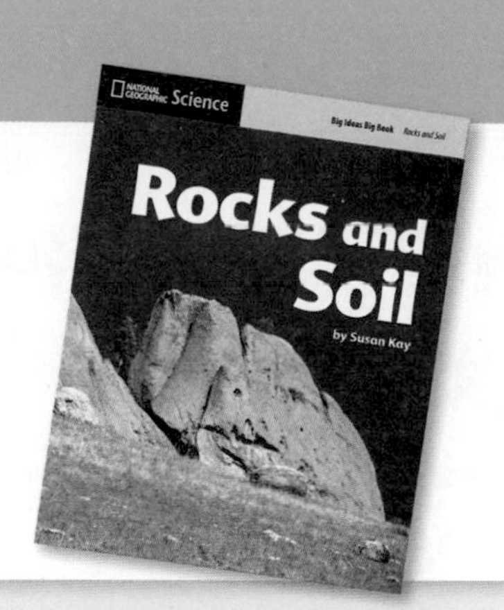

weathering - the breaking apart or dissolving of rocks

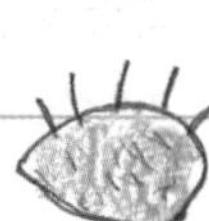

Wind picks up sand and blows it around. The sand rubs against rocks and wears them down.

art by Braedyn, age 7

Have students designate a special section of the science notebook for Science Academic Vocabulary.

- Write the vocabulary words and their definitions on a Science Word Wall for students to copy.
- Encourage students to use the Graphic Organizers from the *Rocks and Soil* Learning Master books or draw their own for recording vocabulary.
    - Students can write the word, draw a picture, write a definition in their own words, and write a sentence using the word.
    - Students can fill in a Word Web.
    - Students can make vocabulary cards or use the Vocabulary Cards Graphic Organizer, writing the word on one side and a picture and/or a definition on the other side.
- Encourage students to write ideas about vocabulary in their science notebook.

Using a Science Notebook for Unit Activities

Students can summarize and synthesize the unit's content with culminating unit entries.

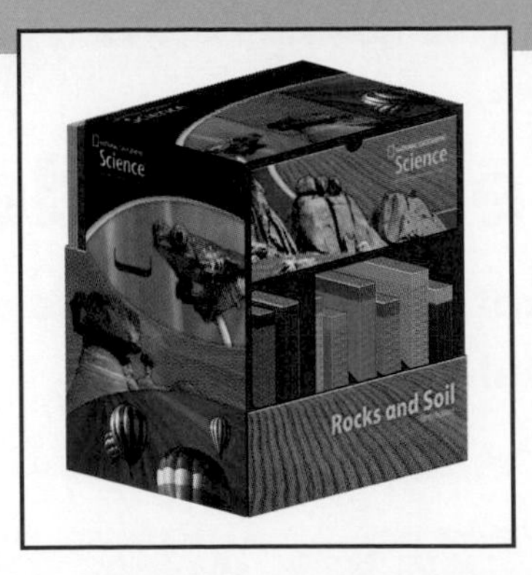

STUDENT REFLECTIONS

At the end of each chapter, help students think about what they learned. Writing will help them understand the Nature of Science (their observations and inferences), the science content, and science inquiry. This helps students relate the three parts of Science to their daily lives. Ask them to write answers to questions such as these in their science notebook:

- What is the main idea of this chapter?
- What is the most surprising thing I learned?
- What is the most important thing I learned?
- What is the soil like where I live?
- What rocks were used to build my home or school?
- What use of soil would I like to learn more about?
- What questions do I have about rocks, soil, or how they are used?

USING THE SCIENCE NOTEBOOK WITH WRITE AND WRAP UP

- Use the science notebook as a place to plan and complete the writing projects found on pages T101–T102.
- Use the science notebook as a place to respond to the Wrap Up *Rocks and Soil* Unit project found on page T103.

What use of soil would I like to learn more about?

I would like to know how to make pottery. Clay is a kind of soil. Some kinds of clay can be used to make pottery. How does clay stay in the same shape? How can I learn more about this?

Big Ideas About Rocks and Soil

Interactive Read Aloud

Science Inquiry

Big Ideas
About Rocks and Soil

Contents

Chapter 1

Chapter 2

Chapter 3

OBJECTIVES

Science

Students will be able to:

- Identify a problem to be solved.
- Predict how trying something new might affect other people.
- Identify ways that science affects people's everyday lives.
- Identify patterns in the natural world.

PROGRAM RESOURCES

- *Rocks and Soil* Unit Launch Video: DVD or Online at myNGconnect.com
- Science at Home Letter (in 7 languages): Learning Masters 1–7, or at myNGconnect.com

Meet the Emerging Explorer

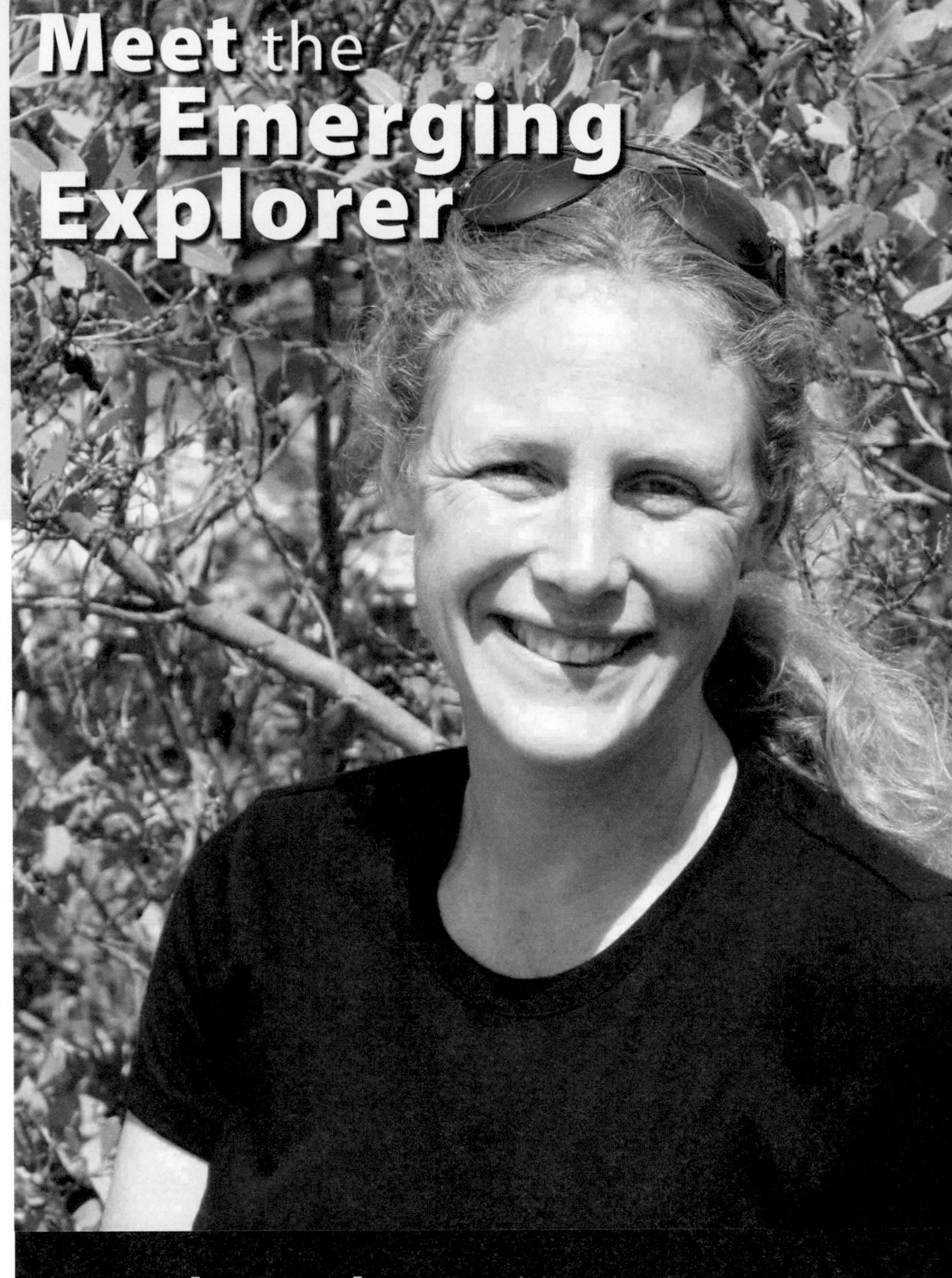

Beverly Goodman is a geo-archaeologist who studies layers of rock and soil at coastlines. She uses skills from archaeology, geology, and anthropology to piece together the history of a coastline, including human activity and what environmental events, like tsunamis, have occurred there. In Caesarea, Israel, Goodman and her team used what they found in the layers of the earth to prove that a tsunami hit the coastline and destroyed an ancient harbor in the first or second century C.E. Goodman hopes that determining the nature and frequency of catastrophic events, like tsunamis, will help us predict when and where future events may strike.

Think Like a Scientist

"Coastal regions present one of the major challenges of our time. I hope I'm collecting clues that will help us avoid catastrophic consequences down the line." — Beverly Goodman, geo-archaeologist

Rocks and Soil Video

Preview the Video

Tell students that they will meet Beverly Goodman, National Geographic Emerging Explorer, in the *Rocks and Soil* video. Share this information with students:

- Beverly Goodman studies the layers of rocks, shells, and soil of the ocean bottom to learn about the history of a coastline.
- Earthquakes that occur under the water can form gigantic waves, called tsunamis, that crash up against the shore.
- When tsunamis hit the coast, they carry material, such as rocks and shells, with them. The rocks and shells pile up where the wave hits.
- Goodman studies the layers of material left on the ocean floor to find out more about the storm and when it struck the shore.

Play the Video

myNGconnect.com

Discuss the Video

Invite students to share what they learned and give their perspectives. You may want to ask some of the following questions:

- What was your favorite part of the video? Why was it your favorite?
- What would you do if you could dive down to the bottom of the ocean?
- What can scientists learn by studying the layers of rock and soil under the ocean, where a tsunami struck?
- Goodman found many things in the ocean bottom where the tsunami struck. Which ones surprised you?
- What do you think would happen to a town if it were struck by a tsunami?
- Why would it help people to know if a tsunami is going to happen where they live?

Science at Home

Distribute the Science at Home Letter on Learning Masters 1–7, or at myNGconnect.com.

Students should take the letter home and

- discuss rocks and soil with their families
- review vocabulary words
- follow the directions to examine soil and discuss what it contains with their families.

CHAPTER 1 ▫ What Can You Observe About Rocks?

LESSON	PACING	OBJECTIVES
1 **Explore Activity** *Investigate Properties of Rocks* pages T1e–T1h **Science Inquiry Book** pages 6–9	**20** minutes	Investigate and Explore (answer a question; make and compare observations; collect and record data; share findings). Observe and measure the properties of rocks.
2 **2A Big Idea and Vocabulary Card** pages T1i–T1j	**20** minutes	**2A** Sort rocks by their properties.
2B Interactive Read-Aloud pages T2–T3	**20** minutes	**2B** Observe and describe rocks and soil.
2C Introduction pages T4–T5	**20** minutes	**2C** Distinguish between living and nonliving things. T Identify nonliving things made by humans and those made by natural events. T
2D Big Idea Question pages T6–T7	**20** minutes	**2D** Recognize that Earth is made up of rocks. T Sort rocks by their properties. T
2E Properties of Rocks pages T8–T9	**20** minutes	**2E** Recognize that rocks come in many sizes and shapes. T Sort rocks by their properties. T
3 **3A Minerals** pages T10–T11	**30** minutes	**3A** Recognize that rocks are made of minerals. T
3B Fossils pages T12–T13	**20** minutes	**3B** Describe the characteristics of fossils. T Infer the type of environment in which fossils formed.
3C People Use Rocks pages T14–T15	**20** minutes	**3C** Identify and describe how people use rocks for buildings, highways, fuels, and other purposes. T
4 **Directed Inquiry** *Investigate More Properties of Rocks* pages T15a–T15d **Science Inquiry Book** pages 10–13	**20** minutes	Investigate through Directed Inquiry (answer a question; make and compare observations; collect and record data; generate questions and explanations based on evidence or observations; share findings; ask questions to increase understanding). Compare and sort rocks according to their properties. Make observations using simple tools and equipment (e.g., magnifiers/hand lenses)

T = Tested Objective

VOCABULARY	RESOURCES	ASSESSMENT
observe **measure**	Science Inquiry Book: *Rocks and Soil* Science Inquiry Kit: *Rocks and Soil* Explore Activity: Learning Master 8	Inquiry Rubric: Assessment Handbook, page 32 Inquiry Self-Reflection: Assessment Handbook, page 35 Reflect and Assess, page T1h
property **texture** **mineral**	Chapter 1 Big Idea Card Vocabulary: Learning Master 9 *Rocks and Soil* Big Ideas Big Book	Before You Move On, pages T5, T7 Assess, page T9
	Extended Learning: Learning Masters 10–11 Share and Compare: Learning Master 12	Chapter Test 1, Assessment Handbook, pages 7–8 Before You Move On, pages T11, T13 Assess, page T15 NGSP ExamView CD-ROM
sort **compare**	Science Inquiry Book: *Rocks and Soil* Science Inquiry Kit: *Rocks and Soil* Directed Inquiry: Learning Masters 13–15	Inquiry Rubric: Assessment Handbook, page 32 Inquiry Self-Reflection: Assessment Handbook, page 36 Reflect and Assess, page T15d

TECHNOLOGY RESOURCES

STUDENT RESOURCES

myNGconnect.com

- Student eEdition
  - Big Ideas Book
  - Science Inquiry Book
  - Become an Expert Books
  - Explore on Your Own Books
- Read with Me
- Sing with Me
- Vocabulary Games
- Enrichment Activities
- Digital Library

National Geographic Kids

National Geographic Explorer!

TEACHER RESOURCES

myNGconnect.com

- Teacher eEdition
  - Big Ideas Book
  - Science Inquiry Book
  - Become an Expert Books
  - Explore on Your Own Books
  - Write About Rocks and Soil Book
  - Online Lesson Planner
  - National Geographic Unit Launch Videos
  - Assessment Handbook
- Presentation Tool
- Digital Library

NGSP ExamView CD-ROM

OBJECTIVES

Science

Students will be able to:

- Investigate and Explore (answer a question; make and compare observations; collect and record data; share findings).
- Observe and measure the properties of rocks.

Science Process Vocabulary

observe, measure

PROGRAM RESOURCES

- Science Inquiry Book: *Rocks and Soil*
- Science Inquiry Book eEdition at myNGconnect.com
- Inquiry eHelp at myNGconnect.com
- Science Inquiry Kit: *Rocks and Soil*
- *Rocks and Soil* Learning Master 8, or at myNGconnect.com
- Inquiry Rubric: Assessment Handbook, page 32, or at myNGconnect.com
- Inquiry Self-Reflection: Assessment Handbook, page 35, or at myNGconnect.com

MATERIALS

Kit materials are listed in italics.
3 rocks; crayons; *hand lens; metric ruler*

❶ Introduce

Tap Prior Knowledge

Remind students that they observe objects and events with their senses. Have them observe things in the classroom with their senses of sight, smell, touch, and hearing. For example, have students close their eyes. Have them feel the smoothness of the desktop, the roughness of a balled up piece of paper, or the shape of a common classroom item, such as an eraser. Have them describe what they feel. Tell students that they can use different senses to observe the properties of rocks.

Connect to Big Idea

- Explain to students that they will observe rocks in this activity. Ask them what they can observe about the rock in the photo on page 6.

Explore Activity

Investigate Properties of Rocks

What are some properties of rocks you can observe?

Science Process Vocabulary

observe verb

When you **observe** something, you use your senses to learn about it.

measure verb

When you want to find out how long or wide something is, you can **measure.**

MANAGING THE INVESTIGATION

Time

20 minutes

Groups

small groups of 4

What to Expect

Students will observe and measure the properties of rocks, such as color, shape, length, and presence of fossils. Students will draw their observations in their science notebooks. They will share their observations with the class.

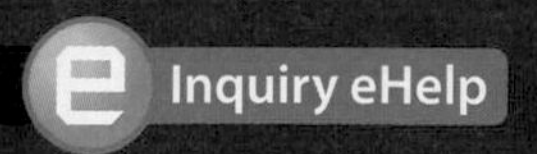

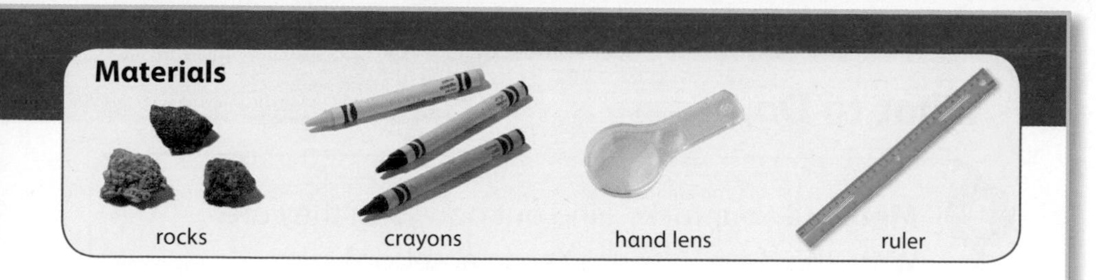

What to Do

1 **Observe** the 3 rocks.

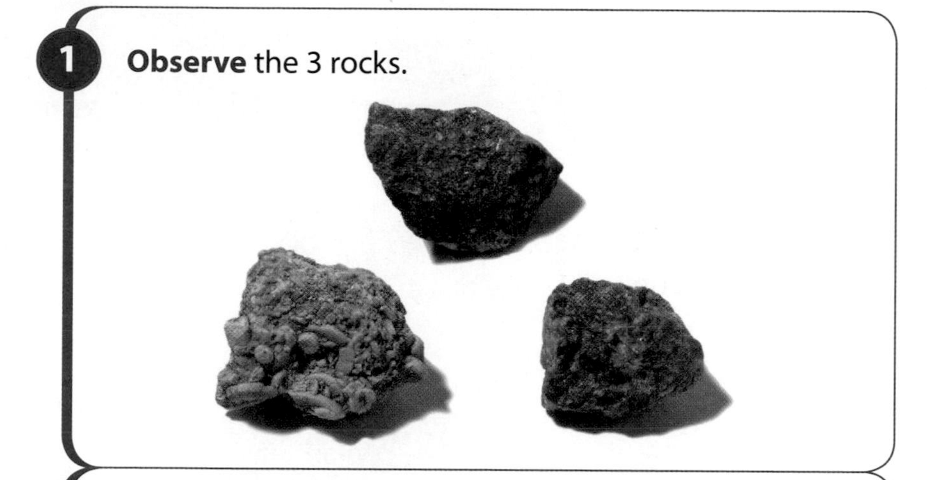

2 What shape and color are your rocks? Trace around your rocks in your science notebook. Color the pictures of your rocks.

7

Teaching Tips

- Make sure students know the meaning of the word *fossil* before beginning the inquiry. Tell them that a fossil is the remains of a plant or animal that died a long time ago. Point out the fossil in the rock on page 6. Tell students that it is actually the pattern in the rock that looks like a leaf. The pattern in the rock is a fossil of an ancient plant.
- Students may find it easier to measure rocks on paper. They can mark on a paper where the longest points are on either side and then measure the distance between the two points.

Introduce, continued

- Have students open their Science Inquiry Books to page 6. Read the Question and invite students to share ideas about the properties of rocks.

❷ Build Vocabulary

Science Process Vocabulary: observe, measure

Use this routine to introduce the words.

1. **Pronounce the Word** Say **observe.** Have students repeat it in syllables.
2. **Explain Its Meaning** Choral read the sentence and the example in the speech balloon. Ask students for another word or phrase that means the same as **observe.** (use senses to learn about something) Say: **Point to the part of the body that you use for your sense of sight.** (Students should point to their eyes.) Repeat the activity for the other senses.
3. **Encourage Elaboration** Ask students to **observe** the rock in the photo. Have them point to the fossil and then add their own observations.

ELL Use Language Frames

Write *I use my sense of ______ to* ***observe*** *the color of a rock.* Ask: **Which sense do you use to look at something?** (sight) Repeat with *I use my sense of ______ to* ***observe*** *the feel of a rock.* (touch)

Repeat for the word **measure.** To encourage elaboration, show students a ruler. Ask: **What can you measure with this ruler?** (my shoe, a sheet of paper, a book) Have students use a metric ruler to find the length of a book.

❸ Guide the Investigation

- Distribute materials. Hold up any unfamiliar item and say its name. Have students match each pictured item to the real item as they say its name.
- Repeat the inquiry Question. Read the inquiry steps on pages 7–8 together with students. Tell students that they will follow these steps to answer the Question. Move from group to group and clarify steps, if necessary.

Guide the Investigation, continued

- In step 2, have students take turns holding the rocks steady while a partner traces them. Students should trace and color all their rocks before going to step 3. For each rock, ask: **What color is the rock? Does it feel smooth or bumpy?** Say: **Make your drawing look as much like the rock as you can.**
- Tell students that shape, color, and size are simple properties. Scientists need to observe more important properties. They might look for layers in rocks, what the texture inside of a rock is like, and other properties to learn about what the rocks are made of and how they formed.
- In step 3, students should measure all 3 rocks and record the measurements with the drawings in their science notebooks. Tell students to measure the longest part of their rocks. Students may also measure any fossils they find. Tell students that this is a more important measurement than the size of the rock.
- In step 4, students should observe the rocks with a hand lens. Ask: **What can you observe with the hand lens that you cannot see without it? What fossils do you see?** Have students draw the fossils that they see. Ask: **How could a hand lens help scientists make better observations?** (It helps them see more details.)
- Tell students that the fossils they see are the remains of animals called *crinoids*. These animals lived in shallow marine habitats. They looked like flowers, with a cluster of waving arms on top of a long stem. The fossils in the rock are fragments of those stems. The fossilized stems are long tubes made up of disk-shaped pieces that can be round, five sided, star shaped, or oval in shape.
- When students share their observations, have them take turns telling about one of their rocks. Ask other students to identify the rock.

❹ Share Results

- Have each group share results with the class. For items 1 and 2, use the Academic Language Frames in the speech balloons for support.

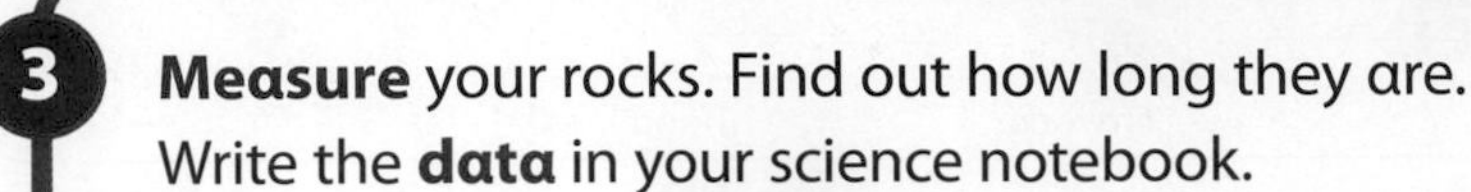

What to Do, continued

3 **Measure** your rocks. Find out how long they are. Write the **data** in your science notebook.

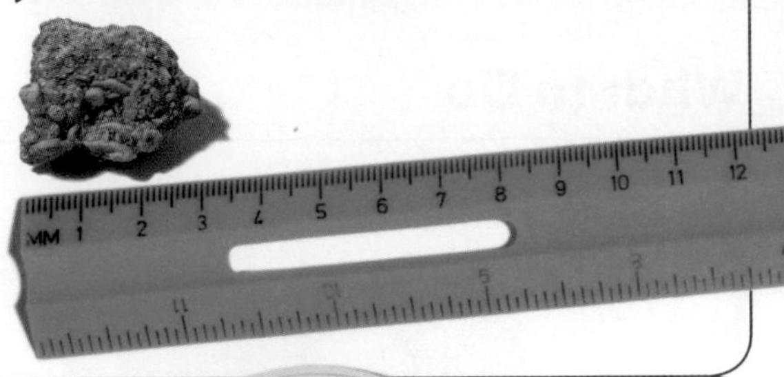

4 Look for fossils in the rocks. Draw any fossils in the rocks.

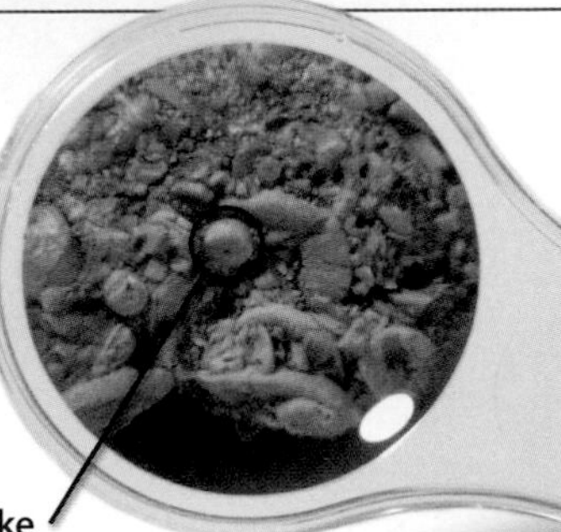

The objects shaped like a circle are fossils.

5 Place your rocks on a table with the rocks from other groups. Share your observations about your rocks with the groups. See if they can find your rocks.

8

Differentiated Instruction

ELL Share Results

BEGINNING

For items 1 and 2, model observing and measuring the length and width of a rock. Write the color and dimensions of the rock. Then point to the data as you ask questions that help students observe the rock's properties. Ask: **What color is the rock? How long and wide is the rock?**

INTERMEDIATE

For items 1 and 2, use Academic Language Frames to help students observe and measure rocks. Write and say: *The color of my rock is ______. The length of my rock is ______.* Have students write, repeat them after you, and then complete the frames.

ADVANCED

Have students review the data that they recorded about one rock. Tell them to list the properties they observed. Ask them to circle the measurable properties on the list, such as length and width. Ask them to sum up all the properties of the rock in one sentence.

Record

Draw your rocks in your science notebook.

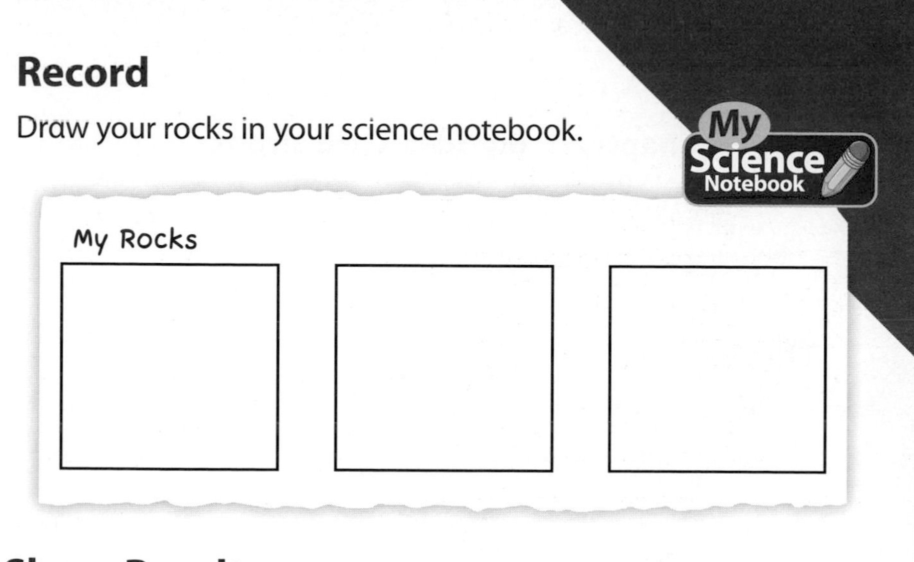

Share Results

1. Tell what you did.

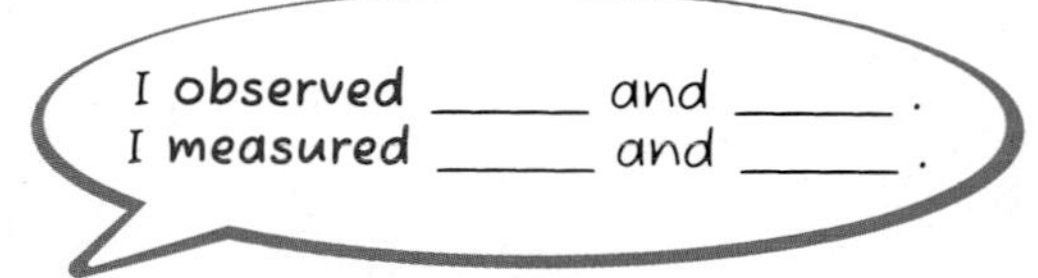

2. Tell about one of your rocks.

Inquiry Rubric at myNGconnect.com	Scale			
The student **observed** the properties of rocks, such as color, size, shape, and presence of fossils.	4	3	2	1
The student traced, made a color drawing of, and **measured** rocks.	4	3	2	1
The student collected and recorded **data** about the properties of rocks.	4	3	2	1
The student **compared** observations about the properties of rocks.	4	3	2	1
The student **shared** observations and **conclusions** with other students.	4	3	2	1
Overall Score	4	3	2	1

Share Results, continued

- Have students compare the information they recorded in their science notebooks. Encourage students to ask classmates for their ideas.

Answers

1. I observed the shape and color of the rocks. I measured the length of the rocks and looked for fossils in the rocks.
2. Possible answer: My rock is brown and 6 cm long.

5 Reflect and Assess

- To assess student work with the Inquiry Rubric shown below, see Assessment Handbook, page 32, or go online to myNGconnect.com.
- Score each item separately and then decide on one overall score.
- Have students use the Inquiry Self-Reflection on Assessment Handbook page 35, or at myNGconnect.com.

6 Extend

Following the activity, lead a classroom discussion about the rocks. Have students tell the differences and similarities between their 3 rocks, including shape, color, length, and the presence of fossils. If time allows, have students choose additional rocks to observe, measure, and draw. If possible, have students examine and record every available rock.

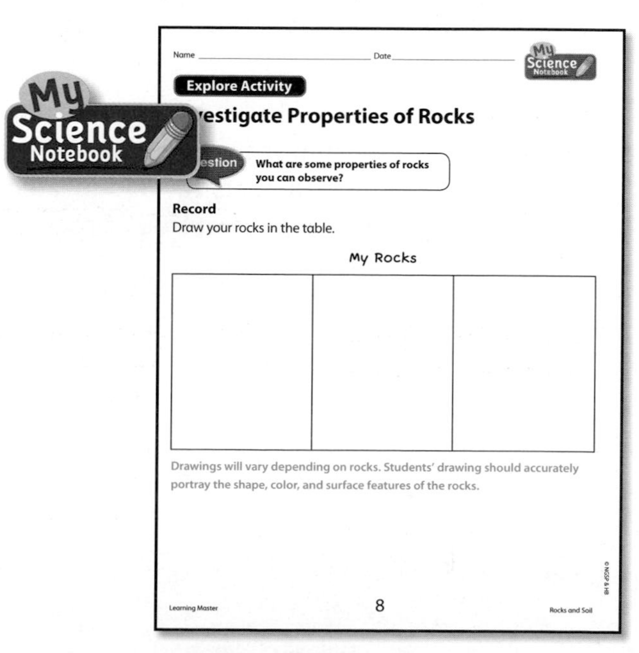

Learning Master 8, or at myNGconnect.com

LESSON 2A ▫ Big Idea and Vocabulary Card

OBJECTIVE

Science

Students will be able to:

- Sort rocks by their properties.

Science Academic Vocabulary

property, texture, mineral

PROGRAM RESOURCES

- Chapter 1 Big Idea Card
- *Rocks and Soil* Learning Master 9, or at myNGconnect.com
- Vocabulary Games at myNGconnect.com

❶ Tap Prior Knowledge

Briefly review the *Rocks and Soil* video. Ask students what they remember about Earth's land and encourage them to talk about some of the ways that people use rocks and soil. Have students give two words to tell about rocks and soil in your area.

❷ Introduce Chapter 1

Big Idea Question

Display the front of the Chapter 1 Big Idea Card and ask students what they see. Read the Question. Explain that any rock can be described by its **properties,** such as color and shape. Tell students that they can learn much about rocks by observing their **properties.**

Show students a rock and challenge them to name as many of its **properties** as they can. Display the **properties** in a list that students can add to later as they learn more about the **properties** of rocks.

Chapter 1 Big Idea Card (front)

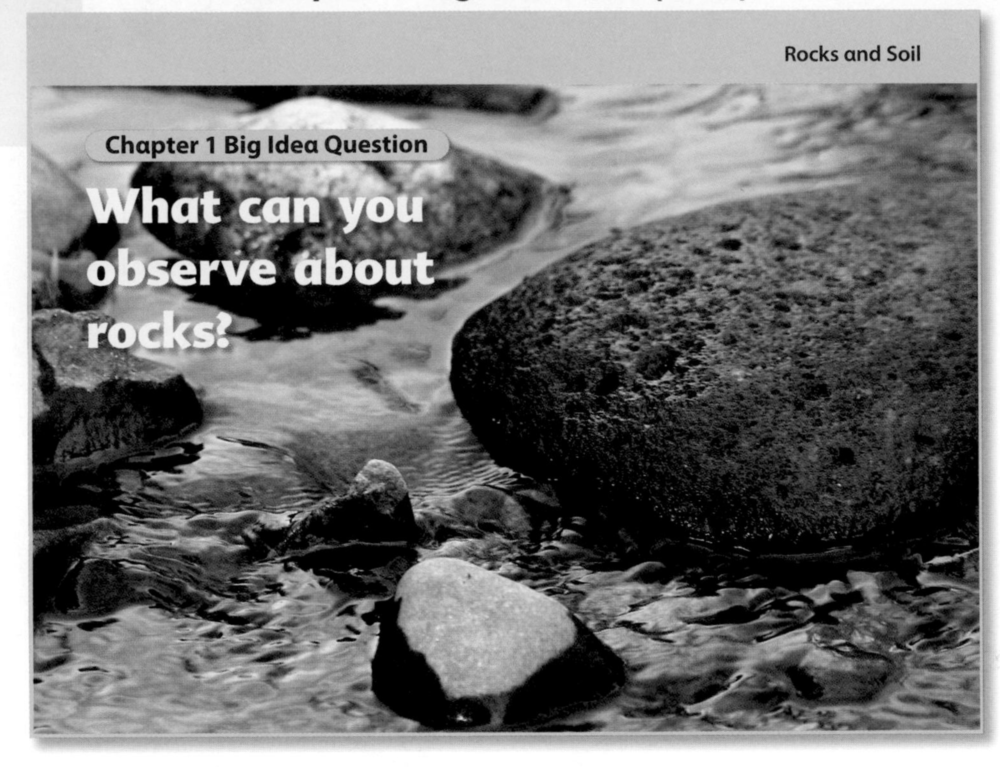

Differentiated Instruction

ELL Vocabulary Support

BEGINNING

Involve students in a chanting rhyme that helps them remember the word *property.*

What I can touch,
And what I can see,
That is called a property.

INTERMEDIATE

Have students draw and color a rock. Have them use this Academic Language Frame to describe one of its properties:

My rock is ______.

ADVANCED

Have students draw and color a rock. Have them make a list of its properties and use this Academic Language Frame to describe it:

My rock is ______, ______, *and* ______.

Chapter 1 Big Idea Card (back)

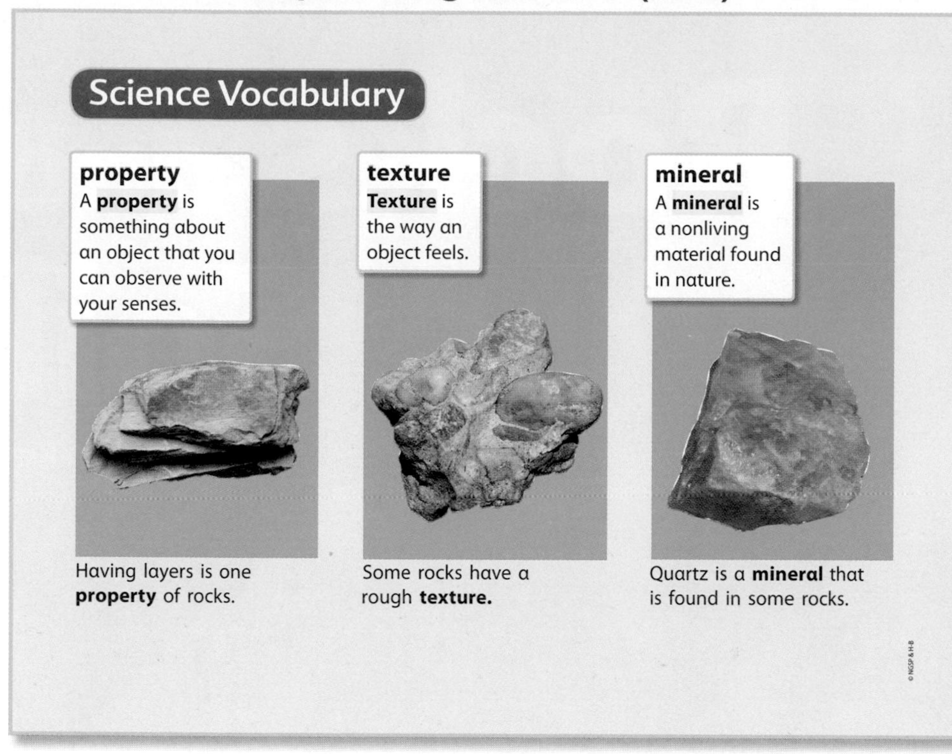

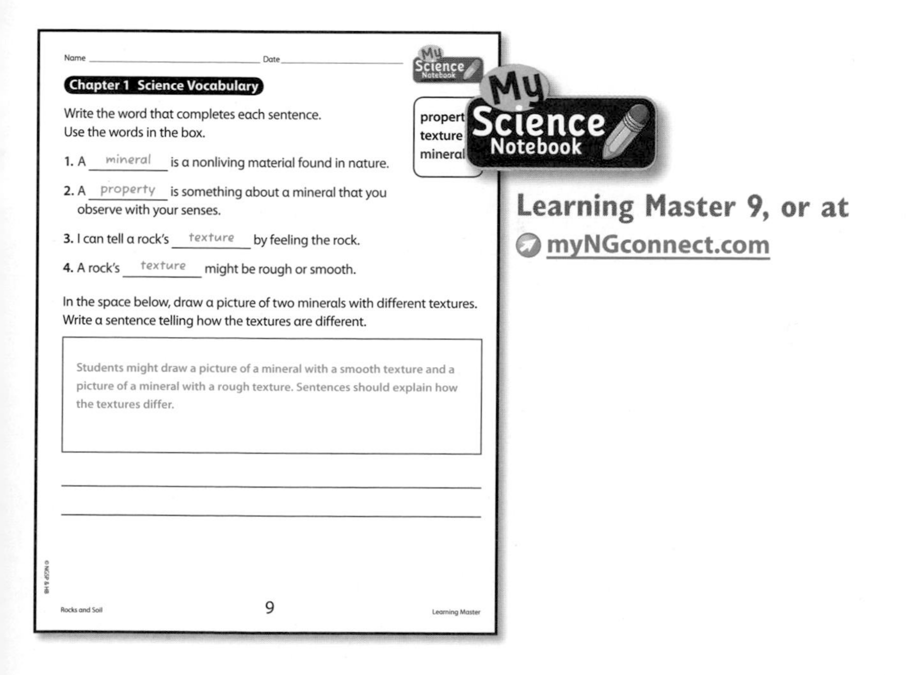
Name _______________ Date _______________

Chapter 1 Science Vocabulary

Write the word that completes each sentence.
Use the words in the box.

property
texture
mineral

1. A mineral is a nonliving material found in nature.
2. A property is something about a mineral that you observe with your senses.
3. I can tell a rock's texture by feeling the rock.
4. A rock's texture might be rough or smooth.

In the space below, draw a picture of two minerals with different textures. Write a sentence telling how the textures are different.

Students might draw a picture of a mineral with a smooth texture and a picture of a mineral with a rough texture. Sentences should explain how the textures differ.

Rocks and Soil 9 Learning Master

Learning Master 9, or at myNGconnect.com

❸ Teach Vocabulary

Display the back of the Chapter 1 Big Idea Card and use this routine to teach each word. For example:

1. **Pronounce the Word** Say **property** and have students repeat it.
2. **Explain Its Meaning** Read the word, definition, sample sentence, and use the photo to explain the word's meaning. Point out the layers on the rock and count them aloud. Say: **This rock has three layers. Having layers is a property.** Ask students to name another **property** of the rock. Say: **Color is also a property of this rock.** Have students compare all three rocks by their colors and whether they have layers.
3. **Encourage Elaboration** Have students compare the rocks in photo 1 and photo 2. Ask: **How are these two rocks alike and different?** (about the same size; different in color, having layers, and texture)

Repeat for the words **texture** and **mineral,** using the following Elaboration Prompts:

- **Which of these is a texture of rock: a rough inside or smooth inside?** (rough inside)
- Point out that the third photo shows a **mineral.** Ask: **What color is the mineral?** (pink)
- **Is a plant a mineral?** (no) **Why not?** (A plant is a living thing.) **What do you think rocks are made of?** (minerals)

Then return students' attention to the photo on the front of the Big Idea Card and invite them to point to the rock that may have air holes. Having air holes is a **property** of some rocks. Then have students compare the two rocks in the foreground, using both words. For example, say: **The properties of the rocks are different. One is red, and one is not. One may have air holes, and the other does not.**

OBJECTIVE

Science

Students will be able to:

- Observe and describe rocks and soil.

Science Academic Vocabulary

property, texture, mineral

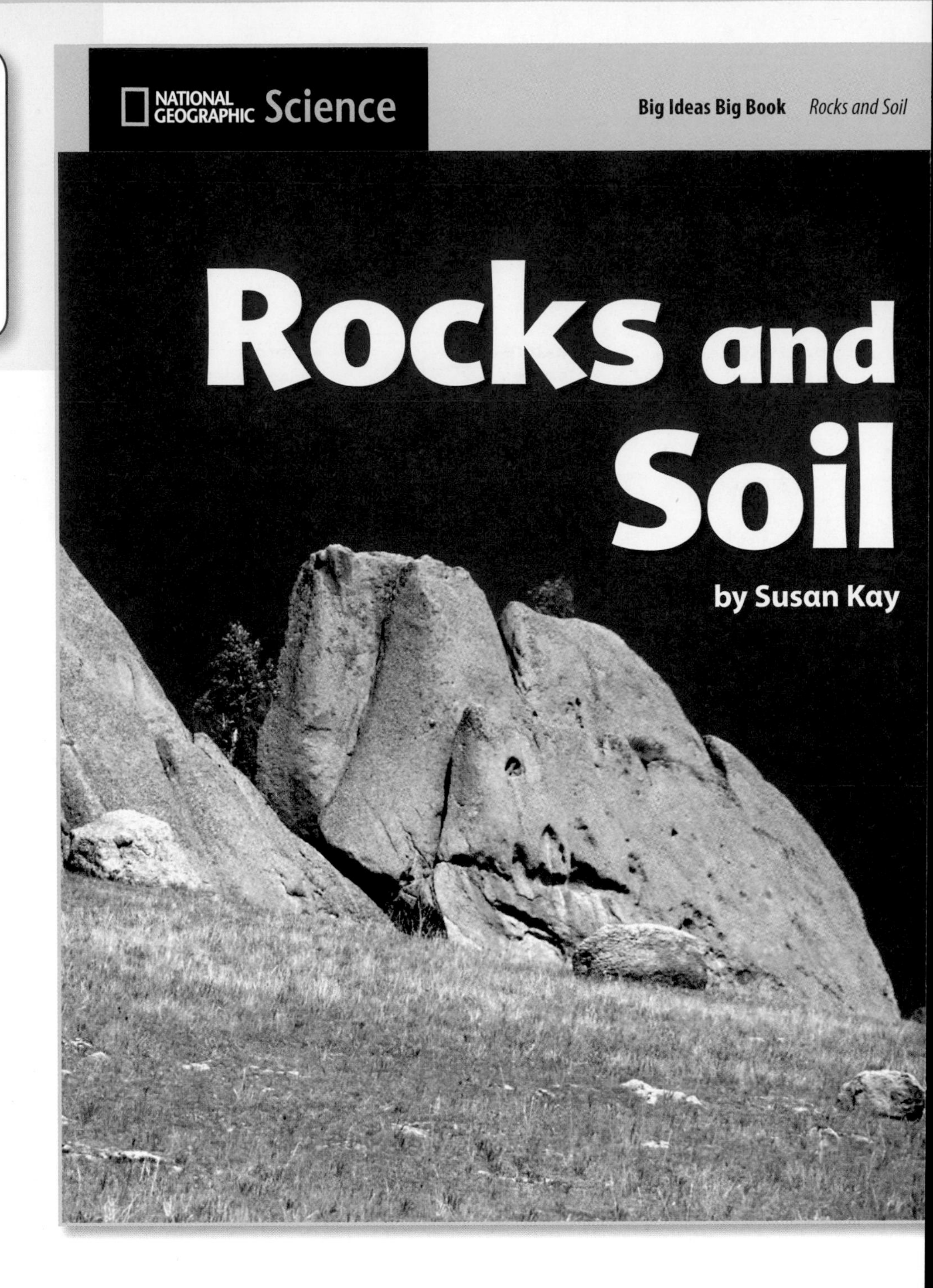

PROGRAM RESOURCES

- *Rocks and Soil* Big Ideas Big Book
- *Rocks and Soil* Big Ideas Big Book eEdition at myNGconnect.com
- Digital Library at myNGconnect.com
- MP3 Read with Me at myNGconnect.com

1 Introduce the Big Ideas Big Book

Title and Author

Display the cover of the Big Ideas Big Book with the front and back covers open. Read the title *Rocks and Soil* and the author's name. Tell students: **This book is about materials that make up Earth.** Ask students to describe what they see on the cover.

Introduce Chapter 1

Big Idea Question

Display the front flap and read the first Big Idea Question. Tell students they will learn the answer when they listen to the Big Ideas Big Book. Point out that students will learn about the other Big Idea Questions later in the unit.

Preview Chapter 1 Vocabulary

Open the front flap and point out the vocabulary words, pictures, and definitions. Tell students they will learn more about the vocabulary words when they listen as the Big Ideas Big Book is read aloud.

Contents

3

❷ Preview the Contents

Connect Contents to the Big Ideas

Point to each color band as you identify the three chapters in this book. Point out the three Big Idea Questions, and tell students that today they will learn the answers to the first question.

❸ Read Chapter 1 Aloud

Use the Table of Contents to locate the Introduction. Turn to page 4 and read the Introduction and Chapter 1 straight through to familiarize students with the chapter content. After reading, encourage students to

- find interesting photos and comment on them
- turn and talk with a partner about a new or surprising idea
- share what they already know about rocks.

Then read through a second time, section-by-section, to teach the Big Idea, vocabulary, and science concepts.

Digital Library

myNGconnect.com

Have students use the Digital Library to find photos of a variety of rocks in their natural settings. You can display the photos using the Presentation Tool.

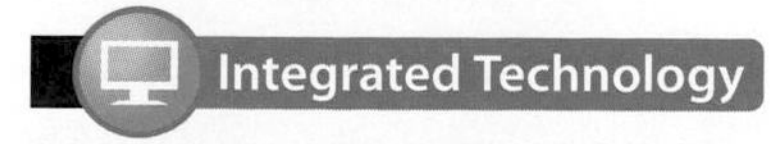

Computer Presentation Students can use the photos to make a video about earth materials.

OBJECTIVES

Science

Students will be able to:

- Distinguish between living and nonliving things. T
- Identify nonliving things made by humans and those made by natural events. T

❶ Introduce

Build Background

Point to a person in the big photo on page 4 and say: **This is a living thing.** Point to a rock in the photo and say: **This is a nonliving thing. The pictures on these pages show lots of living and nonliving things.**

Set the Purpose and Read

- Explain to students that they will learn about living things and nonliving things. Tell them to listen to find out how living and nonliving things are different.
- Then read pages 4–5 aloud.

❷ Teach

Text Features: Photos and Captions

- Point to the caption on page 4. Say: **This is a caption. It tells what the photo is about.**
- Read the caption aloud. Say: **This caption tells you that these are plants, and plants are living things.**
- Read aloud the caption on page 5. Say: **This caption tells you that the photo shows rocks and water, and rocks and water are nonliving things.**

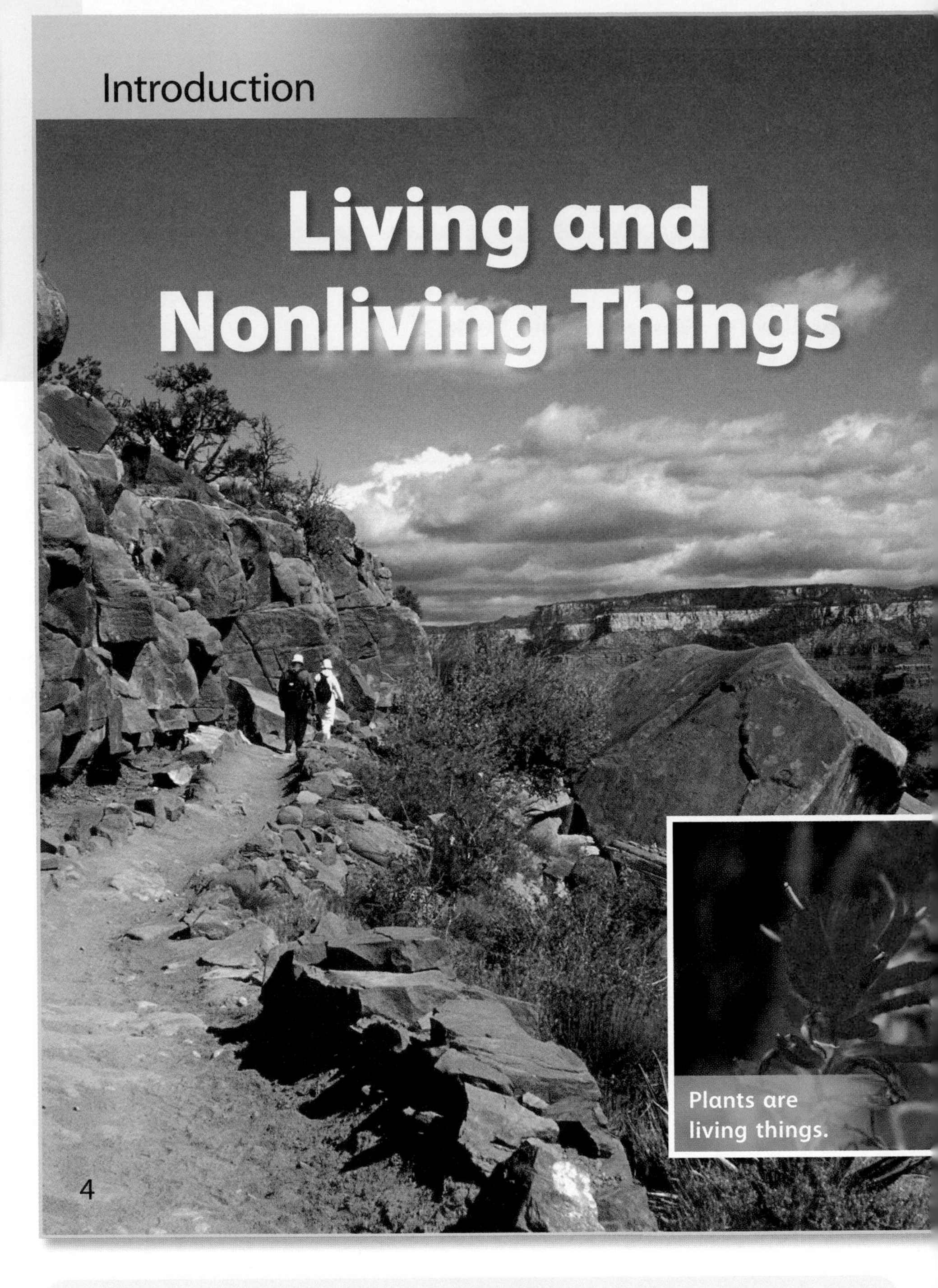

Science Misconceptions

Living or Nonliving? Students might not understand the distinction between living and nonliving things. They might believe that anything that moves is living and anything that has died is nonliving. Explain that living things grow and change, just as they themselves do. To further clarify the difference, point out that things that have died were once living. Stress that nonliving things have never been alive.

Imagine hiking on a nature trail. You see living things, such as plants and animals. You also see nonliving things, such as rocks and water. Rocks and water are part of nature.

The pack on your back is a nonliving thing, too. It is different from the rocks and water, though. It was made by people.

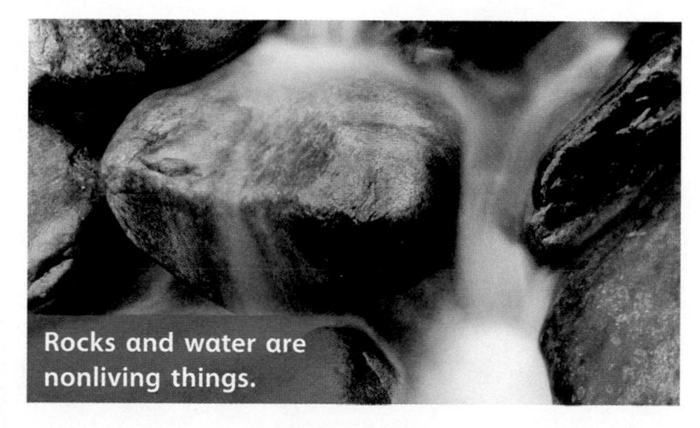

Rocks and water are nonliving things.

5

Teach, continued

Distinguish Between Living and Nonliving Things

- Display pages 4–5. Ask: **What living things do you see?** (flowers, trees, people, plants) Ask: **What nonliving things do you see?** (water, rocks, soil, clouds, sky, people's clothing and backpacks)
- Have students identify living things and nonliving things in the classroom.

Compare Nonliving Things

- Point to a rock in the big photo on page 4. Say: **The rock is nonliving. It is part of nature. It was not made by people.**
- Point to the backpack on each person in the photo on page 4. Ask: **Is a backpack living or nonliving?** (nonliving) **Is it part of nature?** (no) **How do we get backpacks?** (People make them.)
- Ask: **How are the rock and the backpack alike?** (Both are nonliving.) **How are the rock and the backpack different?** (The rock is part of nature. The backpack is made by people.)

Making and Recording Observations

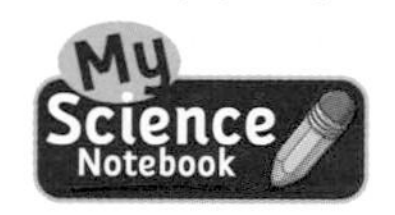

Have students observe again the photos on pages 4 and 5. Then have them record their observations about living things and nonliving things in their science notebook.

Think Like a Scientist Math in Science

Make a Table Tell students to draw or list the nonliving things in the big photo on page 4. Then have them each draw a two-column table. Model drawing the table on the board. Title the table *Nonliving Things*. Label the first column *Made by People*. Label the second column *Part of Nature*. Tell students they will use their lists to fill in the chart. Then have them count the number of things they listed for each category.

» Before You Move On

Ask students:

1. **Observe Do you see living things, nonliving things, or both in the big photo?** (both)
2. **Sort How could you sort the nonliving things in the photo?** (You could sort them according to those made by people and those that are part of nature.)

OBJECTIVES

Science

Students will be able to:

- Recognize that Earth is made up of rocks. T
- Sort rocks by their properties. T

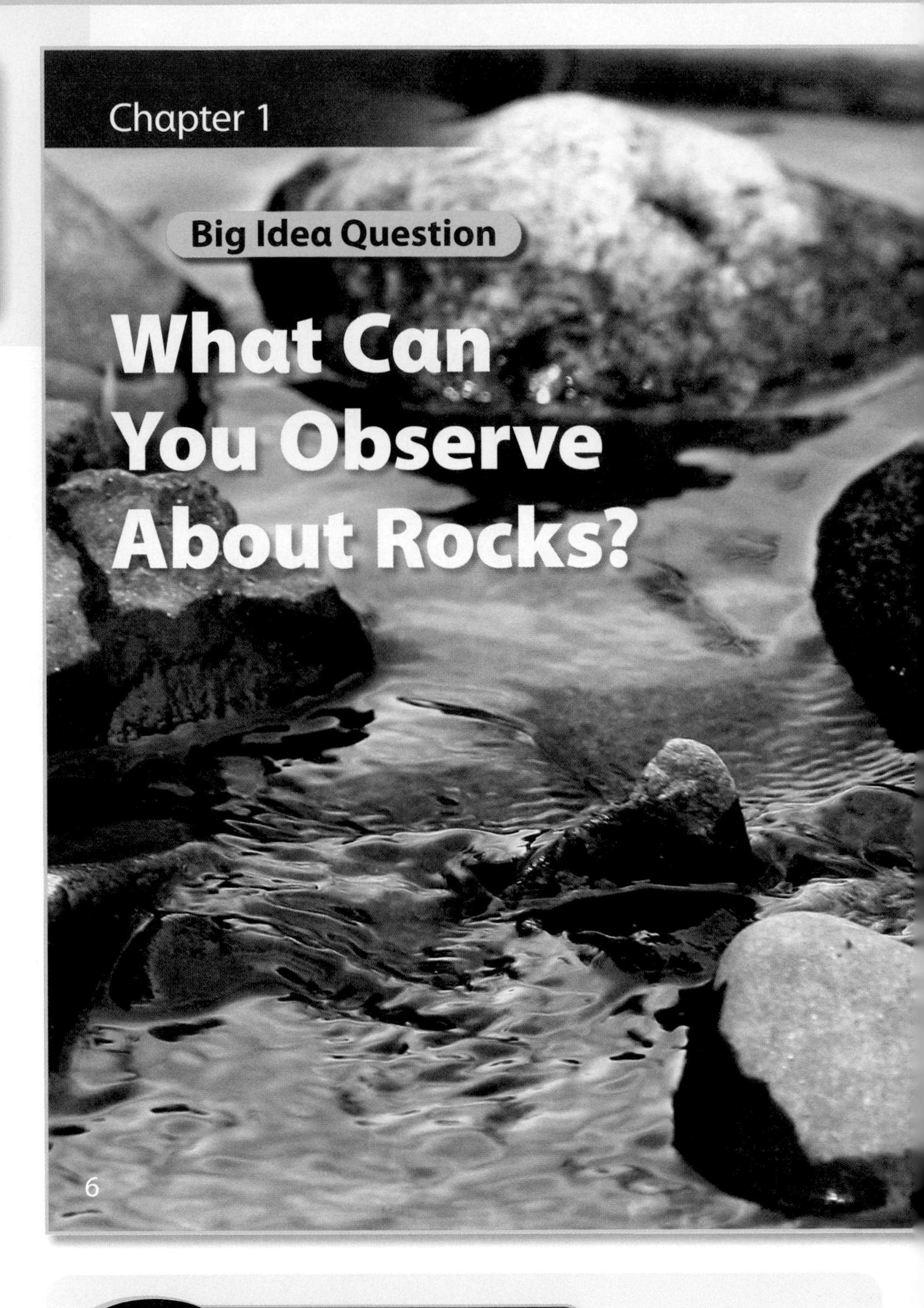

❶ Introduce

Tap Prior Knowledge

Ask: **Where have you seen rocks?** (on the ground, in water) **What do rocks feel like?** (Some rocks feel smooth. Other rocks feel rough. Some rocks are strong. Others are weak and crumbly.)

Focus on the Big Idea

- Read the Big Idea Question and have students echo it.
- Preview pages 8–9, 10–11, 12–13, and 14–15, linking the headings with the Big Idea Question.
- With student input, post a chart that displays the headings.

What Can You Observe About Rocks?

Properties of Rocks

Minerals

Fossils

People Use Rocks

- Have students orally share what they expect to find in each section.
- Then read page 7 aloud.

NATIONAL GEOGRAPHIC Raise Your SciQ!

Egyptian Pyramids People use rocks for many things, including construction. Some of the most famous examples of rock structures are the ancient pyramids in Egypt. The pyramids were made of different types of rock, including limestone. The large stone blocks were likely placed on barges in the Nile River and floated to construction sites. On average, the stones weigh about 2.5 tons—that's about the weight of two cars. The pyramids themselves weigh an estimated 5.4 million tons.

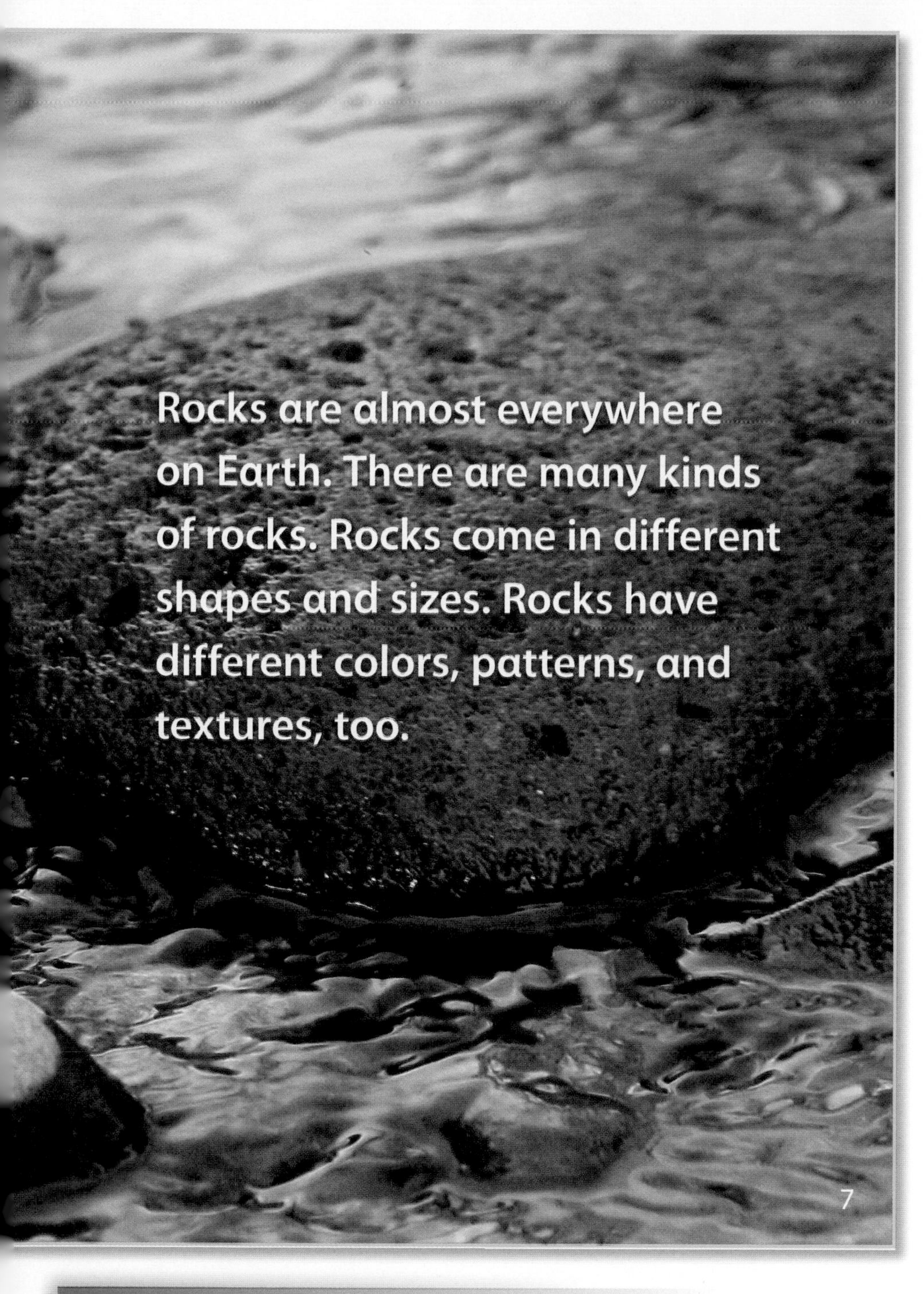

❷ Teach

Recognize What Makes Up Earth

- Hold up a globe. Explain: **The globe is a model of Earth.**
- Point to a continent on the globe. Say: **Rocks, soil, and sand make up this part of Earth.**
- Then point to an ocean on the globe. Say: **There is land under the ocean water. Rocks, soil, and sand make up this part of Earth, too.**
- Explain that rocks can be found in most places.
- Ask: **Are rocks living or nonliving things?** (nonliving)

Comparing Rocks

- Point to the photo. Ask: **What different shapes do the rocks have?** (Some rocks are flat. Some rocks are round.)
- Ask: **What different sizes do the rocks have?** (Some rocks are small, some are medium-sized, and some are large.)

Differentiated Instruction

ELL **Language Support for Comparing Rocks**

BEGINNING

Give students two words, such as *brown* and *gray,* on separate sticky notes that describe rocks in the photo on pages 6–7. Ask them to place the sticky note on the rock it describes.

INTERMEDIATE

Have students study the photo on pages 6–7. Ask them to name the color of one rock. Then ask them to name the color of a different rock.

ADVANCED

Have students select two different rocks in the photo on pages 6–7. Ask them to use describing words to compare the rocks.

» Before You Move On

Ask students:

1. **Recall** **Where can you find rocks?** (Rocks are found almost everywhere on Earth.)
2. **Explain** **Are all rocks the same? Why or why not?** (No, all rocks are not the same. Rocks have different shapes, sizes, colors, patterns, and textures.)

OBJECTIVES

Science

Students will be able to:

- Recognize that rocks come in many sizes and shapes. T
- Sort rocks by their properties. T

Science Academic Vocabulary

property, texture

❶ Introduce

Tap Prior Knowledge

Ask: **What words would you use to tell about rocks?** (Possible answers: *hard, crumbly, gray, brown, round, rough*) Say: **These are all good descriptions of rocks. But you can use other words to describe rocks, too.**

Set the Purpose and Read

- Tell students that the words they used were describing words. Say: **Describing words tell what something is like.**
- Point to the heading and read it aloud. Tell students to listen closely as you read to learn about rock **properties.**
- Then read aloud pages 8–9.

❷ Teach

Science Academic Vocabulary: *property, texture*

- Pronounce the word **property.** Reread the definition. Point out that the table on page 9 lists some **properties** of rocks. Say: **Color is one property of rocks. How would you describe the color of these rocks?** (Students should describe the colors of the rocks on pages 8–9.)
- Point to the word **texture.** Say it aloud. Explain: **Texture is how something feels.** Have students feel the cover of their Big Ideas Book. Ask: **How does it feel?** (smooth) **What is something in the room that might have a rough texture?** (Possible answers: rug, corduroy pants, zipper on coat)

Properties of Rocks

A **property** is something about an object that you can observe with your senses. For example, color and **texture** are properties. Texture is how an object feels. You can sort rocks by their properties.

8

Digital Library

myNGconnect.com

Have students use the Digital Library to find photos of rocks. You can use the  Presentation Tool to display the photos.

Integrated Technology

Computer Presentation Students can use the photos to make a computer presentation about the properties of rocks.

What can you observe about the properties of these rocks?

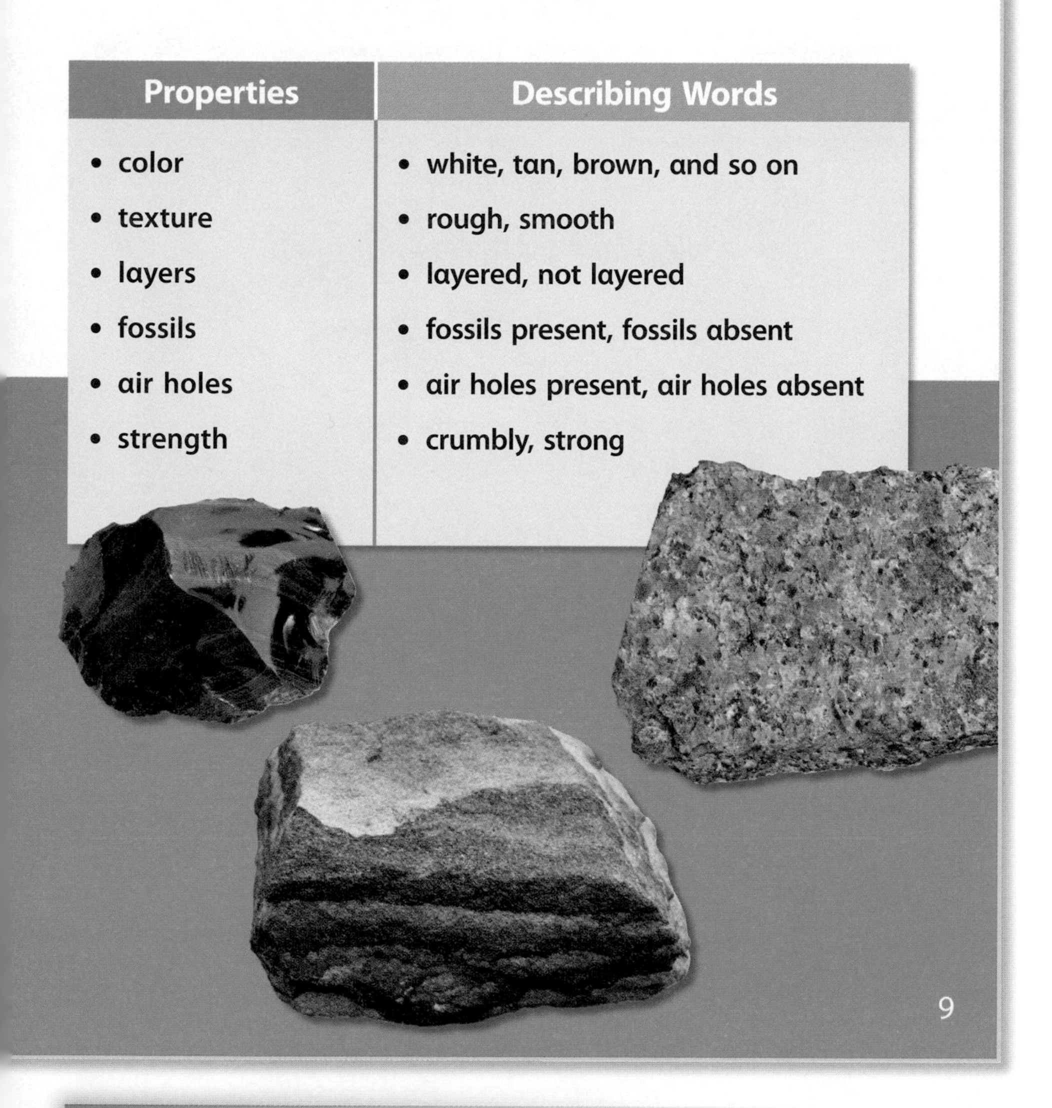

Properties	Describing Words
• color	• white, tan, brown, and so on
• texture	• rough, smooth
• layers	• layered, not layered
• fossils	• fossils present, fossils absent
• air holes	• air holes present, air holes absent
• strength	• crumbly, strong

9

Teach, continued

Sort Information

- Use a chart to clarify the lesson. Say: **Rocks have properties, such as color, size, shape, texture, and having layers.**

Sort Rocks

- Display the photos on pages 8–9.
- Ask: **Which rocks look like they have layers?** (Students should point to the rocks that look like they have layers.) **Which rocks look like they do not have layers?** (Students should point to the rocks that look like they do not have layers.)
- Have students work in pairs to sort the rocks shown in the photos by a different **property.**

❸ Assess

1. **Recall** **What are some rock properties?** (color, texture, layers, fossils, air holes, strength)
2. **Explain** **How would you observe the texture of a rock?** (You would feel it or see it.)
3. **Generalize** **How can you use properties to sort rocks?** (You can group rocks using one property, such as color.)

Differentiated Instruction

ELL Language Support for Sorting Rocks

BEGINNING

Have students look at the different rocks on pages 8–9. Ask questions to help them understand how to sort rocks. For example:

- **Which rocks have layers?**
- **Which rocks have a dark color?**

INTERMEDIATE

Point to a rock on page 8 or page 9 and ask questions that help students sort rocks. For example:

- **What is the color of the rock?**
- **What other rocks have the same color?**

Point out that color is one way to sort rocks.

ADVANCED

Provide Academic Language Frames to help students sort rocks. For example:

- *A _______ is something you can observe.*
- *_______ is a property that tells how a rock feels.*
- *You can _______ rocks by their properties.*

OBJECTIVE

Science

Students will be able to:

- Recognize that rocks are made of minerals. T

Science Academic Vocabulary

mineral

❶ Introduce

Tap Prior Knowledge

- Ask students if they have ever helped make a fruit salad. Ask: **What was added to the fruit salad?** (Possible answers: grapes, pieces of apples, oranges, strawberries, pineapple) Point out that different things are used to make a fruit salad.

Preview and Read

- Say: **Most rocks are made of different things, like a fruit salad is. Some of these things are minerals.**
- Look at the photos on page 10. Read the caption and names of the **minerals** aloud. Have students locate where they think the **minerals** may be in the rock granite. Ask: **Which minerals are often found in granite?** (feldspar, quartz, and mica)
- Repeat for page 11. Ask: **What mineral is the lead in pencils?** (graphite)
- Read pages 10–11 aloud.

Minerals

Rocks are made of **minerals**. A mineral is a nonliving material found in nature. Some rocks are made of just one mineral. Other rocks are made of several minerals.

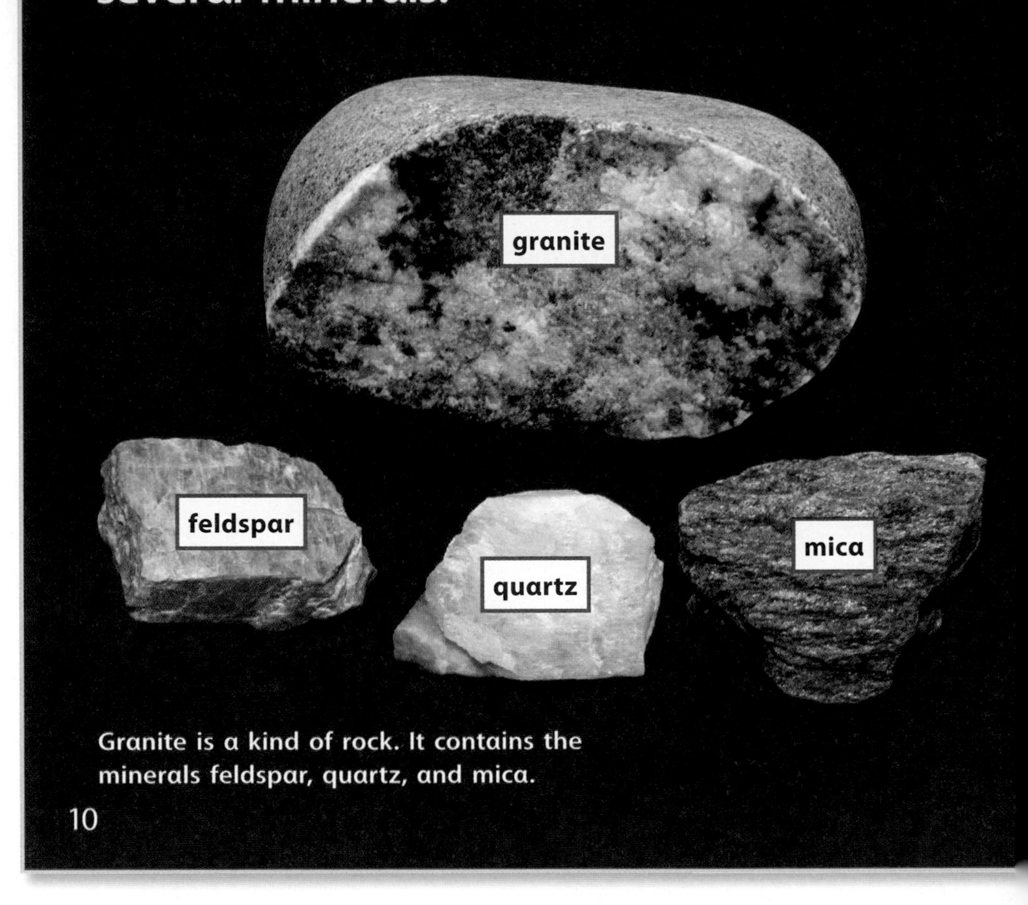

Granite is a kind of rock. It contains the minerals feldspar, quartz, and mica.

10

Extend Learning

MANAGING THE INVESTIGATION

Time

20 minutes

Groups

pairs

PROGRAM RESOURCES

- Learning Masters 10–11, or at myNGconnect.com

MATERIALS

- 4 minerals of different hardness, such as talc, gypsum, feldspar, and quartz
- penny

Sort Minerals by Hardness

Preview	What To Do
 **Question** **How can you sort minerals by hardness?** Explain that a penny is fairly soft. Students will use the penny to attempt to scratch each mineral. They will then sort the minerals into groups based on hardness.	1. Write "Harder" on a notecard. Write "Softer" on a second notecard. 2. Try to scratch one of the minerals with the penny. 3. If the mineral is scratched, place it by the "Softer" notecard. If the mineral is not scratched, place it by the "Harder" notecard. 4. Repeat steps 2 and 3 with the remaining minerals.

Minerals have properties, too. Some minerals are hard, and some are soft. For example, diamond is a very hard mineral. It is so hard that it can cut rocks.

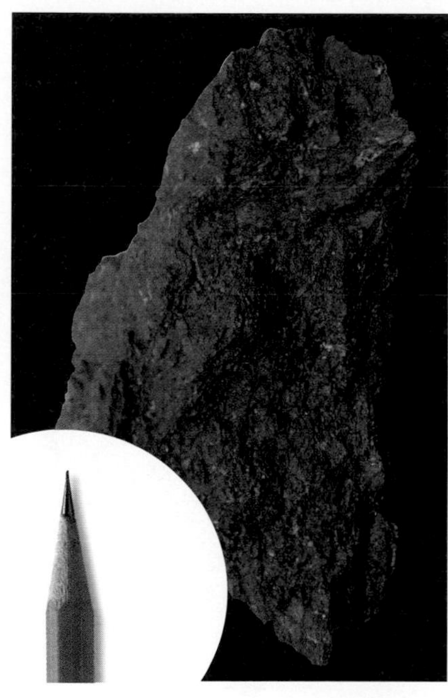

Graphite is a soft, gray mineral. The lead in pencils is made of graphite.

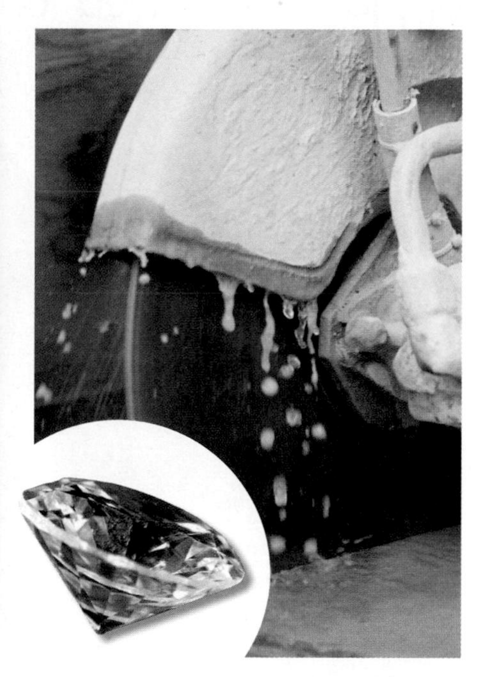

Diamond is a very hard mineral. This spinning saw blade has bits of diamond in it. The blade can cut rocks.

11

❷ Teach

Science Academic Vocabulary: *mineral*

Write the word **mineral.** Repeat its definition. Have students point to the **minerals** on pages 10–11. Ask students to define **mineral** in their own words.

Observe the Composition of Rocks

Have students observe the picture of granite. Tell them granite is a type of rock. Ask: **What are rocks made of?** (minerals) Explain: **The different colors in the granite are from the minerals in the rock.** Then ask: **What are the colors of the minerals that make up this granite?** (white, pink or tan, gray or black)

Drawing Conclusions

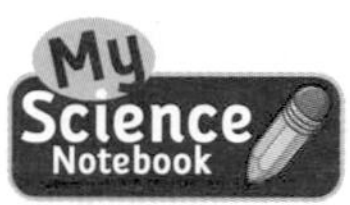

- Read aloud the captions on page 11. Ask: **Which properties of minerals are described in the captions?** (softness, hardness)
- Ask: **Would graphite be used to cut other rocks? Why or why not?** (It would not be used because it is a soft mineral.)
- Have students conclude which **mineral**—graphite or diamond—would cut the other. They can write their conclusions in their science notebook.

» Before You Move On

Ask students:

1. **Recall What are minerals?** (nonliving materials found in nature)
2. **Explain Why do rocks often have different colors?** (They are made of different minerals.)

Name ______ Date ______

Extend Learning

How Can You Sort Minerals by Hardness?

Try to scratch each mineral. Draw them in the correct place in the chart.

	Hard	Soft
Rock 1	Students should draw the two harder minerals in the first column and the two softer minerals in the second column.	
Rock 2		
Rock 3		
Rock 4		

Learning Master 10 Rocks and Soil

My Science Notebook

Learning Masters 10–11, or at myNGconnect.com

Explain Results

Students should explain that

- hardness is a property of some minerals
- some minerals are harder than others
- minerals can be sorted according to their hardness.

LESSON 3B ▫ Fossils

OBJECTIVES

Science

Students will be able to:

- Describe the characteristics of fossils. T
- Infer the type of environment in which fossils formed.

❶ Introduce

Tap Prior Knowledge

Have students recall a time when they may have walked through soft or muddy ground. Ask: **What happened to the ground?** (feet or shoes sank into the ground and probably left footprints)

Set the Purpose and Read

- Read the lesson title. Tell students that fossils are one property that can be used to sort rocks.
- Ask students to listen as you read to learn more about fossils in rocks.
- Then read pages 12–13 aloud.

❷ Teach

Describe Fossils

- Point to the photo of the animal fossil. Read the caption aloud. Ask: **What color is the fossil?** (brown)
- Ask: **What texture is the fossil?** (bumpy)
- Ask: **What does the fossil look like?** (It looks like a seashell.)
- Repeat for the fossil of the plant. Have students describe the color, texture, and appearance of the fossil.

Fossils

Many rocks have a bumpy texture or an interesting pattern. In some rocks, these bumps and patterns might be fossils. Fossils are the remains of animals or plants that lived long ago.

This rock contains a fossil of an animal. The animal lived in the ocean.

This rock contains a fossil of a plant that lived on swampy land.

12

NATIONAL GEOGRAPHIC Raise Your SciQ!

How Fossils Form Fossils form when dead organisms are buried in muddy sediments. Over thousands of years, the sediments harden into rock. Skin, muscles, and other soft parts of organisms decompose quickly and usually do not form fossilized remains. More commonly, fossils come from the hard parts of organisms, such as bones, teeth, and shells. Often scavengers or environmental conditions can destroy even the hard parts of organisms. Thus, an organism has a better chance of becoming fossilized if it is buried relatively quickly under layers of sediment.

Fossils are often found in layers of rock. Scientists study fossils to learn about life in the past.

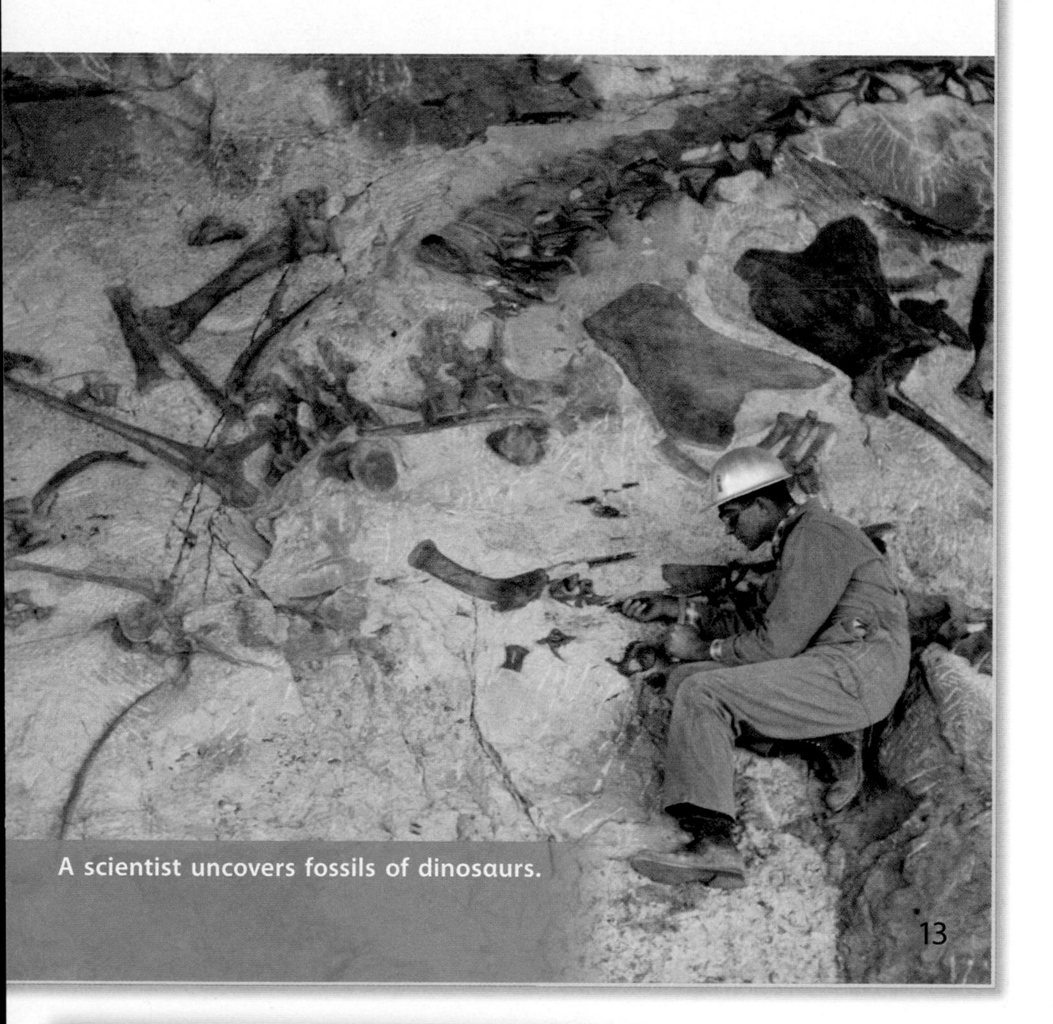

A scientist uncovers fossils of dinosaurs.

13

Teach, continued

Infer Where Fossils Formed

- Say: **Plants or animals can leave a mark in mud in the same way you leave a footprint.**
- Have students look at the photo of the animal fossil on page 12. Tell them: **This is a fossil of a seashell.** Ask: **Where would you expect to find the animal that made this fossil?** (in the ocean)
- Explain: **You can sometimes tell about the place where a fossil formed by observing the fossil.**
- Tell students that some fish fossils were found on dry land. Ask: **What can you infer about the place where the fossil is found?** (The place was once under water.)

Text Features: Photos

- Reread page 13 aloud. Then point to the photo on page 13 and read the caption aloud.
- Tell students that photos and captions can help them better understand ideas in the lesson.
- Say: **The scientist is uncovering fossils of dinosaurs.**
- Ask: **Why does the scientist have to uncover the fossils?** (because the fossils are found in layers of rock)

Making and Recording Observations

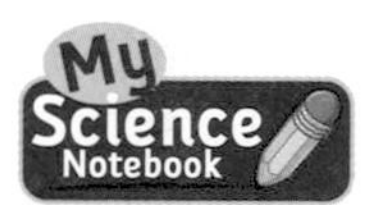

Have students observe dinosaur fossils in the picture. Then have them draw or write descriptions of the dinosaur fossils in their science notebook.

Differentiated Instruction

ELL Language Support for Describing Fossils

BEGINNING

Ask students either/or questions to help them describe fossils. For example, point to the fossil of the animal on page 12. Ask:

Is this a fossil of a plant or an animal? (animal)

INTERMEDIATE

Ask students to choose one of the photos on page 12. Ask them to think of three words to describe the fossil.

ADVANCED

Have partners choose one of the photos on page 12. Ask them to describe the fossil to their partner. Have the partner identify the fossil based on the description.

» Before You Move On

Ask students:

1. **Recall What are fossils?** (the remains of animals or plants that lived long ago)
2. **Explain Why do scientists study fossils?** (They want to learn about life in the past.)

LESSON 3C ▫ People Use Rocks

OBJECTIVE

Science

Students will be able to:

- Identify and describe how people use rocks for buildings, highways, fuels, and other purposes. T

PROGRAM RESOURCES

- *Rocks and Soil* Learning Master 12, or at myNGconnect.com
- Chapter Test 1, Assessment Handbook, pages 7–8, or at myNGconnect.com
- NGSP ExamView CD-ROM

❶ Introduce

Tap Prior Knowledge

Ask students if they have seen buildings that are made of rocks.

Set the Purpose and Read

- Read the lesson title. Ask students to listen as you read to learn about how people use rocks. Then read aloud pages 14–15.

❷ Teach

Identify and Describe How People Use Rocks

- Ask students to recall what they learned about rock properties. Say: **The properties of rocks help determine what rocks are used for.**
- Have students describe how people are using rocks in the photos on pages 14–15.
- Ask: **What tools are people using in the photos?** (tractors, a small pick) Explain: **Rocks have many uses, but people have to use tools to make things from the rocks. What tools do you think were used to make the building in the photo?** (Possible answers: chisel and hammer, some kind of saw)
- Then read pages 14–15 aloud.
- Say: **Rocks are also used to make highways and roads. Some rocks are used to provide the energy we use every day. Coal is a rock that is burned to make electricity.**
- Ask students to identify and describe some ways that rocks are used in their neighborhoods.

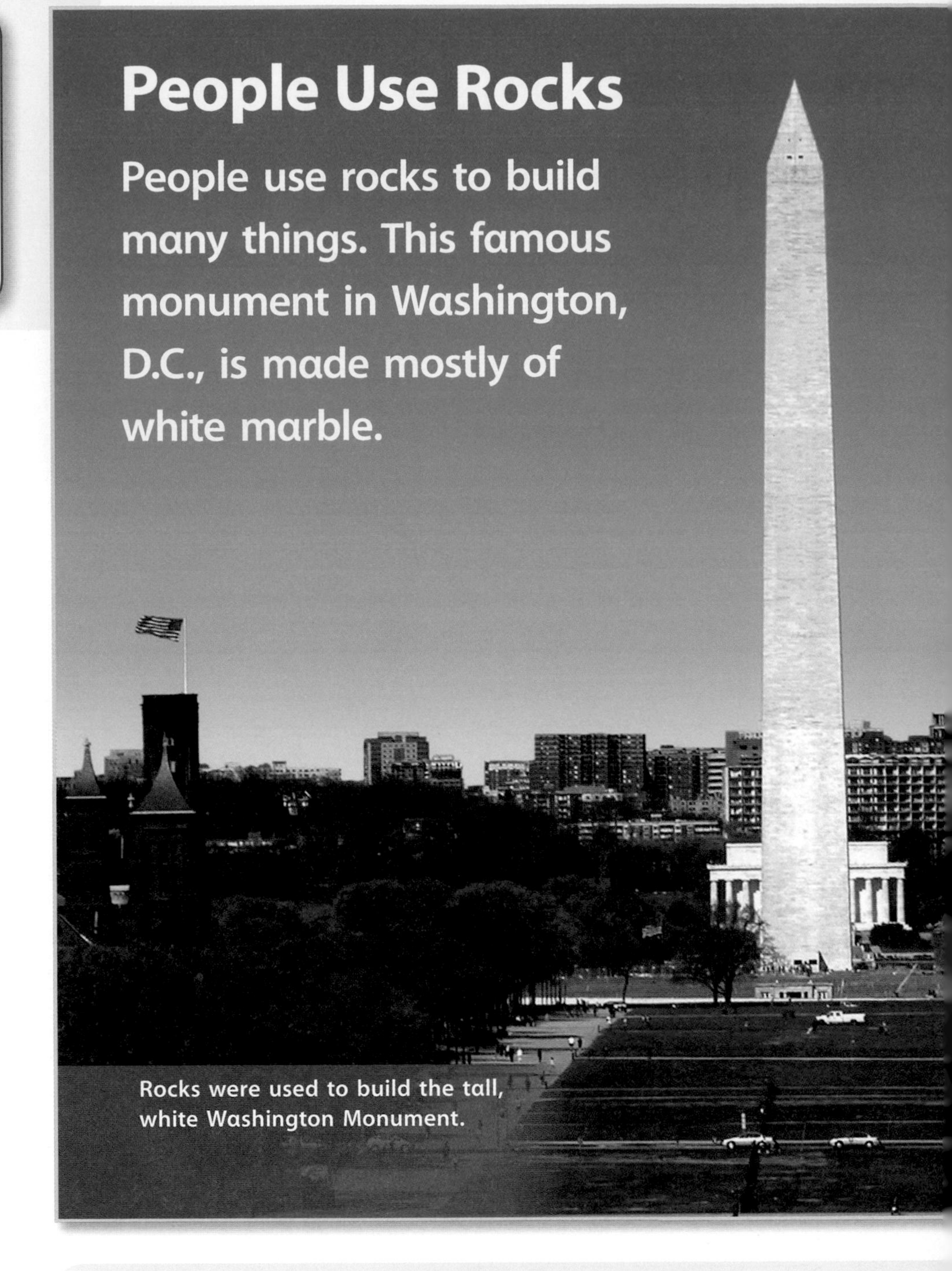

People Use Rocks

People use rocks to build many things. This famous monument in Washington, D.C., is made mostly of white marble.

Rocks were used to build the tall, white Washington Monument.

Share and Compare

Observe Rocks Give partners the Learning Master and a copy of the *Rocks and Soil* small book. Have students read the names of the properties on the chart. Ask them to add one describing word for each property and draw a picture of a rock that shows that property. Partners can use the chart to discuss how they could use rock properties to classify rocks.

My Science Notebook

Name ______ Date ______

Chapter 1 Share and Compare

Rock Properties

Name of Property	Describing Word	Picture of Property
color	tan	
texture	rough	
size	small	
shape	round	
fossils	fossils present	
air holes	air holes present	
layers	layers present	
strength	crumbly	

Answers will vary depending on rocks. Sample answers are provided.

Learning Master 12 Rocks and Soil

© NGSP & HB

Learning Master 12, or at myNGconnect.com

Large rocks are cut into blocks and used to make buildings. Rocks are carved to make statues. Some rocks are cut and polished to make jewelry.

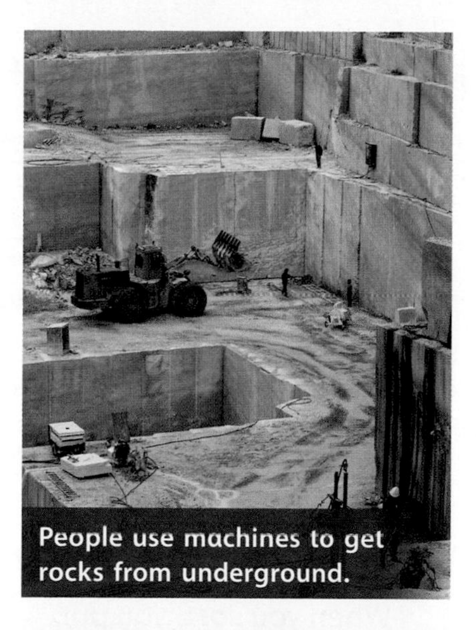
People use machines to get rocks from underground.

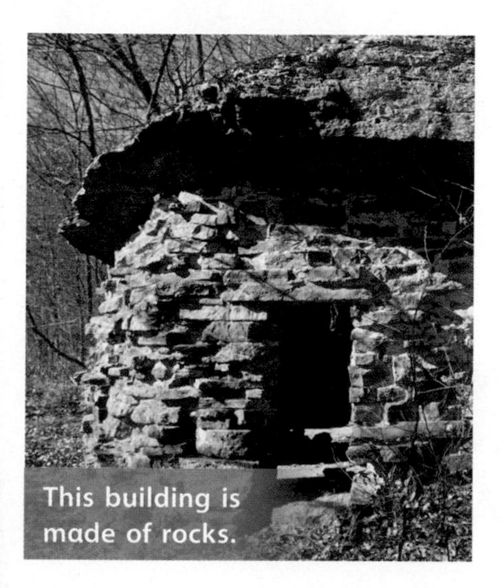
This building is made of rocks.

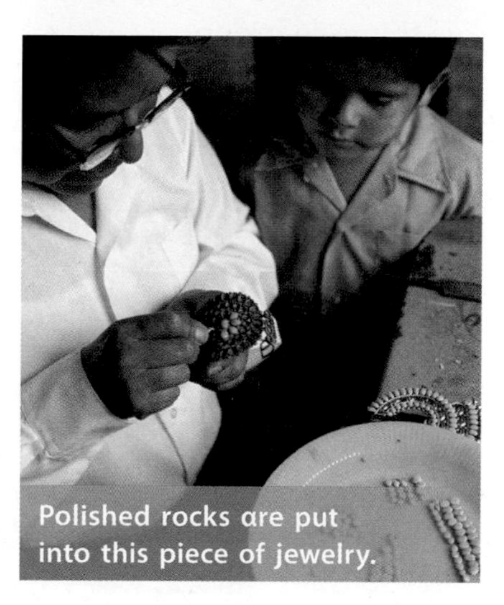
Polished rocks are put into this piece of jewelry.

15

Teach, continued

Summarize the Big Idea

- Display the prediction chart from page T6. Read the Big Idea Question. Then add new information to the chart.
- Ask: **What did you find out in each section? Is this what you expected to find?**

What Can You Observe About Rocks?

Properties of Rocks
Mia Color and texture are properties of rocks.

Minerals
Henry Minerals can be hard or soft.

Fossils
Ela Fossils are the remains of plants or animals from long ago.

People Use Rocks:
Fred Rocks are used for buildings, statues, and jewelry.

Notetaking

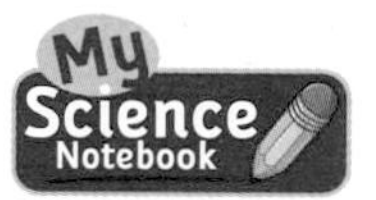

Based on the discussion and the chart, help students develop a statement that sums up the Big Idea. Have students write their statements in their science notebook.

> I can observe properties of rocks and minerals and the ways people use rocks.

Name ______ Date ______ Chapter 1

Chapter Test What Can You Observe About Rocks?

Directions: Read each question. Then choose the correct answer.

1. Which of these are nonliving things?
   Ⓐ rocks
   Ⓑ plants
   Ⓒ animals
2. Which of these is true about rocks?
   Ⓐ Rocks are always small and gray.
   Ⓑ All rocks are large and are smooth.
   Ⓒ Rocks have different sizes and shapes.
3. What is Earth made of?
   Ⓐ air, clouds, and water
   Ⓑ rocks, sand, and soil
   Ⓒ plants and animals
4. Which of these is made by people?
   Ⓐ water
   Ⓑ a mineral
   Ⓒ a backpack
5. Look at the picture of a fossil.
   Which of these shows that this rock is a fossil?
   Ⓐ It is smooth and light.
   Ⓑ It is strong and has air holes.
   Ⓒ It has a pattern of a plant or an animal.
6. What are rocks made of?
   Ⓐ water
   Ⓑ plants
   Ⓒ minerals

GO ON

7 Rocks and Soil Assessment

Chapter Test 1, Assessment Handbook, pages 7–8, or at myNGconnect.com,

or NGSP ExamView CD-ROM

Assess Student Progress Chapter Test 1

Have students complete Chapter Test 1 to assess their progress in this chapter.

3 Assess

1. **List What are two ways that people use rocks?** (Possible answer: People use rocks to make buildings and to make statues.)
2. **Explain How do people get rocks from underground?** (They use machines.)
3. **Infer Why are rocks used to make buildings, homes, and jewelry?** (Rocks are strong; some rocks are beautiful.)

LESSON 4 ▫ Directed Inquiry

OBJECTIVES

Science

Students will be able to:

- Investigate through Directed Inquiry (answer a question; make and compare observations; collect and record data; generate questions and explanations based on evidence or observations; share findings; ask questions to increase understanding).
- Compare and sort rocks according to their properties.
- Make observations using simple tools and equipment (e.g., magnifiers/hand lenses).

Science Process Vocabulary *sort, compare*

PROGRAM RESOURCES

- Science Inquiry Book: *Rocks and Soil*
- Science Inquiry Book eEdition at myNGconnect.com
- Inquiry eHelp at myNGconnect.com
- Science Inquiry Kit: *Rocks and Soil*
- *Rocks and Soil* Learning Masters 13–15, or at myNGconnect.com
- Inquiry Rubric: Assessment Handbook, page 32, or at myNGconnect.com
- Inquiry Self-Reflection: Assessment Handbook, page 36, or at myNGconnect.com

MATERIALS

Kit materials are listed in italics.

6 rocks; hand lens

❶ Introduce

Tap Prior Knowledge

Remind students of the properties of rocks that they observed in the previous inquiry. Ask: **Which properties did you observe?** (color, size, presence of fossils) Say: **In this inquiry, you will use the properties of rocks to compare and sort rocks.**

Directed Inquiry

Investigate More Properties of Rocks

How can you use properties to sort rocks?

Science Process Vocabulary

sort verb

When you **sort,** you put things in groups.

compare verb

When you **compare,** you tell how things are alike and how they are different.

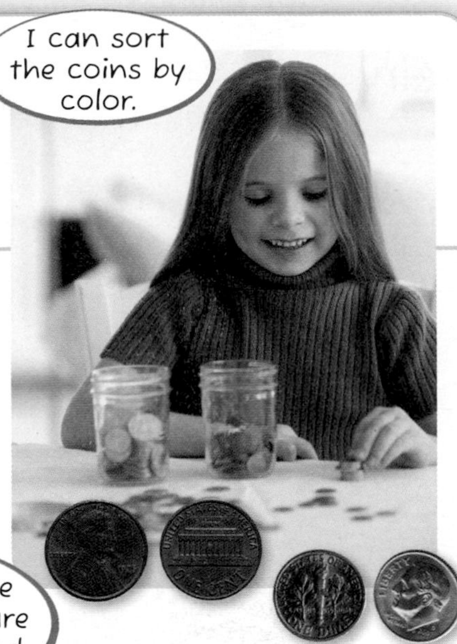

10

MANAGING THE INVESTIGATION

Time

20 minutes

Groups

small groups of 4

Advance Preparation

Arrange the materials on a table before beginning the inquiry. For each group, put 6 rocks in a pile. Recommended rocks include obsidian, pyrite, slate, scoria, sandstone, and rocks with fossils, such as crinoid fossils in limestone.

Teaching Tips

- Before beginning the inquiry, briefly review the properties of rocks already discussed.
- Ask students to volunteer properties as you write and display them where students can refer to them during the inquiry.

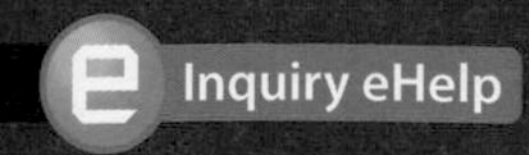

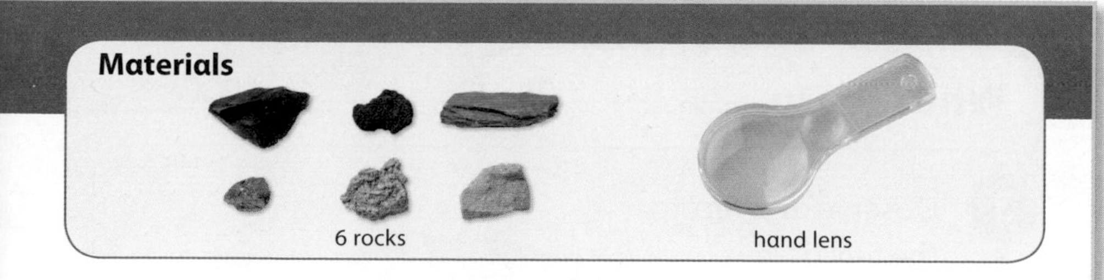

What to Do

1 **Observe** the rocks. Draw a picture of each rock in your science notebook.

2 Use the hand lens to observe fossils in the rocks. Record your observations. **Sort** into groups of rocks without fossils and rocks with fossils.

without fossils

with fossils

11

What to Expect

Students will use a hand lens to observe 6 rocks and compare and sort them by their properties. They will sort the rocks according to texture, presence of fossils, presence of layers, and presence of air holes. They will then sort the rocks into groups based on a property of their choosing. Students will make drawings or write observations explaining how they sorted the rocks.

Introduce, continued

Connect to Big Idea

- Review the Big Idea Question, *What can you observe about rocks?* Explain to students that in this inquiry they will observe rocks and sort them by property. Remind students to observe properties by using their senses.
- Have students open their Science Inquiry Books to page 10. Read the Question and invite students to share ideas about the properties of rocks.

❷ Build Vocabulary

Science Process Vocabulary: sort, compare

Use this routine to introduce the words.

1. **Pronounce the Word** Say **sort.** Have students repeat the word.
2. **Explain Its Meaning** Choral read the sentence and the example in the top speech balloon. Ask students for another way to say **sort.** (group things by properties) Explain that **sorting** objects by properties helps to show how objects are alike and different.
3. **Encourage Elaboration** Have students look at the picture on page 10. Ask: **What is the girl in the picture sorting?** (coins)

ELL Use Language Frames

Write *I* **compare** *how rocks are alike or different before I ___ them into groups.* Have students complete the language frame with the word **sort.**

Repeat for the word **compare.** To encourage elaboration, ask: **What do you do when you compare two objects?** (tell how they are alike and different)

❸ Guide the Investigation

- Distribute materials. Have students match each pictured item to the real item as they say its name.
- Repeat the inquiry Question. Read the inquiry steps on pages 11–12 together with students. Tell students that they will follow these steps to answer the Question. Move from group to group and clarify steps if necessary.

Guide the Investigation, continued

- Have students make a drawing of each rock before they begin using the hand lens. Suggest that students trace around their rock.
- In step 2, have students use the hand lens to help sort the rocks. Ask: **What can you observe on the surface of the rocks?** (holes, layers, fossils) Say: **If there are fossils in the rock, describe them.** See page T1g for information about the crinoid fossils in the rocks. Tell students that these types of properties are more useful to scientists than just knowing size or shape. Scientists can tell more about how the rocks formed.
- In step 3, ask: **How can you observe whether the rocks are rough or smooth?** (by touching the rocks)
- In step 4, ask students to describe the layers in the rocks. Ask: **Are there many layers or just a few? Are the layers wide or thin?**
- In step 6, have students communicate to the class another way they sorted their rocks by presenting the rock drawings in their tables. Have them use the drawings to explain how they sorted the rocks.
- Remind students to record observations in their science notebook each time they sort the rocks.

❹ Explain and Conclude

- Students should examine the data they collected and use these as evidence to develop reasonable explanations for their observations and results. To encourage this, ask questions such as **What do you think?** or **How do you know?**
- As groups share explanations and conclusions, have students ask questions (**Why? How do you know?**) to increase understanding. Students should actively listen for other interpretations and ideas. Discuss possible reasons for any differences in results or explanations.

What to Do, continued

3 Observe and record the feel of the rocks. Sort the rocks by how they feel.

4 Observe and record the layers in the rocks. Sort the rocks by rocks with layers and rocks without layers.

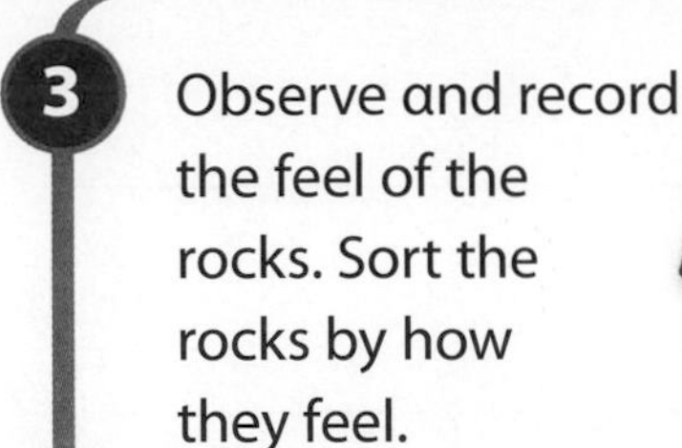

5 Observe and record the air holes in the rocks. Sort the rocks into rocks with air holes and rocks without air holes.

6 Show another way to **compare** and sort the rocks. Write in your science notebook.

12

Differentiated Instruction

ELL Understand Science Process Vocabulary

Provide the following Academic Language Frames for students to complete:

- *When you ______ (compare), you tell how things are alike and how they are different.*
- *When you ______ (sort), you put things into groups.*
- *You can use a hand lens to ______ (observe) the properties of rocks.*
- *You can ______ (record) your observations in your science notebook.*

Record

Write or draw in your science notebook.
Tell about the properties of each rock.

Rock Properties

Drawing of the Rock	Properties of the Rock
Rock 1	without fossils smooth without layers without air holes

Explain and Conclude

1. Did you find any fossils in your rocks? If so, describe them.
2. Was it easier to **sort** by some properties than others? Explain.

Think of Another Question

What else would you like to find out about rock properties? How could you find an answer to this new question?

13

Inquiry Rubric at myNGconnect.com	Scale			
The student **observed** different rocks with and without a hand lens.	4	3	2	1
The student **compared** rocks and **sorted** them according to different properties.	4	3	2	1
The student compared observations about the properties of rocks with others.	4	3	2	1
The student explained which properties were easier to use when sorting than other properties.	4	3	2	1
The student **shared** observations and **conclusions** with other students.	4	3	2	1
Overall Score	4	3	2	1

Explain and Conclude, continued

Answers

1. Answers will vary depending on the appearance and type of fossils in the rocks. Students may have observed round and tube-like shapes of fossilized crinoids.
2. Possible answer: It was easy to sort by presence of air holes because the air holes were easy to see. It was harder to sort by presence of layers because some rocks looked like they might have layers, but it was hard to tell.

5 Find Out More

Think of Another Question

Students should use observations from this investigation to generate other questions. Record student questions for future investigations.

6 Reflect and Assess

- To use the Inquiry Rubric below, see Assessment Handbook, page 32, or myNGconnect.com.
- Score each item separately and then decide on one overall score.
- Have students use the Inquiry Self-Reflection on Assessment Handbook page 36, or at myNGconnect.com.

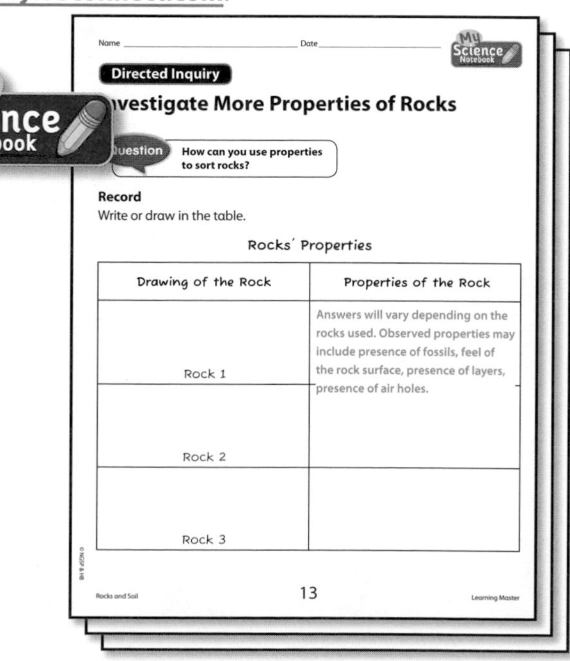
Name Date
Directed Inquiry
Investigate More Properties of Rocks
Question How can you use properties to sort rocks?
Record
Write or draw in the table.

Rocks' Properties

Drawing of the Rock	Properties of the Rock
Rock 1	Answers will vary depending on the rocks used. Observed properties may include presence of fossils, feel of the rock surface, presence of layers, presence of air holes.
Rock 2	
Rock 3	

Rocks and Soil 13 Learning Master

Learning Masters 13–15, or at myNGconnect.com

CHAPTER 2 ▫ How Do Rocks Change?

LESSON	PACING		OBJECTIVES
1 **Directed Inquiry** *Investigate How Rocks Wear Away* pages T15g–T15j **Science Inquiry Book** pages 14–17	**20** minutes		Investigate through Directed Inquiry (answer a question; make and compare observations; collect and record data; generate questions and explanations based on evidence or observations; share findings; ask questions to increase understanding). Observe slow changes to earth materials caused by processes such as weathering by water. Predict and infer how weathering changes rocks.
2 **2A Big Idea and Vocabulary Card** pages T15k–T15l	**20** minutes	**2A**	Describe how rocks change.
2B Interactive Read-Aloud pages T15m–T15n	**20** minutes	**2B**	Describe how rocks change.
2C Big Idea Question pages T16–T17	**20** minutes	**2C**	Describe how wind, water, and ice can change rocks and other earth materials. T Explain the process of weathering.
3 **Weathering** pages T18–T21	**20** minutes		Describe how weathering by flowing water has affected local features. Describe how weathering by ice and wind has affected local features.
4 **4A Erosion** pages T22–T23	**20** minutes	**4A**	Explain how land is changed by erosion from interactions among air, water, and land. T Observe local examples of erosion.
4B New Land pages T24–T25	**20** minutes	**4B**	Recognize how interactions between air and wind can change earth materials.
5 **Think Like A Scientist** *Math in Science: Measuring Liquids* pages T25a–T25d **Science Inquiry Book** pages 18–21	**30** minutes		Identify the tools scientists use to measure liquids. Collect data and create a table. Express quantities using integers. Interpret data in a table.
6 **Guided Inquiry** *Investigate How Water Affects Soil* pages T25e–T25h **Science Inquiry Book** pages 22–25	**15** minutes		Investigate through Guided Inquiry (answer a question; make and compare observations; collect and record data; generate questions and explanations based on evidence or observations; share findings; ask questions to increase understanding; adjust explanations based on feedback). Model how erosion and deposition are caused by interactions between land and water.

T = Tested Objective

VOCABULARY	RESOURCES	ASSESSMENT
predict **infer**	Science Inquiry Book: *Rocks and Soil* Science Inquiry Kit: *Rocks and Soil* Directed Inquiry: Learning Masters 16–18	Inquiry Rubric: Assessment Handbook, page 33 Inquiry Self-Reflection: Assessment Handbook, page 37 Reflect and Assess, page T15j
weathering **soil** **erosion** **gravity**	Chapter 2 Big Idea Card Vocabulary: Learning Master 19 *Rocks and Soil* Big Ideas Big Book	Before You Move On, page T17
		Before You Move On, page T19 Assess, page T21
	Share and Compare: Learning Master 20	Chapter Test 2, Assessment Handbook, pages 9–10 Before You Move On, page T23 Assess, page T25 NGSP ExamView CD-ROM
	Think Like a Scientist: Learning Master 21	Assess, page T25d
predict **plan**	Science Inquiry Book: *Rocks and Soil* Science Inquiry Kit: *Rocks and Soil* Guided Inquiry: Learning Masters 22–24	Inquiry Rubric: Assessment Handbook, page 33 Inquiry Self-Reflection: Assessment Handbook, page 38 Reflect and Assess, page T25h

TECHNOLOGY RESOURCES

STUDENT RESOURCES

myNGconnect.com

- Student eEdition
- Big Ideas Book
- Science Inquiry Book
- Become an Expert Books
- Explore on Your Own Books
- Read with Me
- Sing with Me
- Vocabulary Games
- Enrichment Activities
- Digital Library

National Geographic Kids

National Geographic Explorer!

TEACHER RESOURCES

myNGconnect.com

- Teacher eEdition
- Big Ideas Book
- Science Inquiry Book
- Become an Expert Books
- Explore on Your Own Books
- Write About Rocks and Soil Book
- Online Lesson Planner
- National Geographic Unit Launch Videos
- Assessment Handbook
- Presentation Tool
- Digital Library

NGSP ExamView CD-ROM

OBJECTIVES

Science

Students will be able to:

- Investigate through Directed Inquiry (answer a question; make and compare observations; collect and record data; generate questions and explanations based on evidence or observations; share findings; ask questions to increase understanding).
- Observe slow changes to earth materials caused by processes such as weathering by water.
- Predict and infer how weathering changes rocks.

Science Process Vocabulary

predict, infer

PROGRAM RESOURCES

- Science Inquiry Book: *Rocks and Soil*
- Science Inquiry Book eEdition at myNGconnect.com
- Inquiry eHelp at myNGconnect.com
- Science Inquiry Kit: *Rocks and Soil*
- *Rocks and Soil* Learning Masters 16–18, or at myNGconnect.com
- Inquiry Rubric: Assessment Handbook, page 33, or at myNGconnect.com
- Inquiry Self-Reflection: Assessment Handbook, page 37, or at myNGconnect.com

MATERIALS

Kit materials are listed in italics.

hand lens; sandstone rock; plastic jar (16 oz) with lid; water; safety goggles; *stopwatch; plastic spoon; paper plate*

❶ Introduce

Tap Prior Knowledge

Point out the picture of the water rushing over the rocks on page 14. Explain that rocks in rivers and streams are often smooth and slippery. Ask: **What can you observe in the picture that could cause rocks to become smooth?** (moving water and rocks rubbing or bumping against each other)

Directed Inquiry

Investigate How Rocks Wear Away

Question What happens to sandstone when it is shaken in a jar with water?

Science Process Vocabulary

predict verb

When you **predict,** you explain what you think will happen.

I predict that the water will change the way that the hill looks.

infer verb

You can use what you know to **infer** how rocks are worn away.

I infer that moving water is wearing away these rocks.

14

MANAGING THE INVESTIGATION

Time

20 minutes

Groups

small groups of 4

Teaching Tips

- Check that the lid is screwed on tightly before students shake their jar.
- Make sure students wear safety goggles when shaking the jar.
- Caution students to shake the jar carefully but vigorously to obtain the best results. Group members can take turns shaking the jar.
- Ask students to inform you of any spills. Wipe up spills and wet surfaces immediately.
- Before students do step 4, review how to use a stopwatch. Ask what numbers they will see when 5 minutes have passed.

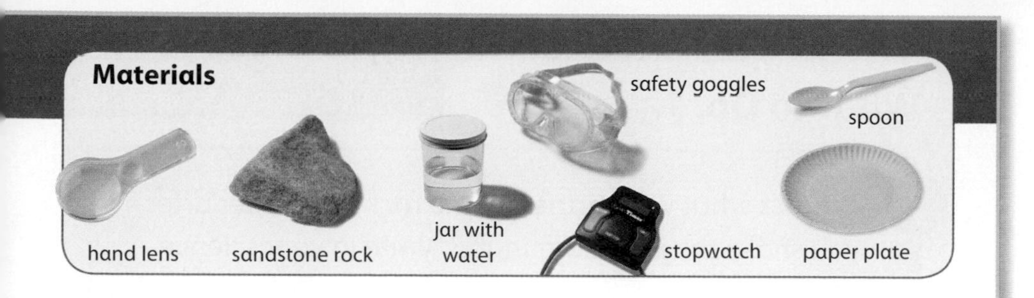

What to Do

1. Use the hand lens to **observe** the sandstone rock. Write in your science notebook.

2. Put the rock in the jar with water. Put on the lid. Observe the water in the jar. Record your observations.

15

What to Expect

Students may predict that the rock will break apart or wear away when it is shaken in water. They may observe that the rock is whole and the water has no pieces of rock in it before they begin shaking the jar. After shaking the jar for 5 minutes, students may not see differences in the rock, but they will see small bits of the rock and sand in the water.

Introduce, continued

Connect to Big Idea

- Review the Big Idea Question, *How do rocks change?* Explain to students that they will observe what happens when sandstone rock is shaken in a jar of water.
- Have students open their Science Inquiry Books to page 14. Read the Question and invite students to tell about a river or waterfall they have visited and what they may have observed about it.

❷ Build Vocabulary

Science Process Vocabulary: predict, infer

Use this routine to introduce the words.

1. **Pronounce the Word** Say **predict.** Have students repeat it in syllables.
2. **Explain Its Meaning** Choral read the sentence and the example. Ask students for another way to say **predict.** (tell what will happen) Explain that a **prediction** is not a wild guess. It is based on what you observe and know.
3. **Encourage Elaboration** Have students look at the picture and **prediction** on page 14. Say: **Imagine water falls on the hill. Predict where the rocks and soil will go.** (They will go to the bottom of the hill.)

ELL Vocabulary Support

Tell students that a **prediction** can be written as an If ... then ... statement. Give students a simple example of an If ... then ... statement. (If a plant is watered, then it will grow.)

Repeat for the word **infer.** To encourage elaboration, say: **Imagine you saw a pile of rocks at the bottom of a hill.** Ask: **What can you infer about the rocks?** (They fell down the hill.)

❸ Guide the Investigation

- Distribute materials. Hold up any unfamiliar item and say its name. Have students match each pictured item to the real item as they say its name.
- Repeat the inquiry Question. Read the inquiry steps on pages 15–16 together with students. Tell students that they will follow these steps to answer the Question. Move from group to group and clarify steps if necessary.

Guide the Investigation, continued

- Have students write their predictions in their science notebooks before beginning the inquiry.
- In step 5, tell students to let the jar sit for a minute before observing it. Ask: **How are the rock and water different than they were before you shook the jar? What do you see in the water? Where do you think it came from?**
- Tell students that this model shows several things that happen in nature. Shaking shows how water moves and erodes rock. The rock hitting the container shows how rocks bump into each other and other hard surfaces during erosion. Small parts breaking off of the rock show how physical weathering works.

❹ Explain and Conclude

- Have students compare observations. Students should examine the data they collected and use them as evidence to develop reasonable explanations.
- Explain to students how to distinguish between empirical observations, or observations made with the senses, and ideas or inferences. Point out that they use observations to make inferences.
- Tell students that wearing away by water is just one way that Earth's surface changes. Point out that freezing and thawing of rocks can cause them to break apart. Ask students to tell about times they have seen rocks broken this way.
- Have students compare their explanations for their results to their prior knowledge and predictions.

Answers

1. Possible answer: The rock was worn away. The water had pieces of rock in it. My prediction was supported.
2. Possible answer: Pieces of the rock wore off the rock.
3. Possible answer: Water breaks off small pieces from rocks. It makes the rocks smaller, smoother, and more rounded.

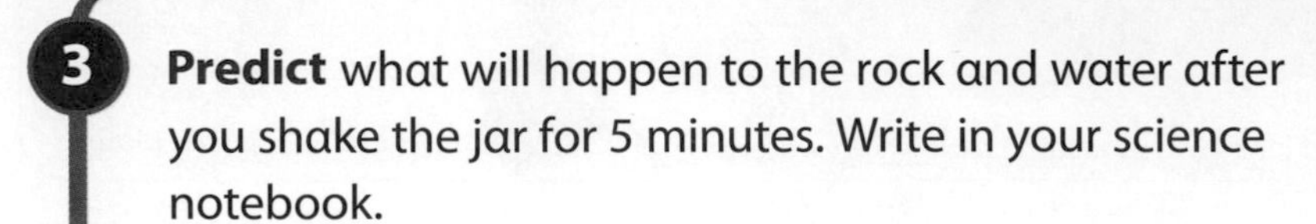

What to Do, continued

3. **Predict** what will happen to the rock and water after you shake the jar for 5 minutes. Write in your science notebook.

4. Put on your safety goggles. Use the stopwatch as you shake the jar for 5 minutes.

5. Use the spoon to put the rock on the paper plate. Observe the rock and the water. Record your observations.

16

Science Misconceptions

How Quickly Do Rocks Change? Most rocks are very hard. Therefore, students often believe that rocks do not change or that they only change when they are subjected to great force. These misconceptions arise in part because students have a difficult time visualizing processes that occur slowly over long periods of time. Stress that the type of weathering and erosion modeled in this inquiry takes place over the course of many years rather than minutes.

Record

Write or draw what happened to the rock and water. Use a table like this one.

	Before Being Shaken	After Being Shaken
Rock		
Water		

Explain Your Results

1. What happened to the rock and water? Do these results support your **prediction?** Explain.
2. What do you think caused the change in the water?
3. What can you **infer** from your results about how water wears away rocks?

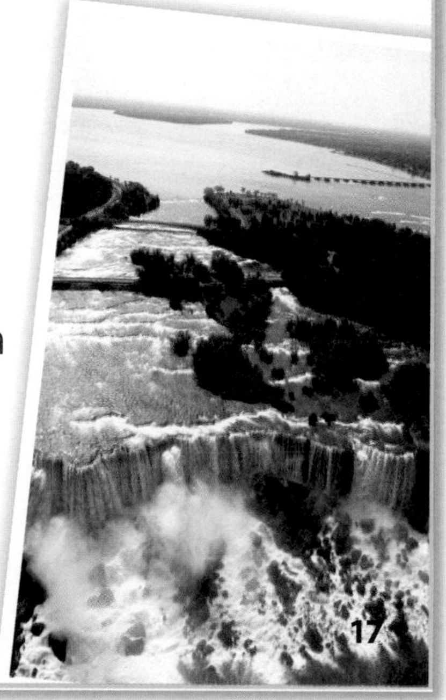

Think of Another Question

What else would you like to find out about how water wears away rocks? How could you find an answer to this new question?

17

Inquiry Rubric at myNGconnect.com	Scale			
The student made a **model** of how moving water affects rocks by shaking a sandstone rock in a jar of water.	4	3	2	1
The student **predicted** what would happen to the rock when shaken in the jar of water.	4	3	2	1
The student **observed** the model and recorded **data.**	4	3	2	1
The student **inferred** from the investigation how water wears away rocks.	4	3	2	1
The student **shared** and **compared** observations and **conclusions** with other students.	4	3	2	1
Overall Score	**4**	**3**	**2**	**1**

5 Find Out More

Think of Another Question

- Students should use observations from this investigation to generate other questions that can be answered using readily available materials.
- Record student questions for possible future investigations.

6 Reflect and Assess

- To assess student work with the Inquiry Rubric shown below, see Assessment Handbook, page 33, or go online to myNGconnect.com.
- Score each item separately and then decide on one overall score.
- Have students use the Inquiry Self-Reflection on Assessment Handbook page 37, or at myNGconnect.com.

Think Like a Scientist How Scientists Work

Explain to students that some scientific investigations are conducted on a smaller scale in a shorter amount of time, which is what students did during this inquiry. This allows scientists to use what they learned as a model to infer about events that take place over hundreds, thousands, or even millions of years.

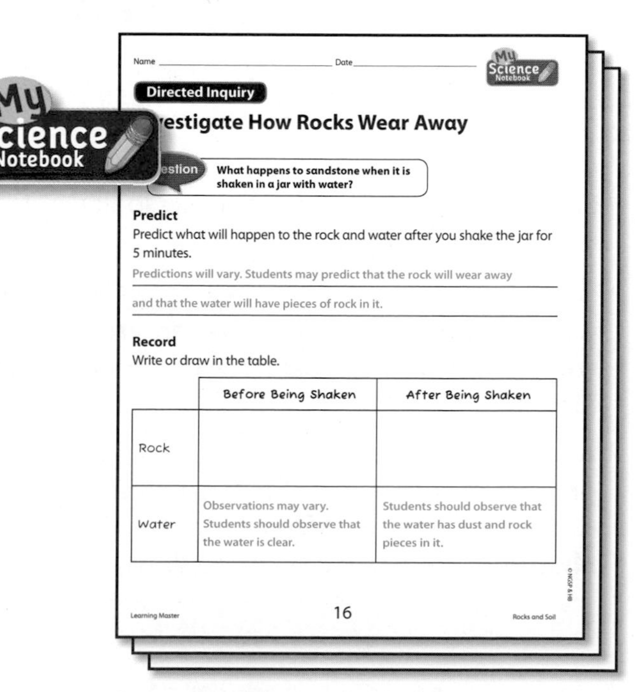
My Science Notebook

Name ______ Date ______

Directed Inquiry

Investigate How Rocks Wear Away

Question: **What happens to sandstone when it is shaken in a jar with water?**

Predict

Predict what will happen to the rock and water after you shake the jar for 5 minutes.

Predictions will vary. Students may predict that the rock will wear away and that the water will have pieces of rock in it.

Record

Write or draw in the table.

	Before Being Shaken	After Being Shaken
Rock		
Water	Observations may vary. Students should observe that the water is clear.	Students should observe that the water has dust and rock pieces in it.

© NGSP & HB

Learning Master 16 Rocks and Soil

Learning Masters 16–18, or at myNGconnect.com

LESSON 2A ▫ Big Idea and Vocabulary Card

OBJECTIVE

Science

Students will be able to:

- Describe how rocks change.

Science Academic Vocabulary

weathering, soil, erosion, gravity

PROGRAM RESOURCES

- Chapter 2 Big Idea Card
- *Rocks and Soil* Learning Master 19, or at myNGconnect.com
- Vocabulary Games at myNGconnect.com

❶ Tap Prior Knowledge

Have students raise their hands if they have ever noticed cracks in a sidewalk. Ask volunteers to describe the cracks. Say: **Sidewalks are made of concrete. Concrete is very hard, like rock. However, concrete is not a rock. What do you think causes it to crack and break?** Guide students to recognize that weather elements, such as water and ice, are often the cause. Tie this back to the main idea. Ask: **Does concrete change or stay the same?** (It changes.) **How does it change?** (by cracking or breaking apart)

❷ Introduce Chapter 2

Big Idea Question

- Display the front of the Chapter 2 Big Idea Card and ask students what they see. Read the Question. Explain that the rock did not always look this way. It was changed gradually, over time.
- Point to the grooves in the rock. Say: **This rock was carved out by wind, water, and sand. It took many, many years for the rock to look like this.**
- Ask: **Is wind still changing the rock in the photo, or is the rock finished changing?** (It is still changing now.) **Why can't we watch it change?** (because it changes so slowly)

Chapter 2 Big Idea Card (front)

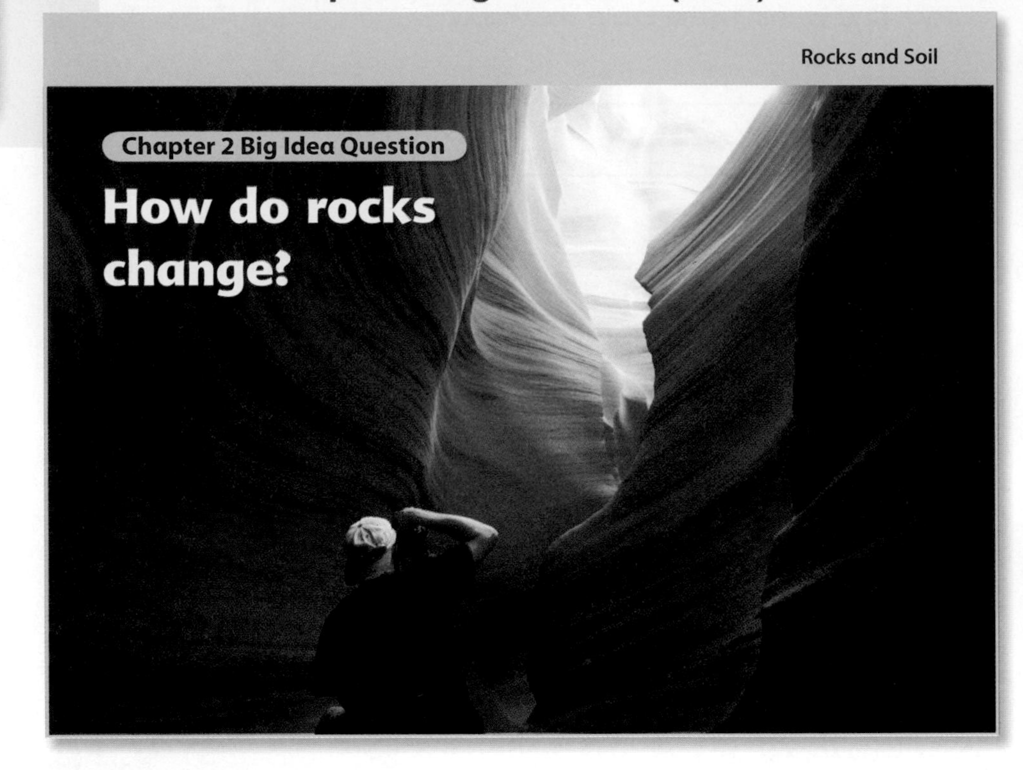

Differentiated Instruction

ELL Vocabulary Support

BEGINNING

Have students draw a picture of small rocks in a stream of water and a second picture of the rocks after they were moved by the water. Have students write and say:

This is erosion.

INTERMEDIATE

Have students draw a picture to help them remember the meaning of each vocabulary word. Provide Academic Language Frames for them to say the meaning to a partner. For example:

- *Erosion is ______.*

ADVANCED

Have students answer the questions *What is erosion?* and *What causes erosion?*

- *Erosion is ______.*
- *______, ______, and ______ cause erosion.*

Chapter 2 Big Idea Card (back)

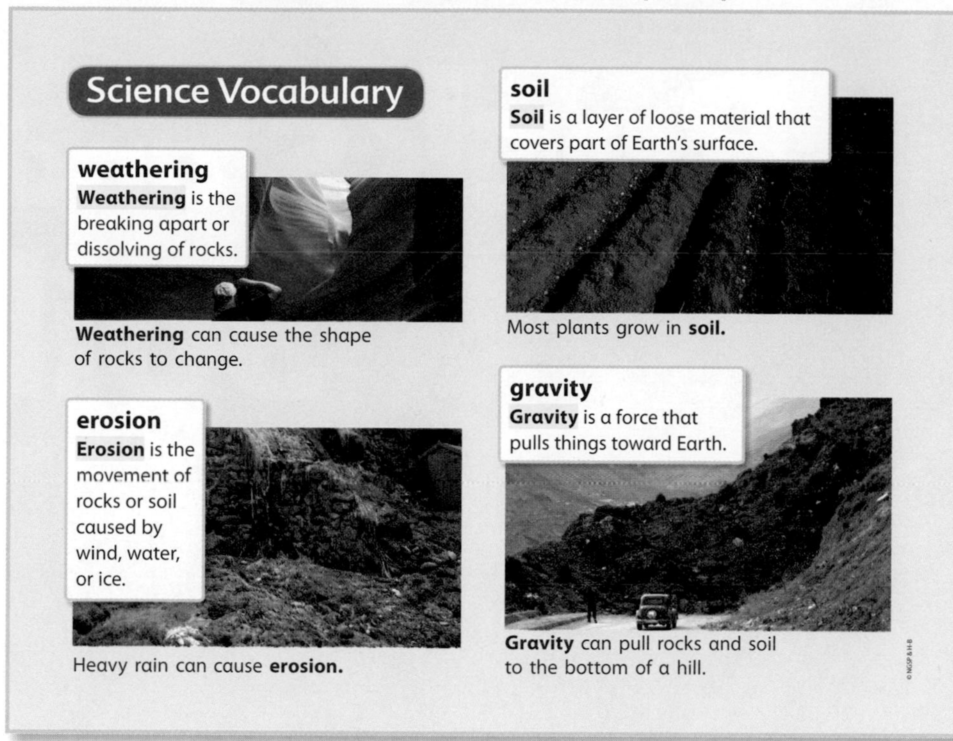

Name ____________ Date ____________

Chapter 2 Science Vocabulary

Circle the word that completes each sentence.

1. Two processes that change rocks are weathering and _______.
   (erosion) soil
2. The process that breaks down rocks is _______.
   (weathering) erosion
3. The force that pulls all things toward Earth is _______.
   weathering (gravity)
4. Clay is a kind of _______.
   (soil) erosion
5. Draw a picture about one of the vocabulary words. Label your picture.

   Drawings will vary.

Rocks and Soil 19 Learning Master

My Science Notebook

Learning Master 19, or at
myNGconnect.com

❸ Teach Vocabulary

Display the back of the Chapter 2 Big Idea Card and use this routine to teach each word. For example:

1. **Pronounce the Word** Say **weathering** and have students repeat it. Say it again in syllables and have students echo each syllable. Then say the whole word again as a group. Ask: **What other word is part of this word?** (weather)
2. **Explain Its Meaning** Read the word, definition, and sample sentence and use the photo to explain the word's meaning. Ask: **How has weathering changed this rock?** (It changed the shape of the rock.)
3. **Encourage Elaboration** Ask: **How has the shape of these rocks changed?** (Possible answer: The rocks look like a deep canyon with swirled walls.)

Repeat for the words **soil, erosion,** and **gravity,** using the following Elaboration Prompts:

- **What is another name you might use for soil?** (dirt) **What is one reason soil is so important?** (Plants grow in it.)
- **What causes erosion?** (wind, water, or ice)
- **When rocks or soil erode, are rocks or soil moved somewhere else or left in one place?** (Rocks or soil are moved somewhere else.)
- **What makes rocks and soil fall to the bottom of a hill?** (gravity)

OBJECTIVE

Science

Students will be able to:

- Describe how rocks change.

Science Academic Vocabulary

weathering, soil, erosion, gravity

PROGRAM RESOURCES

- *Rocks and Soil* Big Ideas Big Book
- *Rocks and Soil* Big Ideas Big Book eEdition at myNGconnect.com
- Digital Library at myNGconnect.com
- MP3 Read with Me at myNGconnect.com

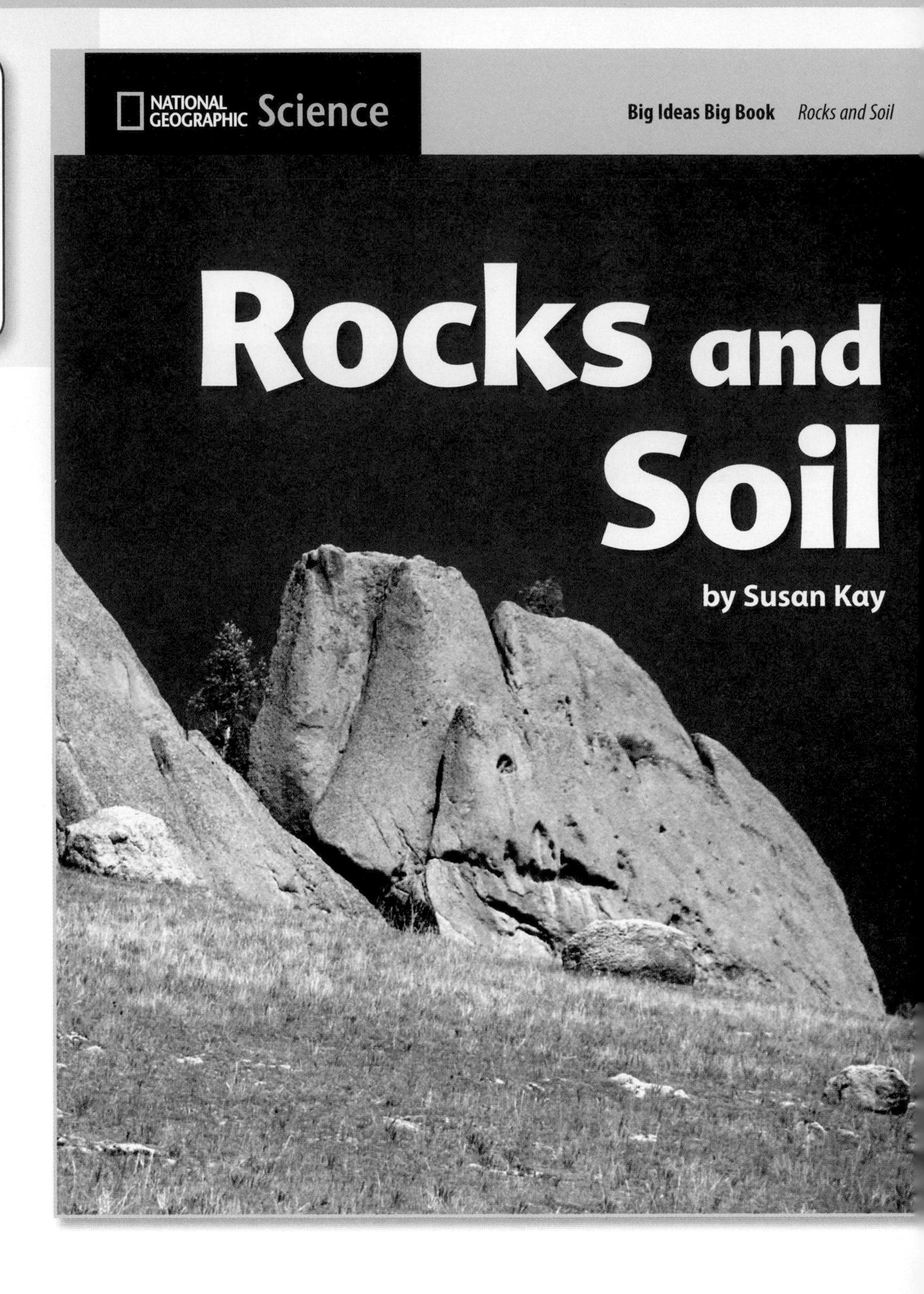

1 Introduce the Big Ideas Big Book

Title and Author

Display the cover of the Big Ideas Big Book with the front and back covers open. Point to the title *Rocks and Soil* and say it aloud. Remind students that this book is about materials that make up Earth. Ask: **What are some properties of the rocks in the photo?** (The rocks are brown. They look like they have different textures.)

Introduce Chapter 2

Big Idea Question

Display the front flap and read the Big Idea Question for Chapter 2. Tell students that they will learn the answer to the question as you read the book aloud. Remind students that they have already learned the answer to the Big Idea Question for Chapter 1. They will learn about the other Big Idea Question later in the unit.

Preview Chapter 2 Vocabulary

Open the front flap and point out the vocabulary words, pictures, and definitions. Tell students they will learn more about the vocabulary words when they listen along as the Big Ideas Big Book is read aloud.

Contents

3

❷ Preview the Contents

Connect Contents to the Big Ideas

Point to each color band as you identify the three chapters in this book. Remind students that you've already read Chapter 1. Call attention to Chapter 2 and the Big Idea Question. Explain that today students will learn the answers to the second Big Idea Question.

❸ Read Chapter 2 Aloud

Use the Table of Contents to locate Chapter 2. Turn to page 16 and read Chapter 2 straight through to familiarize students with the chapter content. After reading, encourage students to

- discuss interesting facts with a partner
- ask questions about topics they would like to know more about
- share their ideas about how rocks change.

Then read through a second time, section-by-section, to teach the Big Idea, vocabulary, and science concepts.

Digital Library

myNGconnect.com

Have students use the Digital Library to find photos showing weathering. You can use the Presentation Tool to display the photos.

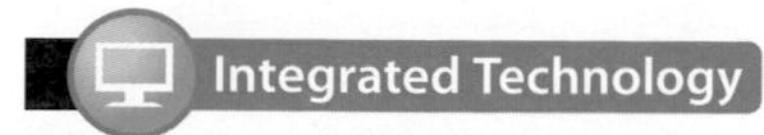

Digital Camera Students can use digital cameras to take photos of examples of weathering near the school or at home.

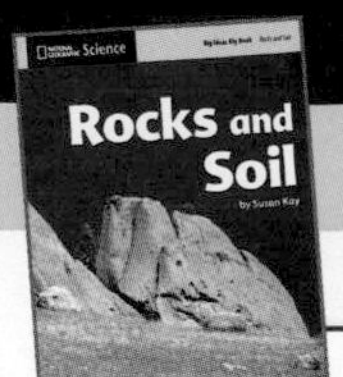

LESSON 2C ▫ Big Idea Question

OBJECTIVES

Science

Students will be able to:

- Describe how wind, water, and ice can change rocks and other earth materials. T
- Explain the process of weathering.

Science Academic Vocabulary

weathering

❶ Introduce

Tap Prior Knowledge

- Ask: **Have you ever seen an old, rusted piece of metal outside? How did it change?** (Possible answer: It rusted and started to crumble into pieces.)
- Say: **The metal was hard and sturdy, yet it changed. Rocks are hard and sturdy, too. How do you think they change?** (Possible answer: Pieces may break off rocks.)

Focus on the Big Idea

- Read the Big Idea Question and have students echo it.
- Preview pages 18–21, 22–23, and 24–25, linking the headings with the Big Idea Question.
- With student input, post a chart that displays the headings.

How Do Rocks Change?

Weathering

Erosion

New Land

- Have students orally share what they expect to find in each section.
- Then read page 17 aloud.

Chapter 2

Big Idea Question

How Do Rocks Change?

16

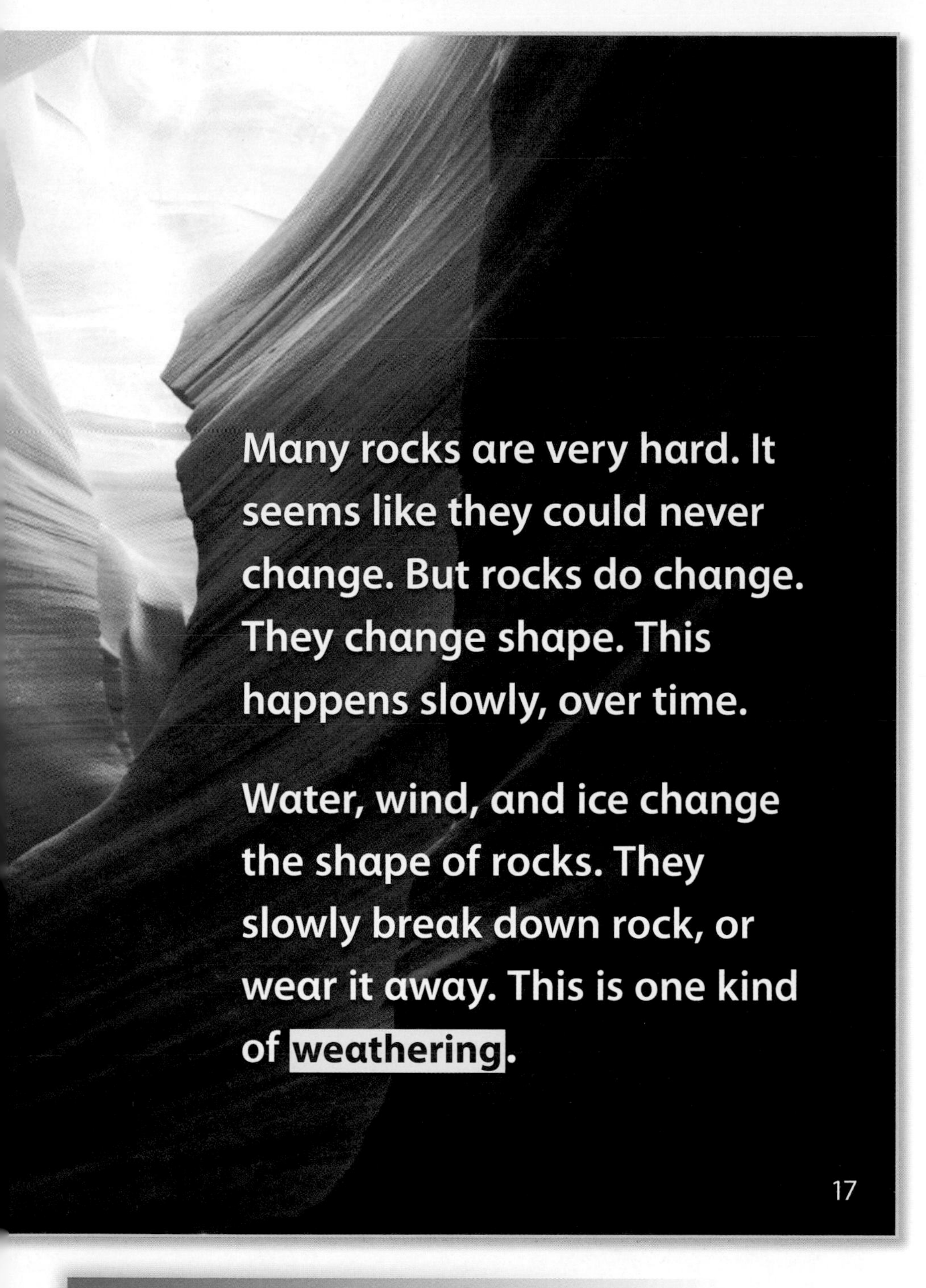

Many rocks are very hard. It seems like they could never change. But rocks do change. They change shape. This happens slowly, over time.

Water, wind, and ice change the shape of rocks. They slowly break down rock, or wear it away. This is one kind of **weathering**.

17

❷ Teach

Science Academic Vocabulary: *weathering*

- Point to the word **weathering.** Reread the definition aloud. Ask: **What does weathering do to rocks?** (It breaks rocks down or dissolves them.)

Explain the Process of Weathering

- Say: **Wind, water, and ice can weather rocks. For example, wind can blow sand against rocks. Over time, wind can break the rocks into smaller pieces. This is called weathering.**
- Tell students to think about rocks in a river. Ask: **What will happen to the rocks if the river water flows over them for a long period of time?** (They will break apart or wear away.)

Differentiated Instruction

ELL Language Support for Explaining Weathering

BEGINNING

Help students explain the process of weathering by asking yes/no questions. For example:, ask

- **Do rocks change? Can the size and shape of rocks change?**
- **Can wind, water, and ice change rocks?**

INTERMEDIATE

Help students explain the process of weathering by asking either/or questions. For example, ask:

- **Does wind cause weathering or do fossils?**
- **Do rocks change or stay the same?**

ADVANCED

Ask students to make a graphic organizer that shows the causes of weathering. Have students include a definition of weathering.

» Before You Move On

Ask students:

1. **List What are three things that can weather rocks?** (water, wind, ice)
2. **Generalize Why do you think weathering happens slowly?** (Some rocks can be strong, so it takes time to break them down.)

LESSON 3 ▫ Weathering

OBJECTIVE

Science

Students will be able to:

- Describe how weathering by flowing water has affected local features.

❶ Introduce

Tap Prior Knowledge

Tell students to picture a river in their mind. Ask: **Does the water always keep moving?** (yes) **Is the moving water powerful?** (yes) **What do you think the moving water does to rocks in the river?** (Possible answer: The moving water wears away parts of the rocks.)

Preview and Read

- Look at pages 18–19. Point to the photos and read the captions aloud.
- Ask: **What do you think happens to rocks when they weather?** (Possible answer: They change by breaking into smaller pieces.)
- Do a demonstration to make sure students understand the concept of dissolving. Put a piece of chalk into a cup of vinegar and stir. Ask: **What happened to the chalk?** (It dissolved.)
- Then read pages 18–19 aloud.

❷ Teach

Sort Information

Use a graphic organizer to help students understand weathering. Say: **Weathering by water can happen in two ways.**

Weathering by Water can

wear away rocks | dissolve rocks

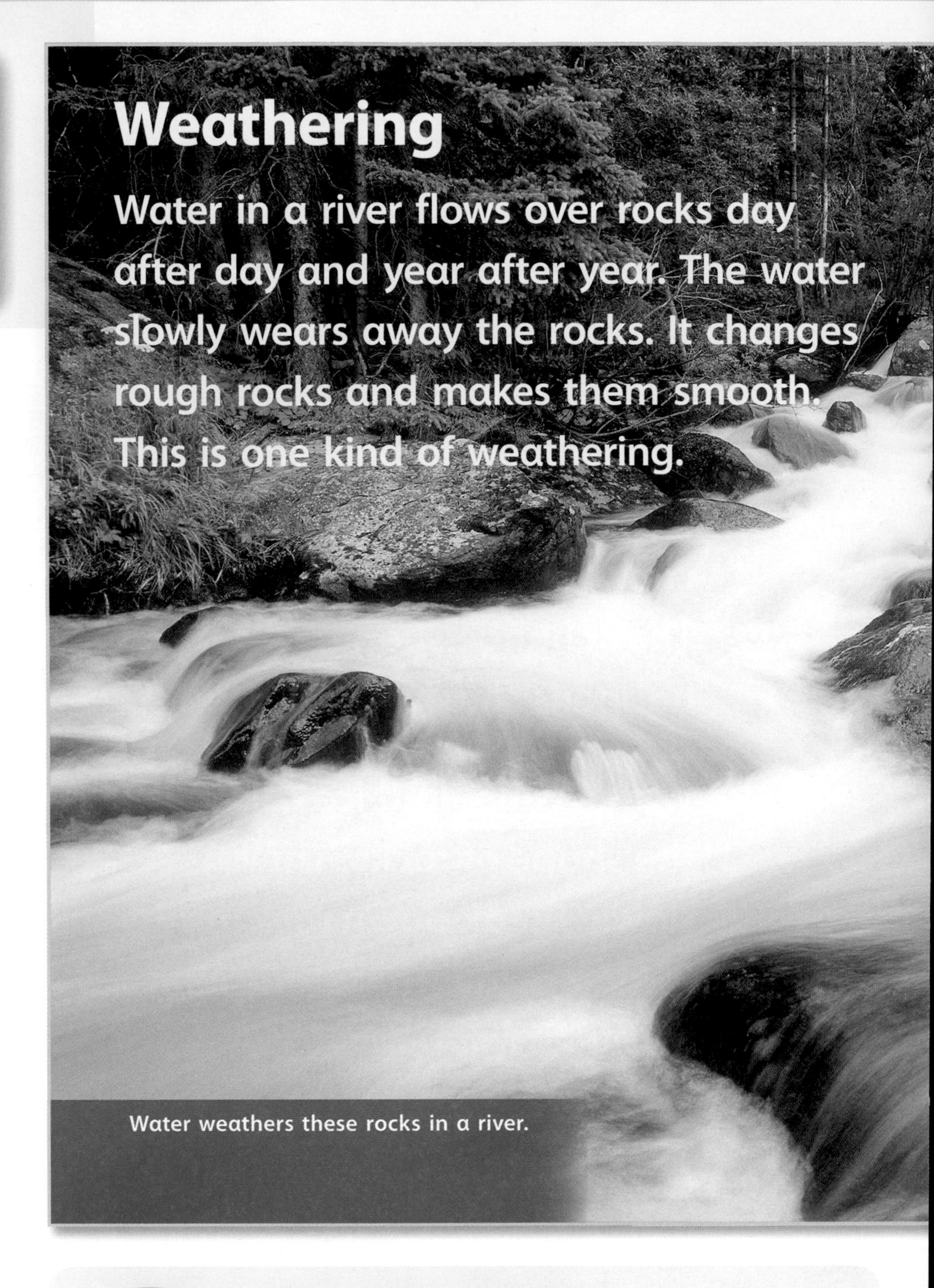

Water weathers these rocks in a river.

NATIONAL GEOGRAPHIC Raise Your SciQ!

Different Types of Weathering Mechanical weathering occurs when wind, water, or ice physically breaks rock into smaller pieces. The chemical composition of the rock does not change. Along with water, wind, and ice, burrowing animals and plant roots can mechanically weather rock. Chemical weathering occurs when chemical reactions dissolve or change rock. The chemical composition of the rock can change. This type of weathering can occur when water mixes with oxygen or carbon dioxide in the air to form an acid that breaks down rock.

There is also another kind of weathering. It happens when water dissolves all or parts of rocks.

Parts of these rocks have dissolved from weathering.

19

Teach, continued

Describe How Weathering by Water Affects Rocks

- Point to the photo on page 18. Say: **Flowing water can change rough rocks. It can break off parts of the rocks and make them smaller.**
- Say: **In one day, a river does not change a rock very much. But over many days and years, the river can wear away rocks.**
- Point to the photo on page 19. Say: **Water can also dissolve rocks.**
- Take students outside to look for examples of weathering by water near the school. Students can also look for examples near their homes, such as the concrete blocks beneath gutter downspouts; these may show wearing away by water. If neither option is possible, take pictures of local weathered features and share them with students.
- Have students describe how weathering by water changed the rocks or features they observed.

Making and Recording Observations

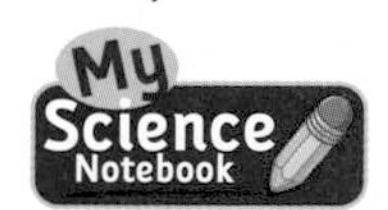

Have students draw or write about their observations of local weathering by water in their science notebook.

Differentiated Instruction

ELL Language Support for Describing Weathering by Water

BEGINNING

Say: **One kind of weathering happens when water wears away rocks.** Have students point to the photo that shows this type of weathering. Repeat for water dissolving rocks.

INTERMEDIATE

Ask students to draw and label before-and-after pictures of a rock that is weathered by water.

ADVANCED

Ask students to draw before-and-after pictures of rocks that have been weathered by water. Have students provide labels and captions and share their pictures.

» Before You Move On

Ask students:

1. **Observe What is water doing to the rocks in the photos?** (weathering the rocks)
2. **Explain In what ways can water weather rocks?** (Water can wear away rocks, or it can dissolve rocks.)

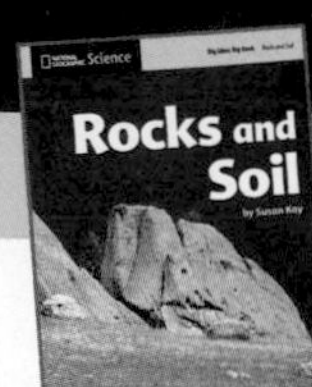

OBJECTIVE

Science

Students will be able to:

- Describe how weathering by ice and wind has affected local features.

Teach, continued

Describe Weathering by Ice and Wind

- Ask: **What happens to water when it freezes?** (It turns into ice.) Say: **You learned how water causes weathering. Ice also can weather rocks.**
- Display the photos on pages 20–21. Say: **In this part of the lesson, you will learn how ice and wind weather rocks.**
- Point to the photo on page 20. Say: **Ice broke the rock apart.** Point to the photo on page 21. Say: **Wind wore the rocks down.** Have students describe the appearance of the weathered rocks.

Sort Information

- Use a graphic organizer to help students understand weathering. Say: **Water, ice, and wind can weather rocks.**

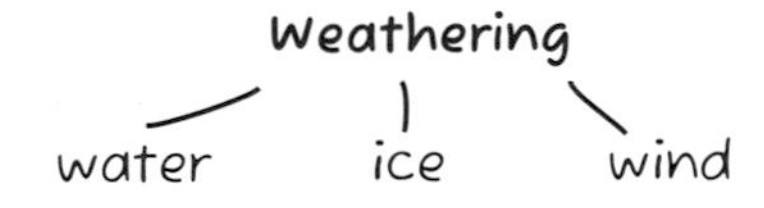

Ice weathers rocks, too. Water gets into cracks in rocks and freezes into ice. The ice pushes on the rock. Over time, rocks break apart.

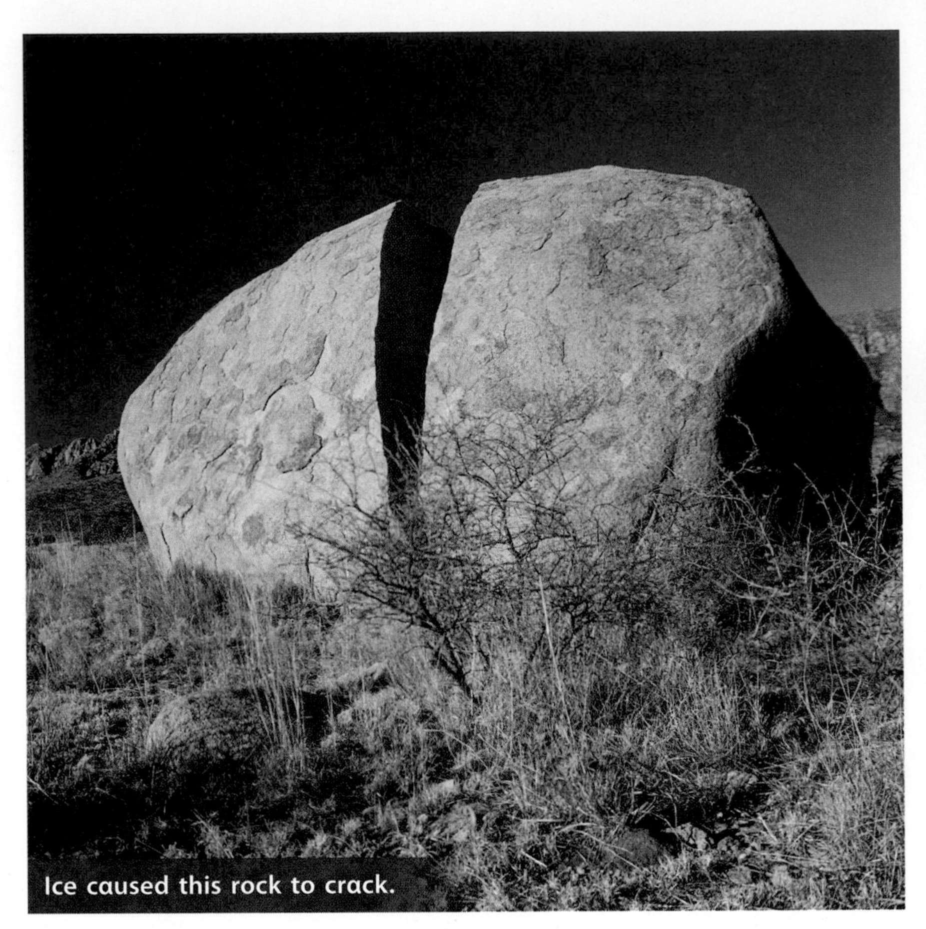

Ice caused this rock to crack.

20

Differentiated Instruction

Extra Support

- Have students role-play how ice breaks rocks apart. Model the concept by pushing your hands out to either side as though you were forcing something apart.
- Repeat the activity for wind. Have students rub their hands together to model how wind wears down rocks.

Challenge

- Have students explore why ice breaks rocks apart. Tell them to place some water in a container. Have them mark the level of the water and then freeze the water. Tell them to recheck the water level.
- Ask: **What happened to the water level?** (It went up.)
- Explain: **Water expands, or gets bigger, when it turns to ice. That is how ice pushes on rocks and breaks them apart.**

Wind also weathers rock. Sometimes the wind picks up sand. It blows the sand over rocks. The wind wears rocks down by rubbing them with sand.

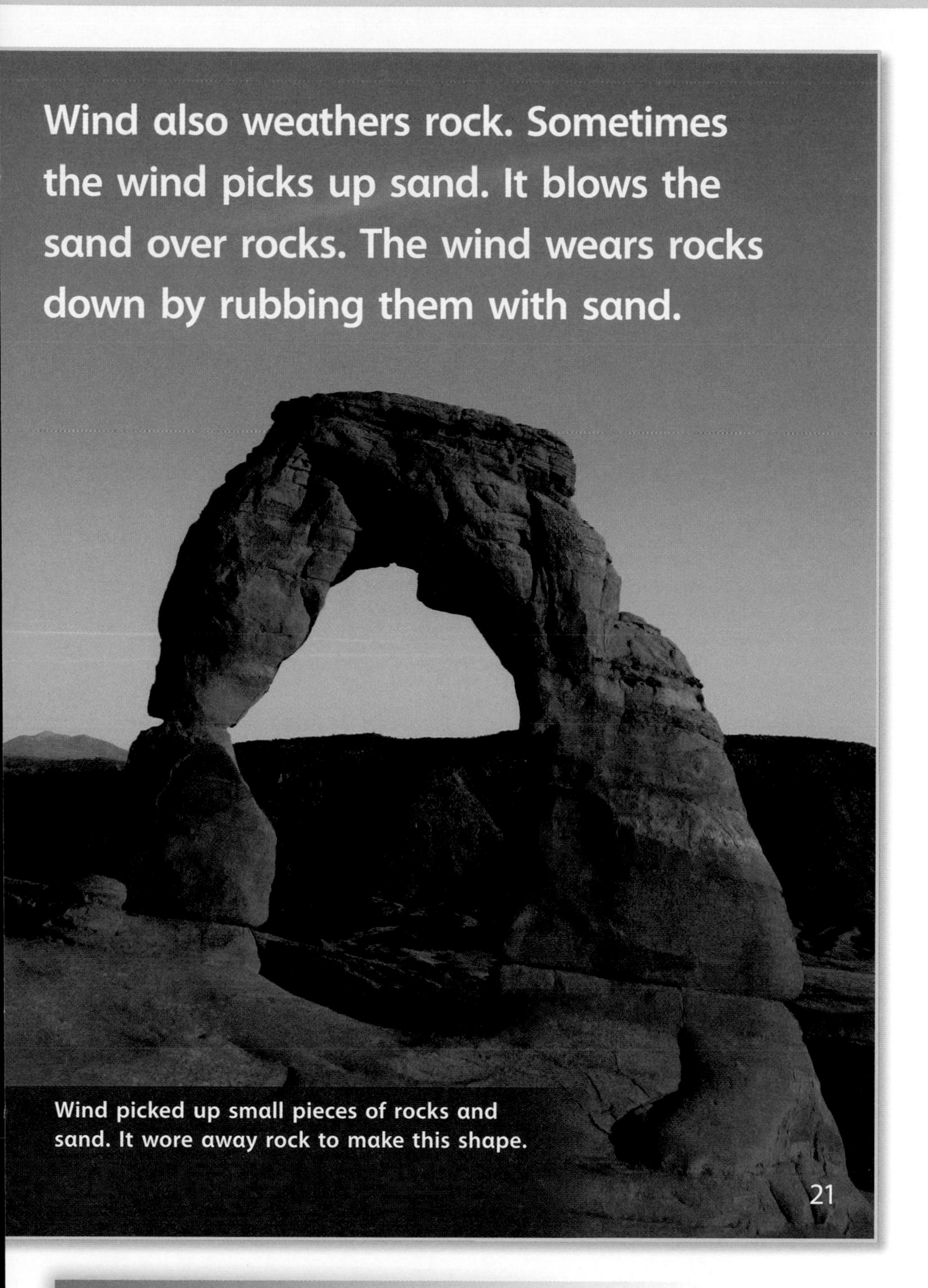

Wind picked up small pieces of rocks and sand. It wore away rock to make this shape.

21

Teach, continued

Describe How Weathering by Ice and Wind Affects Rocks

- Point to the photo on page 20. Say: **Water gets into cracks in rocks and freezes. The ice pushes on the rocks and breaks them apart.**
- Point to the photo on page 21. Say: **Wind blows sand against rocks. Over time, the rocks wear down.**
- Have students look for local examples of weathering by wind and, if possible, ice. Have them describe how weathering changed the shapes or sizes of the features they observed.

Making and Recording Observations

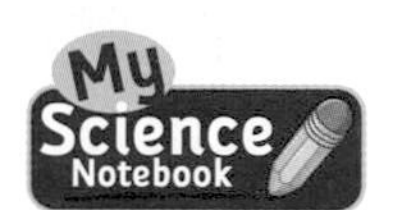

Have students draw or write about their observations of local weathering by ice or wind in their science notebook.

❸ Assess

1. **Identify What can ice do to rocks?** (It can break them apart.)
2. **Compare How do wind and ice weather rocks differently?** (Ice gets into cracks in rocks and pushes them apart. Wind blows sand against rocks to wear them down.)
3. **Infer Which type of weathering might not happen year-round and why?** (Weathering by ice might not happen year-round because temperatures might sometimes be too warm for ice to form.)

Differentiated Instruction

ELL Language Support for Describing Weathering

BEGINNING

Ask questions about the photographs in this section. For example:

- **What caused the weathering of the rock that broke into two pieces?**
- **What caused weathering of the rock on page 21?**

INTERMEDIATE

Provide Academic Language Frames to help students describe weathering by ice and wind. For example:

- *Water can get into the cracks of rocks and ______.*
- *The ______ pushes on the rocks.*
- *The ice breaks apart the ______.*

ADVANCED

Have students sequence the steps that occur when rocks are weathered by ice. They can draw pictures and arrows to show the steps. Have them repeat the activity for weathering by wind.

CHAPTER 2

LESSON 4A ▫ Erosion

OBJECTIVES

Science

Students will be able to:

- Explain how land is changed by erosion from interactions among air, water, and land. T
- Observe local examples of erosion.

Science Academic Vocabulary

soil, erosion

❶ Introduce

Tap Prior Knowledge

Ask students to think about rocks they have seen along a creek, along a beach, or in a field. Ask: **Do you think those rocks were always there?** (probably not) **Did they come from some place else?** (probably) **How do you think they got where they were?**

Preview and Read

- Do a picture walk through pages 22–23. Point to the photos. Say: **Erosion moves the rocks that are broken down by weathering. It moves other materials, too.**
- Then read pages 22–23.

❷ Teach

Science Academic Vocabulary: *soil, erosion*

- Point to the word **soil.** Say: **Soil is a layer of loose material that covers much of Earth's land. You will learn more about soil in the next chapter.**
- Point to the word **erosion.** Repeat its definition. Point out that the same things that cause weathering can cause **erosion.**

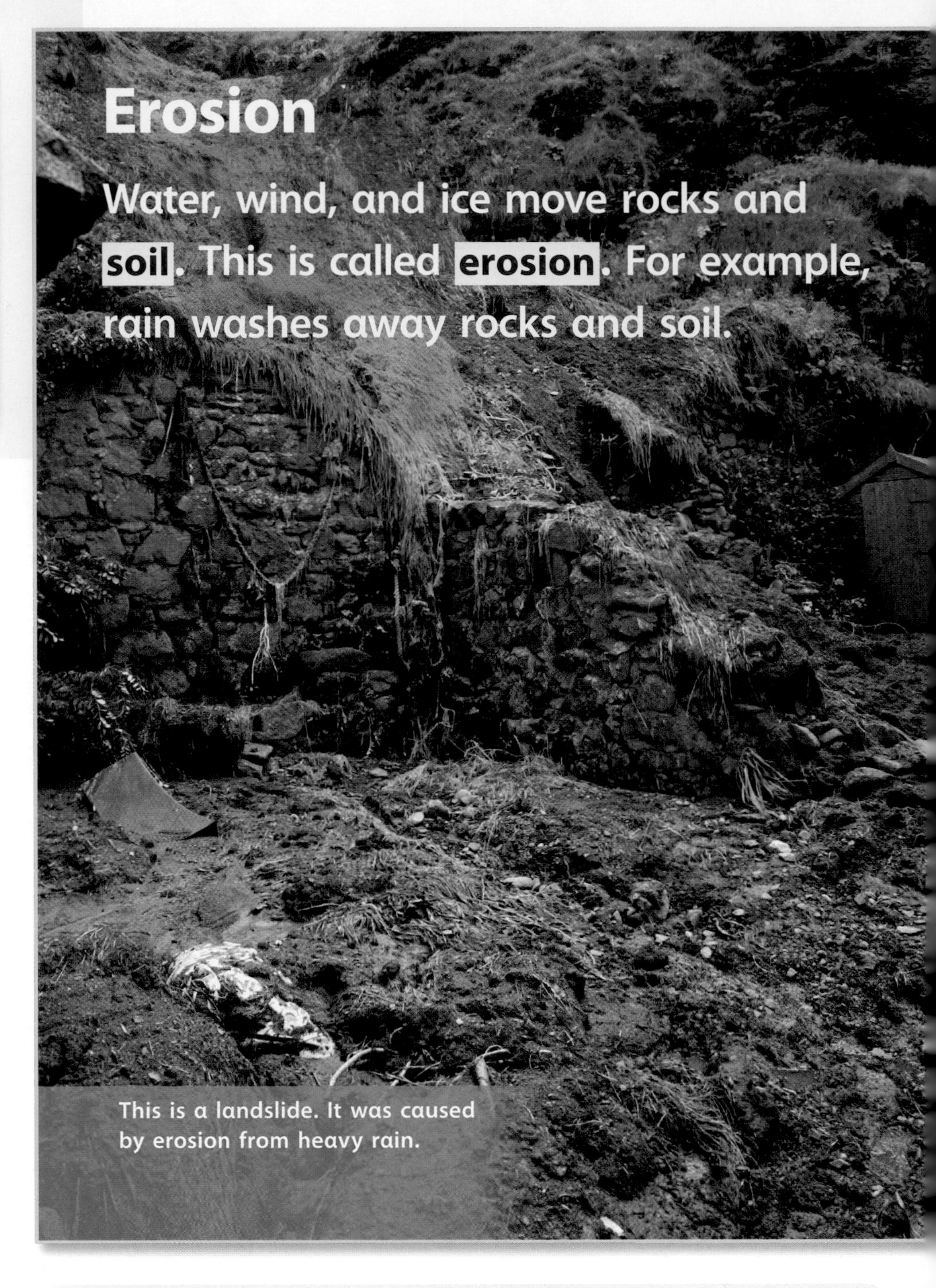

This is a landslide. It was caused by erosion from heavy rain.

NATIONAL GEOGRAPHIC **Raise Your SciQ!**

Glacial Erosion Glaciers can drastically change the landscape. Continental glaciers in particular are powerful agents of erosion. These types of glaciers cover large areas of land. During the last ice age, continental glaciers covered more than 25 percent of Earth's surface. Some of these glaciers were several thousand feet thick. As they moved across parts of the northern United States and Europe, they carved out lakes, changed the course of rivers, flattened mountaintops, and widened valleys. They deposited thick layers of loess, a fine-grained sediment, throughout much of the central United States, giving this area rich soils.

Glaciers move rocks and soil, too. A glacier is a huge piece of slow-moving ice. As it moves, it carries rocks and soil with it. Wind also causes erosion. It blows soil, dust, and sand.

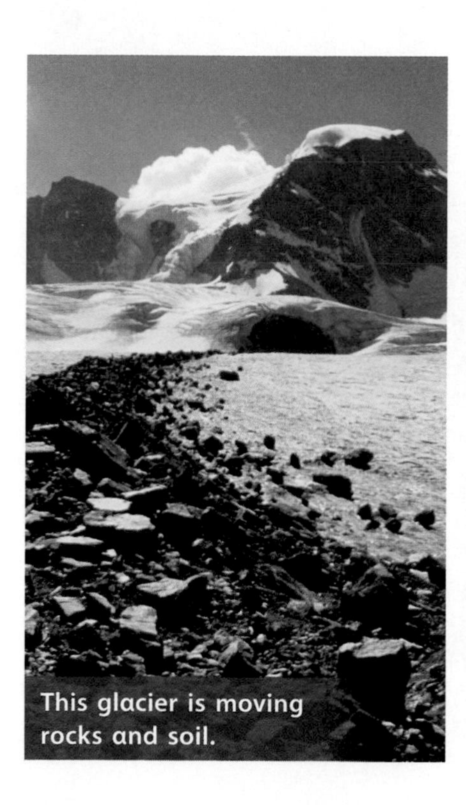

This glacier is moving rocks and soil.

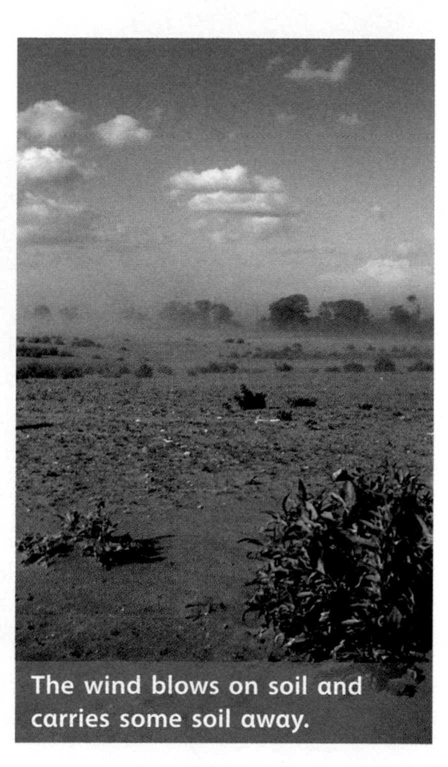

The wind blows on soil and carries some soil away.

23

Teach, continued

Sort Information

Use a graphic organizer to help students understand **erosion.** Say: **Water, glaciers, and wind can erode rocks and soil.**

Explain How Land Is Changed by Erosion

- Point to the photo on page 22. Ask: **What did the water do to the rocks and soil?** (It washed them downward.)
- Point to the photo of the glacier on page 23. Ask: **How is the glacier eroding the land?** (It is moving rocks and soil.)
- Point to the photo of wind **erosion** on page 23. Read the caption aloud. Then ask students to describe in their own words how wind is **eroding** the **soil.**
- Explain that plants help prevent **soil** from washing or blowing away. Their roots hold the **soil** in place.

» Before You Move On

Ask students:

1. **Recall What causes erosion?** (wind, water, and ice)
2. **Compare How does erosion differ from weathering?** (Erosion happens when wind, water, and glaciers move rocks and soil. Weathering can happen when wind, water, and ice break down or wear away rocks or dissolve them.)

Extend Learning

Local Examples of Erosion

Find Out	Think and Do	Describe and Compare
Take students outside on a sunny day to find examples of local features that have been changed by erosion, such as hillsides or riverbanks. Students will likely be able to find examples of water and wind erosion. Depending on your area, they might also find examples of erosion by glaciers.	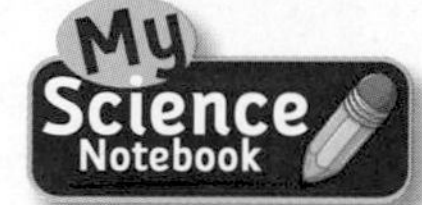 In their science notebook, have students draw and label the features they observed. They should write sentences explaining what caused the erosion and how the erosion changed the feature.	Have volunteers share their findings with the class, including • the names of the features they observed • the type of erosion they observed • how the erosion changed the feature. Ask students to compare and contrast erosion by water, glaciers, and wind.

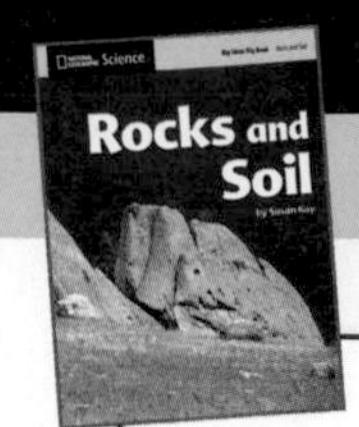

OBJECTIVE

Science
Students will be able to:
- Recognize how interactions between air and wind can change earth materials.

Science Academic Vocabulary *gravity*

PROGRAM RESOURCES
- *Rocks and Soil* Learning Master 20, or at myNGconnect.com
- Chapter Test 2, Assessment Handbook, pages 9–10, or at myNGconnect.com
- NGSP ExamView CD-ROM

Teach, continued

Science Academic Vocabulary: *gravity*
- Point to the word **gravity** and read its definition. Say: **Gravity pulls rocks and soil toward Earth. If rocks and soil are moved to a new place, gravity holds them down and they form new land.**
- Ask: **What causes rocks and soil to move?** (wind, water, and ice) **What does gravity then do to the rocks and soil?** (Gravity moves rocks and soil downhill.)

Summarize the Big Idea
1. Display the prediction chart from page T16. Read the Big Idea Question.
2. Ask: **What did you find out in each section? Is this what you expected to find out?**
3. Then add new information to the chart.

How Do Rocks Change?
Weathering
David Water, ice, and wind weather rocks.
Erosion
Leia Water, wind, and ice move rocks and soil.
New Land
Sayon New land forms when rocks and soil are moved to new places.

New Land

Gravity is a force that pulls things toward Earth. Heavy rains loosened rocks and soil from these mountains. Gravity pulled the rocks and soil downhill.

24

Share and Compare

Compare the Processes that Change Rocks Give partners the Learning Master and a copy of the *Rocks and Soil* small book. Have them complete the Venn diagram to compare weathering and erosion. Check students' work, and then have them write a summary statement of each process under the diagram.

Partners can use their diagrams to discuss how rocks change.

My Science Notebook

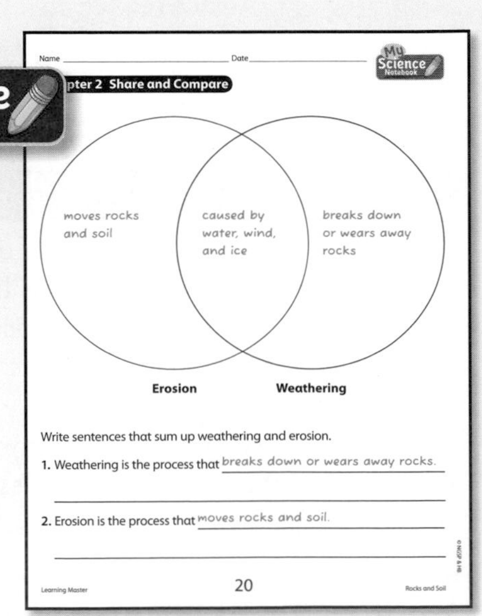
Name Date
Chapter 2 Share and Compare
moves rocks and soil
caused by water, wind, and ice
breaks down or wears away rocks
Erosion
Weathering
Write sentences that sum up weathering and erosion.
1. Weathering is the process that breaks down or wears away rocks.
2. Erosion is the process that moves rocks and soil.
Learning Master 20 Rocks and Soil

Learning Master 20, or at myNGconnect.com

Wind, water, and ice break down and move rocks and soil. Gravity pulls them from the air, water, and ice to the ground. When the rocks and soil are dropped in the same place again and again, new land forms.

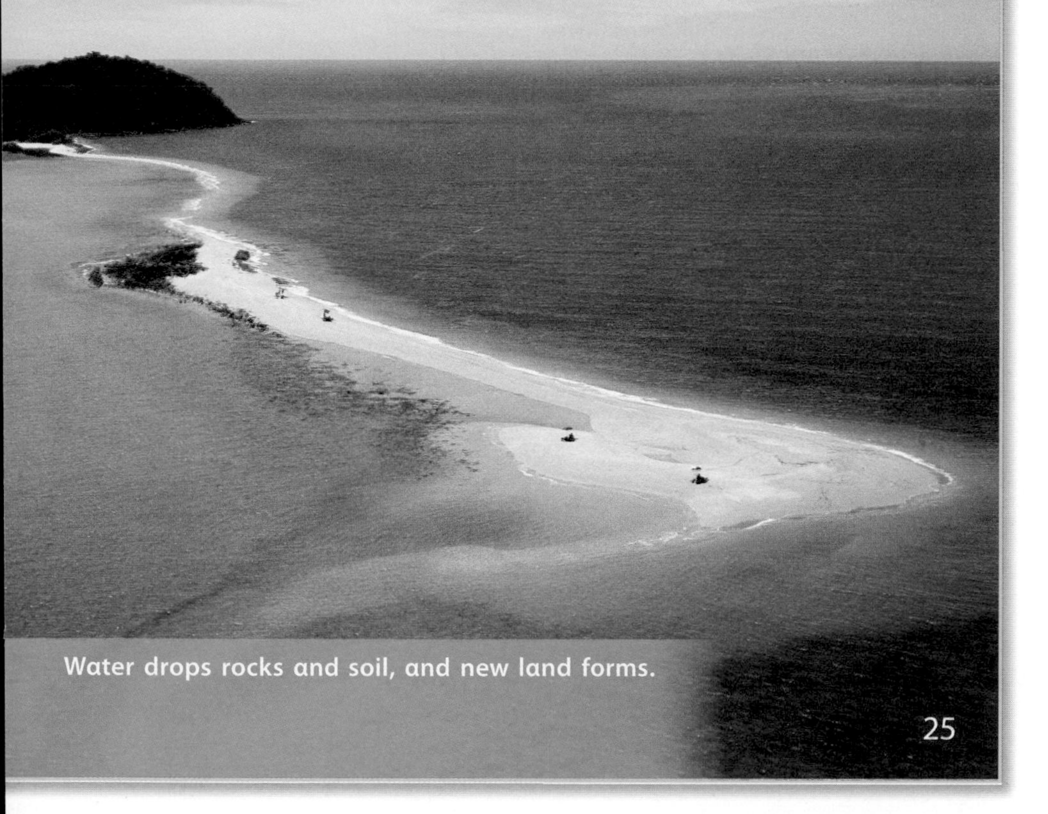

Water drops rocks and soil, and new land forms.

25

Teach, continued

Recording Observations

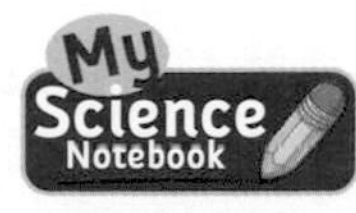

Based on the discussion and the chart, help students develop a statement that sums up the Big Idea. Have students write their statement in their science notebook.

> Weathering breaks down rocks, and erosion carries rock bits to new places.

❸ Assess

1. **Define** **What is gravity?** (a force that pulls things toward Earth)
2. **Summarize** **How might ice and gravity form new land?** (Ice can break down and move rocks and soil. Gravity can pull the rocks and soil to the ground. When the rocks and soil are repeatedly dropped in the same place, new land forms.)
3. **Infer** **When might the formation of new land cause problems? (Hint: Look at the photo on page 24.)** (Possible answer: It would cause problems if the rocks and soil were dropped on roads. The roads would be blocked.)

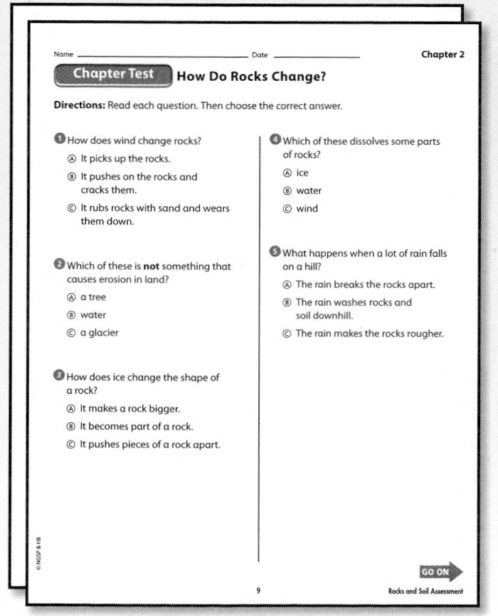

Name ______________ Date ______________ Chapter 2

Chapter Test **How Do Rocks Change?**

Directions: Read each question. Then choose the correct answer.

1. How does wind change rocks?
   Ⓐ It picks up the rocks.
   Ⓑ It pushes on the rocks and cracks them.
   Ⓒ It rubs rocks with sand and wears them down.
2. Which of these is **not** something that causes erosion in land?
   Ⓐ a tree
   Ⓑ water
   Ⓒ a glacier
3. How does ice change the shape of a rock?
   Ⓐ It makes a rock bigger.
   Ⓑ It becomes part of a rock.
   Ⓒ It pushes pieces of a rock apart.
4. Which of these dissolves some parts of rocks?
   Ⓐ ice
   Ⓑ water
   Ⓒ wind
5. What happens when a lot of rain falls on a hill?
   Ⓐ The rain breaks the rocks apart.
   Ⓑ The rain washes rocks and soil downhill.
   Ⓒ The rain makes the rocks rougher.

GO ON

9 Rocks and Soil Assessment

Chapter Test 2, Assessment Handbook, pages 9–10, or at myNGconnect.com,

or NGSP ExamView CD-ROM

Assess Student Progress Chapter Test 2

Have students complete Chapter Test 2 to assess their progress in this chapter.

OBJECTIVES

Science

Students will be able to:

- Identify the tools scientists use to measure liquids.
- Collect data and create a table.
- Express quantities using integers.
- Interpret data in a table.

PROGRAM RESOURCES

Rocks and Soil Learning Master 21, or at myNGconnect.com

❶ Introduce

Tap Prior Knowledge

Ask students if they have ever helped make a recipe or bake something with an adult. Ask: **Why do you measure ingredients before you put them in a mixture?** (to make sure I am using the right amount) Ask if they have used a measuring cup to measure a liquid ingredient when cooking something at home. Explain that scientists measure liquids to make sure that they are using the right amounts in their investigations.

❷ Teach

Measuring Liquids

- Read page 18 aloud with students. Point out the picture. Ask: **What is the scientist doing in the picture?** (measuring rainfall) **Where is the scientist looking as he observes?** (He is looking at the level of the water in the rain gauge.)
- Say: **There are markings on the rain gauge where the scientist is looking.** Ask: **What important ideas can you infer about measuring liquids from looking at this picture?** (It is important to watch the level of the liquid and the markings on the bottle as I measure liquids.)

Math in Science

Measuring Liquids

Scientists sometimes need to measure liquids when doing investigations. They might measure how much rain falls. Scientists would also measure to find out how much water different soils can hold.

Making careful measurements is an important part of science investigations. ▼

18

Scientists often measure amounts of liquids in milliliters. They might use tools like those in the pictures to measure.

Each tool has a scale. A scale is made of lines and numbers that tell how much liquid is in the tool.

▲ A teaspoon holds about 5 milliliters of liquid.

19

Teach, continued

- Read page 19 aloud with students. Tell students that scientists use different units to measure things. Say: **You read that each of the tools has a scale.** Explain that a scale used for measuring something is a series of evenly spaced units.
- Say: **Look at the tools on page 19.** Ask: **What unit is being used to measure the liquids?** (milliliters) **What do you notice about the units on the scales?** (There is a low number at the bottom. The numbers get larger going up the scale.) **What is the importance of these numbers?** Guide students to understand that the numbers and lines represent the amount of liquid in specific units at each marked point.
- Point to the tool at the far left. Ask: **How can you tell how much liquid is in this measuring tool?** (by observing the level of the liquid and reading the number nearest it on the scale)
- Have students look again at the photos of the measuring tools on page 19. Have them read the scales to tell how much liquid is in the flask on the left (about 400 mL) and in the graduated cylinder on the right (about 40 mL).
- Ask: **Why is it hard to tell how much liquid is in the beaker in the middle?** (The beaker is filled past the measuring lines.) **How could you measure 100 mL in the beaker?** (Pour liquid only up to the 100-mL line.)

NATIONAL GEOGRAPHIC Raise Your SciQ!

SI Units Milliliters are part of the International System of Units (SI). Often called the metric system, SI units were first developed in France following the French Revolution and dealt mainly with mass and length. Additional SI units have since been proposed, and the units are continually refined by testing and technology. SI units are used by scientists around the world to ensure a standardized system of measurement. The United States legalized use of the metric system in 1866, but use of the system is not widespread in the general public.

Teach, continued

- Read page 20 aloud with students. Write *milliliters*. Ask: **What is a short way of writing milliliters?** (*ml* or *mL*) Write *ml* and *mL* next to *milliliters*.
- Point to the picture of the measuring cup on page 20. Ask: **How can you tell how much liquid is in the measuring cup?** (by reading the scale and looking at the level of the liquid) **How much liquid is in the measuring cup?** (150 ml)
- Ask students to look closely at the scale on the measuring cup. Ask: **What is the least amount of liquid you could measure with this measuring cup?** (50 ml) **The most?** (250 ml)
- Have students work with a partner to answer the questions on page 20.

What Did You Find Out?

1. milliliters

2. Pour the liquid into the measuring cup. Then observe the level of the liquid and read the scale.

continued

You can use a measuring cup to measure milliliters. The liquid in the measuring cup below is at the line that is labeled 150. That means that the cup has 150 milliliters of liquid.

How do you know that the numbers stand for milliliters? The **ml** beside the 250 stands for **milliliters.** Milliliters can also be written as **mL.**

▶ What Did You Find Out?

1. What unit do scientists often use to measure liquids?
2. How do you use a measuring cup to measure a liquid?

20

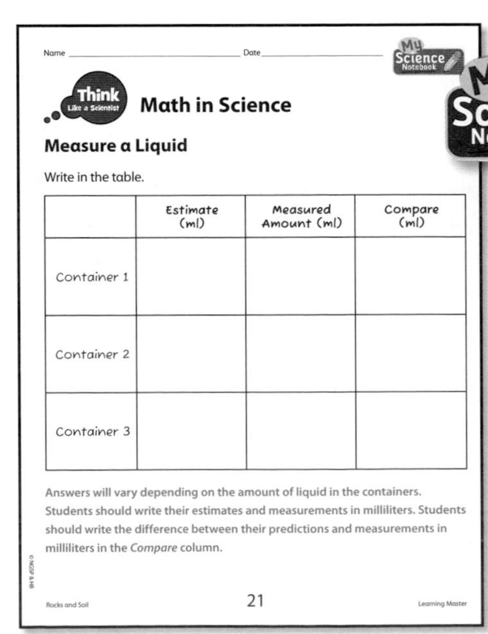
Name ________________ Date ________________

My Science Notebook

Think Like a Scientist — Math in Science

Measure a Liquid

Write in the table.

	Estimate (ml)	Measured Amount (ml)	Compare (ml)
Container 1			
Container 2			
Container 3			

Answers will vary depending on the amount of liquid in the containers. Students should write their estimates and measurements in milliliters. Students should write the difference between their predictions and measurements in milliliters in the *Compare* column.

Rocks and Soil 21 Learning Master

My Science Notebook

Learning Master 21, or at myNGconnect.com

Measure a Liquid

1. Measure some liquids.
   - Put some water in 3 different containers. Estimate how many milliliters of water are in each container.

   - Use a measuring cup to measure the water in each container. Record your data.
   - Compare your estimates to the actual measurements. How close were your estimates?
2. Share your data with others and ask questions about it.

21

Teach, continued

Measure a Liquid

- Read page 21 aloud with students. Have students work in small groups to complete the activity. Give each group 3 containers of different heights and volume and a measuring cup. Make the containers as different in size as possible. Pour approximately 200 ml of water in each container.
- You may wish to add food coloring to the water to make reading the scales easier.
- Ask students to alert you if they spill any water.
- Have students estimate the amount of water in one container and record their estimate. Then have them pour the water from the container into the measuring cup and record the actual measurement. Have students repeat this procedure for the remaining 2 containers. Ask: **Was it easier to estimate larger or smaller amounts?**
- Ask students to write a sentence comparing their estimates to the actual measurements for each container.

❸ Assess

Use Learning Master 21. Answers will vary depending on the amount of liquid in the containers. Have students write their estimates and measurements in milliliters. Have them write the difference between their predictions and measurements in milliliters in the Compare column.

SafetyFirst

Wipe up spills and wet surfaces immediately.

OBJECTIVES

Science

Students will be able to:

- Investigate through Guided Inquiry (answer a question; make and compare observations; collect and record data; generate questions and explanations based on evidence or observations; share findings; ask questions to increase understanding; adjust explanations based on feedback).
- Model how erosion and deposition are caused by interactions between land and water.

Science Process Vocabulary

predict, plan

PROGRAM RESOURCES

- Science Inquiry Book: *Rocks and Soil*
- Science Inquiry Book eEdition at myNGconnect.com
- Inquiry eHelp at myNGconnect.com
- Science Inquiry Kit: *Rocks and Soil*
- *Rocks and Soil* Learning Masters 22–24, or at myNGconnect.com
- Inquiry Rubric: Assessment Handbook, page 33, or at myNGconnect.com
- Inquiry Self-Reflection: Assessment Handbook, page 38, or at myNGconnect.com

MATERIALS

Kit materials are listed in italics.

safety goggles; *plastic tub (20 cm x 30 cm x 10 cm); sandy soil;* 2 books; *measuring cup; paper cup (7 oz); spray bottle (16 oz); clear plastic cup (9 oz);* water

For teacher use: sharpened pencil

1 Introduce

Tap Prior Knowledge

Ask students if they have ever seen water dripping from a faucet. Ask: **What would happen to the flow of the water if you turned on the faucet?** (More water would come out of the faucet at a quicker rate.) Tell students that the way water flows down a hill can be similar to the way water flows from a faucet. Sometimes it flows slowly, and sometimes it flows quickly.

Guided Inquiry

Investigate How Water Affects Soil

Question What happens when you pour water slowly and quickly onto a hill of soil?

Science Process Vocabulary

predict verb

You can use what you already know to **predict** what will happen when you pour water onto soil.

plan noun

You can make a **plan** to find out how moving water affects soil.

22

MANAGING THE INVESTIGATION

Time

20 minutes

Groups

small groups of 4

Advance Preparation

- Measure 3 cups of sandy soil into each tub.
- Use the sharpened end of a pencil to punch 3 holes into the bottom of a 7-ounce paper cup for each group.
- Wipe up spills and wet surfaces immediately.

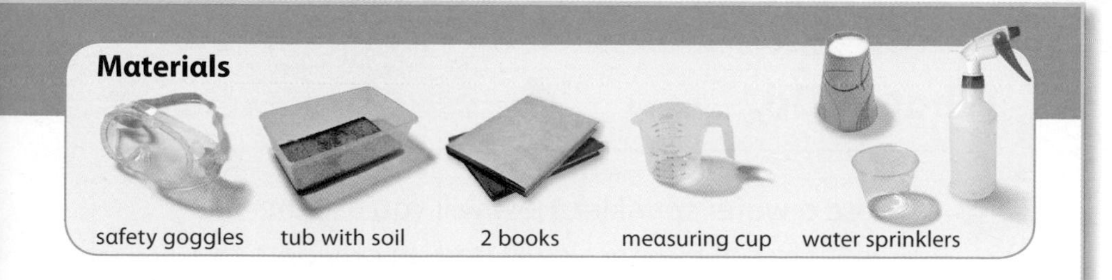

What to Do

1 Put on your safety goggles. Use the soil to make a hill. Put the books under the tub.

2 You will pour water on the hill. **Predict** what will happen to the soil when you pour slowly. Next predict what will happen when you pour quickly. Write your predictions in your science notebook.

23

What to Expect

Students will model soil erosion by pouring water slowly and quickly on a constructed hill of soil. They will predict how changing the flow of the water will affect the hillside. They will choose a sprinkler (a cup with holes, a cup without holes, or a spray bottle) and design a plan to control the flow of water. Students should observe more soil erosion when the water flows quickly and less soil erosion when the water flows slowly.

Introduce, continued

Connect to Big Idea

- Review the Big Idea Question, *How do rocks change?* Explain to students that the surface of Earth changes over time. Remind them how their investigation with the sandstone rock demonstrated how rocks could change when exposed to moving water. Ask them to think about how water could change soil.
- Have students open their Science Inquiry Books to page 22. Read the Question and have students share ideas about how water could change a hill of soil.

❷ Build Vocabulary

Science Process Vocabulary: predict, plan

Use this routine to introduce the words.

1. **Pronounce the Word** Say **plan.** Ask students to say other words that begin with the same sound as **plan.** (play; plant; plot; plus)
2. **Explain Its Meaning** Choral read the sentence. Ask students for another way to say **plan.** (steps to do to get something done)
3. **Encourage Elaboration** Tell students that a **plan** often involves steps. These steps happen in a logical order. Ask: **What would you do first: observe how water moves soil or record how water moves soil?** (observe how water moves soil)

Repeat for the word **predict**. To encourage elaboration, ask students to complete this **prediction: If I drop a cup of water, then _____.** (The water will spill on the floor.)

❸ Guide the Investigation

- Distribute materials. Hold up any unfamiliar item and say its name. Have students match each pictured item to the real item as they say its name.
- Repeat the inquiry Question. Read the inquiry steps on pages 23–24 together with students. Tell students that they will follow these steps to answer the Question. Move from group to group and clarify steps if necessary.
- In step 1, model how to use the books to prop up one end of the tub.

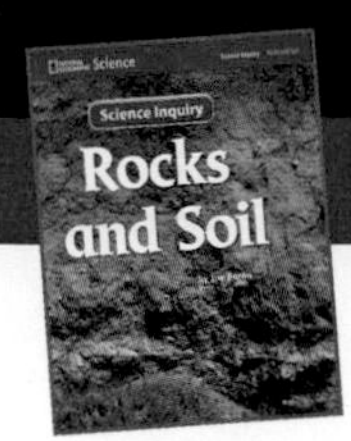

Guide the Investigation, continued

- In step 2, have students use their observations about the soil in the tub to make a prediction.
- In step 3, students will choose among a cup with holes, a cup without holes, or a spray bottle.
- In step 4, remind students to measure carefully. Have them turn to page 20 in their Science Inquiry Book if they need a reminder about how to measure 200 mL of water.
- In step 5, ask: **What can you observe about the soil as you pour water slowly?**
- In step 6, ask: **What can you observe about the soil as you pour water quickly? How is this different from what happened to the soil in step 5?**
- Have students write or record their observations in their science notebooks.

❹ Explain and Conclude

- Have students compare results. Students should then examine the data they collected and use these as evidence to develop reasonable explanations for their observations and results.
- As each group shares explanations and conclusions, encourage students to ask questions to increase understanding. Have students actively listen for other interpretations and ideas. Discuss reasons for any differences in results and explanations.
- Encourage students to suggest alternative explanations. Allow them to adjust their explanations and conclusions. Have students create and record conclusions about their findings.

Answers

1. Possible answer: More soil washed down the hill when I poured the water quickly.
2. Possible answer: Rain can move soil around on the land and make the land look different.
3. Possible answer: Water flowed faster from the cup with holes. Water flowed slower from the sprayer. When water was poured faster, more soil washed down the hill.

What to Do, continued

3. Choose a water sprinkler. How will you use the sprinkler to pour water slowly and quickly onto the hill? Make a **plan.**

4. Put 200 milliliters of water in the measuring cup.

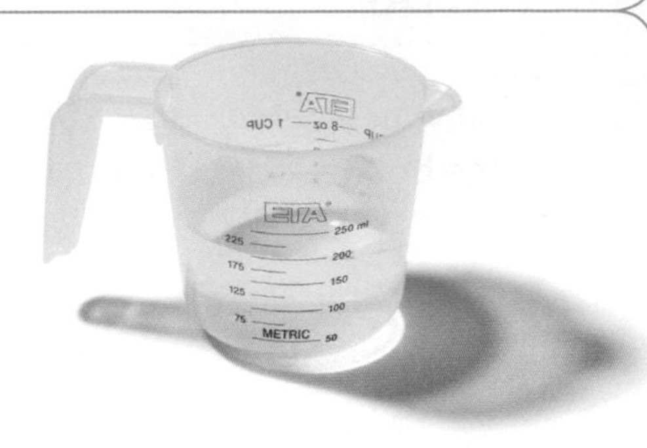

5. Hold the water sprinkler over the model hill. Slowly pour the 200 milliliters of water into your sprinkler. Make the water fall slowly onto the hill. Record your **observations** in your science notebook.

6. Repeat steps 4 and 5. This time make the water fall quickly.

24

MANAGING THE INVESTIGATION

Teaching Tips

- Allow students to test the rate of water flow from the different sprinklers before they choose one and pour water on the hill. Students can hold the sprinklers over a sink to minimize spills.
- Stress that students should use all 200 mL of water.
- In step 5, tell students to move the sprinkler around to different parts of the hill as the water falls.

Record

Write or draw in your science notebook. Use a table like this one.

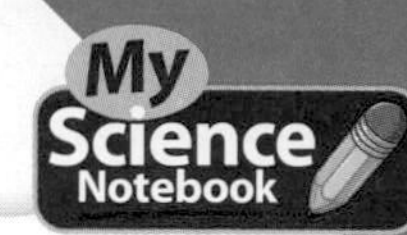

Type of Sprinkler: ______

	What I Predict	What I Observed
Water poured slowly		
Water poured quickly		

Explain Your Results

1. **Compare** how the soil moved when you poured the water slowly and when you poured it quickly.
2. Use your **observations** to explain how rain can affect the land.
3. Compare your results with a group that tested a differernt sprinkler. What **patterns** do you see?

Think of Another Question

What else would you like to find out about how water moves soil? How could you find an answer to this new question?

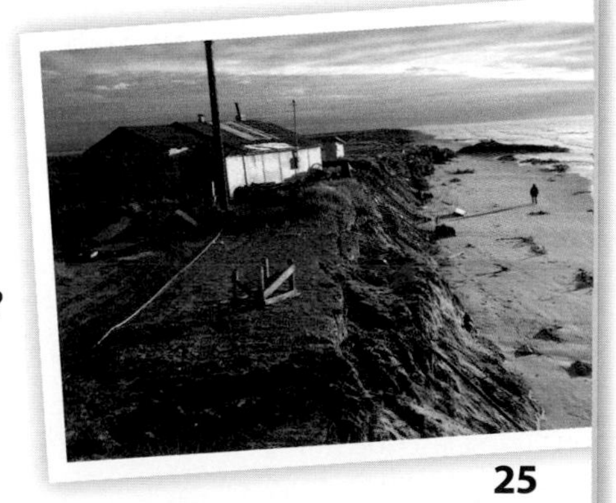

25

Inquiry Rubric at myNGconnect.com	Scale			
The student made a **model** of how moving water affects a hill of soil.	4	3	2	1
The student **predicted** the effects of slowly moving water and quickly moving water on a hill of soil.	4	3	2	1
The student made a **plan** to make **observations** of slowly moving water and quickly moving water on a hill of soil.	4	3	2	1
The student **compared** results with other groups and looked for **patterns.**	4	3	2	1
The student **shared** and compared observations and **conclusions** with other students.	4	3	2	1
Overall Score	4	3	2	1

5 Find Out More

Think of Another Question

- Have students use observations from this investigation to generate other questions that can be answered using readily available materials.
- Record student questions for possible future investigations.

6 Reflect and Assess

- To assess student work with the Inquiry Rubric shown below, see Assessment Handbook, page 33, or go online to myNGconnect.com.
- Score each item separately and then decide on one overall score.
- Have students use the Inquiry Self-Reflection on Assessment Handbook page 38, or at myNGconnect.com.

Think Like a Scientist: How Scientists Work

Tell students that scientists often make models when they can't examine something directly or if something is too large to observe properly. Scientists cannot observe every location on Earth, so models can help them investigate how erosion and other factors change our planet.

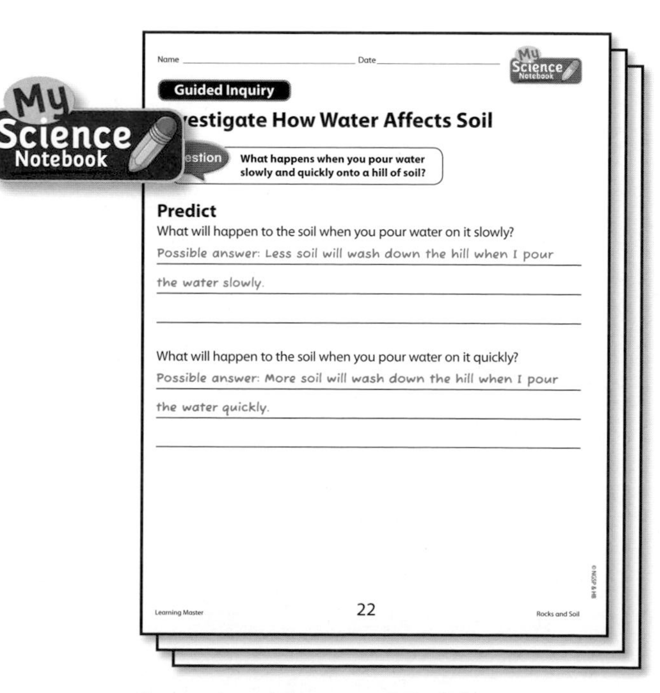
Name ______ Date ______

Guided Inquiry

...estigate How Water Affects Soil

...estion: What happens when you pour water slowly and quickly onto a hill of soil?

Predict

What will happen to the soil when you pour water on it slowly?

Possible answer: Less soil will wash down the hill when I pour the water slowly.

What will happen to the soil when you pour water on it quickly?

Possible answer: More soil will wash down the hill when I pour the water quickly.

Learning Master 22 Rocks and Soil

Learning Masters 22–24, or at myNGconnect.com

CHAPTER 3 ▫ What Can You Observe About Soil?

LESSON	PACING		OBJECTIVES
1 Guided Inquiry *Investigate Soil Properties* pages T25k–T25n **Science Inquiry Book** pages 26–29	**30** minutes		Investigate through Guided Inquiry (answer a question; make and compare observations; collect and record data; generate questions and explanations based on evidence or observations; share findings; ask questions to increase understanding; adjust explanations based on feedback). Investigate how different soils retain water.
2 **2A Big Idea and Vocabulary Card** pages T25o–T25p	**20** minutes	**2A**	Describe how small pieces of rock can be the basis of soil. Describe how people use soil.
2B Interactive Read-Aloud pages T25q–T25r	**20** minutes	**2B**	Describe how small pieces of rock can be the basis of soil.
2C Big Idea Question pages T26–T27	**20** minutes	**2C**	Describe how small pieces of rock can be the basis of soil. T Classify soil types based on color, texture (size of particles), and the ability to retain water. T Describe how people use soil.
2D How Soil Is Formed pages T28–T29	**20** minutes	**2D**	Describe how small pieces of rock and dead plant and animal parts can be the basis of soil and explain the process by which soil is formed.
3 **3A Properties of Soil** pages T30–T31	**20** minutes	**3A**	Classify soil types based on color, texture (size of particles). T
3B People Use Soil pages T32–T35	**20** minutes	**3B**	Classify soil types based on the ability to retain water, and the ability to support the growth of plants. T Describe how people use soil. Identify how soil is used in manufacturing and construction. T
4 **Conclusion** pages T36–T37	**20** minutes		Recognize that Earth is made up of rocks. Rocks come in many sizes and shapes. Describe how wind, water, and ice can change rocks and other earth materials. T Describe how small pieces of rock can be the basis of soil. T
5 Open Inquiry *Do Your Own Investigation* pages T37a–T37b **Science Inquiry Book** pages 30–31 **Investigation Model** pages T37c–T37f	**40** minutes		Investigate through Open Inquiry. Generate questions to investigate. Plan investigations. Make and compare observations; collect and record data. Generate questions and explanations based on evidence or observations. Share findings; ask questions to increase understanding; adjust interpretations based on feedback.
6 **Think Like A Scientist** *How Scientists Work: Using Tools to Observe* pages T37g–T37j **Science Inquiry Book** pages 32–35	**30** minutes		Describe how tools help scientists to make better observations.

T = Tested Objective

VOCABULARY	RESOURCES	ASSESSMENT
compare **investigate**	Science Inquiry Book: *Rocks and Soil* Science Inquiry Kit: *Rocks and Soil* Guided Inquiry: Learning Masters 25–28	Inquiry Rubric: Assessment Handbook, page 34 Inquiry Self-Reflection: Assessment Handbook, page 39 Reflect and Assess, page T25n
humus	Chapter 3 Big Idea Card Vocabulary: Learning Master 29 *Rocks and Soil* Big Ideas Big Book	Before You Move On, page T27 Assess, page T29
	Share and Compare: Learning Master 30	Chapter Test 3, Assessment Handbook, pages 11–12 Before You Move On, pages T31, T33 Assess, page T35 NGSP ExamView CD-ROM
		Assessment Handbook: Unit Test, pages 16–22 NGSP ExamView CD-ROM
fair test	Science Inquiry Book: *Rocks and Soil* Science Inquiry Kit: *Rocks and Soil* Open Inquiry: Learning Masters 31–34 Investigation Model: Learning Masters 35–36	Inquiry Rubric: Assessment Handbook, page 34 Inquiry Self-Reflection: Assessment Handbook, page 40 Reflect and Assess, pages T37b, T37f
	Think Like a Scientist: Learning Master 37	Assess, page T37j

TECHNOLOGY RESOURCES

STUDENT RESOURCES

myNGconnect.com

- **Student eEdition**
  - Big Ideas Book
  - Science Inquiry Book
  - Become an Expert Books
  - Explore on Your Own Books
- **Read with Me**
- **Sing with Me**
- **Vocabulary Games**
- **Enrichment Activities**
- **Digital Library**

National Geographic Kids

National Geographic Explorer!

TEACHER RESOURCES

myNGconnect.com

- **Teacher eEdition**
  - Big Ideas Book
  - Science Inquiry Book
  - Become an Expert Books
  - Explore on Your Own Books
  - Write About Rocks and Soil Book
  - Online Lesson Planner
  - National Geographic Unit Launch Videos
  - Assessment Handbook
- **Presentation Tool**
- **Digital Library**

NGSP ExamView CD-ROM

OBJECTIVES

Science

Students will be able to:

- Investigate through Guided Inquiry (answer a question; make and compare observations; collect and record data; generate questions and explanations based on evidence or observations; share findings; ask questions to increase understanding; adjust explanations based on feedback).
- Investigate how different soils retain water.

Science Process Vocabulary

compare, investigate

PROGRAM RESOURCES

- Science Inquiry Book: *Rocks and Soil*
- Science Inquiry Book eEdition at myNGconnect.com
- Inquiry eHelp at myNGconnect.com
- Science Inquiry Kit: *Rocks and Soil*
- *Rocks and Soil* Learning Masters 25–28, or at myNGconnect.com
- Inquiry Rubric: Assessment Handbook, page 34, or at myNGconnect.com
- Inquiry Self-Reflection: Assessment Handbook, page 39, or at myNGconnect.com

MATERIALS

Kit materials are listed in italics.

safety goggles; *hand lens; sandy soil; humus; clay soil; 3 paper plates; soil property card (Learning Master 26); plastic spoon; funnel; clear plastic cup (10 oz);* paper towel; *measuring cup;* water (100 mL)

For teacher use: newspapers; marker

❶ Introduce

Tap Prior Knowledge

Ask students if they have ever worked in a garden. Ask: **What is one way that people use soil?** (to grow plants) Say: **Soils that hold too much water or too little water are not good for growing plants. Soils that hold the right amount of water are best for growing plants.**

Guided Inquiry

Investigate Soil Properties

Question **Which kind of soil can hold the most water—sandy soil, humus, or clay soil?**

Science Process Vocabulary

compare verb

You can **compare** different types of soil by telling how they are alike and different.

investigate verb

You can **investigate** to find out how or why something works the way it does.

26

MANAGING THE INVESTIGATION

Time

30 minutes

Groups

small groups of 4

Advance Preparation

- Make a copy of the soil property card (Learning Master 26) for each group.
- Cover desks, tables, or other working surfaces with newspapers to minimize mess and clean up.
- Prepare soil for each group: Label 3 paper plates *A, B,* and *C.* Place 5 spoonfuls of sandy soil on plate A, 5 spoonfuls of humus on plate B, and 5 spoonfuls of clay soil on plate C.
- If there is a sink in the classroom, have students use water from the faucet. Another option is setting aside a pitcher of water for the investigation.
- Wipe up spills and wet surfaces immediately.

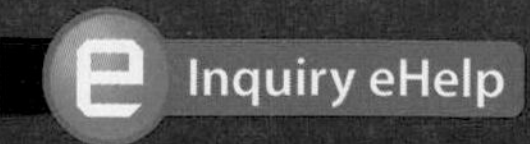

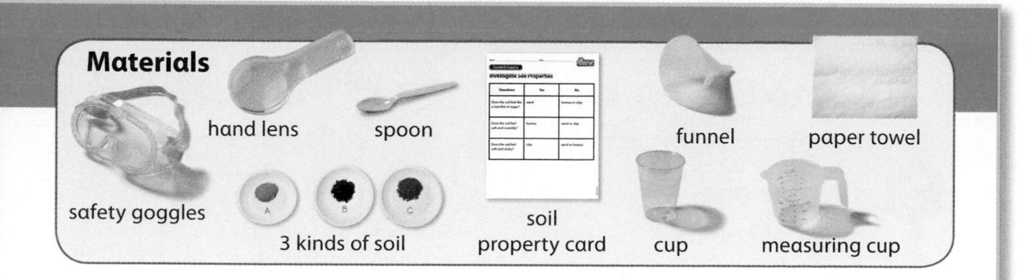

Do a Fair Test

Write your plan in your science notebook.

Make a Prediction

In this investigation, you will test sandy soil, humus, and clay soil. Which kind of soil holds the most water? Write your **prediction.**

Plan a Fair Test

What one thing will you change?
What will you observe or measure?
What will you keep the same?

What to Do

1. Put on your safety goggles. **Observe** the soils with the hand lens. Use the soil property card to tell which soil is sandy, humus, or clay. Write in your science notebook.

27

What to Expect

Students will use Learning Master 26, the soil property card, to identify the different soils by texture. They will then test one soil's ability to hold water. They can also test additional soils if time allows. When students compare their results with other groups, they should find that sandy soil holds the least water and clay soil holds the most water. Humus holds a moderate amount of water.

Teaching Tips

- After students identify the soils in step 1, suggest they relabel the paper plates; plate A should be labeled *Sandy*, plate B should be labeled *Humus*, and plate C should be labeled *Clay*.
- To save time, have different groups test different soils. Give students about 10 minutes to test each soil. Make sure groups use a clean, dry paper towel and 100 mL of water for each test.

Introduce, continued

Connect to Big Idea

- Review the Big Idea Question, *What can you observe about soil?* Explain to students that like rocks and minerals, soils have different properties, such as texture and color. Explain that in this inquiry students will compare different kinds of soil and their ability to hold water.
- Have students open their Science Inquiry Books to page 26. Read the Question and invite students to share ideas about different kinds of soil they have observed or experienced in activities such as building sand castles or working with pottery clay.

❷ Build Vocabulary

Science Process Vocabulary: compare, investigate

Use this routine to introduce the words.

1. **Pronounce the Word** Say **investigate.** Have students repeat it in syllables.
2. **Explain Its Meaning** Choral read the sentence. Ask students for another way to say **investigate.** (find out why things happen)
3. **Encourage Elaboration** Ask: **What are some things you would like to investigate about soil?** (I want to know what soils are made of or what different soils are used for.)

Repeat for the word **compare.** To encourage elaboration, ask students to look at the picture on page 26. Say: **Compare the colors of the soils.**

❸ Guide the Investigation

- Distribute materials. Hold up any unfamiliar items. Have students match each photo to the real item.
- Repeat the inquiry Question. Read the inquiry steps on pages 27–28 together with students. Tell students that they will follow these steps to answer the Question. Move from group to group and clarify steps if necessary.
- In step 1, point to the questions and answers on the soil property card as you demonstrate how to use the card.
- In addition to observing with the hand lens, encourage students to observe how each of the soils smells.

Guide the Investigation, continued

- In step 2, demonstrate how to line the funnel with the paper towel and place the funnel in the cup. Display a completed soil tester for students to see.
- In step 3, explain to students that it is important that all the water that goes through the funnel should be collected in the cup.
- In step 4, tell students when 10 minutes have elapsed. Ask: **Do you think all the water you poured into the soil being tested is now in the cup? If not, where do you think the water is?**
- In step 6, help students analyze the results for all groups that tested each kind of soil. Ask: **How are the results in each group alike? How are they different?** Guide students in forming a conclusion about the water-holding capacity of each soil type. Then discuss how each group's results compare with those conclusions.
- If time permits, ask students to repeat the investigation and compare their results. Ask them what they think caused any differences.

❹ Explain and Conclude

- Students should examine the data they collected and use these as evidence to develop reasonable explanations for their observations and results.
- As each group shares explanations and conclusions, encourage students to ask questions to increase understanding. Have students actively listen for other interpretations and ideas and discuss possible reasons for any differences.
- Encourage students to suggest alternative explanations and allow them to adjust explanations and conclusions as needed. Have students create and record individual conclusions about group findings.

Answers

1. Sand let the most water run through it.
2. Clay held the most water.
3. Possible response: Humus would be best for a garden because it doesn't hold too much water or too little water.

What to Do, continued

2 Choose one type of soil to test. Make a soil tester with that soil.

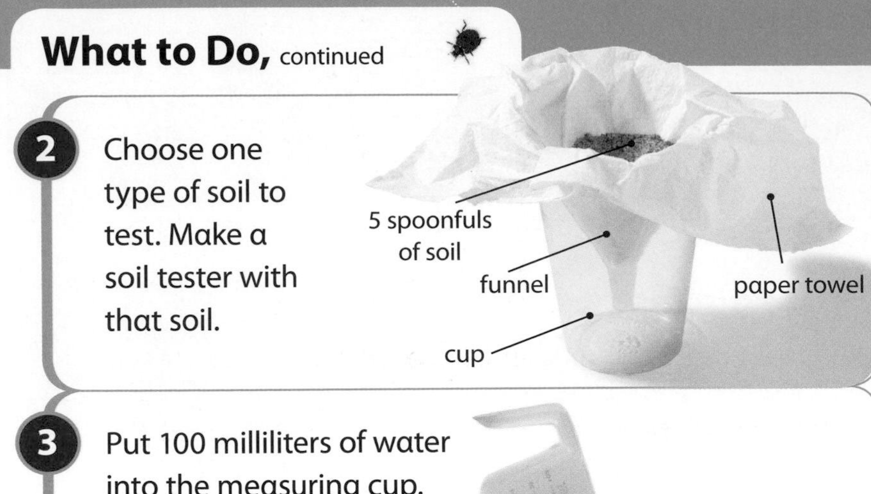

3 Put 100 milliliters of water into the measuring cup. Slowly pour the water onto the soil.

4 Wait 10 minutes. Remove the funnel and soil. Use the measuring cup to **measure** the water in the cup. Record your **data.**

5 **Compare** your results with the results of other groups. What **patterns** do you see? Write in your science notebook.

28

NATIONAL GEOGRAPHIC Raise Your SciQ!

Soil Surveys Many states publish soil maps that show the types of soil found in an area. Scientists conduct soil surveys to determine soil types. A soil survey is a field study in which scientists dig holes and take soil samples from a particular area. They observe and record the sample's properties and conduct further tests to identify the soil type. The resulting soil maps can be used to make recommendations for land use. For example, construction on hillsides made of clay soils must take into account that these soils turn slippery when wet.

Record

Write in your science notebook.
Use a table like this one.

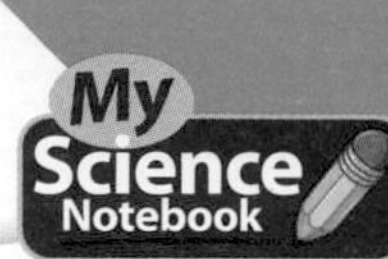

Soil	Observations	Type of Soil	How Much Water in Measuring Cup
A			
B			
C			

Explain and Conclude

1. Which soil let the most water go through it?
2. Which soil held the most water?
3. Which soil do you think would be best for a garden? Why?

Think of Another Question

What else would you like to find out about soil properties? How could you find an answer to this new question?

29

Inquiry Rubric at myNGconnect.com	Scale			
The student **observed** different types of soil and **predicted** how the soils would hold water.	4	3	2	1
The student planned a **fair test** by changing only the type of soil.	4	3	2	1
The student collected and recorded **data** about how different soils hold water.	4	3	2	1
The student **inferred** that the best type of soil for a garden is one that doesn't hold too much or too little water.	4	3	2	1
The student **shared** and **compared** observations and **conclusions** with other students.	4	3	2	1
Overall Score	4	3	2	1

5 Find Out More

Think of Another Question

- Have students use their observations to generate other questions. Have them use the question stems, *What happens when…*, *What would happen if…*, or *How can I/we…* to form testable questions.
- Record student questions for possible future investigations.

6 Reflect and Assess

- To assess student work with the Inquiry Rubric shown below, see Assessment Handbook, page 34, or go online to myNGconnect.com.
- Score each item separately and then decide on one overall score.
- Have students use the Inquiry Self-Reflection on Assessment Handbook page 39, or at myNGconnect.com.

Think Like a Scientist: How Scientists Work

Tell students that scientific investigations should yield similar conclusions when repeated. Point out that combining class data is a way of repeating the investigation, since all student groups used the same method.

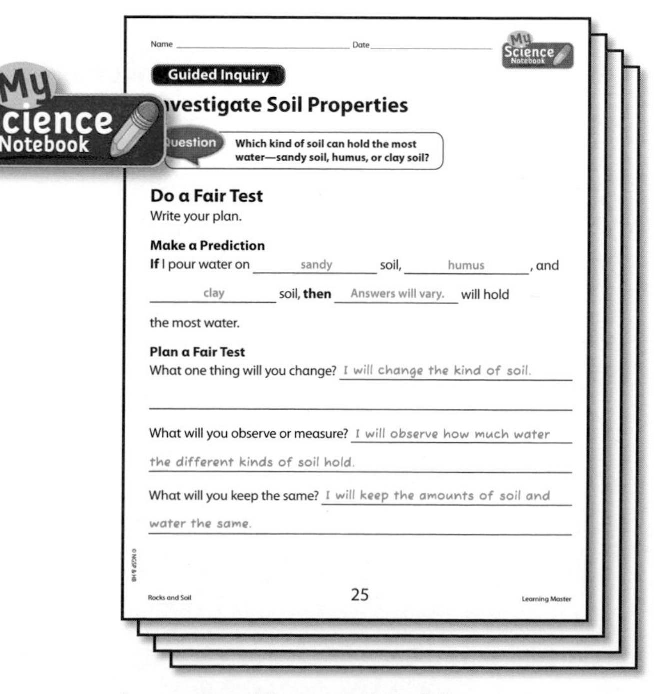
My Science Notebook

Name ______ Date ______

Guided Inquiry

nvestigate Soil Properties

uestion: Which kind of soil can hold the most water—sandy soil, humus, or clay soil?

Do a Fair Test
Write your plan.

Make a Prediction
If I pour water on sandy soil, humus, and clay soil, then Answers will vary. will hold the most water.

Plan a Fair Test
What one thing will you change? I will change the kind of soil.

What will you observe or measure? I will observe how much water the different kinds of soil hold.

What will you keep the same? I will keep the amounts of soil and water the same.

Rocks and Soil 25 Learning Master

Learning Masters 25–28, or at myNGconnect.com

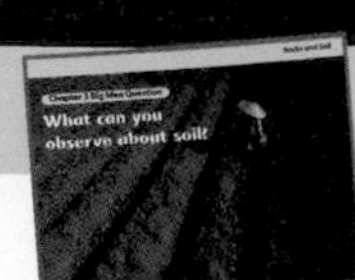

LESSON 2A ▫ Big Idea and Vocabulary Card

OBJECTIVES

Science

Students will be able to:

- Describe how small pieces of rock can be the basis of soil.
- Describe how people use soil.

Science Academic Vocabulary *humus*

PROGRAM RESOURCES

- Chapter 3 Big Idea Card
- *Rocks and Soil* Learning Master 29, or at myNGconnect.com
- Vocabulary Games at myNGconnect.com

❶ Tap Prior Knowledge

Have students raise their hands if they have ever planted something in the ground. Ask two or three volunteers to describe how the soil looked and felt. Then have the class compare the descriptions.

❷ Introduce Chapter 3

Big Idea Question

- Display the front of the Chapter 3 Big Idea Card and ask students what they see. Read the question. Explain that the person in the photo is a farmer who is using soil to grow food.
- Ask: **What color is the soil?** Point out the dead plant matter visible near the bottom of the photo. Remind students that this soil is a combination, or mixture, of dead plant and animal matter, along with small pieces of rock. Explain that you know this because of the dark brown color of the soil.

Chapter 3 Big Idea Card (front)

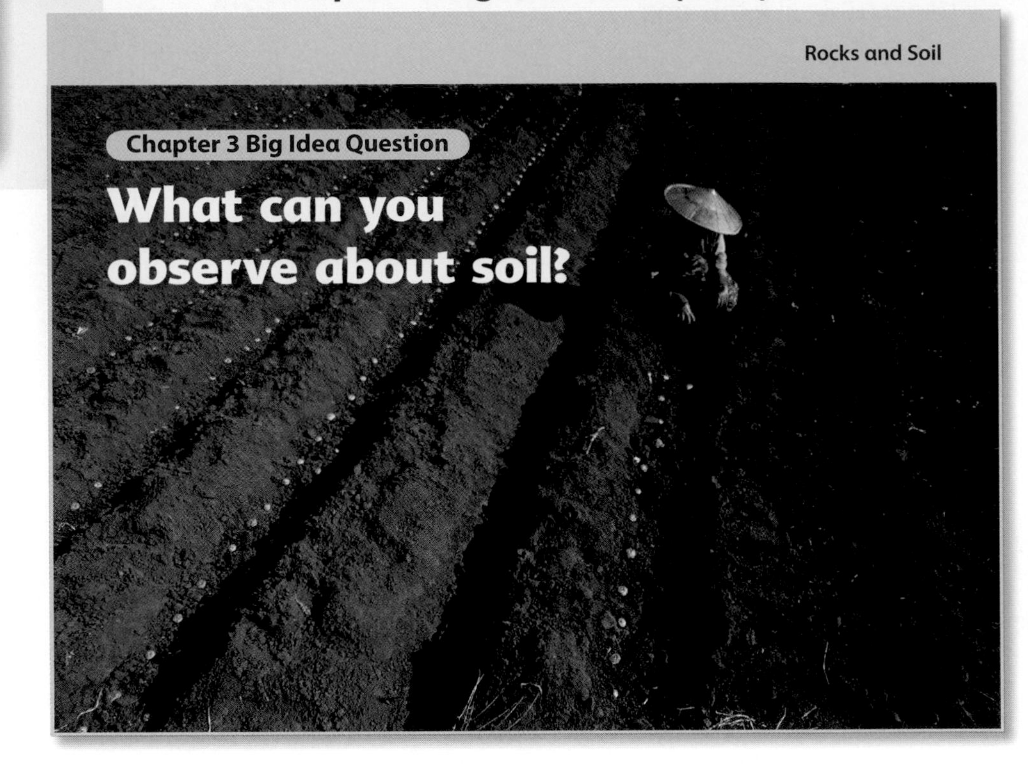

Differentiated Instruction

ELL Vocabulary Support

BEGINNING

Have students draw pictures of humus. Look for the use of dark colors in students' drawings. Help them label their drawings.

INTERMEDIATE

Have students draw and label pictures of humus that show what it is made of (bits of rocks and bits of decayed plants and animals). Have students tell about their drawings with this Academic Language Frame:

Humus is made of ______, ______, and ______.

ADVANCED

Have students draw pictures of humus that show what it is made of (bits of rocks and bits of dead plants and animals). Have them write a caption for their drawings.

Chapter 3 Big Idea Card (back)

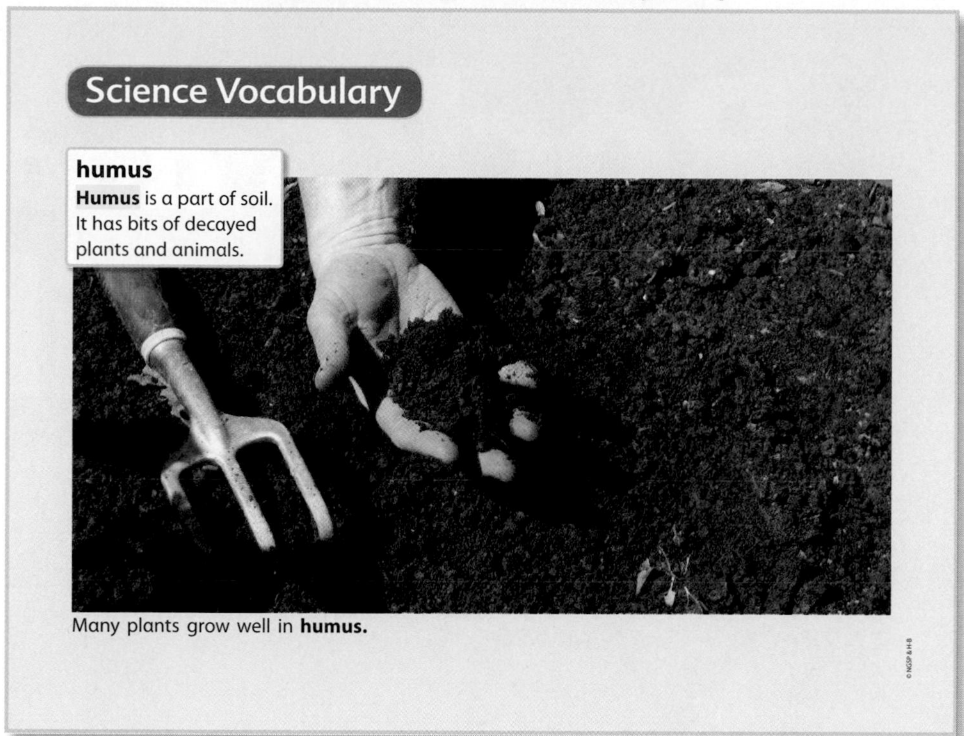

❸ Teach Vocabulary

Display the back of the Chapter 3 Big Idea Card and use this routine to teach each word. For example:

1. **Pronounce the Word** Say **humus** and have students repeat it. Say it again in syllables as students echo each syllable. Then say the whole word again as a group.
2. **Explain Its Meaning** Read the word, definition, and sample sentence and use the photo to explain the word's meaning. Say: **Humus is the best kind of soil for growing plants.**
3. **Encourage Elaboration** Ask: **What is the texture of humus?**

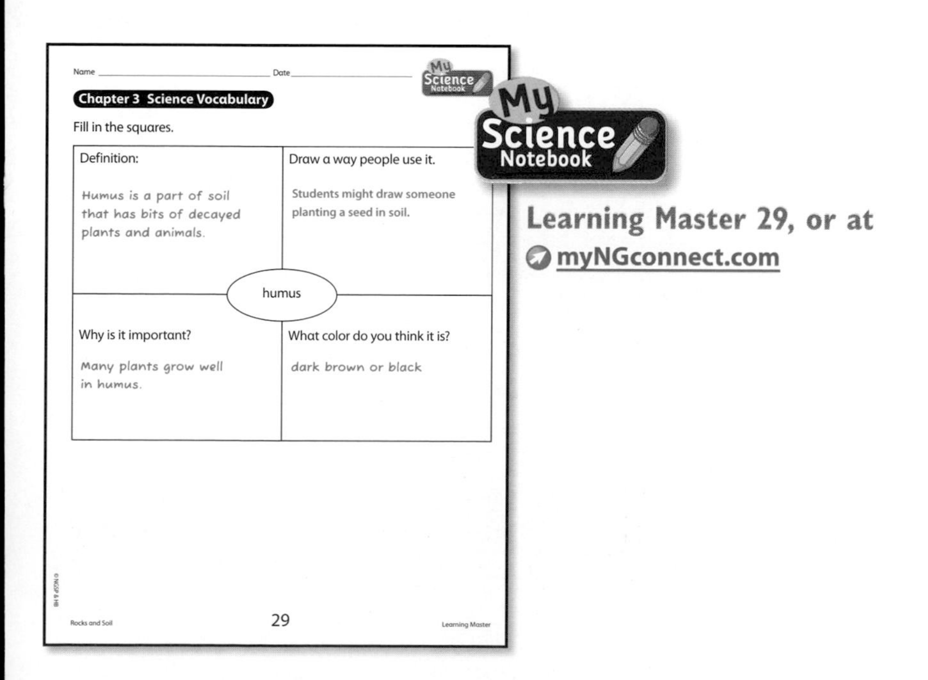

Name ______________ Date ______________

My Science Notebook

Chapter 3 Science Vocabulary

Fill in the squares.

Definition:	Draw a way people use it.
Humus is a part of soil that has bits of decayed plants and animals.	Students might draw someone planting a seed in soil.
humus	
Why is it important?	What color do you think it is?
Many plants grow well in humus.	*dark brown or black*

Rocks and Soil 29 Learning Master

My Science Notebook

Learning Master 29, or at myNGconnect.com

OBJECTIVE

Science

Students will be able to:

- Describe how small pieces of rock can be the basis of soil.

Science Academic Vocabulary *humus*

PROGRAM RESOURCES

- *Rocks and Soil* Big Ideas Big Book
- *Rocks and Soil* Big Ideas Big Book eEdition at myNGconnect.com
- Digital Library at myNGconnect.com
- MP3 Read with Me at myNGconnect.com

❶ Introduce the Big Ideas Big Book

Title and Author

Display the cover of the Big Ideas Big Book with the front and back covers open. Point to the title *Rocks and Soil* and say it aloud. Ask: **What is this book about?** (rocks and soil, Earth's land) **What is soil?** (loose material that covers much of Earth's land)

Introduce Chapter 3

Big Idea Question

Display the front flap and read the Big Idea Question for Chapter 3. Tell students that the answer to the question is in the chapter. Remind them that they have already learned the answers to the first two Big Idea Questions. This is the last Big Idea Question in the unit.

Preview Chapter 3 Vocabulary

Open the front flap and point out the vocabulary word, picture, and definition. Tell students they will learn more about the vocabulary word when they listen as the Big Ideas Big Book is read aloud.

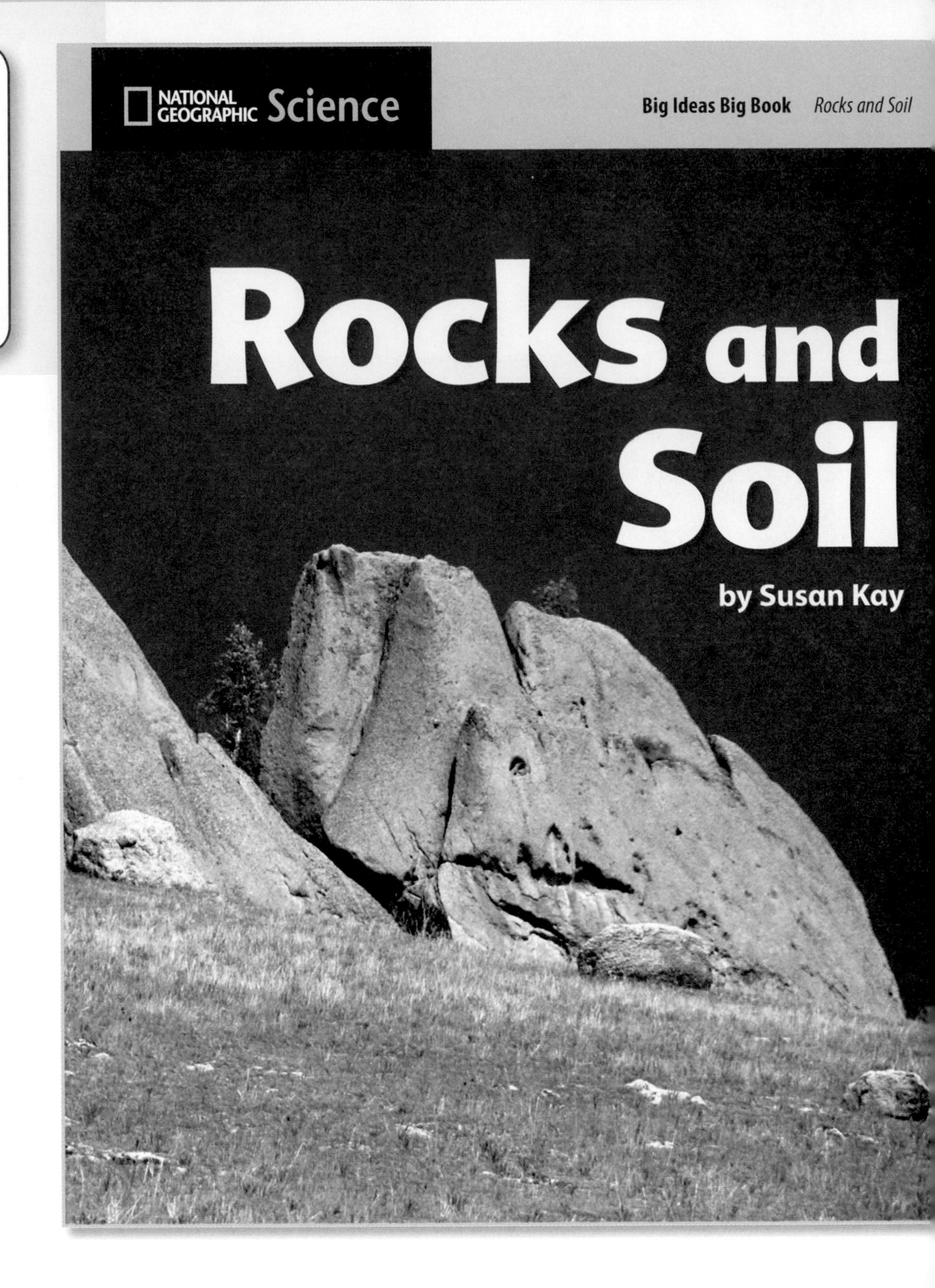

Contents

3

❷ Preview the Contents

Connect Contents to the Big Ideas

Point to each color band as you identify the three chapters in this book. Remind students that you've already read Chapters 1 and 2. Ask: **What was Chapter 1 about?** (rock properties) **What was Chapter 2 about?** (how rocks change) Call attention to Chapter 3 and the Big Idea Question in the Table of Contents. Read aloud each lesson title in the chapter. Tell students that today they will learn the answer to the third Big Idea Question.

❸ Read Chapter 3 Aloud

Use the Table of Contents to locate Chapter 3. Turn to page 26 and read Chapter 3 straight through to familiarize students with the chapter content. After reading, encourage students to

- write down notes or make drawings about interesting facts
- talk to a partner about what they expect to learn
- share their ideas about how people use soil

Then read through a second time, section-by-section, to teach the Big Idea, vocabulary, and science concepts.

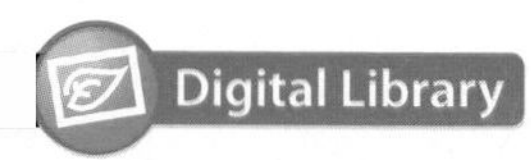

Digital Library

myNGconnect.com

Have students use the Digital Library to find photos of a variety of different-looking soils. Use the Presentation Tool to share the photos.

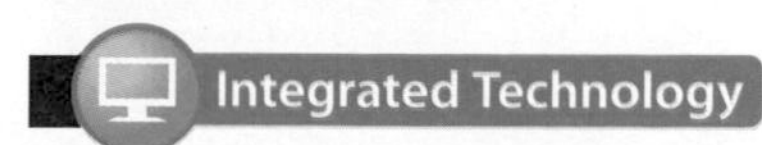

Integrated Technology

Computer Presentation Help students use the photos to make a computer presentation about the different types of soil discussed in the Big Ideas Big Book.

OBJECTIVES

Science

Students will be able to:

- Describe how small pieces of rock can be the basis of soil. T
- Classify soil types based on color, texture (size of particles), and the ability to retain water. T
- Describe how people use soil.

1 Introduce

Tap Prior Knowledge

- Ask students if they have ever grown fruits, vegetables, or flowers in a garden. Do they remember the color and feel of the soil?
- Ask volunteers to describe the soil in their gardens, including what it looks like and feels like.

Focus on the Big Idea

- Read the Big Idea Question aloud and have students echo it.
- Preview pages 28–29, 30–31, and 32–35, linking the headings with the Big Idea Question.
- With student input, post a chart that displays the headings.

What Can You Observe About Soil?

How Soil is Formed

Properties of Soil

People Use Soil

- Have students orally share what they expect to find in each section.
- Then read page 27 aloud.

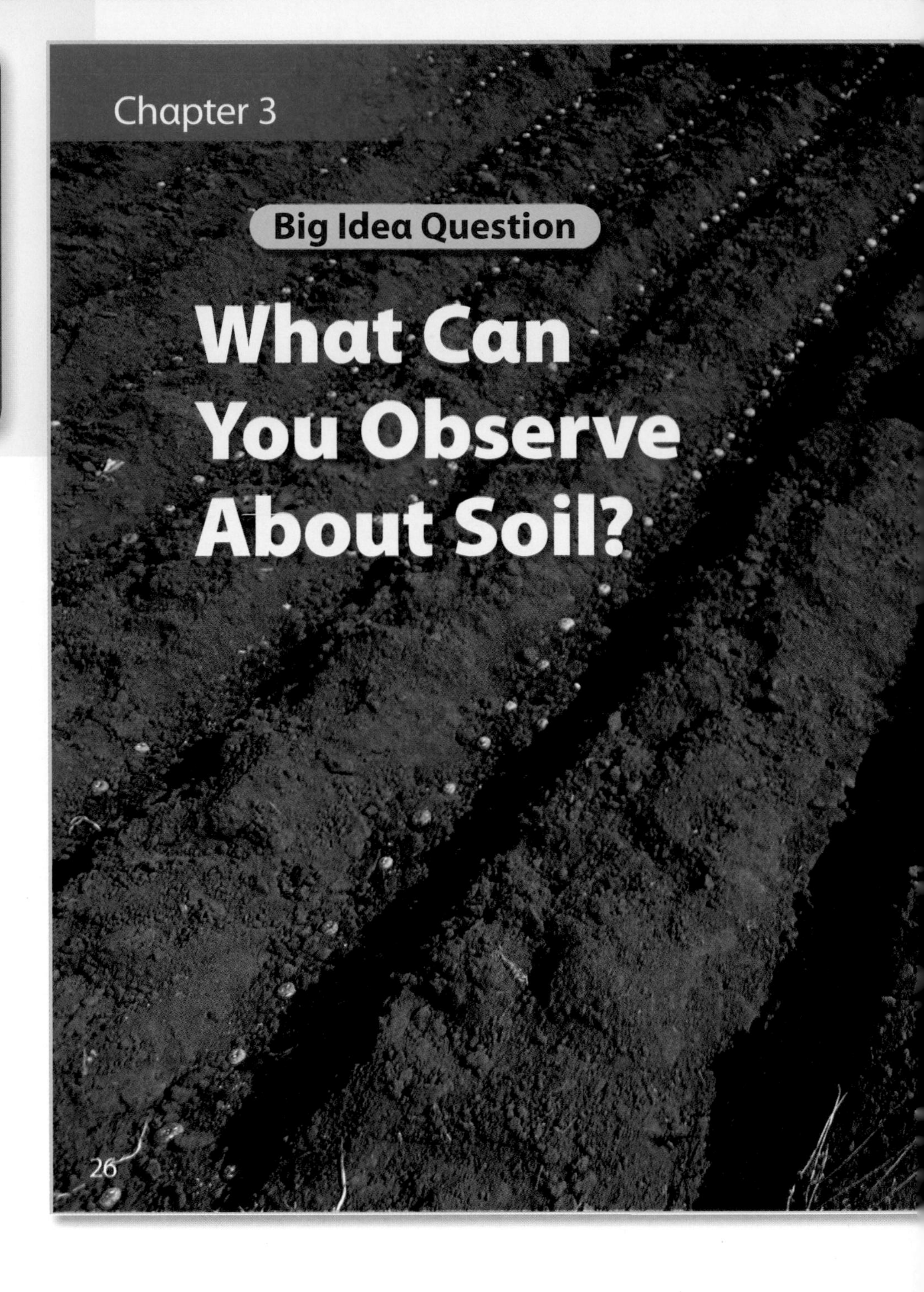

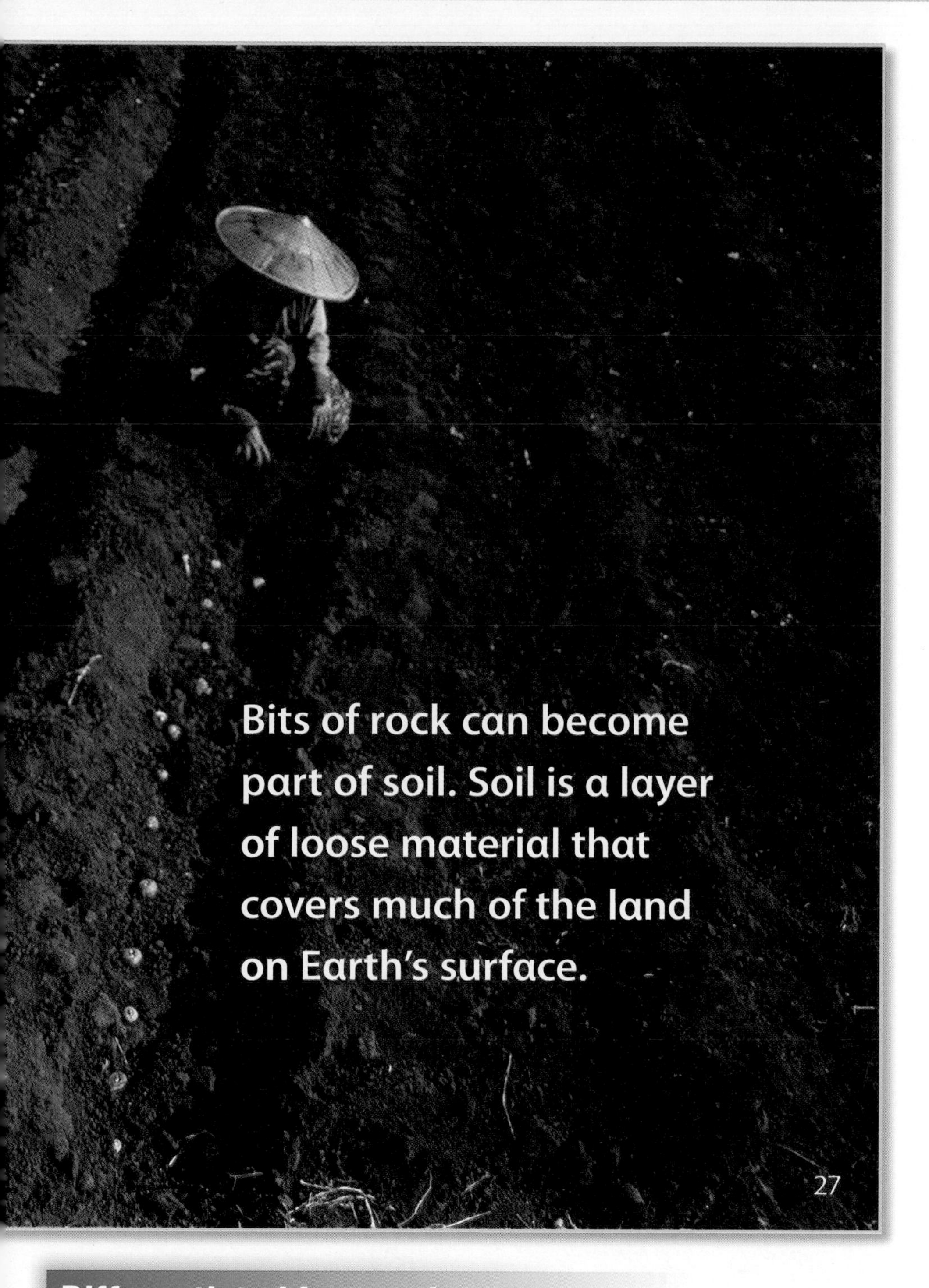

❷ Teach

Explain a Use of Soil

- Ask: **When a bulldozer digs into the ground, what is the first thing it digs into?** (soil)
- Direct students' attention to the photo. Ask: **How would you describe this soil?** (dark brown, crumbly) **What else do you notice about the soil?** (It's dug in rows.) **Why do you think the soil is dug in rows?** (Crops are being planted.) **What's one important way that people use soil?** (to grow crops for food)

Describe the Make-Up of Soil

- Ask students to recall and explain how rocks are broken down by weathering. Explain: **These weathered bits of rock get smaller and smaller. They lay on the ground and in the ground. What do you think they become part of?** (soil)
- Say: **You will learn more about the make-up of soil in this chapter.**

Making and Recording Observations

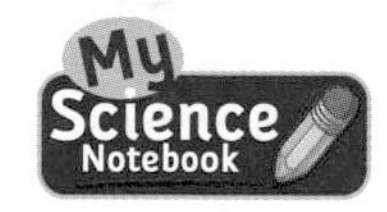

Have students draw or write about their observations of soil in their science notebook. Tell students to separate their observations from ideas they may have about soil. For example, descriptions of color, texture, and other soil properties are observations. These are different from ideas about what they think soil is made of. Model how to write observations neatly in a chart and how to write ideas below the chart.

Differentiated Instruction

Extra Support

Bring in a soil sample. Let students examine the sample. Ask them to name at least three properties of the soil.

Challenge

Have students examine a sample of soil. They can moisten the soil to determine its ability to hold water. Have them make tables that describe the properties of the soil, such as color, texture, and ability to hold water. Each table should include a title, columns, and rows.

» Before You Move On

Ask students:

1. **Recall What loose material covers much of Earth's land?** (soil)
2. **Explain How does weathering help make soil?** (Weathering breaks down rocks. These bits of rocks can become part of soil.)

LESSON 2D ▫ How Soil Is Formed

OBJECTIVE

Science

Students will be able to:

- Describe how small pieces of rock and dead plant and animal parts can be the basis of soil and explain the process by which soil is formed.

Science Academic Vocabulary *humus*

❶ Introduce

Tap Prior Knowledge

Ask students if they have ever dug a hole in the ground. Have them describe what they saw. Ask questions to guide students' descriptions. For example:

- **Did you see earthworms?**
- **Did you see small rocks?**
- **What else did you see?**

Preview and Read

- Display the photos on pages 28–29. Say: **The photos show things that are found in soil. Soil forms when these things mix.**
- Then read pages 28–29 aloud.

❷ Teach

Science Academic Vocabulary: *humus*

Point to the word **humus.** Reread its definition. Show students a photo of decaying leaves on a forest floor. Explain: **These leaves are decaying. That means they are breaking down into humus.** Have students define **humus** in their own words.

Describe the Composition of Soil

- Point to the photo of leaves and earthworms on page 29. Read the caption aloud. Ask: **What is happening to the leaves?** (They are decaying.) Ask: **What will the leaves become when they decay?** (humus)
- Point to the photo of **humus** on page 28. Say: **Humus is part of soil. It is bits of dead animals and plants that have decayed, or rotted.**

How Soil Is Formed

Bits of rock, air, and water are parts of soil. They are nonliving. The small bits of rock in soil come from the weathering of bigger rocks. **Humus** is part of soil, too.

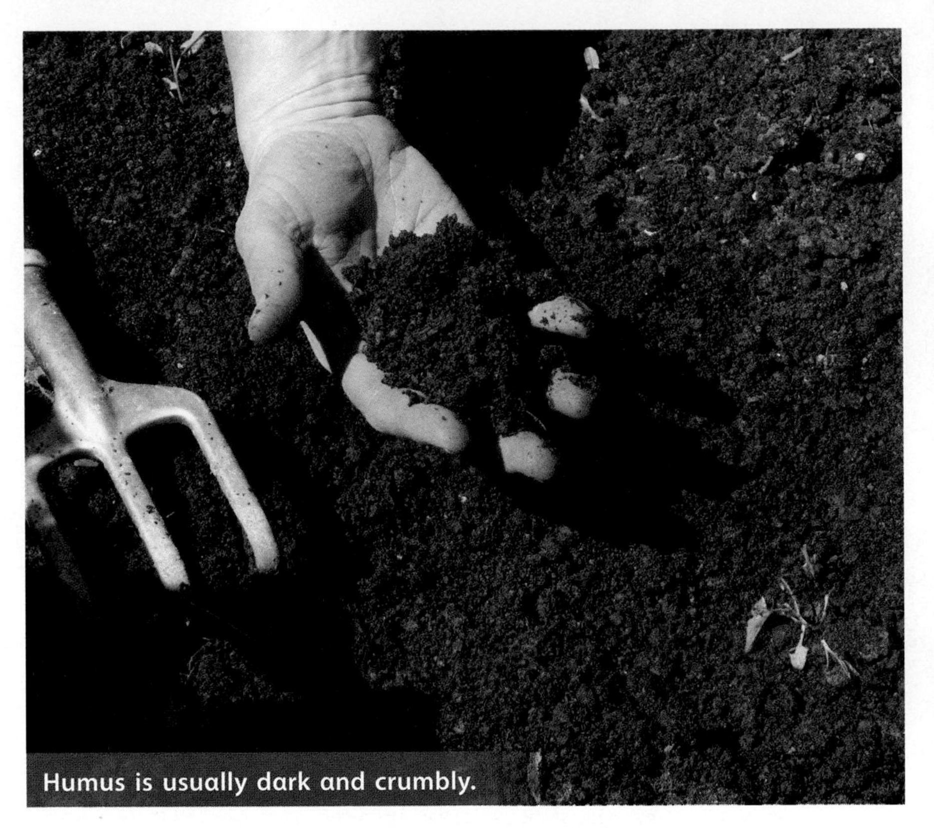

Humus is usually dark and crumbly.

28

NATIONAL GEOGRAPHIC Raise Your SciQ!

Soil Horizons Soil is made of different layers. These layers are called horizons. The top layer of soil is known as the A horizon, or simply topsoil. It contains the most humus and is usually darker than lower layers. The next deepest layer of soil is the B horizon. It has less humus than the A horizon and thus is lighter and less fertile. The bottom layer, or C horizon, contains partially weathered rock. Beneath the C horizon is solid rock.

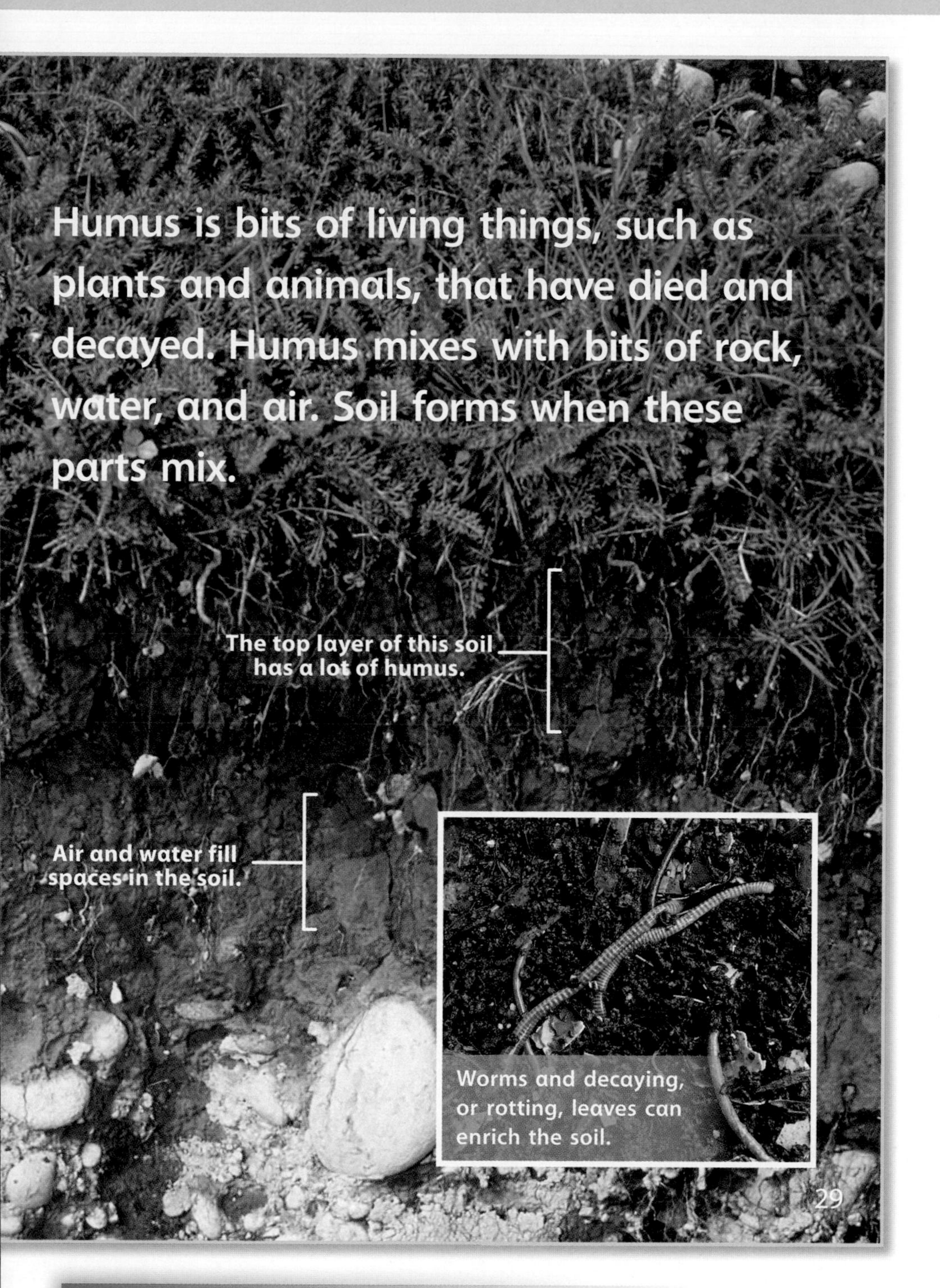

Teach, continued

- Display the photo of soil on page 29. Point to one caption. Say: **The lines by this caption are called brackets. They tell you which part of the photo the caption is about.**
- Then read the captions aloud. Ask: **What other things are found in soil?** (air, water, and bits of rock)

Explain How Soil Forms

- Ask: **Where do the bits of rock in soil come from?** (weathered rocks) **Where does humus come from?** (decayed plants and animals)
- Ask: **What forms when water, air, humus, and bits of rock mix?** (soil)

❸ Assess

1. **Define What is humus?** (a part of soil that contains bits of living things that have died and decayed)
2. **Classify Which things in soil are nonliving? Which things are living or come from living things?** (Bits of rock, air, and water are nonliving. Earthworms are living, and humus comes from living things.)
3. **Infer Why does the top layer of soil usually have the most humus?** (Animals and plants usually die near the surface. The decayed bits stay close to the top of the soil.)

Differentiated Instruction

ELL Language Support for Describing Soil

BEGINNING

Ask yes/no questions to monitor students' understanding of soil. For example:

- **Are bits of rock found in soil?**
- **Are water and air in soil?**
- **Is humus part of soil?**

INTERMEDIATE

Provide Academic Language Frames to help students describe the composition of soil. For example:

- *Nonliving parts of soil include ______, ______, and ______.*
- *______ and ______ fill spaces in the soil.*

ADVANCED

Have students describe soil. Ask:

- **What is found in humus?**
- **What forms when humus mixes with bits of rock, water, and air?**

OBJECTIVE

Science

Students will be able to:

- Classify soil types based on color, texture (size of particles). T

❶ Introduce

Tap Prior Knowledge

- Remind students that a property is something about an object that you can observe with your senses. Have students describe properties of the soil near school or their homes.
- Make a list of the properties that students name.

Set the Purpose and Read

- Point to the photos of the different soils on page 31. Say: **Different types of soils have different properties.**
- Then read pages 30–31 aloud.

❷ Teach

Text Features: Photos, Labels, and Captions

- Tell students that labels tell what a photo mostly shows. Captions tell more about a photo.
- Display the photos on page 31. Ask students to point to each soil type as you read its label aloud.
- Then read each caption aloud. Ask: **What were the captions about?** (the color and texture of different soils)

Properties of Soil

There are different kinds of soil. Each kind has different properties. Color and texture are two properties of soil.

Soil that has a lot of clay is sticky when it is wet.

30

Think Like a Scientist: Math in Science

Make Charts

Ask students to make graphic organizers in their science notebook that show the color and texture of each type of soil. Model how to do the first graphic organizer for students.

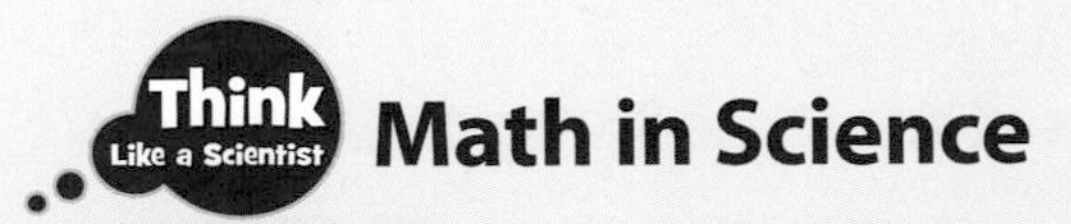

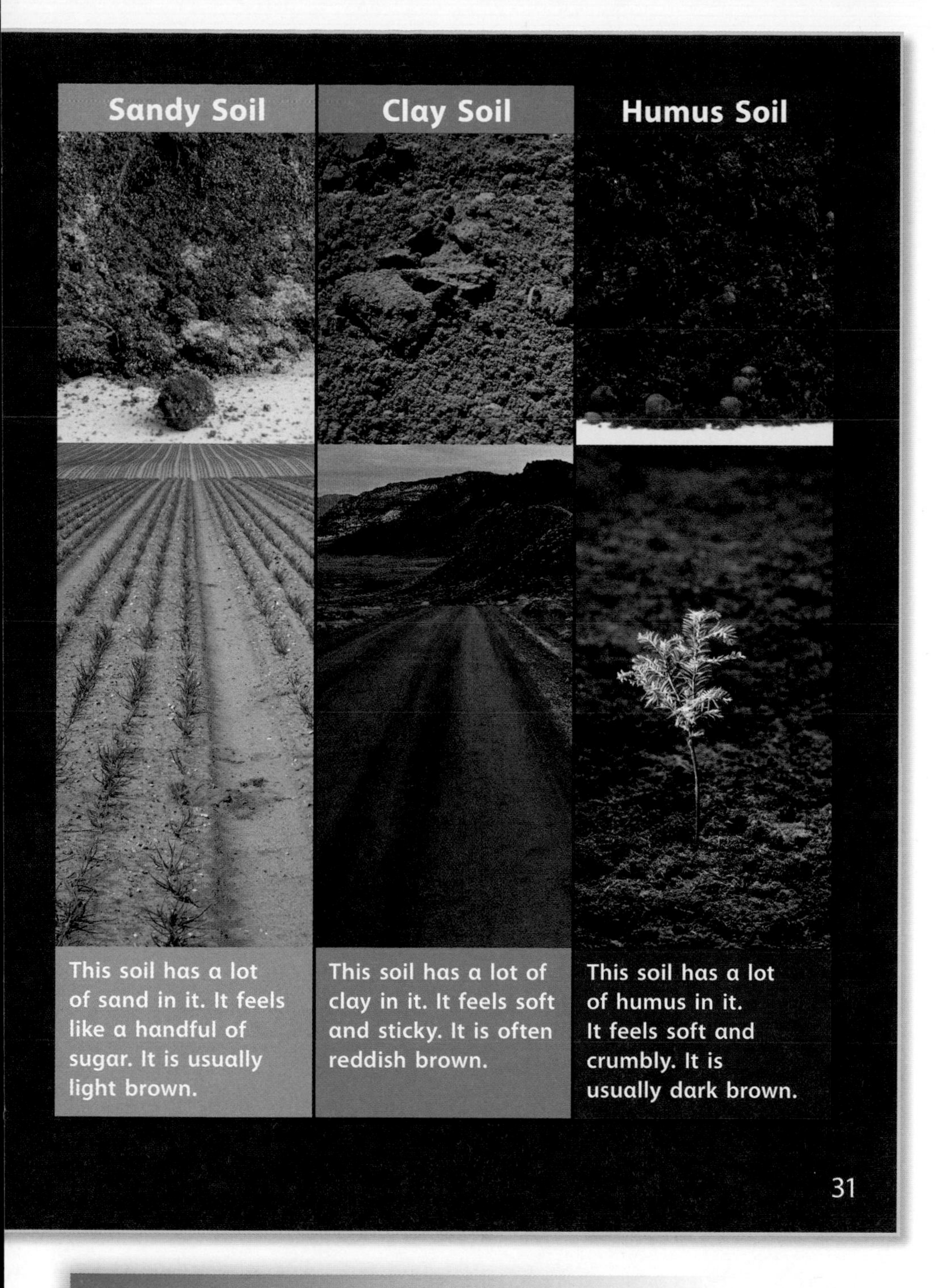

Teach, continued

Classify Soil Types By Color and Texture

- Explain: **Soils are made of different-sized particles. The size of these particles determines the texture of the soil. Clay soils have very small particles. Humus soils have small particles. Sand soils have the biggest particles.**
- Point to the photos on page 31. Reread the labels and captions aloud. Explain: **You can use the properties of color and texture to classify soils.**
- Tell students to imagine that they have a soil that feels like sugar. Ask: **Would you classify the soil as sand, clay, or humus?** (sand) **What property did you use to classify the soil?** (texture)
- Tell students to imagine that they have a soil that is reddish brown. Ask: **Would you classify the soil as sand, clay, or humus?** (clay) **What property did you use to classify the soil?** (color)

Differentiated Instruction

ELL Language Support for Classifying Soils

BEGINNING

Help students classify soils by asking questions as you point to the photos. For example:

- **Is the sandy soil reddish brown or light brown?**
- **Is clay soil gray or reddish brown?**
- **Is humus soil reddish brown or dark brown?**

INTERMEDIATE

Provide Academic Language Frames to help students classify soils. For example:

- _______ *soil is often light brown. It feels like* _______.
- _______ *soil is often reddish brown. It feels* _______ *and* _______.

ADVANCED

Have students draw pictures that compare sand, clay, and humus soil. Students should include captions that describe the texture of each soil type.

» Before You Move On

Ask students:

1. **Recall What are three kinds of soil?** (sandy soil, clay soil, and humus soil)
2. **Compare How do the textures of the soils differ?** (Sandy soil feels like sugar. Clay soil feels soft and sticky. Humus soil feels soft and crumbly.)

OBJECTIVES

Science

Students will be able to:

- Classify soil types based on the ability to retain water, and the ability to support the growth of plants. T
- Describe how people use soil.

❶ Introduce

Tap Prior Knowledge

Ask students if they have ever eaten a vegetable, such as a carrot, corn, a potato, and so on. Ask: **Where did the food come from?** (farm or garden) Prompt students to relate what they may know about growing food to what they learned about sandy, clay, and humus soils.

Set the Purpose and Read

- Point to the heading "People Use Soil" and read it aloud. Say: **The first part of this chapter is about how people use soil for growing plants. In the next part of the chapter, we'll learn about other soil uses.**
- Then read pages 32–33 aloud.

❷ Teach

Text Features: Connect Visuals and Text

- Remind students that photos and captions can help explain ideas in the lesson.
- Display the photos on pages 32–33. Read the captions aloud.
- Say: **The chapter tells us that some soils are better for growing plants than others. The photos and captions explain why this is true.**
- Ask: **Which soil is best for growing most plants?** (humus)
- Ask: **Why is humus good for growing plants?** (It holds the right amount of water for most plants.)

People Use Soil

People use soil for many things. People use soil to grow plants for food. Some kinds of soil are better for growing food than others.

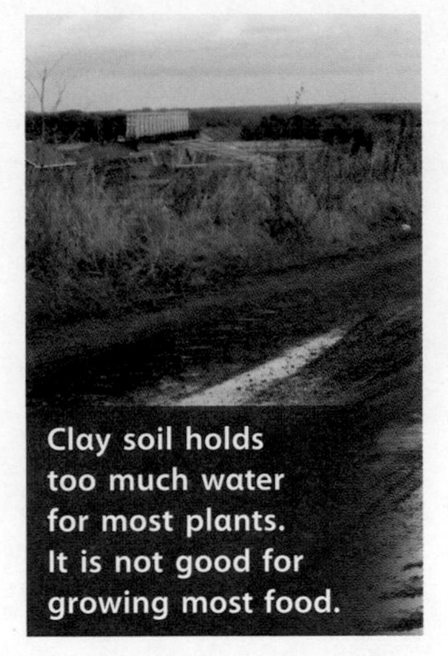

Clay soil holds too much water for most plants. It is not good for growing most food.

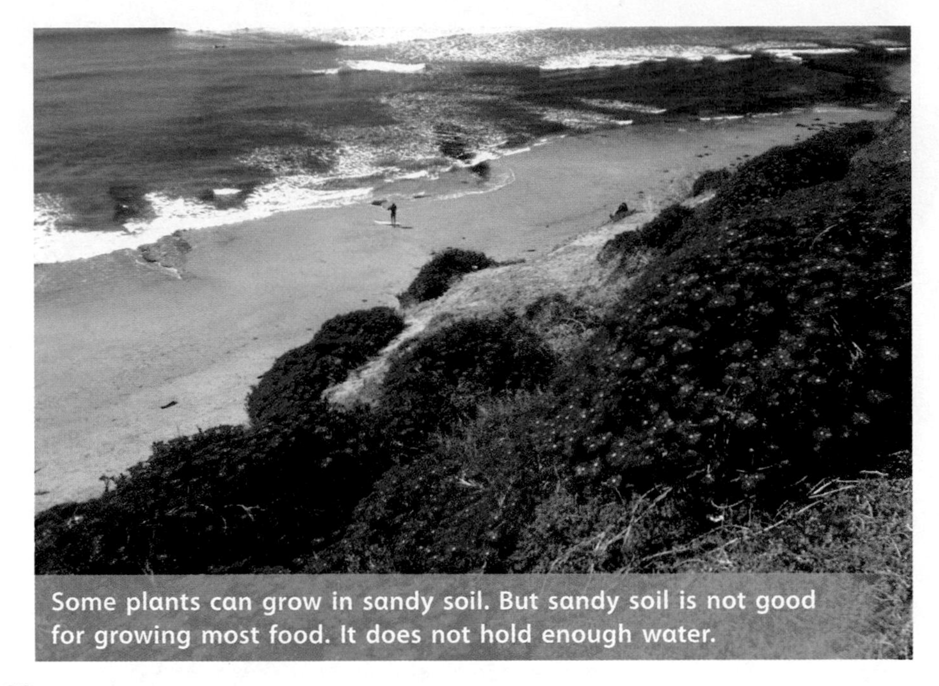

Some plants can grow in sandy soil. But sandy soil is not good for growing most food. It does not hold enough water.

32

NATIONAL GEOGRAPHIC Raise Your SciQ!

How Soil Is Important for Some Plants Unlike animals, most plants make their own food. Plants use sunlight, water, and carbon dioxide to make food in a process called photosynthesis.

Plant roots take in water and nutrients from the soil. The nutrients help plants grow. Fertilizers add nutrients to the soil.

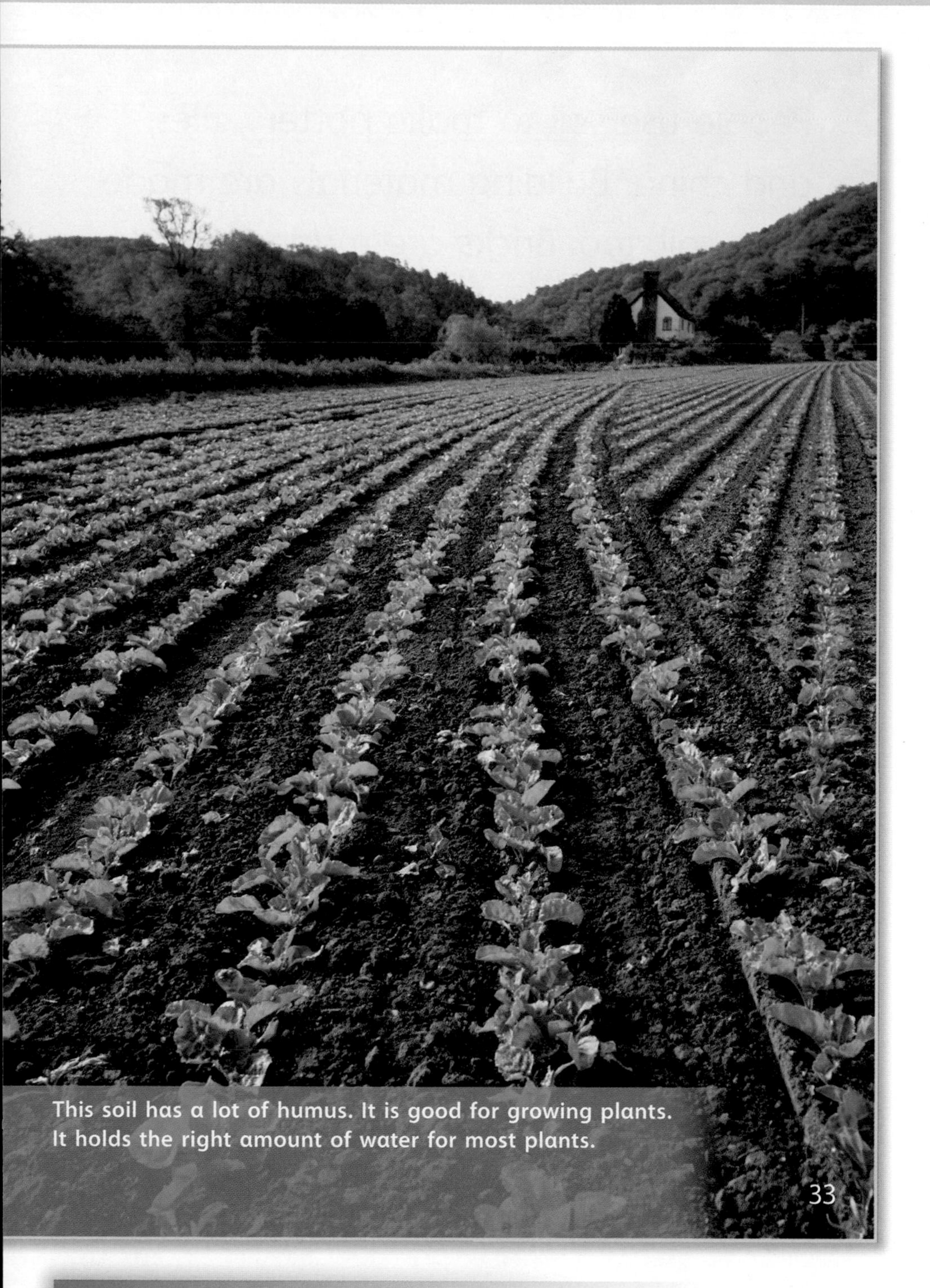

This soil has a lot of humus. It is good for growing plants. It holds the right amount of water for most plants.

33

Teach, continued

Classify Soils

- Reread page 32. Ask: **What do people use to grow plants?** (soil)
- Point to the photo on page 33. Say: **The plants in this photo are used as food.**
- Read the captions on pages 32–33. Ask: **Would clay be good for growing food? Why or why not?** (No, clay is not good for growing food because it holds too much water.)
- Ask: **Would sandy soil be good for growing food? Why or why not?** (No, sandy soil would not be good for growing food because it does not hold enough water.)
- Ask: **Why is food grown in humus?** (because humus holds the right amount of water for most plants)
- Explain that areas with good soil for growing plants are valuable throughout the world. These geographic areas have been developed to produce food and other products that we need.

Making Charts

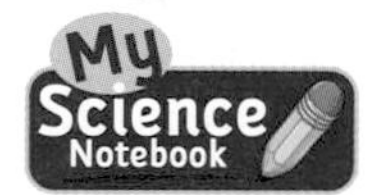

In the science notebook, have students make a chart that classifies soils according to the ability to hold water and grow plants.

Differentiated Instruction

ELL Language Support for Classifying Soils

BEGINNING

Reread the captions. Then say:

Point to the photo of the soil that holds too much water. Point to the photo of the soil that holds too little water. Point to the photo of the soil that holds the right amount of water for growing plants.

INTERMEDIATE

Provide Academic Language Frames to help students classify soils. For example:

- *People often use ______ to grow plants.*
- *______ soil holds too much water to grow most plants.*
- *______ soil holds the right amount of water for growing most plants.*

ADVANCED

Have students each make a graphic organizer that compares the ability of different soils to retain water and grow plants. The organizers can vary but should correspond to the descriptions given in the captions on pages 32–33.

» Before You Move On

Ask students:

1. **Name What is one way that people use soil?** (Possible answer: to grow food)
2. **Apply Which soil would you use to grow plants? Why?** (Possible answer: I would use humus soil because it holds the right amount of water for most plants.)

OBJECTIVE

Science

Students will be able to:

- Identify how soil is used in manufacturing and construction. T

PROGRAM RESOURCES

- *Rocks and Soil* Learning Master 30, or at myNGconnect.com
- Chapter Test 3, Assessment Handbook, pages 11–12, or at myNGconnect.com
- NGSP ExamView CD-ROM

Teach, continued

Identify How Soil Is Used for Building and for Making Things

- Ask students to raise their hands if they live in a building made of brick. Ask them to raise their hands if they have a driveway or sidewalk made of concrete. Have students identify how soil is used around their neighborhoods.
- Read page 34 aloud. Show students photos of china and tiles. Ask: **What is used to make these things?** (soil) **What would you use to make bricks?** (clay) **What would you use to make concrete?** (sand)

Summarize the Big Idea

- Display the chart from page T26. Read the Big Idea Question.
- Ask: **What did you find out in each section? Is this what you expected to find?** With students, add new information to the chart.

People use soil to make pottery, tiles, and china. Building materials are made from soil, too. Bricks are made from clay. Concrete is made from sand.

These colorful pottery jars are made of clay.

34

Share and Compare

My Science Notebook

Classify Soils Give students the Learning Master and a copy of the *Rocks and Soil* small book. Have them find pictures of different soil types in Chapter 3. Tell them to add the names of the soils to the chart in the correct column. Check their work and then have them write a description of each soil type.

Partners can use the charts to discuss how soils are used.

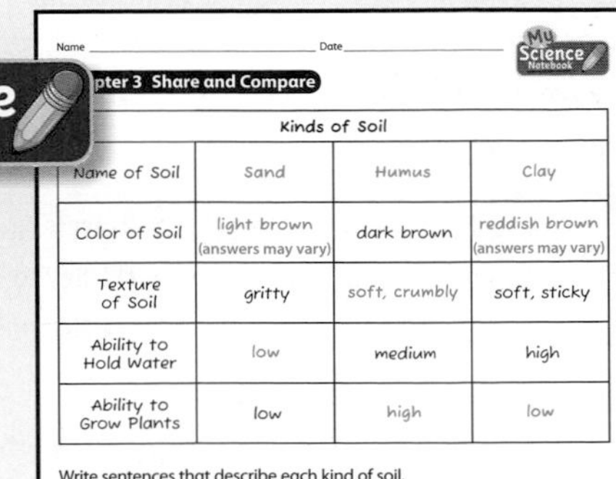

Name ______ Date ______

My Science Notebook

...pter 3 Share and Compare

Kinds of Soil			
Name of Soil	Sand	Humus	Clay
Color of Soil	light brown (answers may vary)	dark brown	reddish brown (answers may vary)
Texture of Soil	gritty	soft, crumbly	soft, sticky
Ability to Hold Water	low	medium	high
Ability to Grow Plants	low	high	low

Write sentences that describe each kind of soil.

1. Sand soil is light brown and feels gritty like sugar. It does not hold much water and is not good for growing plants.
2. Humus soil is dark brown and feels soft and crumbly. It holds the right amount of water and is good for growing plants.
3. Clay soil is reddish brown and feels soft and sticky. It holds too much water and is not good for growing plants.

Learning Master 30 Rocks and Soil

Learning Master 30, or at myNGconnect.com

People also use soil for building. Soil is the firm base under many homes and roads.

A new house will be built on this soil.

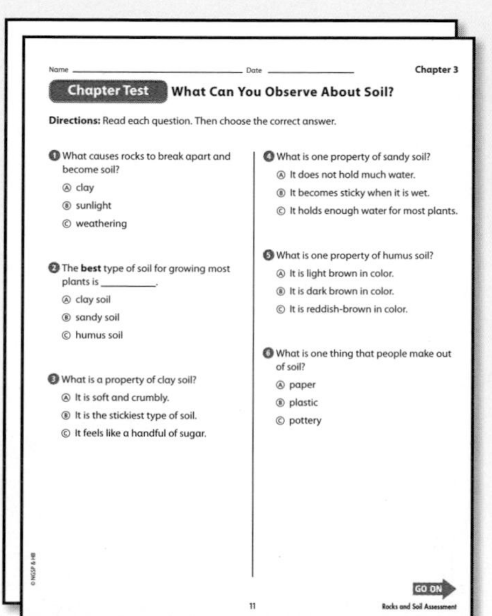

Name ______ Date ______ Chapter 3

Chapter Test **What Can You Observe About Soil?**

Directions: Read each question. Then choose the correct answer.

1. What causes rocks to break apart and become soil?
   - Ⓐ clay
   - Ⓑ sunlight
   - Ⓒ weathering
2. The **best** type of soil for growing most plants is ______.
   - Ⓐ clay soil
   - Ⓑ sandy soil
   - Ⓒ humus soil
3. What is a property of clay soil?
   - Ⓐ It is soft and crumbly.
   - Ⓑ It is the stickiest type of soil.
   - Ⓒ It feels like a handful of sugar.
4. What is one property of sandy soil?
   - Ⓐ It does not hold much water.
   - Ⓑ It becomes sticky when it is wet.
   - Ⓒ It holds enough water for most plants.
5. What is one property of humus soil?
   - Ⓐ It is light brown in color.
   - Ⓑ It is dark brown in color.
   - Ⓒ It is reddish-brown in color.
6. What is one thing that people make out of soil?
   - Ⓐ paper
   - Ⓑ plastic
   - Ⓒ pottery

GO ON

11 Rocks and Soil Assessment

Chapter Test 3, Assessment Handbook, pages 11–12, or at myNGconnect.com,

or NGSP ExamView CD-ROM

Assess Student Progress Chapter Test 3

Have students complete Chapter Test 3 to assess their progress in this chapter.

Teach, continued

What Can You Observe About Soil?

How Soil Is Formed
Kate Rock, air, water, and humus form soil.

Properties of Soil
Juan Color, texture, and ability to hold water are properties of soil.

People Use Soil
Emanuela People use soil to grow things and for building.

Notetaking

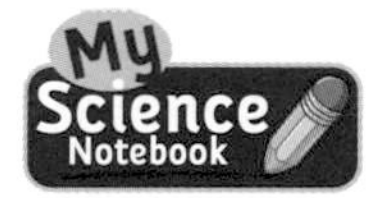

Based on the discussion and the chart, help students develop a statement that sums up the Big Idea. They can write their statements in their science notebook.

You can observe soil properties, such as color, texture, ability to hold water, and ability to grow plants.

❸ Assess

1. **Recall What are three uses for soil?** (growing food, building homes and roads on soil, making materials from soil)
2. **Explain What are clay and sand used for?** (Clay is used to make brick and pottery. Sand is used to make concrete.)
3. **Infer What kind of soil would you use for growing a garden? Why?** (Humus; it holds the right amount of water for growing plants.)

OBJECTIVES

Science

Students will be able to:

- Recognize that Earth is made up of rocks. Rocks come in many sizes and shapes.
- Describe how wind, water, and ice can change rocks and other earth materials. T
- Describe how small pieces of rock can be the basis of soil. T

Science Academic Vocabulary

property, texture, mineral, weathering, soil, erosion, gravity, humus

PROGRAM RESOURCES

- Unit Test, Assessment Handbook, pages 16–22, or at myNGconnect.com
- NGSP ExamView CD-ROM
- Big Idea Cards

❶ Sum Up Big Ideas

- Students have now learned about the three Big Ideas in the unit. Display all the three Big Idea Cards and read each Big Idea Question to students.
- Then read the Conclusion on page 36 to summarize the Big Ideas.
- Have students match each paragraph of the text with the Big Idea Question on the Big Idea Card.

Conclusion

Earth's Rocks and Soil

Rocks have properties, such as color, texture, and layers. People use rocks in many ways. For example, people use rocks for buildings and jewelry.

Weathering changes rocks. Wind, water, and ice can wear down rocks or break them apart. Water can dissolve all or parts of rocks.

Soil is made up of bits of rock, air, water, and humus. People use soil in many ways. People grow food in soil. They build homes and roads on soil. They make building materials from soil.

36

Review Science Academic Vocabulary

Science Academic Vocabulary Tell students that scientists use special words when describing their work to others. For example:

property	texture	mineral	weathering
soil	erosion	gravity	humus

Have students write the list in their science notebook and use each word in a sentence that tells about earth materials. Encourage students to share their sentences with a classmate.

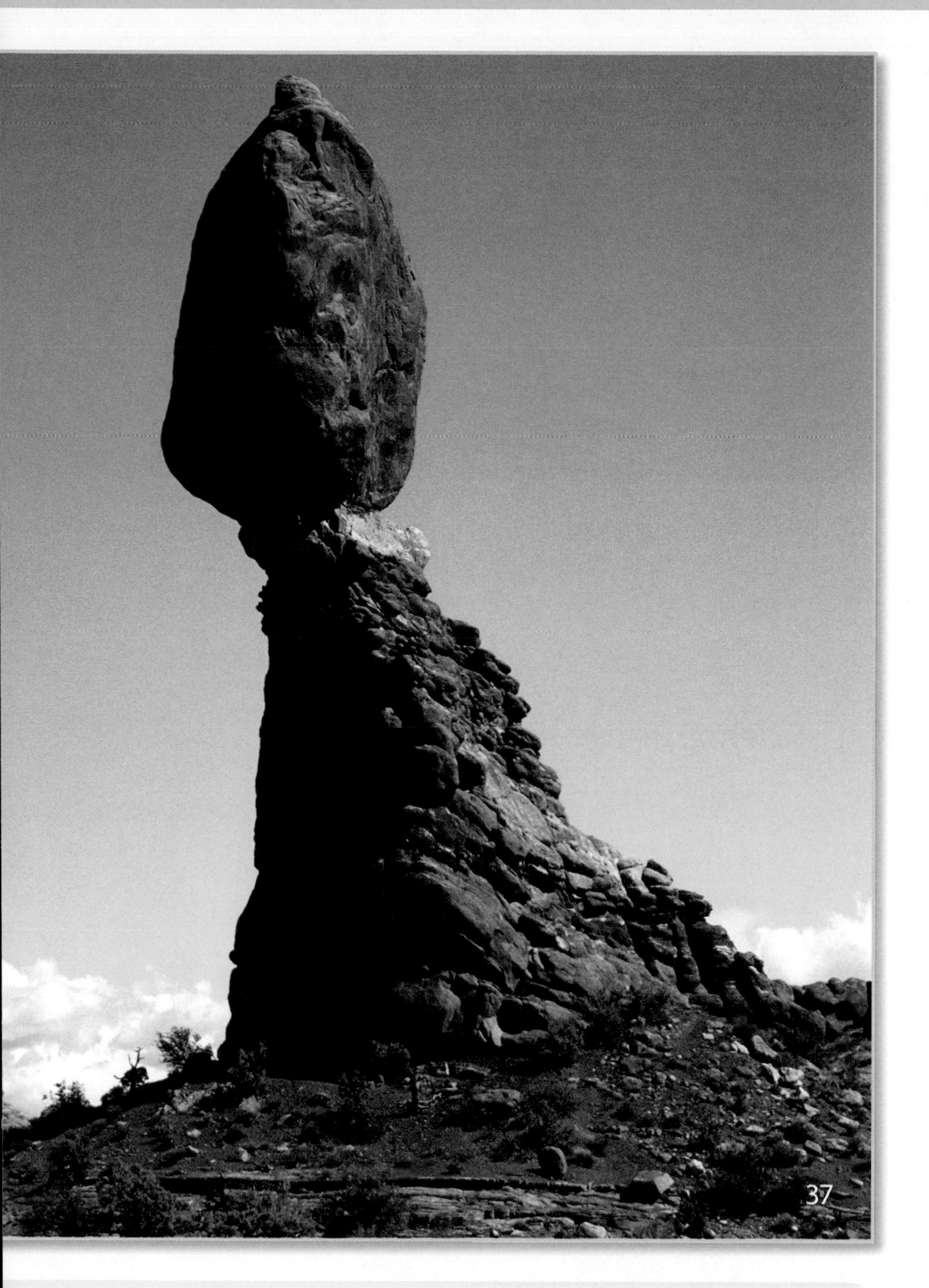

❷ Discuss Big Ideas

Notetaking

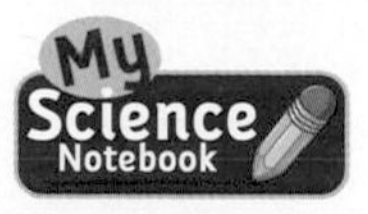

Have students write in their science notebook to show what they know about the Big Ideas. Have them:

1. Write three **properties** of a rock.
2. Tell how **weathering** and **erosion** can change rocks.
3. Tell how weathered materials can help form **soil.**
4. Tell what things they can observe about **soil.**
5. Discuss and share their writing with the class.

❸ Assess Big Ideas

1. **Big Idea 1 What can you observe about rocks?** (You can observe rock properties and the ways people use rocks.)
2. **Big Idea 2 How do rocks change?** (Rocks change as they are weathered and eroded by ice, water, and wind.)
3. **Big Idea 3 What can you observe about soil?** (You can observe soil properties, such as color, texture, ability to hold water, and ability to grow plants. You can observe uses for soil.)

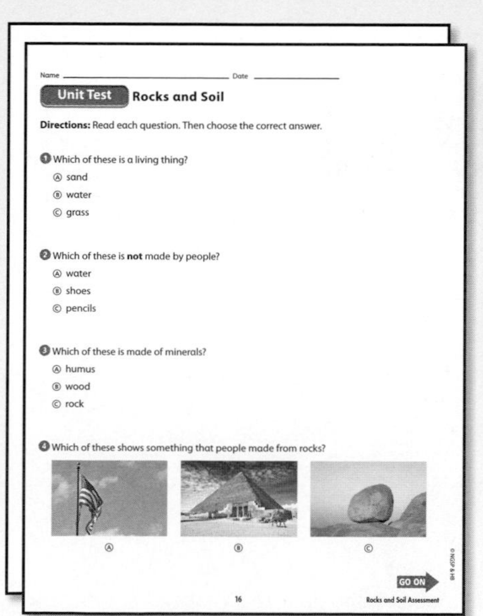

Name ______________________ Date ____________

Unit Test **Rocks and Soil**

Directions: Read each question. Then choose the correct answer.

1. Which of these is a living thing?
   Ⓐ sand
   Ⓑ water
   Ⓒ grass

2. Which of these is **not** made by people?
   Ⓐ water
   Ⓑ shoes
   Ⓒ pencils

3. Which of these is made of minerals?
   Ⓐ humus
   Ⓑ wood
   Ⓒ rock

4. Which of these shows something that people made from rocks?
   Ⓐ Ⓑ Ⓒ

GO ON

© NGSP & HB

16 Rocks and Soil Assessment

Unit Test, Assessment Handbook, pages 16–22, or at myNGconnect.com,

or NGSP ExamView CD-ROM

Assess Student Progress Unit Test

Have students complete their Unit Test to asses their progress in the unit.

OBJECTIVES

Science

Students will be able to:

- Investigate through Open Inquiry.
- Generate questions to investigate.
- Plan investigations.
- Make and compare observations; collect and record data.
- Generate questions and explanations based on evidence or observations.
- Share findings; ask questions to increase understanding; adjust interpretations based on feedback.

Science Process Vocabulary *fair test*

PROGRAM RESOURCES

- Science Inquiry Book: *Rocks and Soil*
- Science Inquiry Book eEdition at myNGconnect.com
- Inquiry eHelp at myNGconnect.com
- *Rocks and Soil* Learning Masters 31–34, or at myNGconnect.com
- Inquiry Rubric: Assessment Handbook, page 34, or at myNGconnect.com
- Inquiry Self-Reflection: Assessment Handbook, page 40, or at myNGconnect.com

MATERIALS

Materials will vary based on students' choices of investigations. See page T37c for materials for the Sample Question and Steps.

❶ Introduce

- In Open Inquiry, students ask questions, then make plans for investigations to answer the questions.
- Have students open their Science Inquiry Books to page 30. Read the sample questions and have students choose one or make up a question of their own. Students may use the Open Inquiry Checklist in their Inquiry Books as they plan and conduct their investigations.
- On pages T37c–T37f, the Sample Question and Steps can be used if you prefer to give students more direct guidance in designing an investigation.

Open Inquiry

Do Your Own Investigation

Question **Choose a question or make up one of your own to do your investigation.**

- How can you find out if a mineral is harder than a penny?
- How can you show how wind moves different kinds of soil?
- What happens if you grow some lima bean seedlings in sandy soil and some lima bean seedlings in humus soil?

Science Process Vocabulary

fair test noun

In a **fair test,** you change only one thing and keep everything else the same.

I changed the kind of soil. Everything else is the same.

30

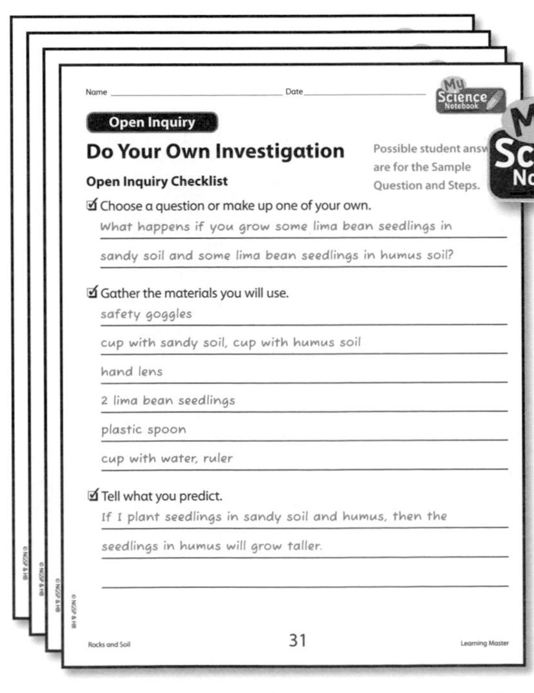

Name ____ Date ____

Open Inquiry

Do Your Own Investigation

Possible student answers are for the Sample Question and Steps.

Open Inquiry Checklist

☑ Choose a question or make up one of your own.
What happens if you grow some lima bean seedlings in sandy soil and some lima bean seedlings in humus soil?

☑ Gather the materials you will use.
safety goggles
cup with sandy soil, cup with humus soil
hand lens
2 lima bean seedlings
plastic spoon
cup with water, ruler

☑ Tell what you predict.
If I plant seedlings in sandy soil and humus, then the seedlings in humus will grow taller.

Rocks and Soil 31 Learning Master

My Science Notebook

Learning Masters 31–34, or at myNGconnect.com

Open Inquiry Checklist 

Here is a checklist you can use when you investigate.

- ☐ Choose a **question** or make up one of your own.
- ☐ Gather the materials you will use.
- ☐ Tell what you **predict.**
- ☐ Plan a **fair test.**
- ☐ Make a **plan** for your investigation.
- ☐ Carry out your **plan.**
- ☐ Collect and record **data.** Look for **patterns** in your data.
- ☐ Explain and **share** your results.
- ☐ Tell what you **conclude.**
- ☐ Think of another question.

31

Differentiated Instruction

ELL Understand Science Process Vocabulary

BEGINNING

Have students look at the picture on page 30. Reread the speech balloon aloud. Ask: **What changed in this fair test?** (the type of soil)

INTERMEDIATE

Have students look at the picture on page 30 and read the speech balloon silently to themselves. Ask: **What changed in this fair test?** (the type of soil)

ADVANCED

Ask students if the following is a fair test. Say: **Jim wanted to find out which soil held the most water. He poured different amounts of water on different soils.** Ask: **Is this a fair test? Why or why not?** (It is not a fair test because Jim changed two things instead of one [water and soil].)

❷ Build Vocabulary

Science Process Vocabulary: fair test

Use this routine to introduce the word.

1. **Pronounce the Word** Say **fair test.** Have students repeat it by sounding out each word.
2. **Explain Its Meaning** Choral read the sentence and speech balloon. Ask students for another phrase that means the same as **fair test.** (investigation in which only one thing is changed)
3. **Encourage Elaboration** Ask: **What kind of investigation might not involve a fair test?** (one that is based only on observations)

❸ Guide the Investigation

Guide students in the process of developing and carrying out their investigations. For a model of the Open Inquiry investigation, see pages T37e and T37f for sample student responses. Students may also use other inquiry activities in the Science Inquiry Book as models for their investigations.

❹ Explain and Conclude

Have students share the results of their investigations and their conclusions with other students. You may use the Sample Question and Steps as a model. See page T37e for guidance on explaining results.

❺ Find Out More

Encourage students to use observations made in their investigations to generate other questions that could be studied through scientific investigations. See page T37f for information on generating questions.

❻ Reflect and Assess

- To assess student work with the Inquiry Rubric shown on page T37f, see Assessment Handbook, page 34, or go online to myNGconnect.com.
- Score items separately and then decide on one overall score.
- Have students use the Inquiry Self-Reflection on Assessment Handbook page 40, or at myNGconnect.com.

LESSON 5 ▫ Investigation Model

OBJECTIVES

Science

Students will be able to:

- Investigate through Open Inquiry.
- Generate questions to investigate.
- Plan investigations.
- Make and compare observations; collect and record data.
- Generate questions and explanations based on evidence or observations.
- Share findings; ask questions to increase understanding; adjust interpretations based on feedback.

PROGRAM RESOURCES

- Science Inquiry Book: *Rocks and Soil*
- Science Inquiry Book eEdition at myNGconnect.com
- Inquiry eHelp at myNGconnect.com
- Science Inquiry Kit: *Rocks and Soil*
- *Rocks and Soil* Learning Masters 31–36, or at myNGconnect.com
- Inquiry Rubric: Assessment Handbook, page 34, or at myNGconnect.com
- Inquiry Self-Reflection: Assessment Handbook, page 40, or at myNGconnect.com

MATERIALS

Kit materials are listed in italics.

2 plastic cups (9 oz); sandy soil; humus; hand lens; plastic spoon; cup (10 oz); water; *metric ruler*

For teacher use (advance preparation): *2 lima bean seeds;* paper towel; *resealable plastic bag;* marker; masking tape

1 Introduce

Tap Prior Knowledge

- Ask: **What have you observed that all plants need in order to grow?** (water, sunlight) Explain that in addition to water and sunlight, plants need nutrients, such as minerals, that are found in soil. Tell students that in this investigation they will grow bean plants in two different soils to see in which soil the plants grow best.

Name ______________________ Date ______________________

My Science Notebook

SAMPLE QUESTION AND STEPS

Investigate Soil

What happens if you grow some lima bean seedlings in sandy soil and some lima bean seedlings in humus soil?

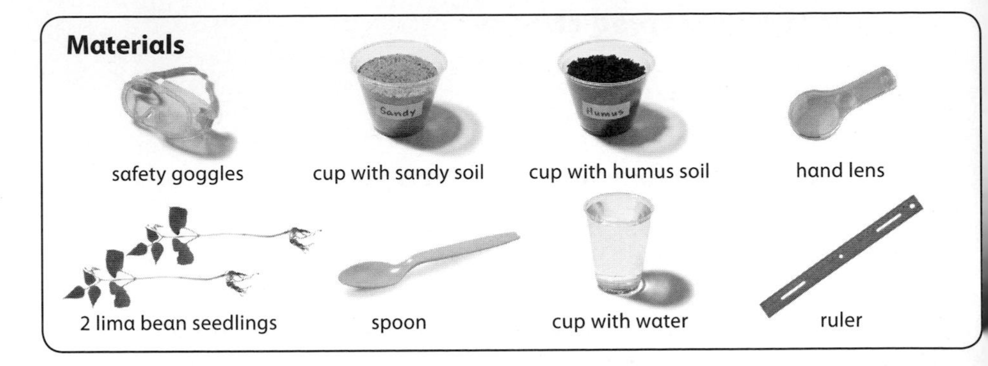

What to Do

1. Put on your safety goggles. Use the hand lens to **observe** each type of soil.

MANAGING THE INVESTIGATION

Time

40 minutes

Groups

small groups of 4

Advance Preparation

- Place the lima bean seeds on a wet paper towel in a resealable plastic bag 3–5 days before the activity or until they sprout. Have students plant these seedlings. Sprout enough lima bean seedlings for each group.
- Provide a sunny location, such as a windowsill, for the seedlings.
- Put 4 ounces of sandy soil in the first cup. Put 4 ounces of humus in the second cup. Label the first cup *Sandy* and the second cup *Humus.*

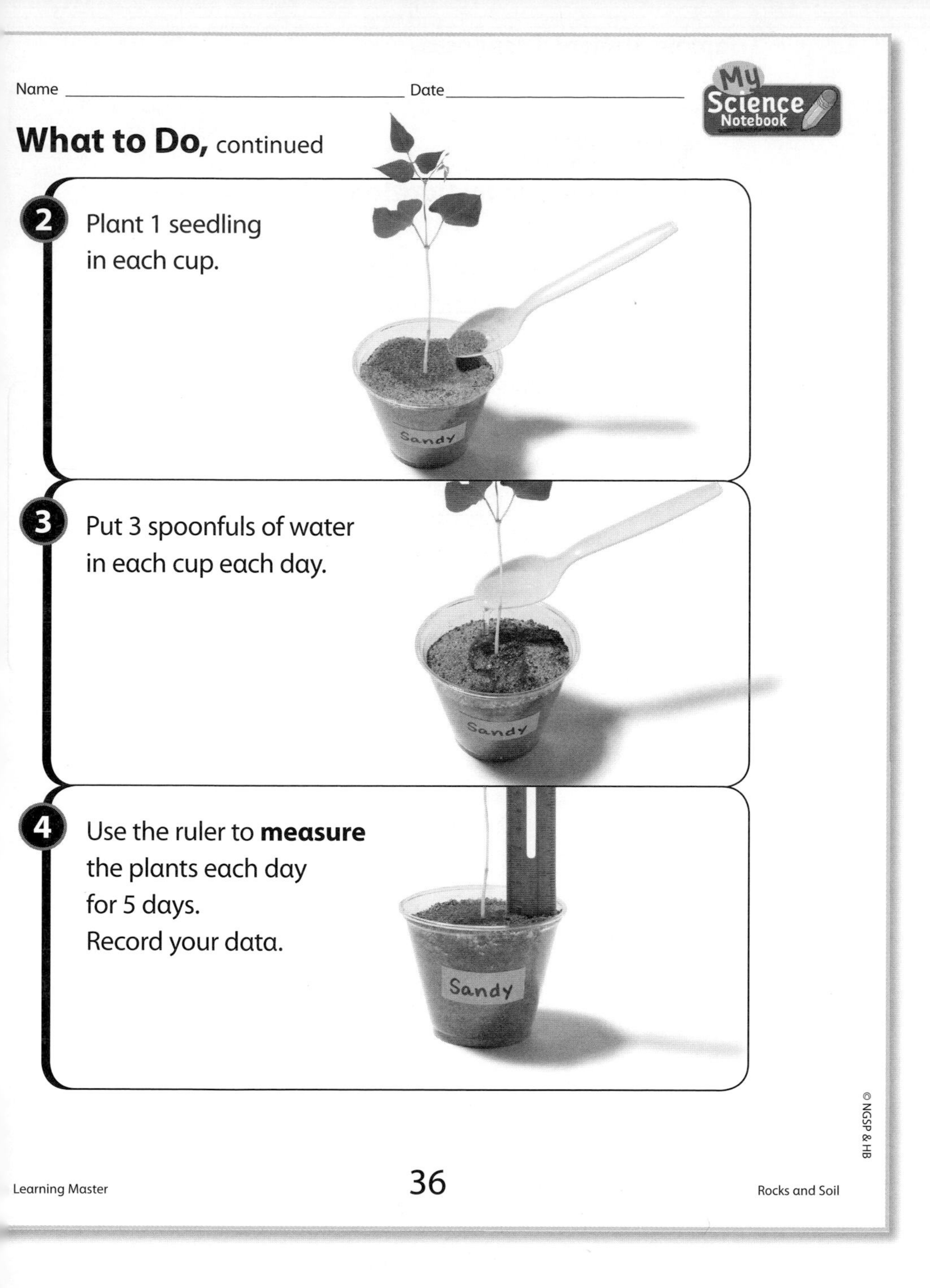

Name _______________ Date _______________

My Science Notebook

What to Do, continued

2 Plant 1 seedling in each cup.

3 Put 3 spoonfuls of water in each cup each day.

4 Use the ruler to **measure** the plants each day for 5 days. Record your data.

Learning Master 36 Rocks and Soil

Introduce, continued

- Ask: **Do you think that some soils might be better for plants to grow in than others?** (yes) **What can you infer about a soil that grows plants better than another soil?** (It holds water better. The material it is made of has more nutrients.) Explain to students that some soils have more nutrients than others and are better for growing plants.

Sample Question and Steps

- Use the Sample Question and Steps as a procedure that students can use to practice the steps of an Open Inquiry investigation. Provide as much guidance as needed, keeping in mind that the goal is for students to learn how to make their own plans to answer questions through scientific investigations.
- Have students use the Open Inquiry Checklist on the Student Inquiry Book page 31. This checklist also appears on Learning Masters 31–34. Students may use these Learning Masters to make a record of their investigations.

Connect to Big Idea

- Review the Big Idea Question, *What can you observe about soil?* Explain to students that observing and knowing the properties of different types of soil can help determine which soils are best for growing plants.
- Distribute Learning Masters. Have students read the question on Learning Master 35. Ask students if they have ever planted seeds in soil. Have them discuss how they might be able to tell which of two soils is better for growing a lima bean plant.

❷ Guide the Investigation

- Distribute materials.
- Guide students in writing their predictions. Students should write their predictions as If… then… statements. Accept all reasonable responses. See sample student responses on page T37e.
- Guide students in planning a fair test. Students should list what they will change, what they will observe or measure, and what they will keep the same. See sample student responses on page T37e.

What to Expect

Students will plant the seedlings in cups containing different soils. Each cup will contain the same amount of soil. Students will give the seedlings the same amount of water and sunlight. They will measure the seedlings each day for a week. Seedlings planted in humus soil should grow taller.

Teaching Tips

- Suggest that students measure and water seedlings at the same time each day. Students should record their data immediately after taking measurements.
- The number of days needed for appropriate plant growth will vary depending on the growing conditions. Allow time for the plants to display observable differences.
- If this inquiry is done during late spring, students can take seedlings home to plant in their gardens.

Rocks and Soil

Guide the Investigation, continued

- Assist students as necessary to develop a list of steps for their investigation. Stress that the steps should be able to be repeated by anyone without additional instruction. See sample student responses on page T37e.
- Guide students as they set up and do their investigations.
- Assist students in completing a table for recording data. See sample table on page T37f.

❸ Explain and Conclude

- Have students compare observations of individual and group results.
- Students should then examine the data they collected and use these as evidence to develop reasonable explanations for their observations and results. To encourage this, ask questions such as: **What do you think?** or **How do you know?**
- As each group shares explanations and conclusions, encourage students to ask questions (Why? How do you know?) to increase understanding. Students should actively listen for other interpretations and ideas. Discuss possible reasons for any differences in results and explanations.
- Encourage students to suggest alternative explanations if needed. Allow students to adjust their explanations and conclusions as needed. Have students create and record individual conclusions about group findings.

Sample Student Responses

Name ______ Date ______ My Science Notebook

Open Inquiry

Do Your Own Investigation

Possible student answers are for the Sample Question and Steps.

Open Inquiry Checklist

☑ Choose a question or make up one of your own.

What happens if you grow some lima bean seedlings in sandy soil and some lima bean seedlings in humus soil?

☑ Gather the materials you will use.

safety goggles
cup with sandy soil, cup with humus soil
hand lens
2 lima bean seedlings
plastic spoon
cup with water, ruler

☑ Tell what you predict.

If I plant seedlings in sandy soil and humus, then the seedlings in humus will grow taller.

Name ______ Date ______ My Science Notebook

Open Inquiry continued

☑ Plan a fair test.

What one thing will you change? I will change the kind of soil.

What will you observe or measure? I will observe and measure how tall the plants grow.

What will you keep the same? I will keep the kind of plant and the amount of sunlight and water the same.

☑ Make a plan for your investigation.

1. Put on safety goggles. Use the hand lens to observe each type of soil.
2. Plant 1 seedling in each cup.
3. Put 3 spoonfuls of water in each cup each day.
4. Use the ruler to measure the plants each day for 5 days. Record your data.

Name ______________________ Date ______________________

My Science Notebook

Open Inquiry continued

☑ Carry out your plan.

☑ Collect and record data. Look for patterns in your data.

Day	Height of Seedling in Sandy Soil (cm)	Height of Seedling in Humus Soil (cm)
1		
2		
3		
4		
5		

Students should observe that the plant in humus soil grew taller than the plant in sandy soil.

Name ______________________ Date ______________________

My Science Notebook

Open Inquiry continued

☑ Tell what you conclude. Plants grow better in humus soil than in sandy soil.

☑ Explain and share your results. The plant in humus soil grew tallest. The plant in sandy soil did not grow as tall.

☑ Think of another question. How can you make soils better for growing plants?

❹ Find Out More

Think of Another Question

- Students should use observations from this investigation to generate other questions that can be answered using readily available materials. Use the question stems, *What happens when…*, *What would happen if…*, or *How can I/we…* to form testable questions.
- Record student questions for possible future investigations.

❺ Reflect and Assess

- To assess student work with the Inquiry Rubric shown below, see Assessment Handbook, page 34, or go online to myNGconnect.com.
- Score each item separately and then decide on one overall score.
- Have students use the Inquiry Self-Reflection on Assessment Handbook page 40, or at myNGconnect.com.

Inquiry Rubric at myNGconnect.com	Scale			
The student generated or chose a **question** to investigate.	4	3	2	1
The student planned a **fair test** by changing only one thing.	4	3	2	1
The student made and compared **observations** and collected and recorded **data.**	4	3	2	1
The student formed a **conclusion** and explained results based on evidence from the collected data and observations.	4	3	2	1
The student **shared** observations and conclusions with other students.	4	3	2	1
Overall Score	**4**	**3**	**2**	**1**

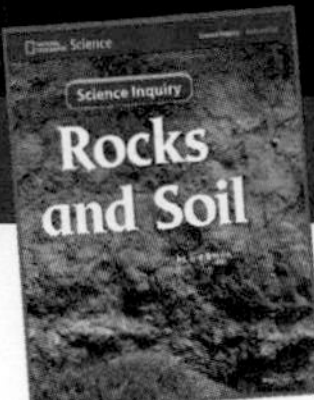

OBJECTIVE

Science

Students will be able to:

- Describe how tools help scientists to make better observations.

PROGRAM RESOURCES

- Science Inquiry Book: *Rocks and Soil*
- Science Inquiry Book eEdition at myNGconnect.com
- *Rocks and Soil* Learning Master 37, or at myNGconnect.com

❶ Introduce

Tap Prior Knowledge

Remind students how they used a hand lens when they investigated rocks. Ask: **What could you observe with the hand lens that you could not see with your eyes alone?** (tiny fossils, layers, holes) **What other tools have you used to investigate rocks and soil?** (metric ruler, measuring cups) Explain that scientists use many different tools to help them observe and measure objects that they investigate.

❷ Teach

- Read page 32 aloud with students. Ask: **What tool would you use to make things look bigger?** (magnifying glass or hand lens) **What things might you observe with a hand lens?** (fossils, soil, leaves, rocks) **How does observing carefully with a hand lens help you gain knowledge about the soil?** (I can observe details that I can't see by using only my eyes.)
- If possible, give students hand lenses to use. Have them examine some common materials they may find in their desks or look at print in a textbook. Have them practice focusing the lens and looking at details.
- Point out that scientists often use a magnifying glass or hand lens when working in the field or outside a laboratory. Explain to students that a hand lens isn't as powerful as a microscope, but it does offer a much closer look than looking with eyes alone.

How Scientists Work

Using Tools to Observe

Scientists use tools to help them make better observations. You also use tools when you do science investigations.

You can use a magnifying glass to make things look bigger. A magnifying glass is also called a hand lens. It helps scientists study small and large objects, like fossils.

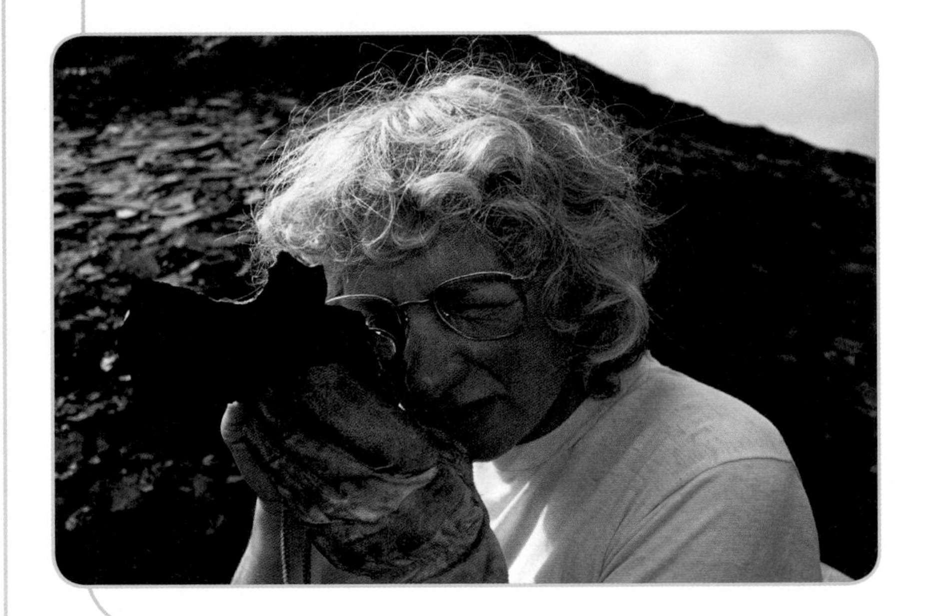

32

A balance is a tool that can help you compare the weights of objects. Why is this tool called a balance? When you balance the pans, the objects in the two pans have the same weight.

You can use a balance to compare the weight of almost any objects that will fit on the balance. You might compare rocks, water, or even tiny insects in the soil.

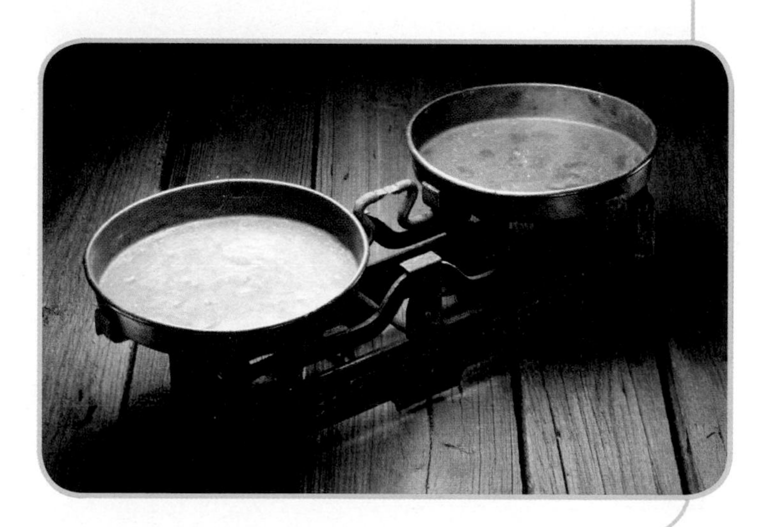

People have used balances such as this one for a long time. ▶

33

Teach, continued

- Read page 33 aloud with students. Point out the top photo on page 33. Ask: **What can you use a balance for?** (to compare weights of objects) **Why do you think this tool is called a balance?** (When the two pans balance, the weights on both sides are the same.)
- Explain to students that they have used a balance to compare the weights of two objects. Point out that they have used a balance to find out which of two objects is heavier or lighter. Ask: **Did you find out the exact weight of either of the two objects?** (no)
- Have students review how to use a balance to compare the weights of some common objects in the classroom.

NATIONAL GEOGRAPHIC Raise Your SciQ!

Soil Samples on Mars On May 25, 2008, NASA's Phoenix Lander arrived on Mars to collect and analyze soil samples from the surface of the planet. Scientists were eager to investigate whether Mars could support plant life. One way to do this was to determine if water had ever been present in the soil. Samples were scooped into a tiny oven and heated to 982 degrees C (1,800 degrees F), releasing water vapor. This test confirmed that water had once been present in the sample. Other tests showed soil samples to have a pH level between 8 and 9, close to ocean water's pH of 8.2. Further soil analysis showed samples to contain mineral nutrients, such as magnesium, sodium, and potassium, that would support plant life.

Teach, continued

- Read page 34 aloud with students. Point to the thermometer in the picture. Ask: **What is the name for this tool?** (thermometer) **What information can you learn by using a thermometer?** (how hot or cold something is)
- Review with students how to read a thermometer. Have students observe thermometers that have been set out at room temperature. Remind students that the *F* on the left side of the thermometer stands for *Fahrenheit*, and the *C* on the right stands for *Celsius*. Have students practice reading the thermometers and stating the room temperature in degrees Fahrenheit and degrees Celsius. Ask: **What is the temperature of the soil on page 34 in degrees Fahrenheit?** (about 61 degrees) **In degrees Celsius?** (about 16 degrees)
- Have students work with a partner to answer the questions on page 34.

What Did You Find Out?

1. Scientists use tools to help them make better observations.
2. Three tools scientists use are a magnifying glass or hand lens, a balance, and a thermometer. A magnifying glass or hand lens makes things look bigger. You can compare weight with a balance. A thermometer measures temperature.

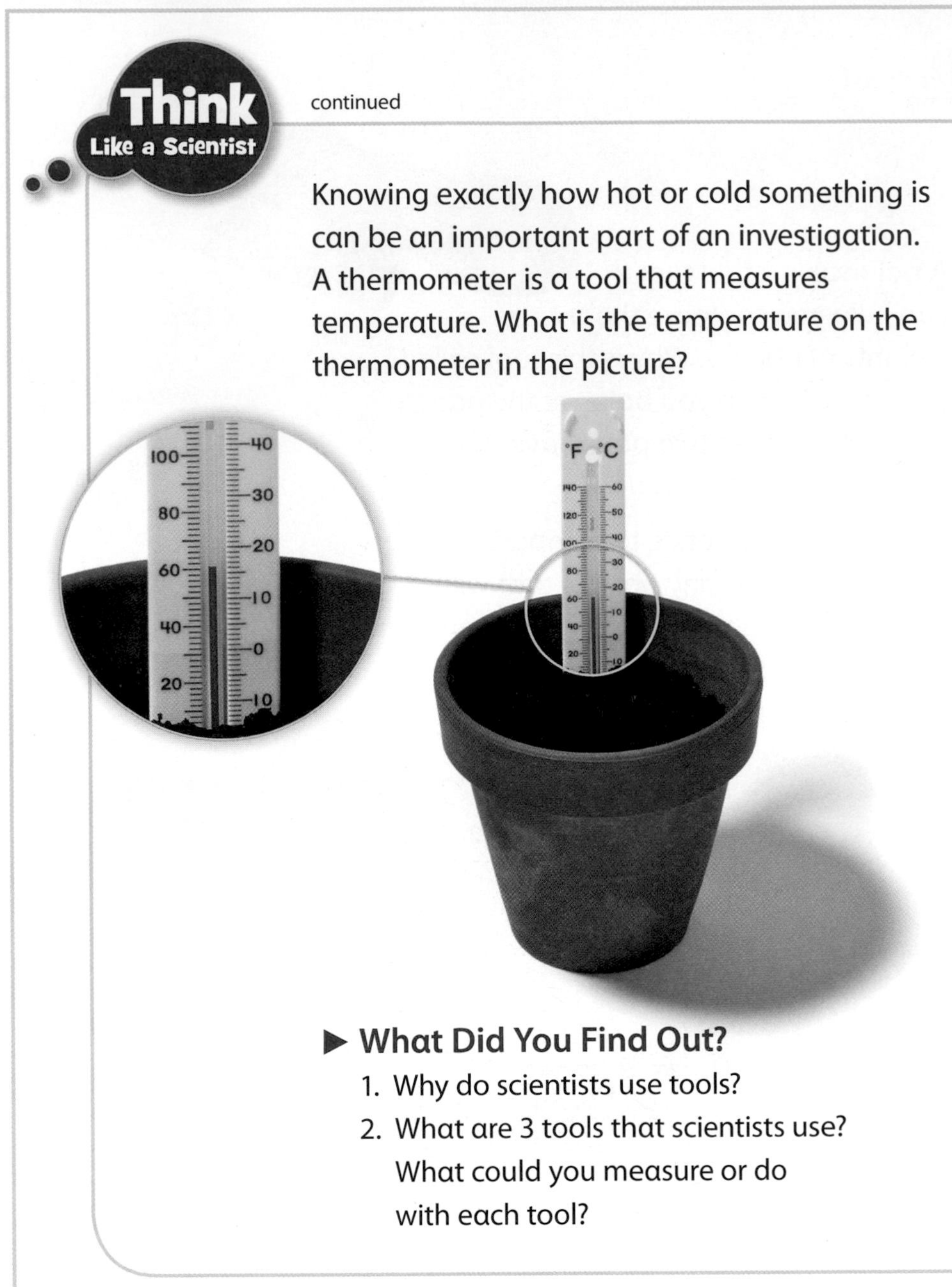

Think Like a Scientist continued

Knowing exactly how hot or cold something is can be an important part of an investigation. A thermometer is a tool that measures temperature. What is the temperature on the thermometer in the picture?

▶ **What Did You Find Out?**

1. Why do scientists use tools?
2. What are 3 tools that scientists use? What could you measure or do with each tool?

34

Name ______ Date ______

Think Like a Scientist **How Scientists Work**

Use Tools to Observe

1. What did you observe?
Answers will vary. Students will likely have observed rocks or soil.

2. How did the hand lens help you make better observations?
Possible answer: The hand lens helped me to see details in the rock that I couldn't see with my eyes alone.

Rocks and Soil 37 Learning Master

My Science Notebook

Learning Master 37, or at myNGconnect.com

Use Tools to Observe

You can use tools to study rocks and soil. First, find a rock or some soil to observe. Observe it without a hand lens. Then, use a hand lens to observe the rock or soil again.

- Tell what you observed.
- Tell how the hand lens helped you to make better observations.

35

Teach, continued

Use Tools to Observe

- Read page 35 aloud with students. Students can complete the inquiry in pairs or small groups. Make sure each student has access to a hand lens.
- Students can observe the rocks and soil samples from previous activities, or they can choose different objects to study. Remind students that hand lenses help them to see small details, so they might want to choose objects with interesting patterns or textures.
- Have students share their observations with the class. They should tell how using the hand lens helped them make better observations.

❸ Assess

Use Learning Master 37. Students should draw or write about what they observed. They should tell what they observed and explain how using the hand lens helped them to make better observations. For example, students will likely have observed rocks or soil and may have discovered that the hand lens helped them to see details in the rock that they couldn't see with their eyes alone.

Rocks and Soil

Use the Song Card to wrap up the *Rocks and Soil* Big Ideas Big Book.

Before you sing together, point out the unit vocabulary in the song.

Sing the song and then:

- Look for answers to this Big Idea Question: How do rocks change?
- Have students identify the phrases in the song that describe erosion. (rock flew by, strong wind, big rainfall) Then ask students to name the force that caused the rock to fall downhill instead of uphill. (gravity)
- Have students tell what else can move rocks and soil. (ice) Then have students sing the song again, substituting the word *glacier* for *rainfall*.

Song Card (front)

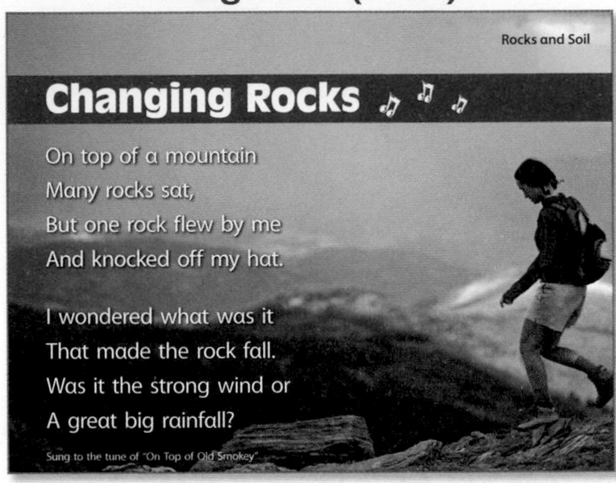

- Look for answers to these Big Idea Questions:
  What can you observe about rocks?
  How do rocks change?
  What can you observe about soil?
- Divide students into two or more groups. Choose words from each verse that one group will sing and words that the other group will sing. For example, one group sings "Rocks become," and the other group sings "weathered."

Song Card (back)

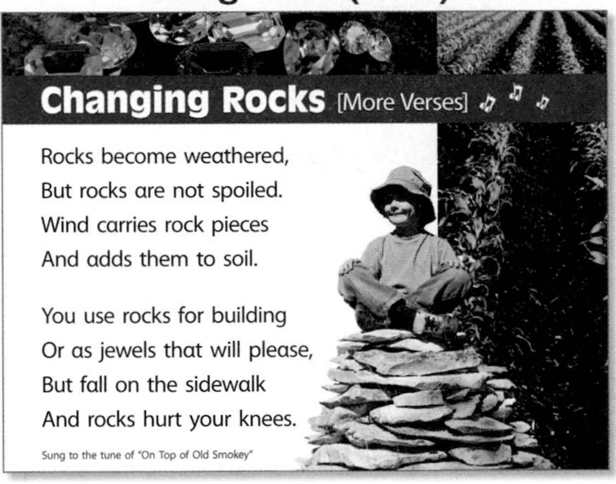

Sing with Me

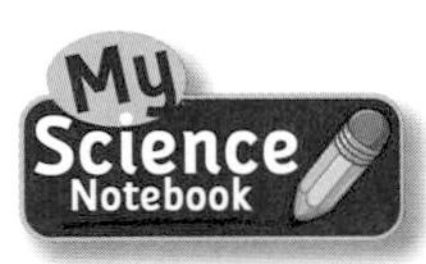

Learning Master 38, or at myNGconnect.com

Name ____________ Date ____________

Rocks and Soil Song

Draw a picture that goes with the unit song, *Changing Rocks*.

On top of a mountain
Many rocks sat,
But one rock flew by me
And knocked off my hat.
I wondered what was it
That made the rock fall.
Was it the strong wind or
A great big rainfall?
Sung to the tune of "On Top of Old Smokey"

One big idea I learned about in this unit is ____________
Possible answer: how rocks change.

Learning Master 38 Rocks and Soil

Read Informational Text

Become an Expert Books

Explore on Your Own Books

Contents

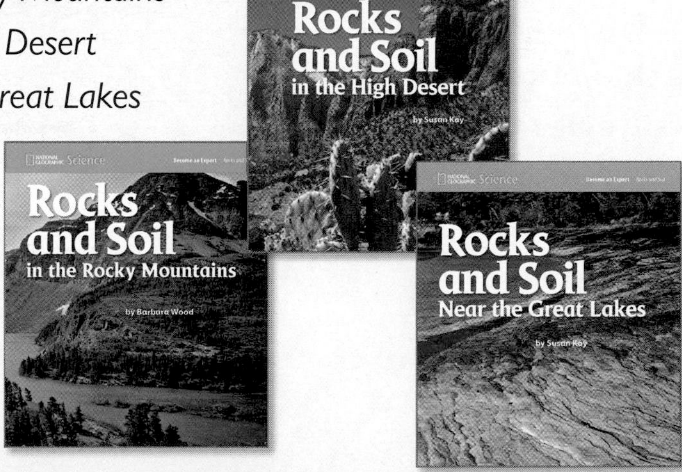

eEdition at myNGconnect.com

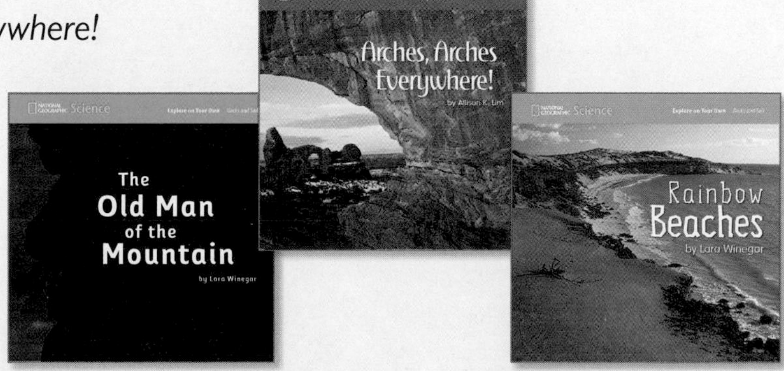

eEdition at myNGconnect.com

Science Through Literacy

Teaching students reading comprehension strategies can help them access science content and support their scientific inquiries. National Geographic Science focuses on four key reading comprehension strategies.

You may choose to review or teach one or more of the strategies using the Mini-Lessons on pages T42–T45, as appropriate for your students.

Reading Comprehension Strategies

Preview and Predict

- Look over the text.
- Form ideas about how the text is organized and what it says.
- Confirm ideas about how the text is organized and what it says.

Monitor and Fix Up

- Think about whether the text is making sense and how it relates to what you know.
- Identify comprehension problems and clear up the problems.

Make Inferences

- Use what you know to figure out what is not said or shown directly.

Sum Up

- Pull together the text's big ideas.

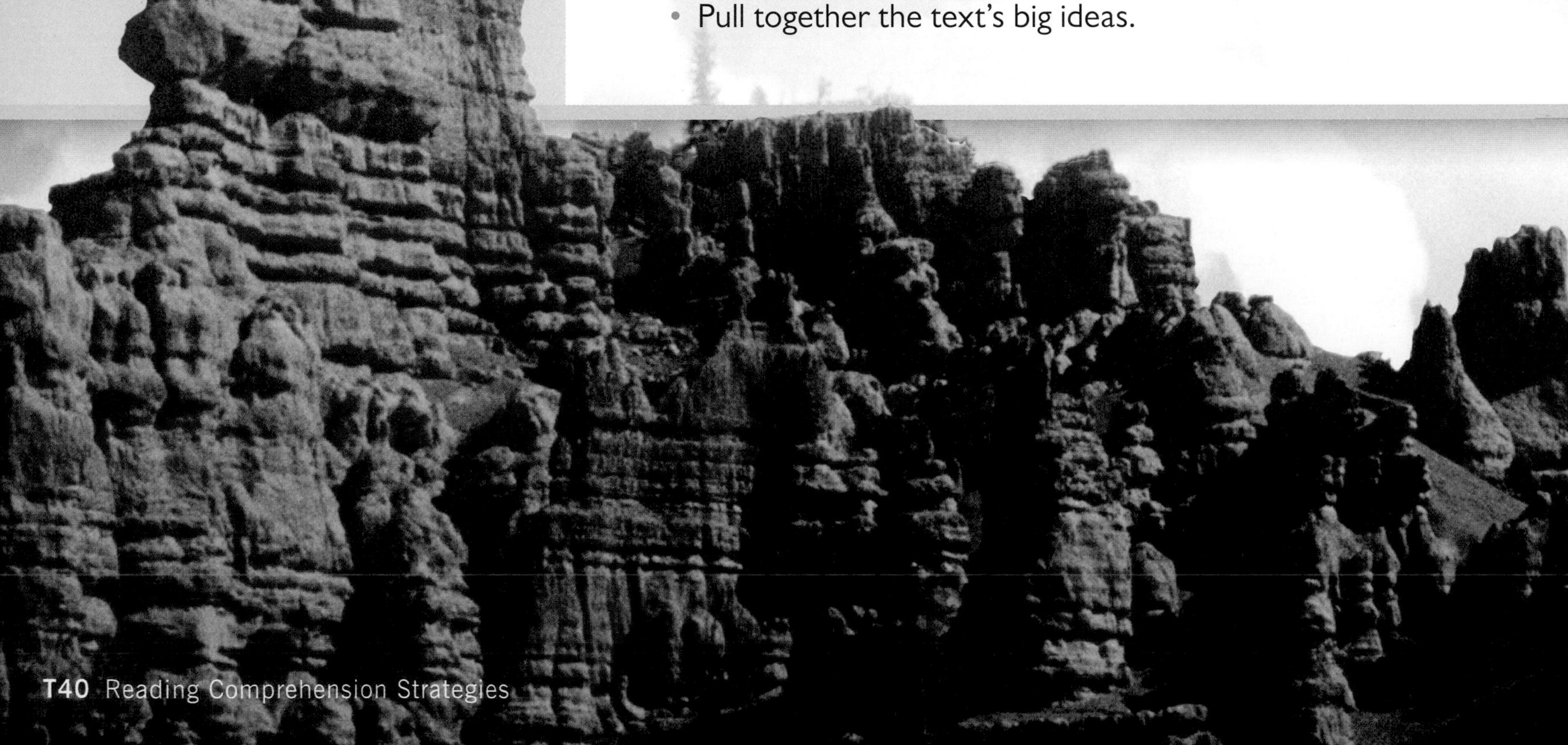

Five-Step Model

For each reading comprehension strategy you teach, we recommend that you follow this five-step model.

1 Describe the Strategy

Explain what the strategy is and when and how to use it.

2 Model the Strategy

Show students how to use the strategy by thinking aloud as you read.

3 Collaboratively Use the Strategy

Work with students to jointly apply the strategy.

4 Guide Application of Multiple Strategies

Gradually release responsibility to small groups of students to use the strategy, along with other strategies they have learned.

5 Support Independent Application of Multiple Strategies

Continue releasing responsibility to students to use strategies they have learned when they are reading on their own.

Preview and Predict Mini-Lesson

To teach this strategy, use *Rocks and Soil in the Rocky Mountains*.
Readers mainly use this strategy before and during reading.

1 Describe the Strategy

Preview

Tell students that previewing is something that good readers do to get ready to read. Say: **You can preview by looking over the text. This helps you get an idea of what the text is mostly about and how it is organized.** Draw on background knowledge and give examples of previewing outside the classroom (for example, watching movie previews and looking at a map before traveling).

Predict

Tell students that predicting is forming ideas about what you will read. You predict by forming ideas about how the text is organized and what it says.

2 Model the Strategy

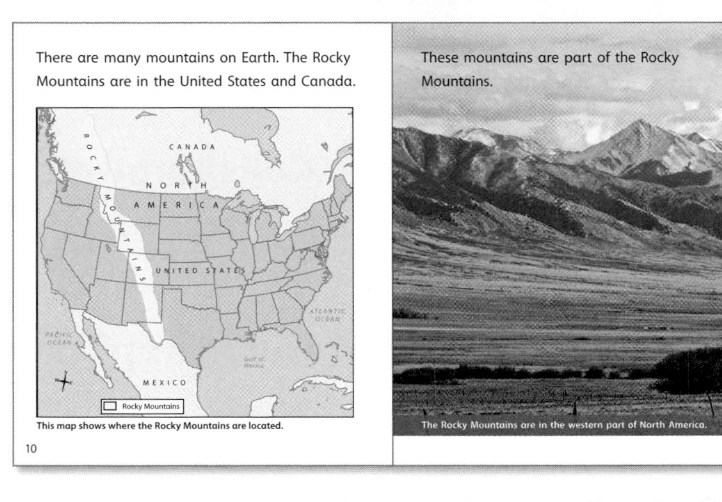

Use *Rocks and Soil in the Rocky Mountains* to model how to preview. Read the title from the cover and then turn to pages 8–9. Point to the heading and the photo. You might say: **From the title of the book and the heading and photo, I know that the book is about mountains.**

Model how to make a prediction. You might say: **My preview leads me to predict that I will learn more about mountains and, in particular, the Rocky Mountains.**

Turn to pages 10–11. Say: **As I continue reading, I will see if I can confirm my prediction.** Point to the map and its label on page 10. Say: **My prediction is confirmed. The map tells me where to find the Rocky Mountains.**

Then explain to students that the use of strategies should be ongoing. You might say: **As I keep reading, I will preview more information and make and confirm more predictions.**

3 Collaboratively Use the Strategy

Begin handing over the strategy to students. Select a point midway through the book. Remind students to use section heads, vocabulary words, and their background knowledge to make another prediction. Work together with students to apply the strategy.

See pages T46 and T91 for suggestions for guided and independent applications of the strategy.

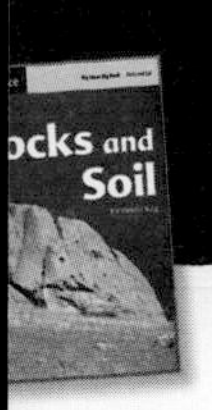

Monitor and Fix Up Mini-Lesson

To teach this strategy, use the Big Ideas Big Book.
Readers mainly use this strategy during reading.

1 Describe the Strategy

Monitor and Fix Up

Tell students that when you monitor your reading, you pay attention to whether or not the text makes sense and stop at confusing parts. Then you take steps to fix up, or figure out, what you don't understand. You might look back or look forward in the text.

Even good readers sometimes don't understand, but good readers stop and fix up, or figure out, what they don't understand.

2 Model the Strategy

Use *Rocks and Soil* Chapter 1 to model how to monitor your reading and fix up any confusion about the text. Turn to page 8. Read the text aloud to students. You might say: **I'm not sure I understand what it means to sort rocks by their properties. When I look at the table, I see some describing words listed next to each property. For example, the words *rough* and *smooth* are next to the property *texture*.**

Reread the text on page 8 aloud to students. Say: **Now that I read it again, I think I understand. I can use describing words to sort rocks by their properties. For example, I can sort rocks according to whether the texture is rough or smooth.**

Explain to students that the use of strategies should be ongoing. You might say: **As you read, you should monitor your reading. Stop if you don't understand something. Use strategies, such as rereading, to fix up the parts that are confusing.**

Properties of Rocks

A **property** is something about an object that you can observe with your senses. For example, color and **texture** are properties. Texture is how an object feels. You can sort rocks by their properties.

What can you observe about the properties of these rocks?

Properties	Describing Words
• color	• white, tan, brown, and so on
• texture	• rough, smooth
• layers	• layered, not layered
• fossils	• fossils present, fossils absent
• air holes	• air holes present, air holes absent
• strength	• crumbly, strong

8 9

3 Collaboratively Use the Strategy

Begin handing over the strategy to students. Direct students to pages 10–11 in *Rocks and Soil*. Work together with students to apply the strategy to parts that might be confusing.

See pages T46 and T91 for suggestions for guided and independent applications of the strategy.

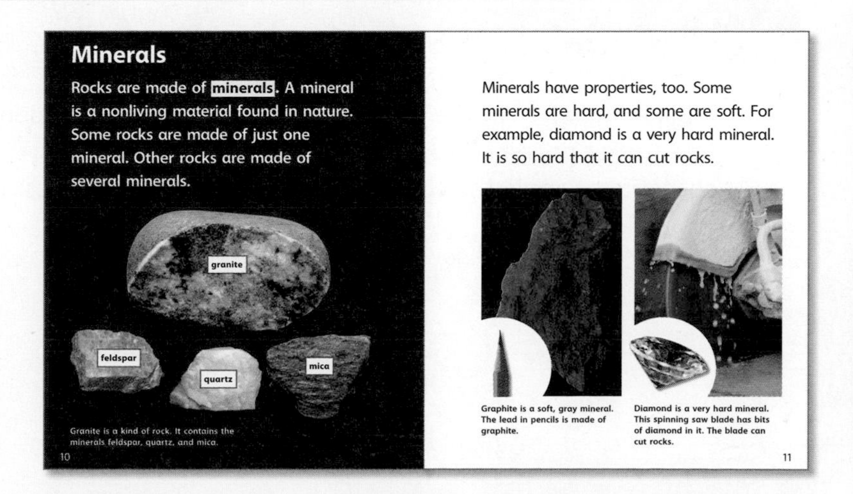
Minerals

Rocks are made of **minerals**. A mineral is a nonliving material found in nature. Some rocks are made of just one mineral. Other rocks are made of several minerals.

Granite is a kind of rock. It contains the minerals feldspar, quartz, and mica.

10

Minerals have properties, too. Some minerals are hard, and some are soft. For example, diamond is a very hard mineral. It is so hard that it can cut rocks.

Graphite is a soft, gray mineral. The lead in pencils is made of graphite.

Diamond is a very hard mineral. This spinning saw blade has bits of diamond in it. The blade can cut rocks.

11

Make Inferences Mini-Lesson

To teach this strategy, use the Big Ideas Big Book.
Readers mainly use this strategy during reading.

1 Describe the Strategy

Make Inferences

Tell students that when you make an inference you combine what the text says with what you know to arrive at new understandings that are not directly stated.

Making inferences helps you better understand what you read, so you can learn more science.

How to Make Inferences

I read ________.

I know ________.

And so ________.

2 Model the Strategy

Reread the text on page 11. Ask: **How can what I already know help me learn something new?** Say something like: **I read that hardness is an example of mineral properties. I know color is a property of rocks. I see a variety of colors in the mineral photos. And so I think color is a property of minerals.**

You can make an inference by thinking:
I read ________. I know ________.
And so ________.

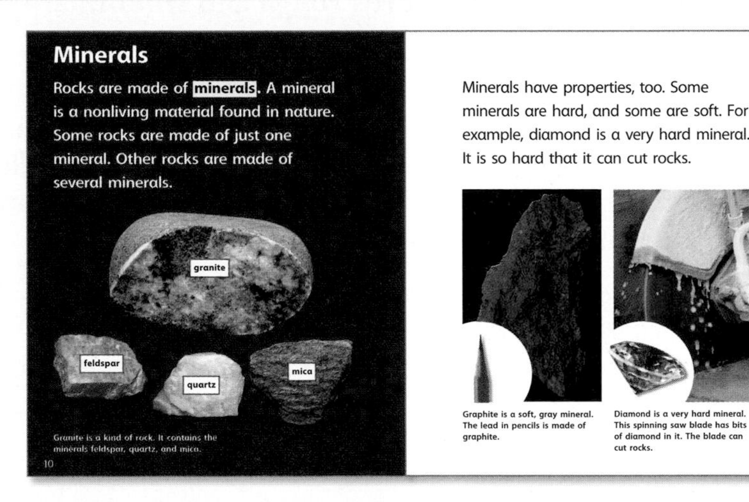

Minerals

Rocks are made of **minerals**. A mineral is a nonliving material found in nature. Some rocks are made of just one mineral. Other rocks are made of several minerals.

Granite is a kind of rock. It contains the minerals feldspar, quartz, and mica.

10

Minerals have properties, too. Some minerals are hard, and some are soft. For example, diamond is a very hard mineral. It is so hard that it can cut rocks.

Graphite is a soft, gray mineral. The lead in pencils is made of graphite.

Diamond is a very hard mineral. This spinning saw blade has bits of diamond in it. The blade can cut rocks.

11

3 Collaboratively Use the Strategy

Begin handing over the strategy to students. Direct students to another page in *Rocks and Soil*. Work together with students to apply the strategy using the sentence frames:

I read ________. I know ________.
And so ________.

Prompt students to share self-knowledge or world knowledge that connects with the text. Then lead them to share how this connection adds to their understanding.

See pages T46 and T91 for suggestions for guided and independent applications of the strategy.

Sum Up Mini-Lesson

To teach this strategy, use the Big Ideas Big Book.
Readers mainly use this strategy after reading.

1 Describe the Strategy

Sum Up

Tell students that when you sum up, you pull together the big ideas in a text so that you take away what is most important.

2 Model the Strategy

Open the *Rocks and Soil* book to the Chapter 1 opener on pages 6–7. Read the question. You might say: **To sum up this chapter, I need to tell what is most important. I'll review the headings, photos, and text to help me remember what I read.**

Model reviewing the chapter, and then say: **What is most important in this chapter is that you can observe properties of rocks. Size, shape, color, and texture are some of the properties of rocks.**

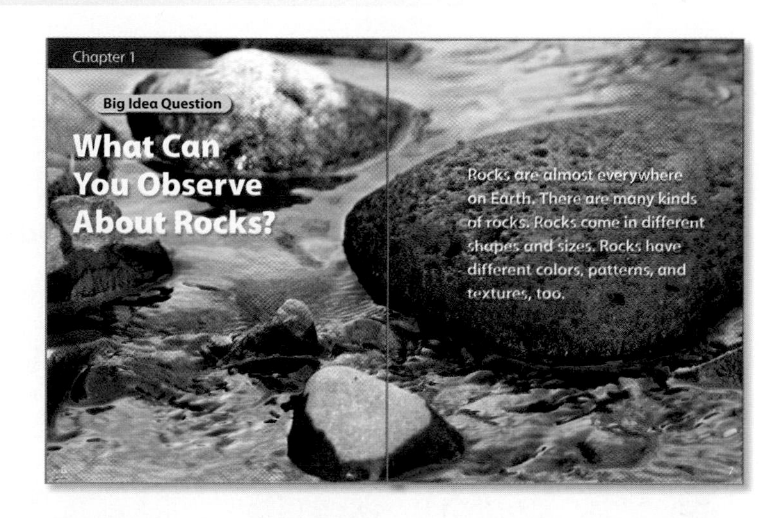

3 Collaboratively Use the Strategy

Begin handing over the strategy to students. Direct students to the Chapter 2 opener on pages 16–17 in *Rocks and Soil*. Work together with students to apply the strategy to this chapter.

See pages T46 and T91 for suggestions for guided and independent applications of this strategy.

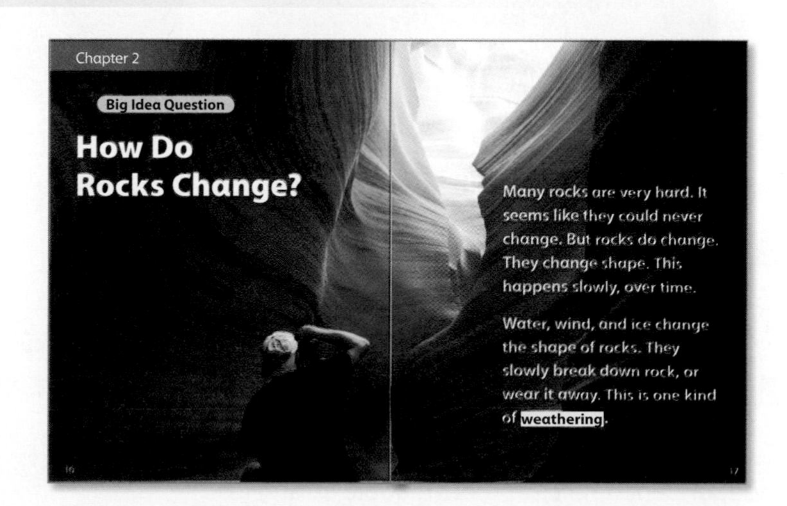

 Guide Application of Multiple Strategies

Read Informational Text in Small Groups

The Become an Expert books provide important opportunities for students to

- deepen their science content knowledge as they focus on the Big Ideas
- learn to apply multiple reading comprehension strategies as they read.

You may choose to have students read pages from the Become an Expert books silently to themselves. You may want to have students stop reading periodically so that you can teach and lead a group discussion. The following pages have notes to support your teaching of science concepts and comprehension strategies. Use these notes for the pages where you choose to stop.

BECOME AN EXPERT BOOKS ▫ *Small Group*

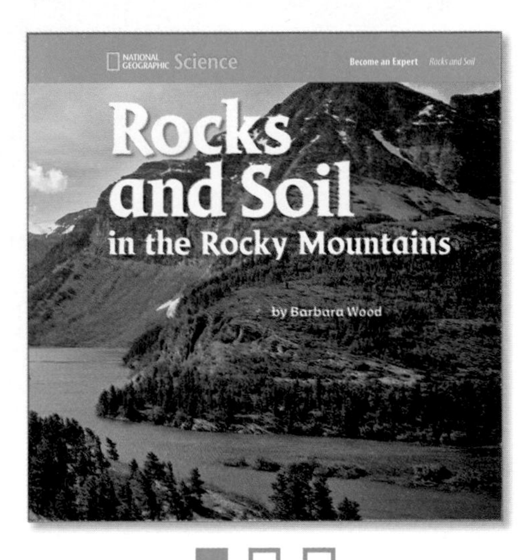

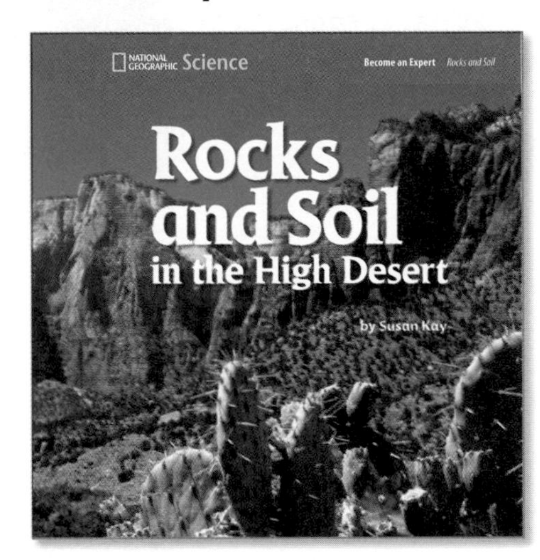

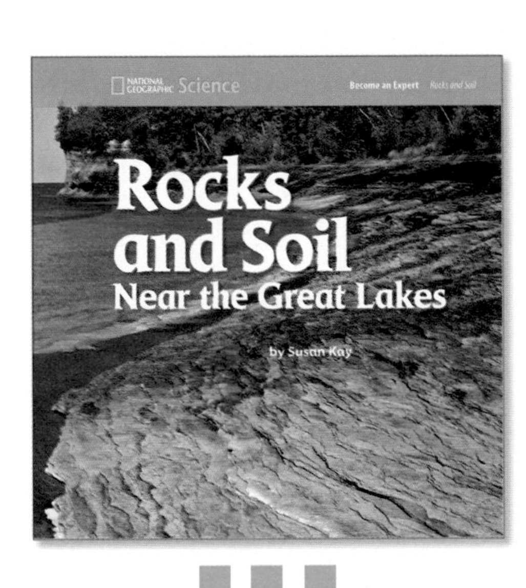

eEdition at myNGconnect.com

Preview: Independent Reading

See page T91 to read more about how to support independent application of multiple strategies as students read Explore on Your Own books. Facsimiles of the Explore on Your Own pages are shown on pages T92–T94.

EXPLORE ON YOUR OWN BOOKS ▫ Independent

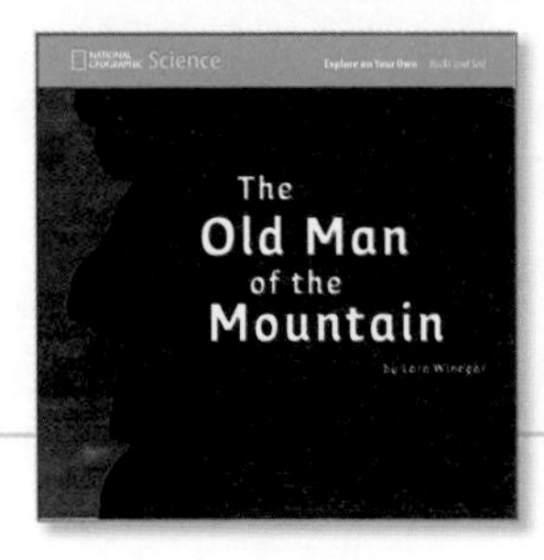

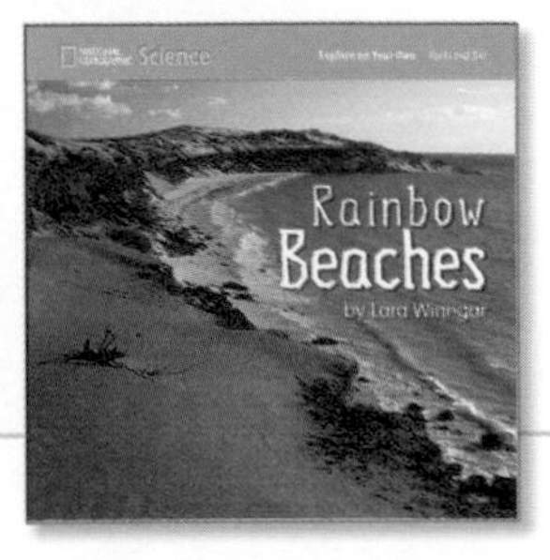

eEdition at myNGconnect.com

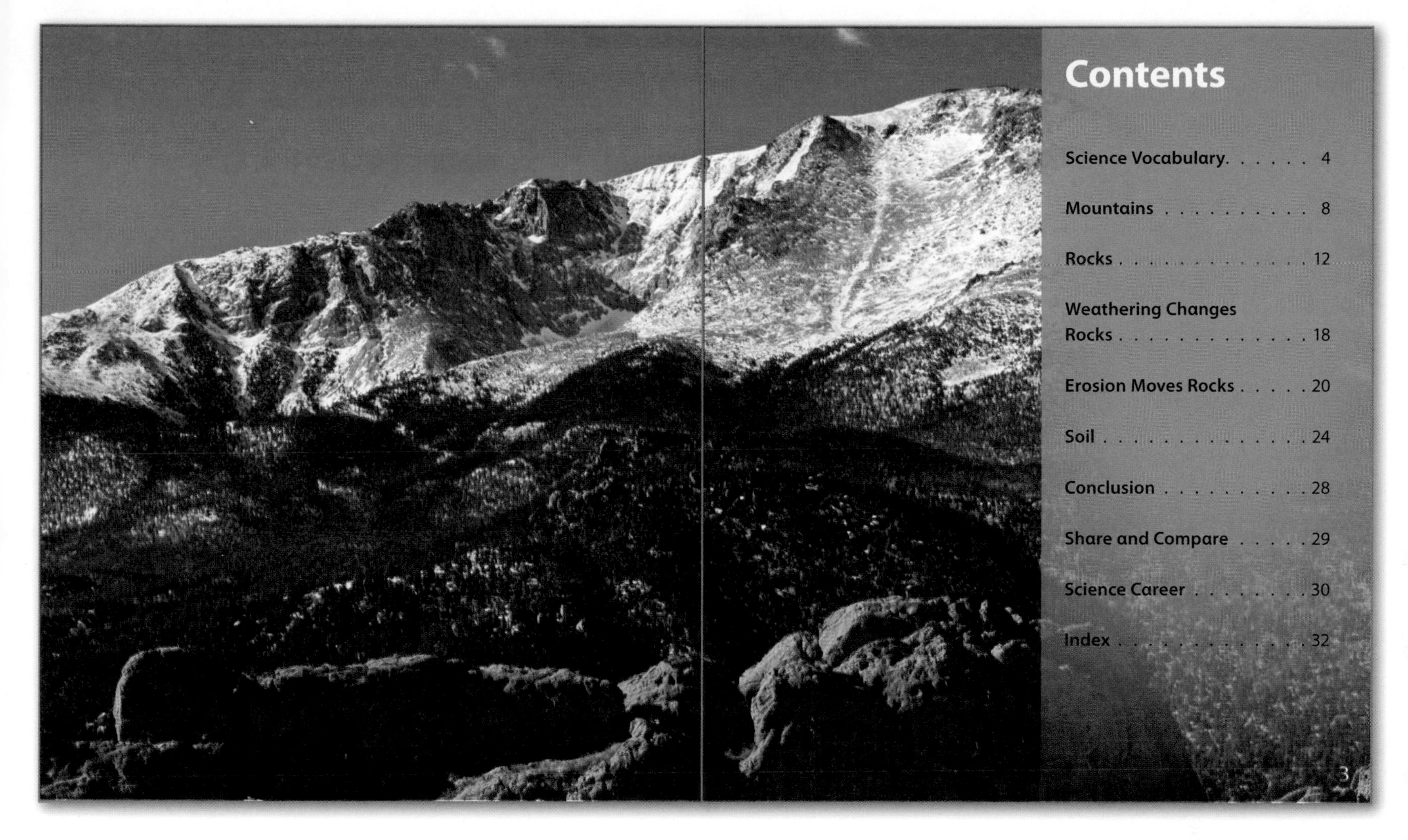

Use the Table of Contents

Preview

Ask students to preview the book by looking at the Table of Contents. Discuss how the book is organized. You may also want to look through the book with them.

Point to the word *Contents* on page 3.

- Say: **The table of contents shows what's inside a book. Use it to learn what is in a book and to find where parts of the book start.**
- Draw attention to the entries listed in the Table of Contents.
- Model looking for an entry on a particular topic and then turning to a page where an entry begins.
- Then have pairs work together; one partner identifies a topic he or she would like to read about, and the other tells the page number where it begins.
- Circulate and help students who are having difficulty.

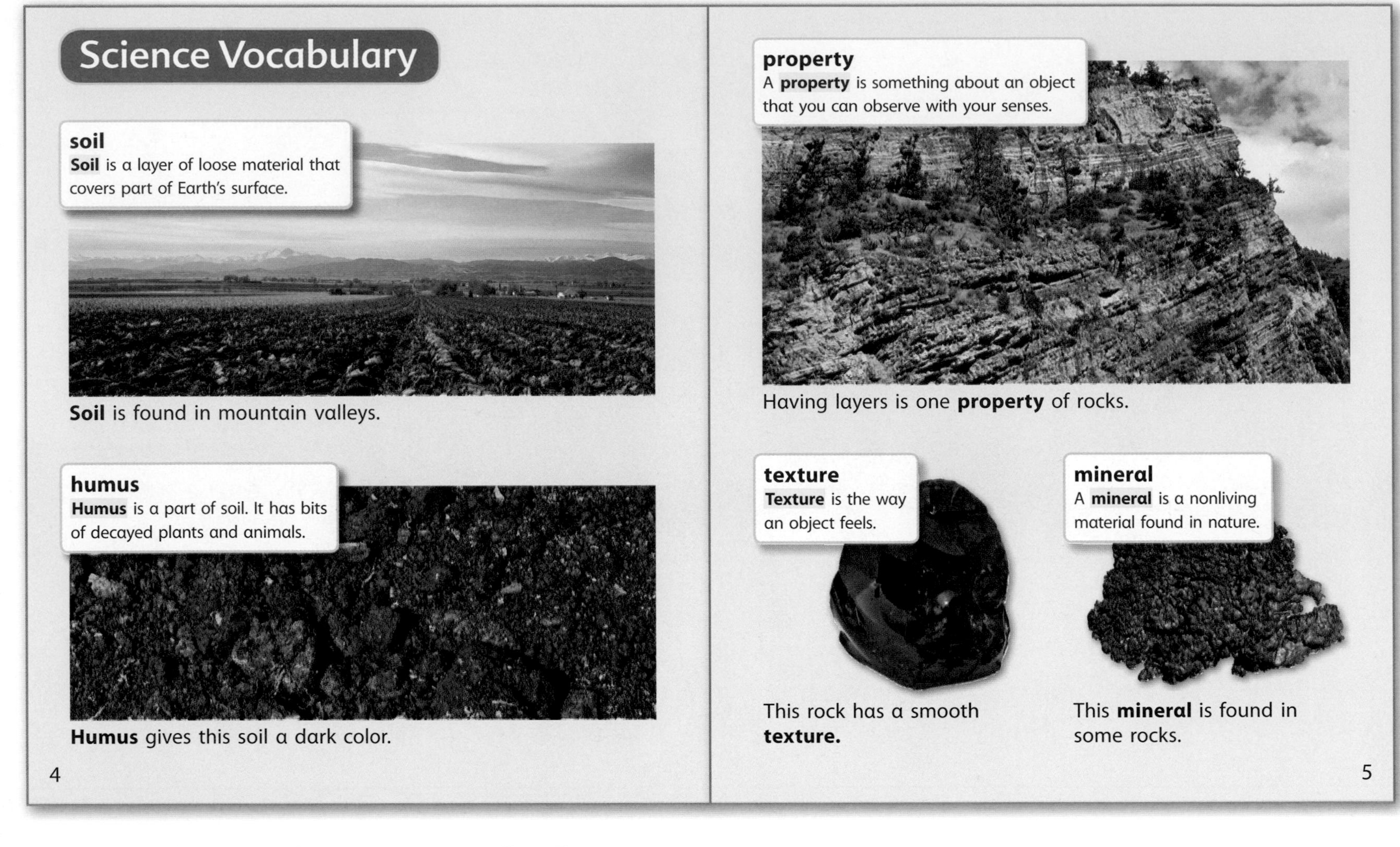

Review Science Vocabulary

Review the vocabulary that was introduced in the Big Ideas Big Book. Then use the following suggestions to relate the words to key science concepts.

- **soil** Point to the first photo. Ask: **Where have you seen soil?** (Possible answers: in my yard, in a garden, at a construction site)
- **humus** Read aloud the definition at the bottom of page 4. Then point to the photo. Ask: **What do you see that contains humus?**
- **property** Say: **We can describe things by naming properties. Look at page 5. What are the properties of the rock cliff?** (It has layers. It is a tan color.)
- **texture** Point to the granite pictured at the bottom of page 5. Ask: **How would you describe the texture of this granite?** (bumpy, rough)
- **mineral** Read aloud the definition of **mineral.** Point to the photo and ask: **Is this mineral living or nonliving?** (nonliving)

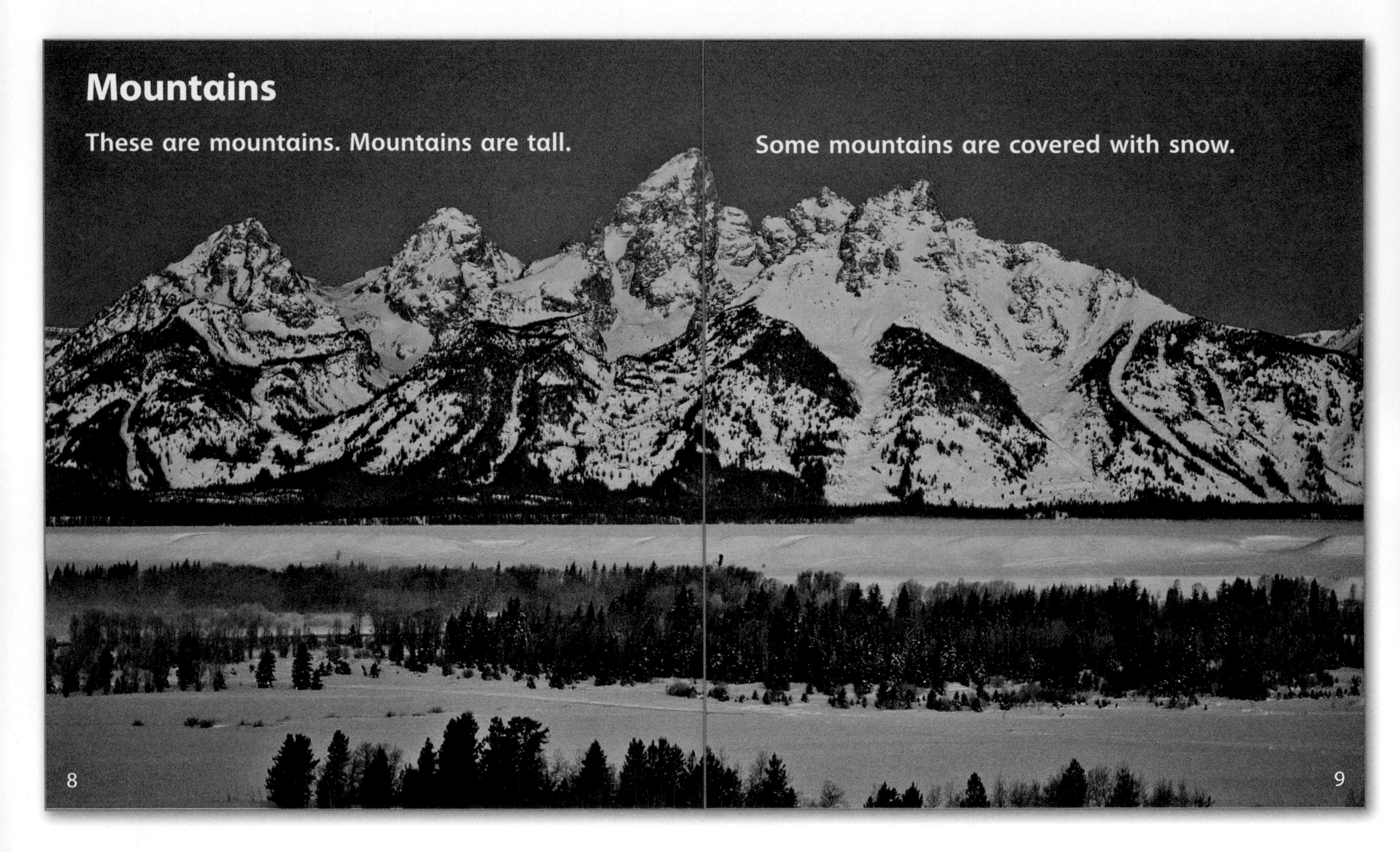

Access Science Content

Preview and Predict

Remind students to use the section heads, vocabulary words, and their background knowledge to make predictions. Circulate and ask students about predictions they may have.

Recognize Mountains

Students can use a photo to learn about mountains.

- Have students look at the photo on pages 8–9. Ask: **What do you see in the photo?** (trees, snow, mountains, sky) **Which is taller, a tall tree or a mountain?** (mountain) Say: **The pointed tops of the mountains are called peaks.** Have students point to the highest peak in the photo.
- Ask: **What is on the mountains?** (snow) Explain: **Even if there is no snow at the bottom of a mountain, there may be snow at the top. The temperature is usually colder at the top of a mountain.**

There are many mountains on Earth. The Rocky Mountains are in the United States and Canada.

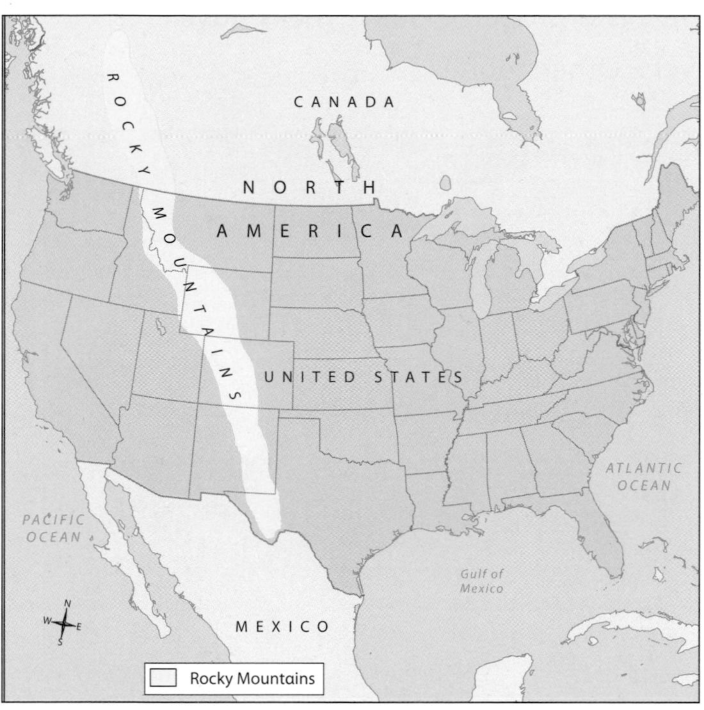

This map shows where the Rocky Mountains are located.

10

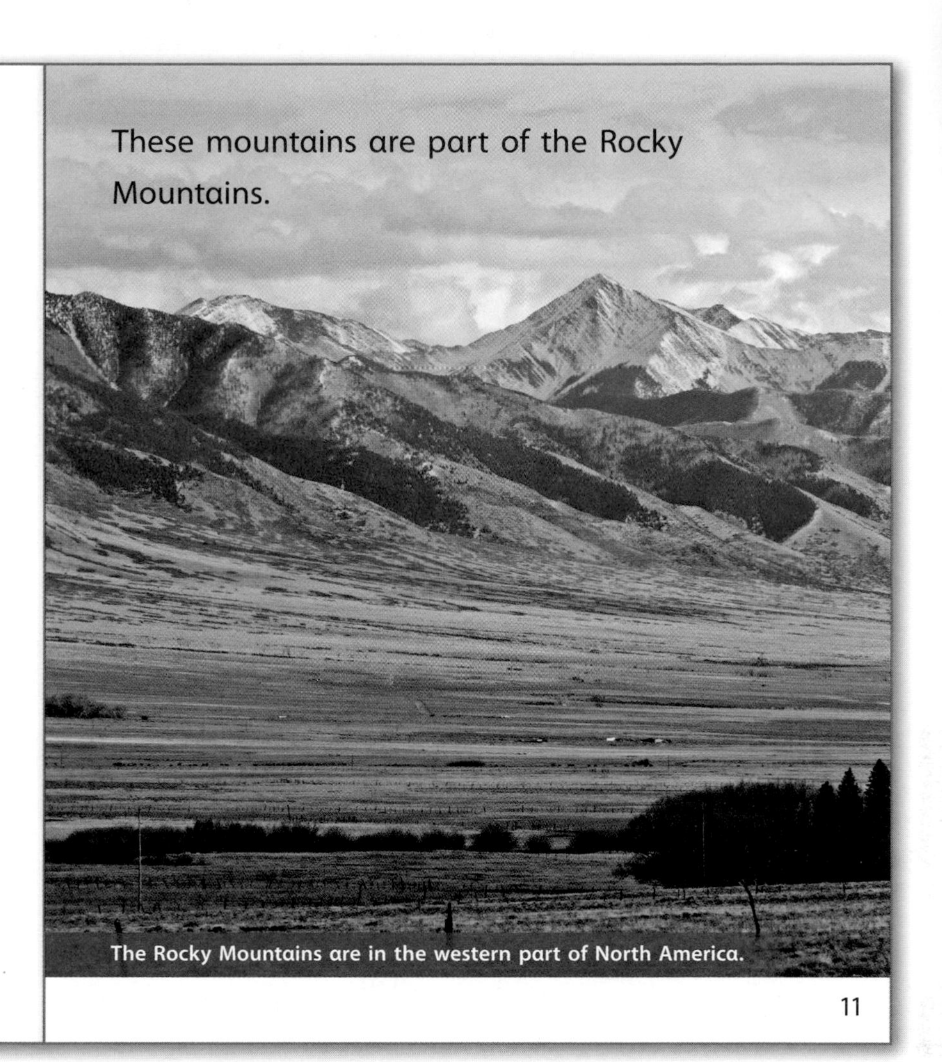

The Rocky Mountains are in the western part of North America.

11

Access Science Content

Describe the Rocky Mountains

Help students study a map and photo to learn about the Rocky Mountains.

- Have students look at the map on page 10. Ask: **What color shows the location of the United States?** (green) **What country is north of the continental United States?** (Canada)
- Ask: **What does the yellow area on the map show?** (the Rocky Mountains) Say: **The Rocky Mountains stretch for miles through the United States and Canada.** Locate your state on the map and determine if the Rocky Mountains run through parts of your state.
- Read aloud the caption on page 11 and have students study the photo. Ask: **How would you describe the Rocky Mountains?** (tall, steep, snowy peaks, ridges) Point out that people visit the Rocky Mountains to enjoy the beautiful scenery and to ski, fish, hike, or hunt. Bighorn sheep, moose, bear, elk, chipmunks, and other animals live in the mountains or in the grassy valleys between the mountains.

Text Features: Maps

Work with students to find and use the map features, including the map key and compass rose.

Assess

1. **Name What high mountains stretch from near the southern border of the United States into Canada?** (the Rocky Mountains)
2. **Interpret Maps Are the Rocky Mountains in the eastern or western part of the United States and Canada?** (western)

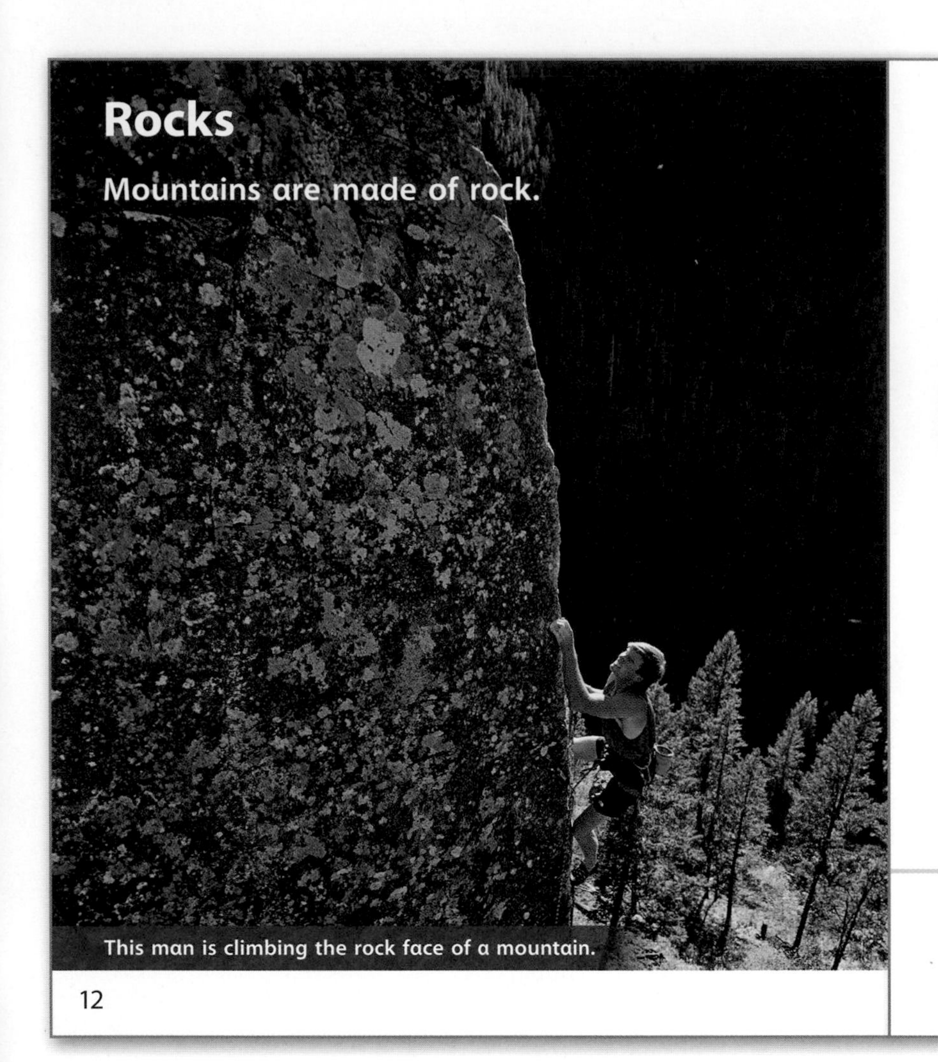

This man is climbing the rock face of a mountain.

12

Rocks have different **properties.** Having layers is a property. Some rocks have layers. Others don't.

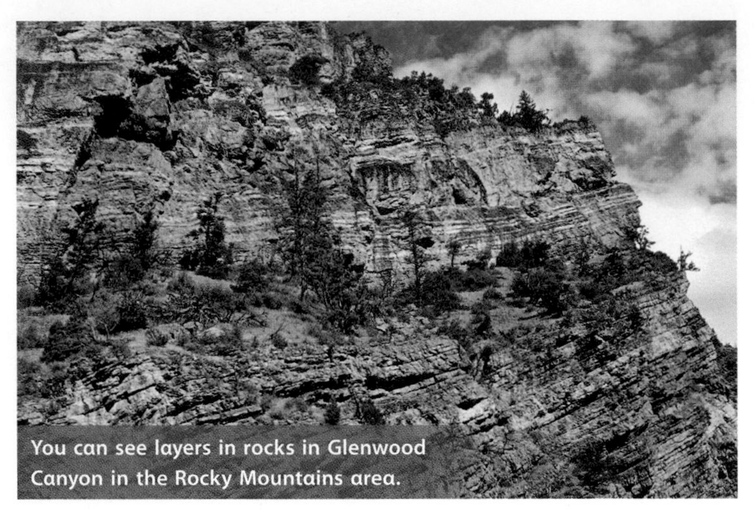
You can see layers in rocks in Glenwood Canyon in the Rocky Mountains area.

property
A **property** is something about an object that you can observe with your senses.

13

Access Science Content

Recognize that Mountains Are Rock

Guide students to realize that mountains are made of rock and that rock can be layered.

- Point to the man on page 12. Ask: **What is this man doing?** (climbing, rock climbing) Say: **Mountains are not easy to climb. They are made of rock. Climbers fasten metal devices into cracks in the rock. Then they attach ropes for climbing safely.**
- Explain: **Layers are a property of some rocks.** Have students look closely at the photos and point out the layered rock photographed on page 13.

〉Monitor and Fix Up

Ask: **Was anything you just read confusing to you?** (Possible answer: I thought *property* was something you owned.) **How did you work it out?** (Possible answer: I reread the definition on the page and thought about what I knew already. Then I decided that *property* has more than one meaning.)

Text Features: Highlighting

Remind students to pay special attention to highlighted words as they read. Explain that words that are highlighted are often especially important, and in this book highlighted words are defined at the bottom of the page. Have students point out the highlighted word **properties** on page 13 and read the corresponding definition.

There are many kinds of rocks in the Rocky Mountains.

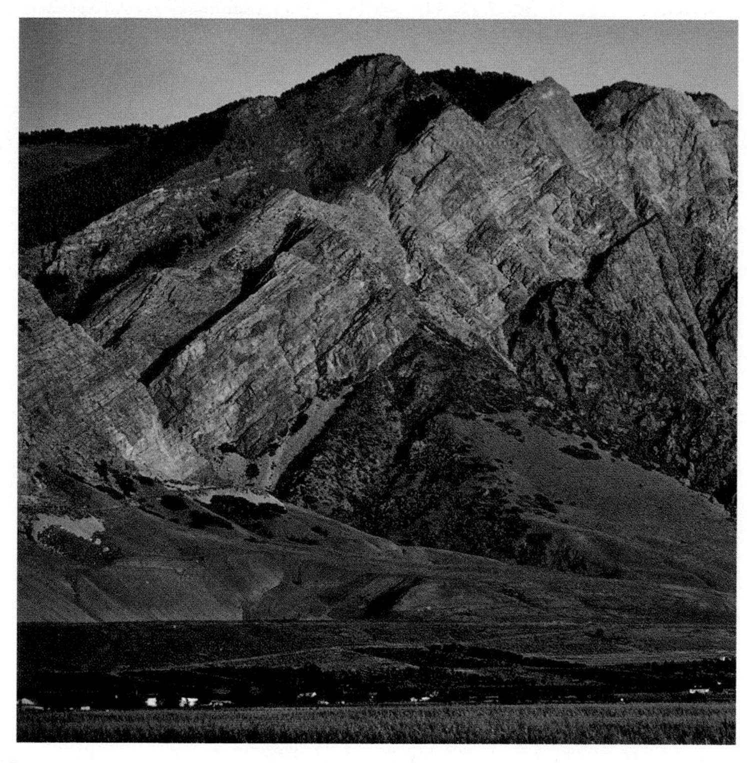

14

Color and **texture** are properties of rocks. Rocks may have a smooth or a rough texture. Having layers is also a property of some rocks.

Properties	Words That Describe Properties
color	orange, white, black
layers	layered, not layered
texture	rough, smooth

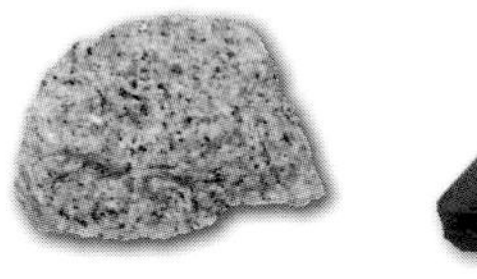

different colors

some layers

smooth texture

texture
Texture is the way an object feels.

15

Access Science Content

Describe Properties of Rock

Students view photos of rocks and describe color, **texture,** and layers.

- Read aloud the definition of **texture.** Explain: **You can touch a rock to tell if it has a smooth or rough texture. Sometimes you can judge the texture by viewing the rock or a photo of the rock.**
- Have students study the chart. Ask: **What do the columns of the chart show?** (three kinds of properties, words describing these properties) **What are some words to describe texture?** (rough, smooth)

Differentiated Instruction

ELL Language Support for Describing Properties

BEGINNING

Ask yes/no questions about the rocks on pages 14–15.

Is color a property of this rock? Is this rock smooth?

INTERMEDIATE

Ask either/or questions about the rocks on pages 14–15.

Is its color white or black? Is this rock rough or smooth?

ADVANCED

Have students use Academic Language Frames to describe a rock's color, texture, and layers.

The ____ is ____. The ____ is ____. It is ____.

Real-World Connections

Take students on a short walk to observe rocks in the playground or near the school. Have students examine the rocks and describe their properties, including their color, **texture,** and layers.

Minerals can be found in rocks. Minerals have properties, too.

copper

diamond

mineral
A **mineral** is a nonliving material found in nature.

16

Minerals can be soft or hard. Soft or hard is a property.

zinc

silver

17

Access Science Content

Recognize that Minerals Have Properties

Help students realize that rocks contain **minerals,** which have properties such as softness or hardness.

- Read aloud the definition of **mineral** at the bottom of page 16. Then have students point to the **minerals** shown on the spread as you name them.
- Say: **Minerals have properties. Wire made from copper can bend easily. Is copper soft or hard?** (soft) **Almost nothing can scratch diamond. Is diamond soft or hard?** (hard)

Assess

1. **Name Which word describes a rock's texture, *rough* or *layered?*** (*rough*)
2. **Explain Jed says, "Grass is a mineral." Is Jed's statement correct? Explain your answer.** (No, because minerals are nonliving materials, and grass is living.)

Weathering Changes Rocks

Weathering can change rocks. Weathering can break apart or dissolve rocks over time. For example, water moves across rocks and breaks off tiny bits.

Over time, water will make these rocks smooth.

weathering
Weathering is the breaking apart or dissolving of rocks.

18

Wind blows on rocks and breaks off tiny bits, too. Water and wind change the shapes of the rocks.

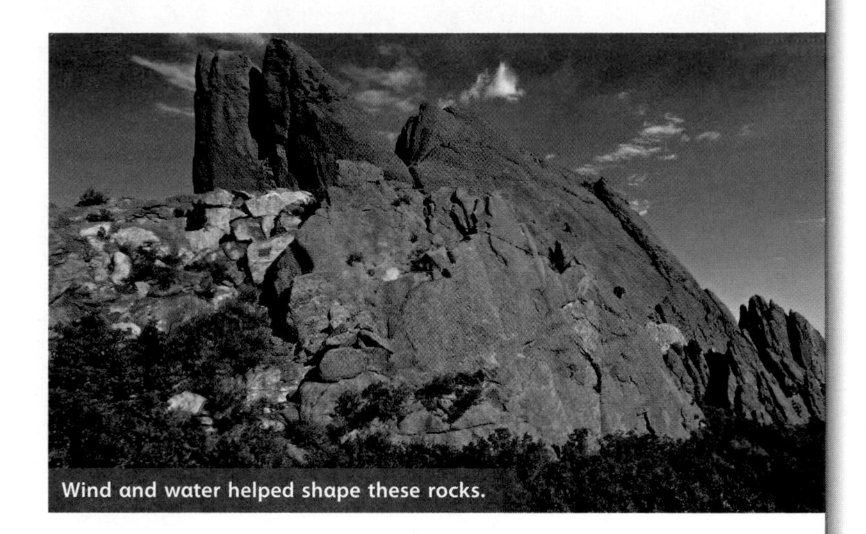

Wind and water helped shape these rocks.

19

Access Science Content

Observe Changes Caused by Weathering

Students can use photos to discover how **weathering** changes rocks.

- Point to various rocks in the photo on page 18. Ask: **How would you describe the texture of these rocks?** (Some rocks are smooth, and some are rough and bumpy.)
- Read aloud the definition of **weathering.** Direct attention back to the photo. Explain: **The moving water breaks off tiny bits of rock.** Ask: **How do you think this weathering will change the texture of these rocks as time goes on?** (It will make the rocks smoother.)
- Have students look at the photo on page 19. Read aloud the caption. Ask: **Do you think weathering shaped the mountains quickly or over many years?** (over many years) **Do you think these mountains will continue to change shape?** (yes) **Why do you think this?** (Wind and water will continue to break off tiny bits of rock.)

Assess

1. **Name What term means the breaking apart or dissolving of rock?** (weathering)
2. **Draw Conclusions Maria finds a smooth, egg-shaped rock in a stream and says, "I guess this rock has been here a long time!" Does her guess make sense? Explain your answer.** (Yes, it's likely the rock was smoothed by the running water, and this weathering would have taken many years.)

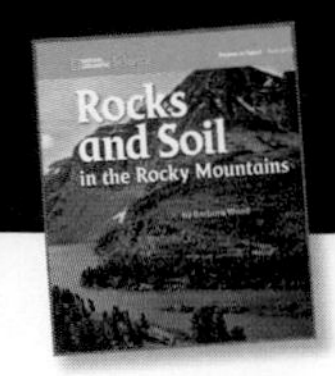

Erosion Moves Rocks

Water and wind can also move rocks.

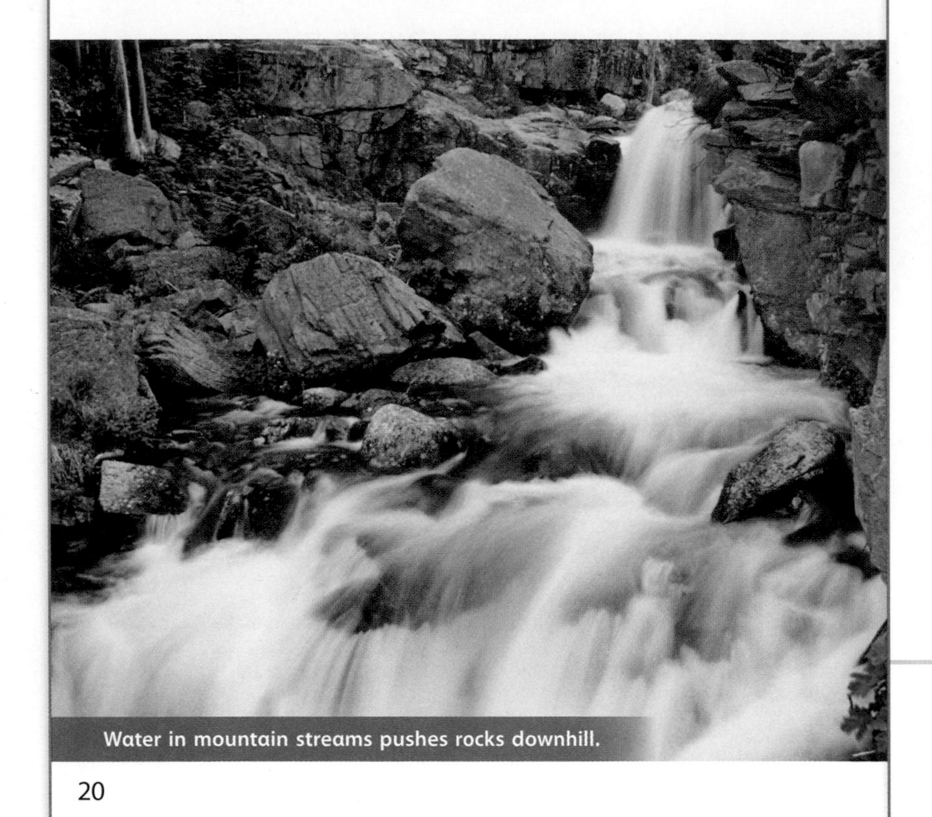

Water in mountain streams pushes rocks downhill.

20

Strong winds blow tiny bits of rock and sand. This movement of rocks and soil is **erosion.**

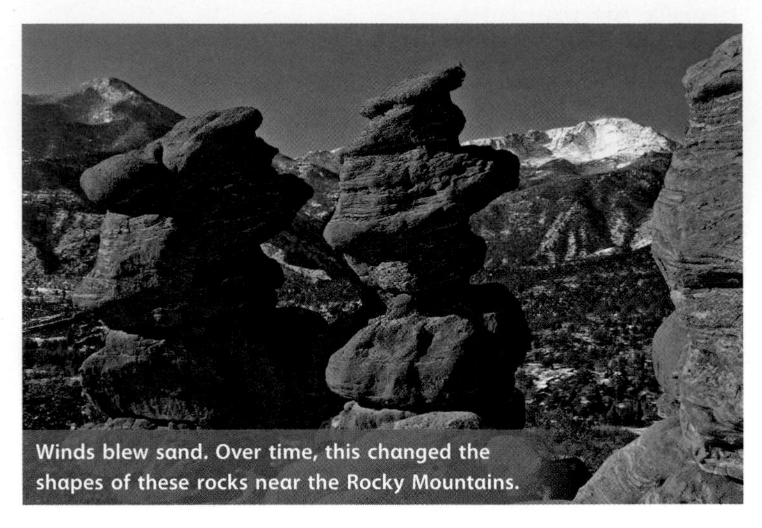

Winds blew sand. Over time, this changed the shapes of these rocks near the Rocky Mountains.

erosion
Erosion is the movement of rocks or soil caused by wind, water, or ice.

21

Access Science Content

Recognize that Erosion Moves Rocks

Help students use photos to discover that rocks can move due to **erosion** by wind and water.

- Read aloud the heading. Ask: **Which two words tell what erosion does?** (moves rocks) Have students read the text on the top of page 21 and ask: **What else does erosion move?** (soil)
- Have students look at the photos on pages 20–21. Ask: **Which photo shows rocks being moved by water?** (photo on page 20) **Which rocks have odd shapes because of wind erosion?** (red rocks on page 21)

Monitor and Fix Up

Ask if any students found themselves confused about the difference between weathering (pages 18–19) and **erosion** (pages 20–21). Discuss possible fix-up strategies. Let them know that one strategy is for them to reread and explain the difference to themselves: weathering breaks or dissolves rocks, and **erosion** moves rocks.

Some mountains have glaciers. Glaciers can move rocks. This is erosion, too.

This frozen ice of the glacier moves downhill.

22

Sometimes glaciers melt. Then **gravity** pulls the rocks from the ice to the ground.

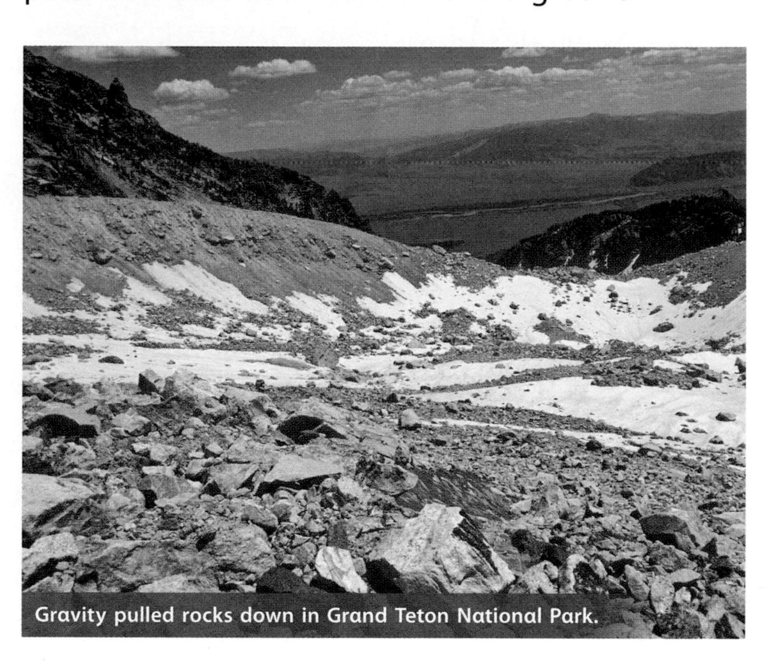

Gravity pulled rocks down in Grand Teton National Park.

gravity

Gravity is a force that pulls things toward Earth.

23

Access Science Content

Identify Ways that Rock Moves

Students can discover the role of glaciers and **gravity** in the erosion process.

- Point to the glacier on page 22. Explain: **This sheet of ice is a glacier. It forms when snow builds up in a mountain valley and turns to ice. The ice gets so heavy that the glacier starts moving down the valley.** Ask: **What is being carried by this glacier?** (rocks)
- Read aloud the definition on page 23. Point to the photo. Ask: **As the glacier melts, what does gravity do to the rocks?** (pulls them to Earth)
- Summarize: **During the erosion process, wind, water, and glaciers move rocks. Gravity pulls the rocks downward.**

Recording Observations

Work with students to list forces that move rocks or soil.

What moves rocks?	
wind	glaciers
water	gravity

Assess

1. **Recall What happens to rock during the erosion process?** (It is moved.)
2. **Explain How does a mountain stream cause erosion?** (The water of the stream pushes loose rocks along as it flows downhill.)

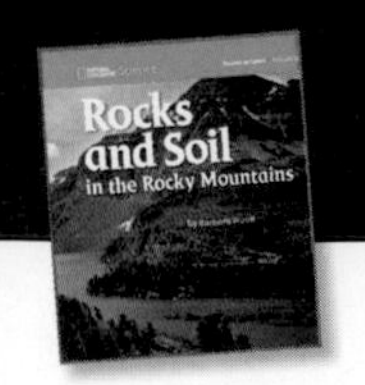

Soil

Much of the **soil** in mountain areas is in valleys. Small bits of rock are part of soil.

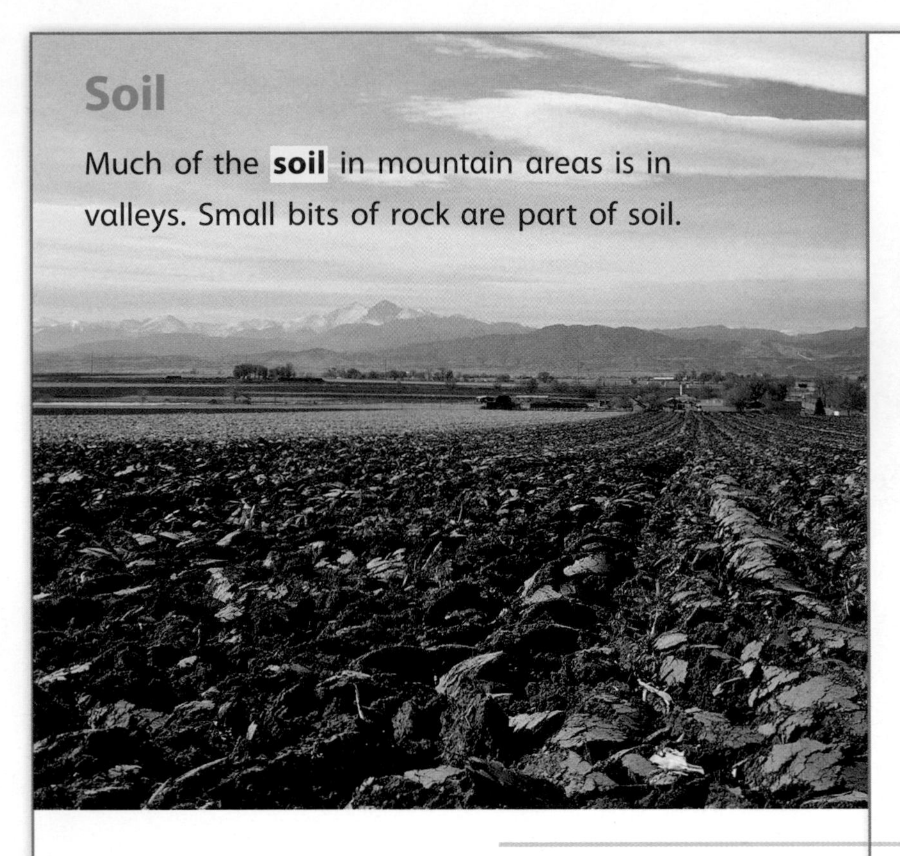

soil
Soil is a layer of loose material that covers part of Earth's surface.

24

Humus is part of soil, too.

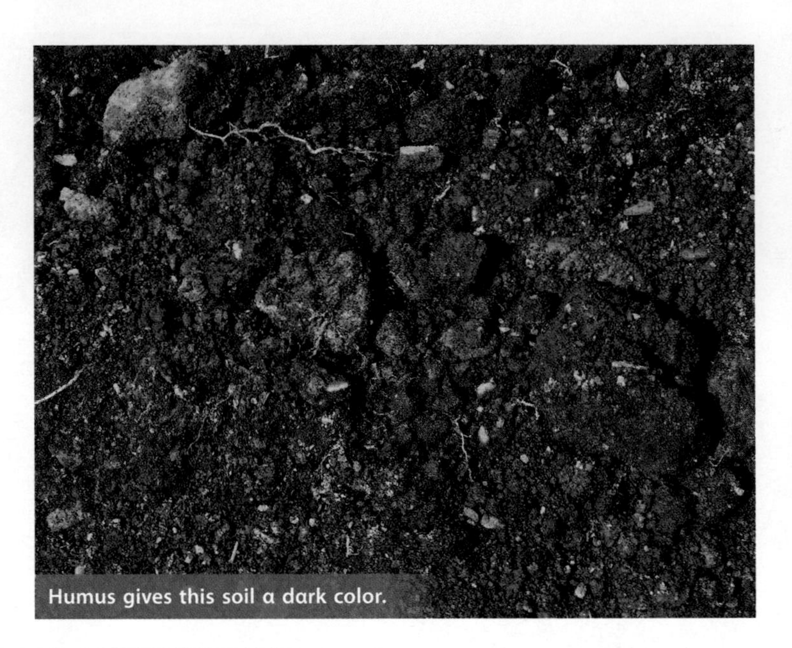
Humus gives this soil a dark color.

humus
Humus is a part of soil. It has bits of decayed plants and animals.

25

Access Science Content

Describe Soil

Help students use photos and definitions to describe **soil** and its components.

- Read aloud the definition of **soil.** Ask: **What do you see in the lower part of the photo on page 24?** (soil) Point out the ridges or rows. Say: **Seeds are planted in rows in this soil.**
- Say: **Soil contains bits of rock. It also contains humus.** Read the definition at the bottom of page 25. Have students study the photo on page 25. Ask: **What do you see in this soil?** (small rocks, bits of rock or sand, tiny plant roots, brown humus)

〉Make Inferences

Read aloud the first sentence on page 24. Ask students to share new ideas they can figure out from reading this page. (Students may infer that the components of **soil** are carried by erosion from the mountains down to the valleys.)

Color and texture are properties of soil. Soil made of very small bits of rocks feels smooth. Soil made of larger bits of rocks feels rough.

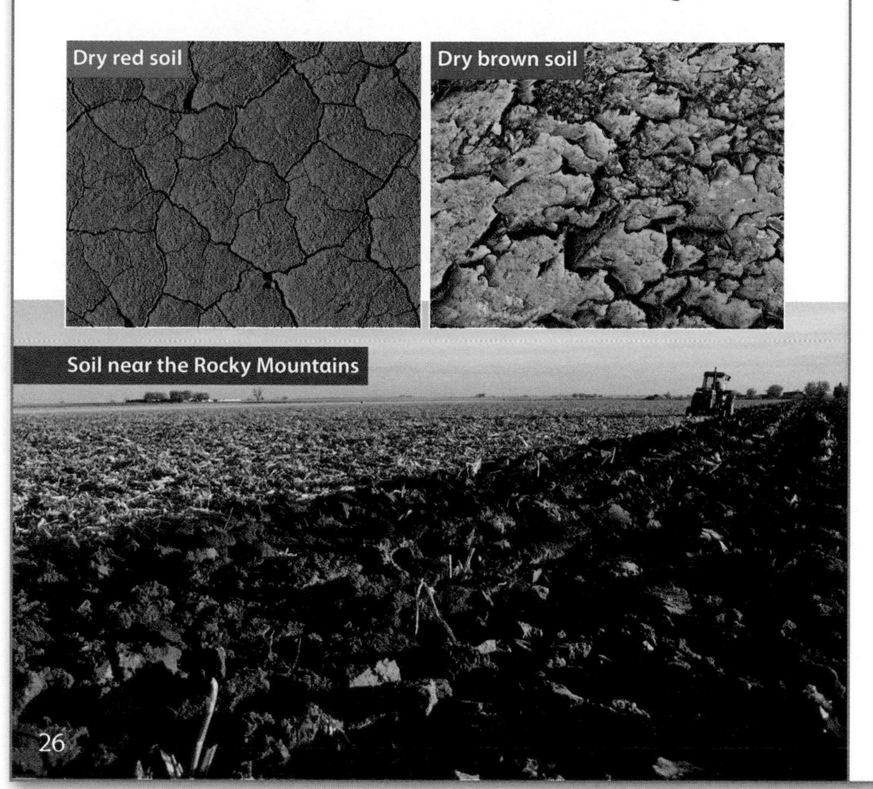

Dry red soil

Dry brown soil

Soil near the Rocky Mountains

26

Look at this soil. How would you describe it? How would it feel?

27

Access Science Content

Recognize Properties of Soil

Lead a discussion about the properties of the different soils pictured on the spread.

- Invite students to look at the array of soils pictured on pages 26–27. Say: **There are many different kinds of soil. Each soil has its own properties, including a particular color and texture.**
- Lead a discussion about each of the different soils. Have students describe each soil's color and texture (rough or smooth). If students do not mention it, point out that dry soils may have surface cracks. Remind students that humus typically gives soil a dark brown color.

Real-World Connections

Display a sample of local soil. Have students describe it and compare its color and texture to the soils pictured on pages 26–27.

Assess

1. **Recall What does humus contain?** (bits of decayed plants and animals)
2. **Infer Mark says the soil at his house is light brown. Do you think it contains a lot of humus? Explain your answer.** (No, because humus gives soil a dark brown color.)

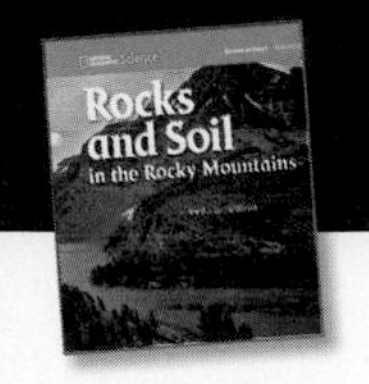

Conclusion

The Rocky Mountains are made of rock. Valleys between mountains often have soil. Rocks and soil have properties, such as color and texture. Weathering and erosion can change rocks to soil over time.

Think About the Big Ideas

1. What can you observe about rocks in the Rocky Mountains?
2. How do rocks change?
3. What can you observe about soil?

28

Following the **Conclusion** section of the *Become an Expert* book, rearrange groups to begin the ***Share and Compare*** section on page T89.

Conclusion

Sum Up

Tell students that a conclusion helps sum up the big ideas in a book. Have students restate the conclusion in their own words.

Answer the Big Idea Questions

Encourage students to sum up what they learned in the book and then share responses to the questions aloud.

1. **What can you observe about rocks in the Rocky Mountains?** (They have different colors and contain a variety of minerals. Some are layered.)
2. **How do rocks change?** (Water or wind can weather rocks, or break them apart. Water, wind, or glaciers can erode rocks, or move them.)
3. **What can you observe about soil?** (Much of it is in mountain valleys. It contains small bits of rock and dark brown humus.)

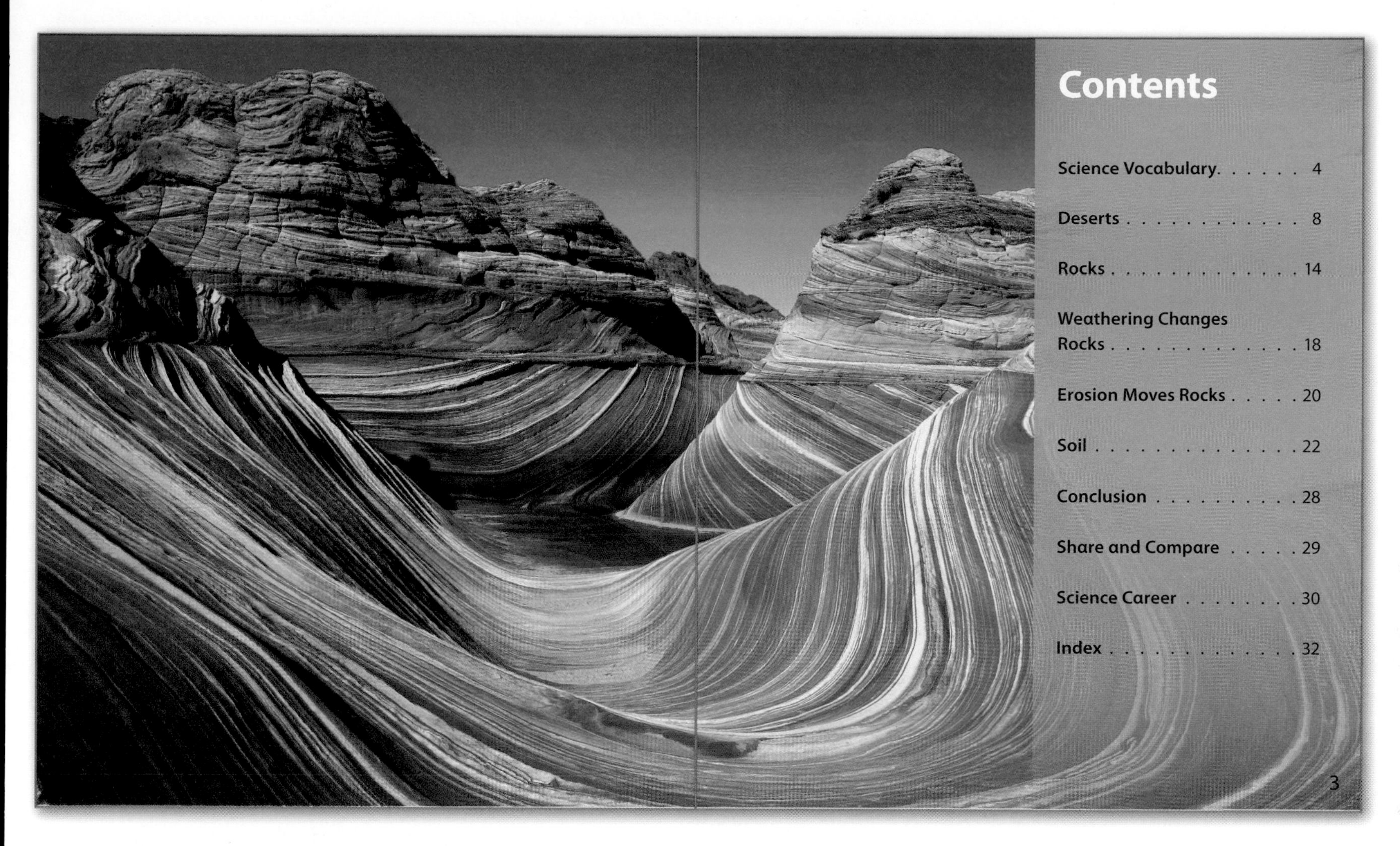

Contents

3

Use the Table of Contents

Preview

Ask students to preview the book by looking at the Table of Contents. Discuss how the book is organized. You may also want to look through the book with them.

Point to the word *Contents* on page 3.

- Say: **The Table of Contents shows what's inside a book. Use it to learn what is in a book and to find where parts of the book start.**
- Draw attention to the entries listed in the Table of Contents.
- Model looking for an entry on a particular topic and then turning to a page where an entry begins.
- Then have pairs work together; one partner identifies a topic he or she would like to read about, and the other tells the page number where it begins.
- Circulate and help students who are having difficulty.

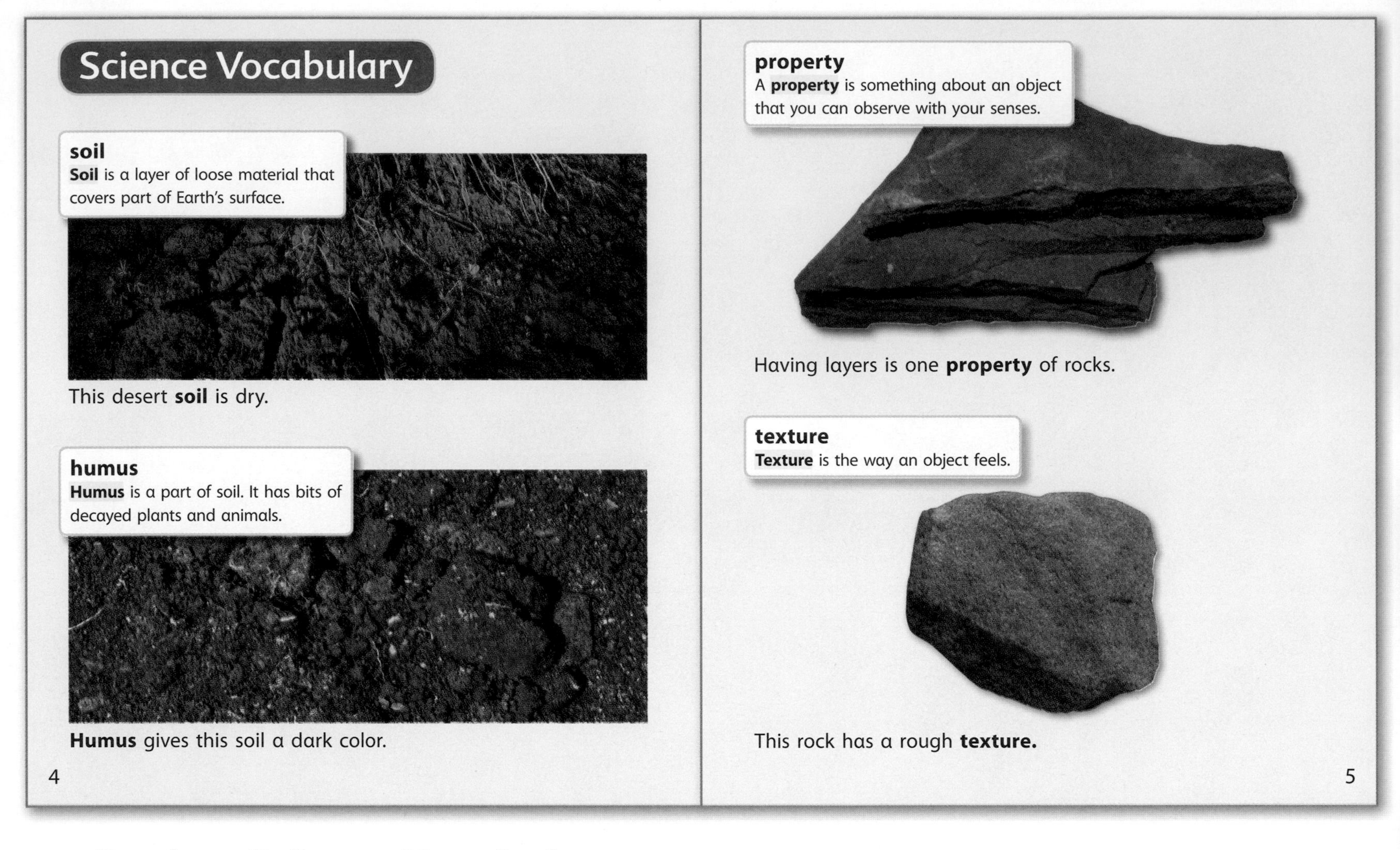

Review Science Vocabulary

Review the vocabulary that was introduced in the Big Ideas Big Book. Then use the following suggestions to relate the words to key science concepts.

- **soil** Point to the first photo. Ask: **Does the soil in this photo look soft and moist, or does it look dry and crusty?** (dry and crusty)
- **humus** Read aloud the definition and explain that **humus** gives soil a dark brown color. Ask students to locate and point to the photo that shows soil containing a lot of **humus.** (bottom of page 4)
- **property** Say: **You can use your senses to observe properties of rocks.** Point to the photo at the top of page 5. Ask: **What properties can you observe about these rocks?** (layers, color, size, shape) **If I had a sample of a real rock, what other sense could I use to examine the rock?** (touch)
- **texture** Point to the photo at the bottom of page 5. Say: **Imagine you are running a finger over this rock.** Ask: **What is the texture?** (rough)

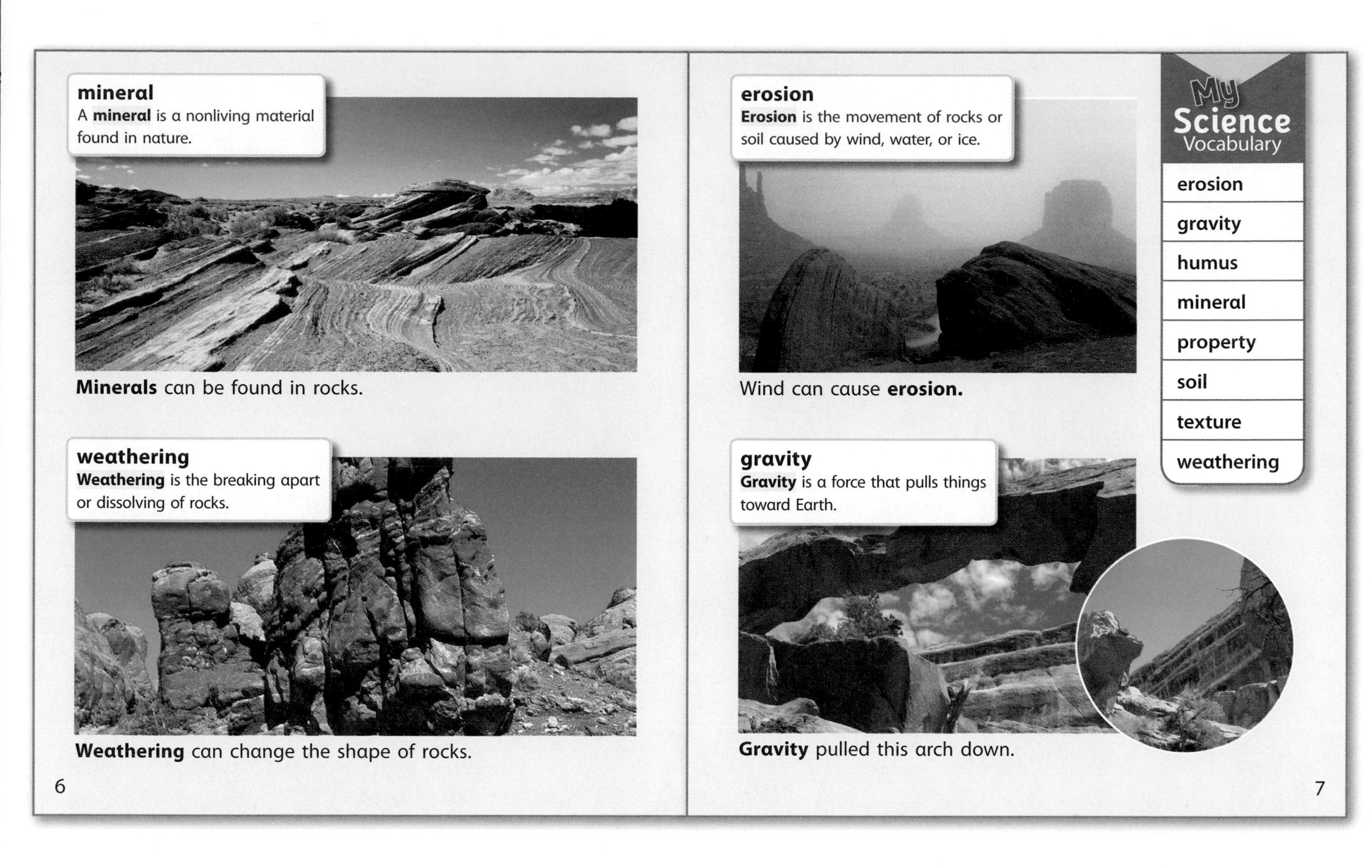

- **mineral** Read aloud the definition at the top of page 6 and point to the photo. Say: **These rocks contain minerals. Are minerals living things?** (no)
- **weathering** Point to the photo at the bottom of page 6. Say: **Weathering has broken off or dissolved bits of these rocks.** Ask students to share their thoughts about how rocks may have looked before **weathering.**
- **erosion** Have students look at the photo at the top of page 7. Ask: **What is the wind blowing through the air?** (bits of red rock or red soil) Say: **This movement of rocks or soil is erosion.**
- **gravity** Ask: **What is the arch on page 7 made from?** (rock) **What force can pull the rocks of a weak arch to the ground?** (gravity)

My Science Vocabulary

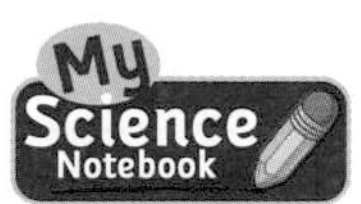

Have students copy the word list into their science notebook. Have students illustrate or explain in their own words their understanding of each new word.

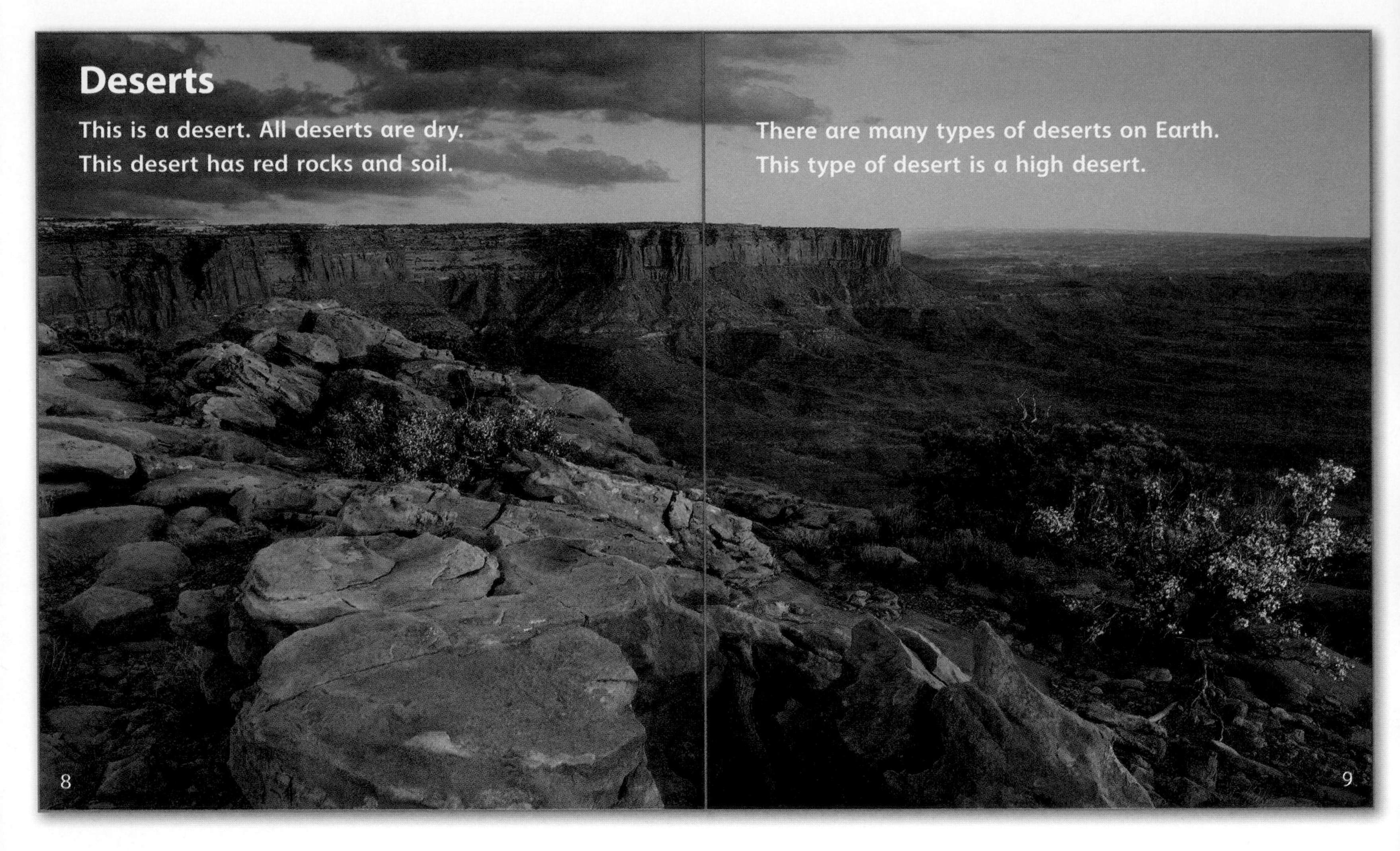

Access Science Content

Preview and Predict

Remind students to use the section heads, vocabulary words, and their background knowledge to make predictions. Circulate and ask students about predictions they have made.

Recognize a High Desert

Help students realize that the photo on pages 8–9 shows a high desert.

- Encourage students to share what they picture when they think of a desert. Have students compare their ideas with the photo on pages 8–9.
- Say: **The photo shows a high desert. It is in an area high above the level of the oceans. All deserts, high or low, are dry.**
- Ask: **What clues in the photo tell you this desert is dry?** (only a few scrubby plants, no visible water, soil looks dry and rocky)

Real-World Connections

Explain that much of the high desert gets fewer than ten inches (25 cm) of rain per year. Help students use books or the Internet to find your local annual rainfall and compare it with that number.

A high desert is hot and dry, but it gets cold weather, too. Sometimes it even gets rainstorms! Some high deserts get snow.

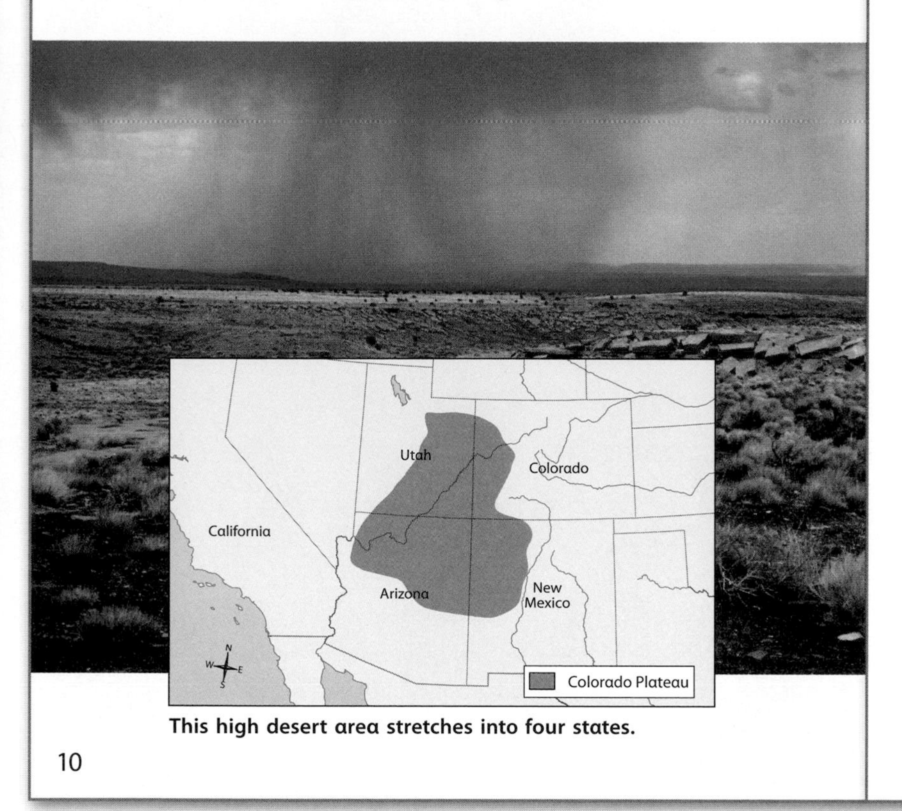

This high desert area stretches into four states.

10

There is a lot of sand in this desert. Sand is tiny bits of rock.

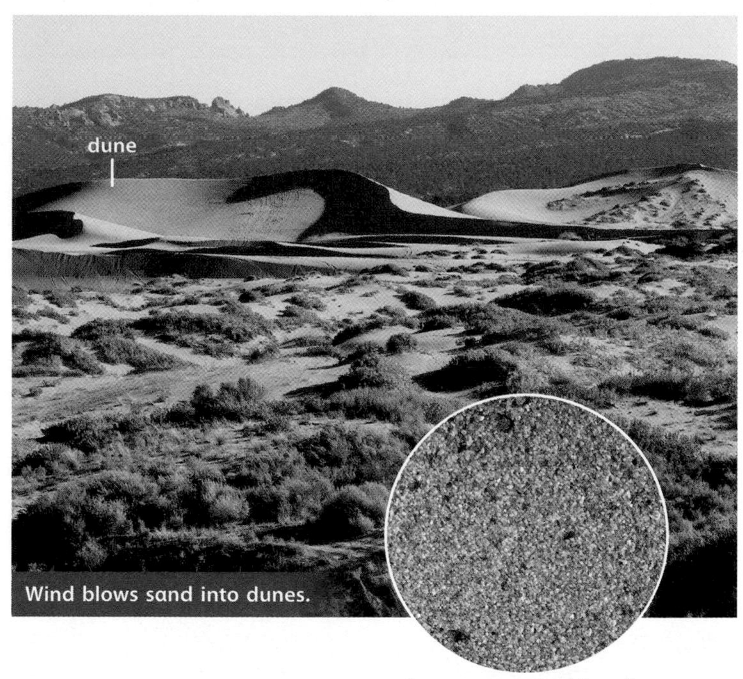

Can you see the bits of rock in this sand?

11

Access Science Content

Describe a High Desert

Students can use a map and photos to describe the high desert area of the Colorado Plateau.

- Have students study the map. Ask: **What does the orange area show?** (Colorado Plateau) Point out that the corners of four states meet in this area. Ask: **Can you name these states?** (Utah, Colorado, Arizona, New Mexico) On a large United States map, show the southwest location of the four states and point out the Colorado River and the Grand Canyon.
- Have students locate the sand dune in the photo on page 11. Say: **Desert winds blow the sand. There are few plants to hold the sand in place.** Have students look for bits of rock in the close-up view of sand.

Make Inferences

Ask students how what they already know can help them learn something new on these pages. (Possible answer: The sand is mostly reddish in color because the rocks in the area are mostly red.)

Text Features: Maps

Work with students to find and use the map features, including the map key and compass rose.

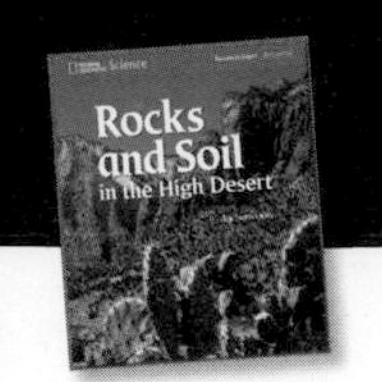

There are many things to see in this high desert. You may see valleys between mountains, or you may see canyons. A canyon is a deep valley with steep sides.

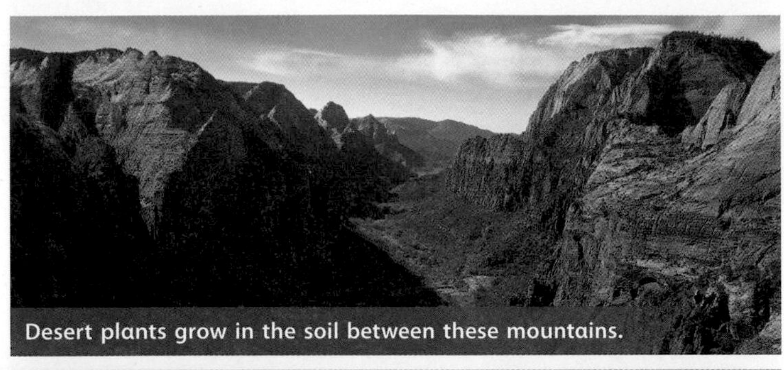

Desert plants grow in the soil between these mountains.

These deep canyons are made of rock.

12

You may see arches made of rock. The arches look like sculptures in this desert.

13

Access Science Content

Describe Natural Features of the Desert

Students can use photos to learn about natural features of the high desert.

- Invite students to view the photos and comment on their favorite scenery. Ask: **Where were these photos taken?** (high desert)
- Have students look closely at the photo at the top of page 12. Ask: **Where do plants grow in this valley?** (in soil) Say: **The words *deep* and *steep* describe a canyon.** Have students point out some of the steep, almost vertical walls in the canyon photo on page 12.

Differentiated Instruction

ELL Language Support for Describing Deserts

BEGINNING	INTERMEDIATE	ADVANCED
Ask yes/no questions about the photos on pages 12–13: **Is this a valley?** **Is this a canyon?** **Is this an arch?**	Have students use Academic Language Frames to name natural features of the high desert: *You can see ____ in the high desert.*	Have students use Academic Language Frames to describe natural features: *You can see ____ in the high desert. They have ____.*

Text Features: Captions

Have students locate the first caption on page 12. Read it aloud. Ask: **What did you learn from the caption?** (Desert plants can grow between mountains.) Remind students to refer to captions for extra information as they read.

Assess

1. **Recall What is sand made of?** (bits of rock)
2. **Compare and Contrast How is a canyon different from other valleys?** (It is deep with very steep sides.)

Rocks

You can observe the **properties** of desert rocks. Some rocks have layers. Having layers is a property.

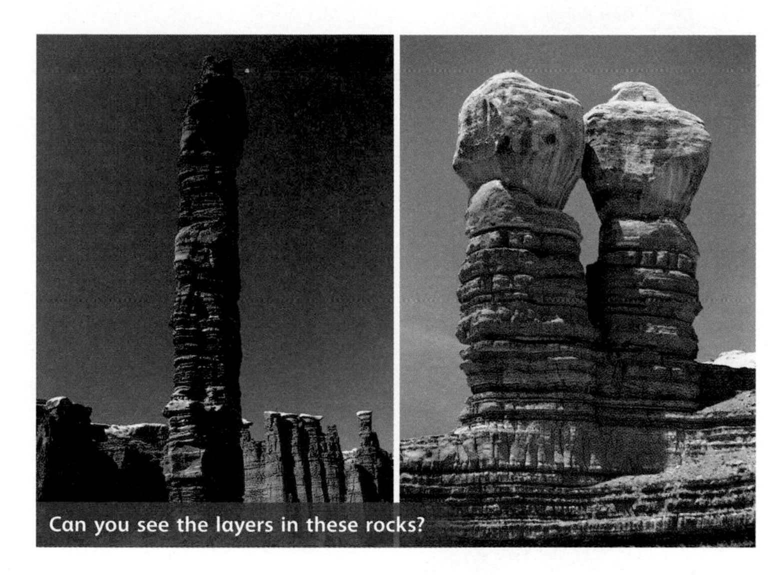
Can you see the layers in these rocks?

property
A **property** is something about an object that you can observe with your senses.

14

Color and **texture** are properties, too. Texture is how an object feels.

Properties	Words That Describe Properties
color	black, orange, pink
layers	layered, not layered
texture	rough, smooth

pink and black color

some layers

rough texture

texture
Texture is the way an object feels.

15

Access Science Content

Observe Properties of Desert Rocks

Students can view photos to observe **properties** of rocks found in the high desert.

- Read aloud the definition at the bottom of page 14. Point to the first photo and say: **One property of this rock is layers.** Ask students to run a finger along the layers of the rocks shown in the second photo on page 14.
- Say: **Another property of rocks is texture.** Read aloud the definition at the bottom of page 15. Ask: **Which words on the chart describe texture?** (rough, smooth) **Which words on the chart describe the property of color?** (black, orange, pink)
- Ask: **How would you describe the properties of the rocks on page 15?** (Students should describe the rocks' colors, whether the rocks are rough or smooth, and whether they have layers.)

Text Features: Tables

Have students locate the columns and rows of the table. Read aloud each column heading and explain how to interpret the data in the column. Have students use the table to get information. For example, ask: **What are some words that describe the property of layers?**

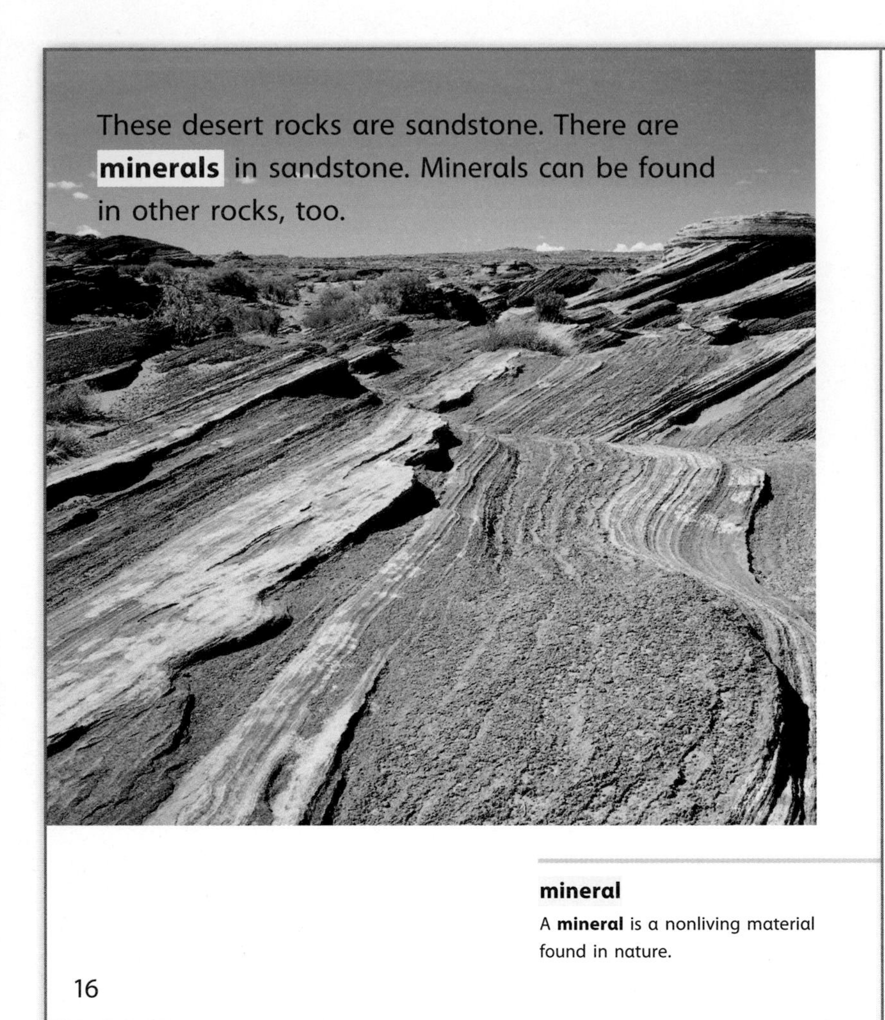

These desert rocks are sandstone. There are **minerals** in sandstone. Minerals can be found in other rocks, too.

mineral
A **mineral** is a nonliving material found in nature.

16

Minerals have properties. Minerals can be different colors. They can also be hard or soft. How would you describe these minerals?

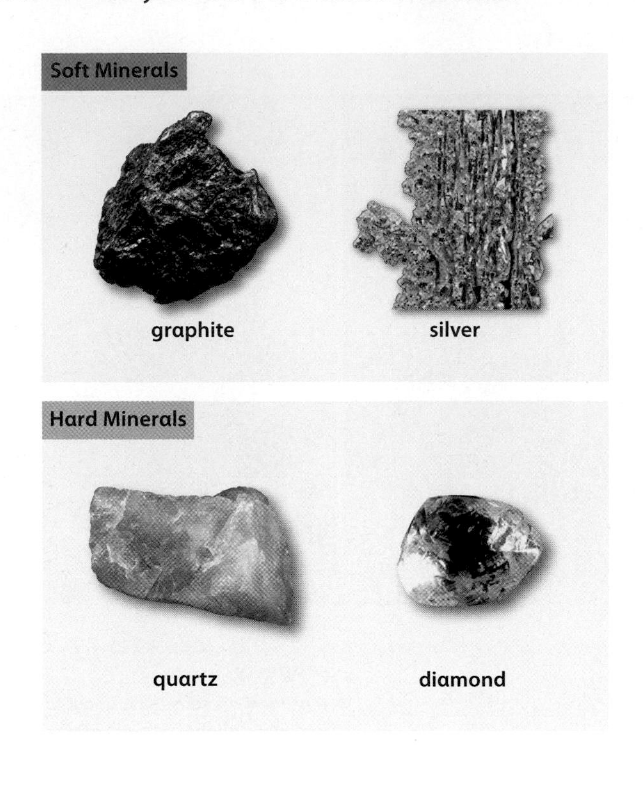

17

Access Science Content

Describe Properties of Minerals

Introduce **minerals.** Then have students describe the properties of the **minerals** pictured on page 17. (Students might describe the color, shape, size, and texture of the **minerals.**)

- Point to the photo on page 16. Say: **These rocks are sandstone. Sandstone, like other rocks, contains minerals.** Read the definition at the bottom of the page.
- Explain: **Minerals have properties, such as color and how hard or how soft they are.** Have students look at the **minerals** on page 17. Read the first heading and point to the corresponding **minerals.** Say: **Graphite and silver are soft minerals.** Repeat with the hard **minerals.**

Assess

1. **Name What do we call nonliving materials such as quartz, silver, graphite, and diamond?** (minerals)
2. **Apply Devin says, "This rock looks like a stack of pancakes." What property is Devin describing?** (layers)

Weathering Changes Rocks

These sandstone shapes didn't always look like this. Wind and water changed their shape.

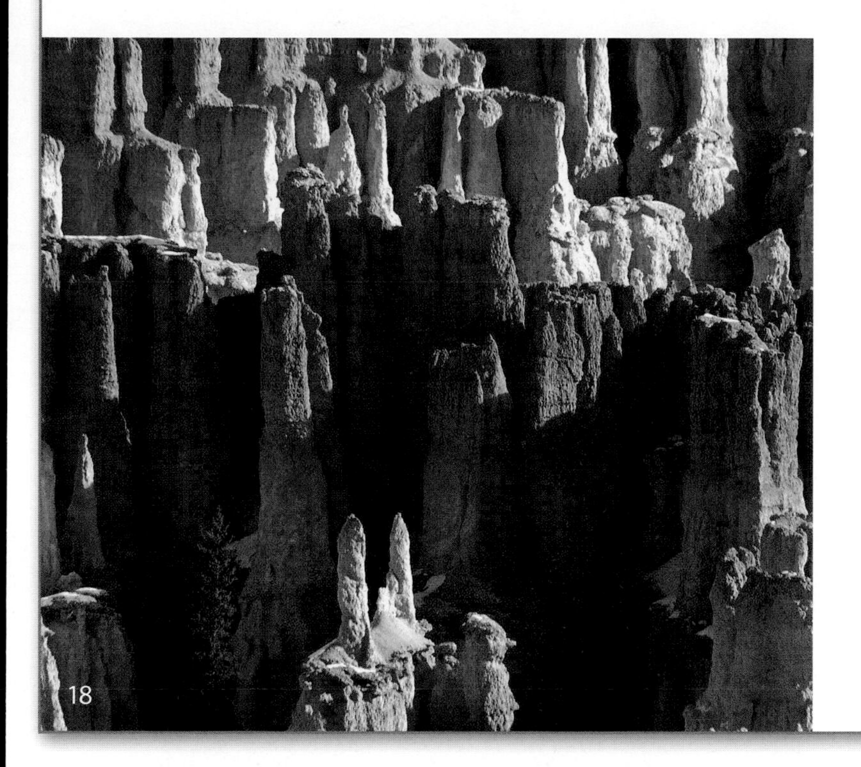

18

Wind breaks off tiny bits of rock. Water can break off tiny rocks. Water can dissolve rocks too. This is called **weathering.**

Wind weathers rocks.

Water weathers rocks.

weathering
Weathering is the breaking apart or dissolving of rocks.

19

Access Science Content

Observe Changes Caused by Weathering

Help students use photos to discover how **weathering** changes rocks.

- Have students compare the sandstone shapes on page 18 to those on page 16. Say: **Over time, wind and water shapes sandstone in different ways.**
- Read the definition of **weathering** and have students view the first photo on page 19. Ask: **How do you think the rock looked before it was so weathered by wind?** (It was probably more solid.) Point to the other photo: **What weathered these rocks?** (water) Say: **Water can break off bits of rock, or it can slowly dissolve rock.**

Assess

1. **Name Name something besides water that can weather desert rocks.** (wind)
2. **Explain How does water weather rocks?** (It breaks them apart, or it dissolves them.)

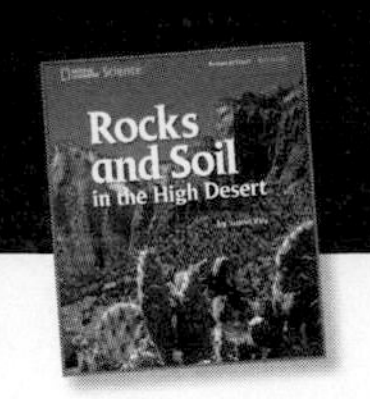

Erosion Moves Rocks

Wind moves loose bits of rocks and sand. Water moves loose rocks and sand, too. This is called **erosion.**

Wind erodes rocks.

Water erodes rocks.

erosion
Erosion is the movement of rocks or soil caused by wind, water, or ice.

20

Weathering and erosion can make arches in the desert very thin. **Gravity** can pull them to the ground.

This is how the arch above looked after it fell.

gravity
Gravity is a force that pulls things toward Earth.

21

Access Science Content

Recognize Ways that Rocks Can Be Moved

Students can study photos to discover that wind and water **erode** rocks and **gravity** pulls rocks downward.

- Read aloud the heading on page 20. Ask: **Which words in the heading explain what erosion does?** (moves rocks) Read aloud the definition at the bottom of the page. Ask: **What makes the rocks move?** (wind, water, ice)
- Have students study the photos on page 20 and identify the agents of **erosion.** Ask: **What is moving or eroding rocks in the first photo?** (wind) **How do you know?** (There are tiny bits of reddish rock in the air.) **What is eroding rocks in the second photo?** (water, the stream)
- Say: **Gravity plays a role in moving rocks. It pulls things toward Earth.** Point out the "before" and "after" photos on page 21. Ask: **What did gravity do to the arch?** (pulled it down) Explain: **If an arch becomes weak, the pull of gravity can collapse it.**

Assess

1. **Define What is gravity?** (a force that pulls things toward Earth)
2. **Contrast In the weathering process, rock breaks or dissolves. How does the erosion process differ?** (In the erosion process, rock moves.)

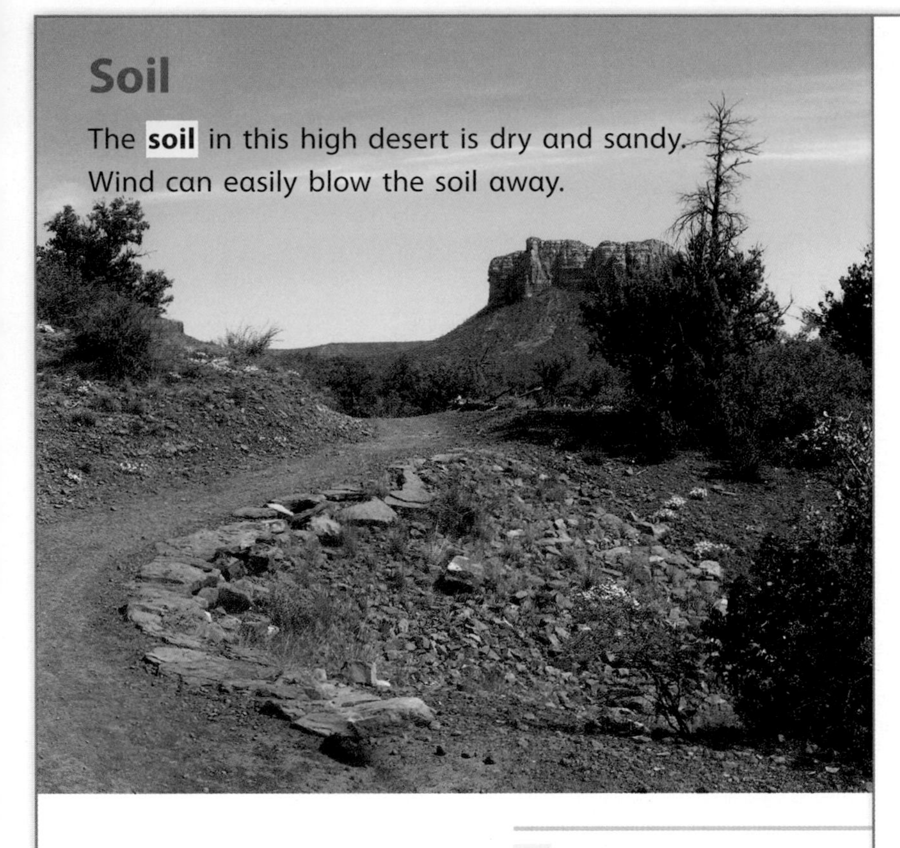

Soil

The **soil** in this high desert is dry and sandy. Wind can easily blow the soil away.

soil
Soil is a layer of loose material that covers part of Earth's surface.

22

But some desert soil has a dark crust that helps the soil hold in water. The crust helps protect the soil from erosion.

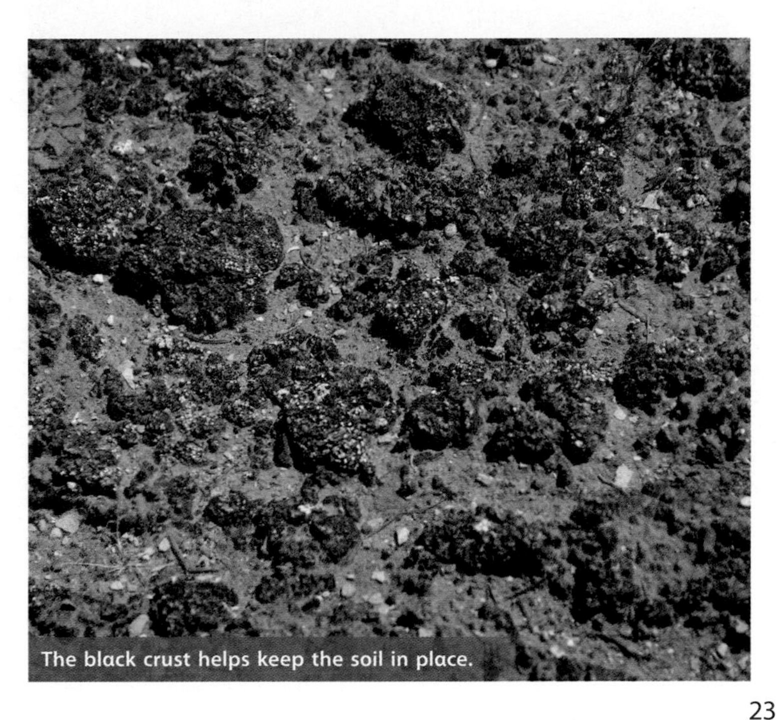

The black crust helps keep the soil in place.

23

Access Science Content

Compare Two Desert Soils

Students can use photos to compare two different types of desert **soil.**

- Read aloud the definition of **soil.** Direct students' attention to the photos on pages 22–23. Say: **These photos show two kinds of desert soil.**
- Ask: **If you blow on sugar, what happens?** (It scatters.) Point to the **soil** on page 22 and say: **This dry, sandy soil is sugarlike. Wind can easily erode it.**
- Say: **Some desert soil is not so easily eroded.** Ask: **What helps keep the soil pictured on page 23 in place?** (the crusty surface)

Desert soil has a lot of sand in it. It does not have much **humus.** Few plants can grow in this soil.

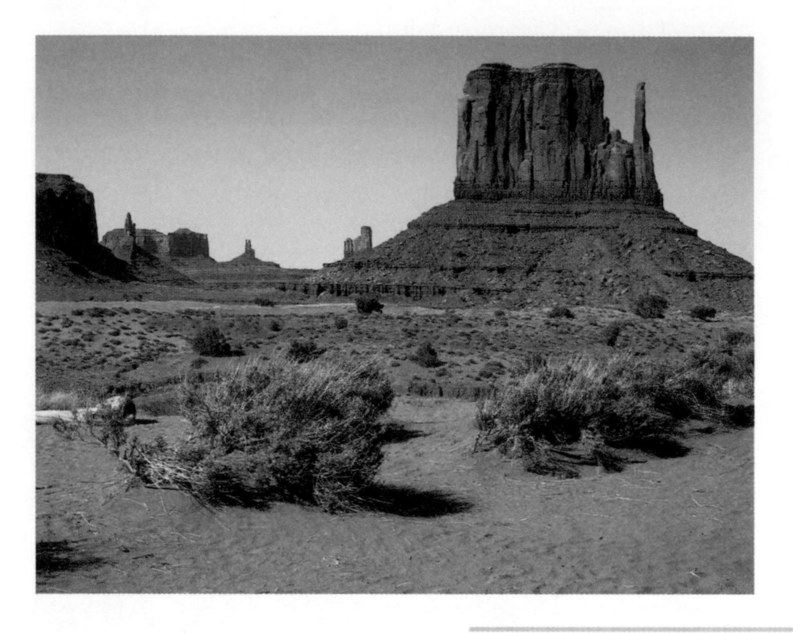

humus
Humus is a part of soil. It has bits of decayed plants and animals.

24

Unlike desert soil, most plants grow well in garden soil. Garden soil has a lot of humus.

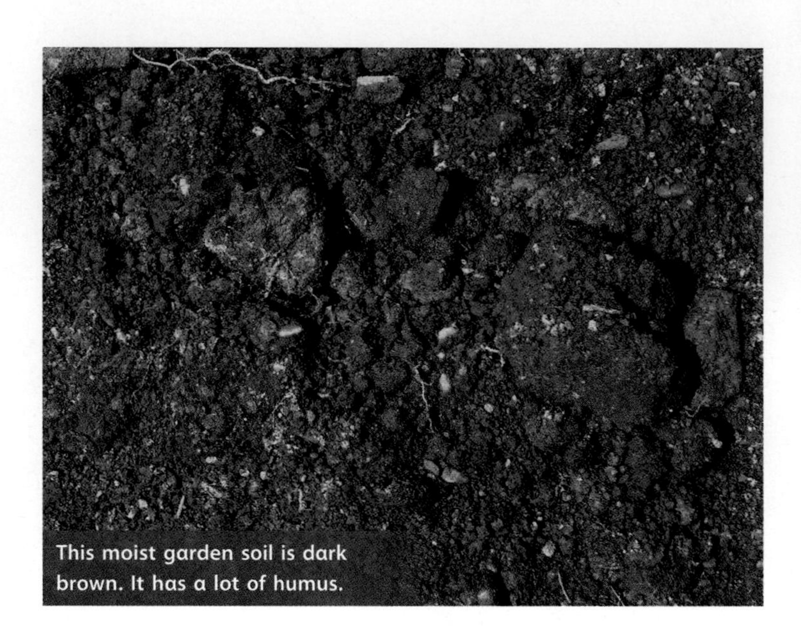

This moist garden soil is dark brown. It has a lot of humus.

25

Access Science Content

Compare Desert Soil and Garden Soil

Students can use photos to compare the composition of desert soil and garden soil.

- Explain: **The photo on page 24 shows desert soil, but the photo on page 25 shows garden soil.**
- Have students look closely at the soil pictured on page 24. Ask: **How would you describe this soil?** (dry with a lot of red sand) **Do you see a lot of grass or other plants?** (no) Explain: **The type of soil affects how well plants can grow. Many plants need soil that contains a dark brown material called humus.** Read aloud the definition at the bottom of page 25.
- Point to the photo on page 25. Ask: **What do you see in this soil?** (small rocks, sand, tiny plant roots, brown humus) Explain: **Humus holds water. Plants grow well in this soil.**

Recording Observations

Ask students to suggest words that describe typical desert and garden soils. Record the words in a T Chart.

Desert Soil	Garden Soil
few plants grow	plants grow well
a lot of sand	a lot of humus
	dark brown

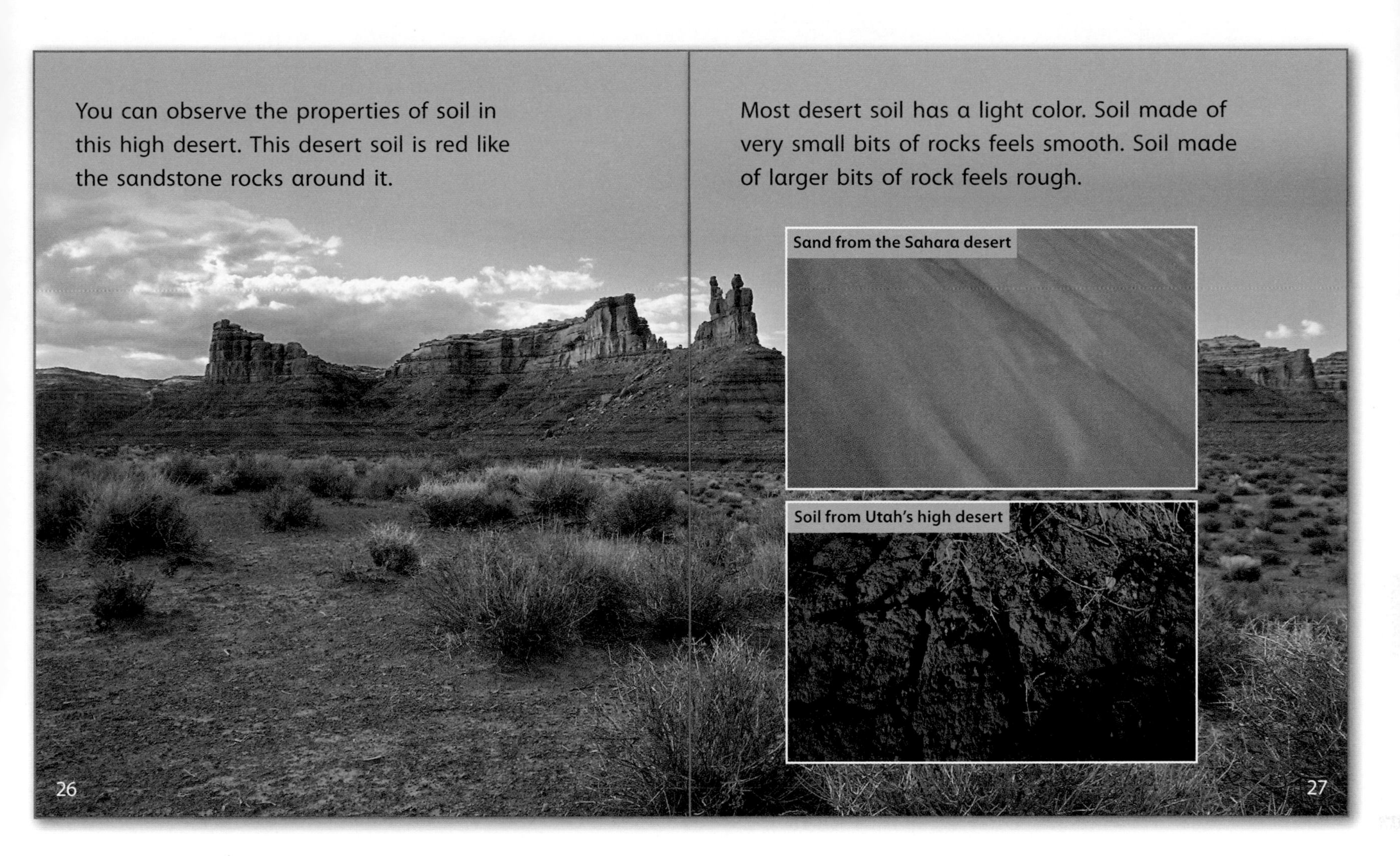

Access Science Content

Observe Properties of High Desert Soil

Students can view photos to observe properties of soil in a high desert and compare these properties to the Sahara.

- Have students look at the photo on pages 26–27. Ask: **What do you see in this high desert?** (red rocks and soil, sky, a few plants) Point out that the second inset photo shows a close-up view of the soil. Ask: **How would you describe the soil?** (red, rough in texture)
- Say: **Most deserts do not have red soil.** Have students look at the first inset photo. Explain: **The Sahara is a big desert in Africa.** Ask: **What color is the sand in the Sahara?** (light brown) Have students say sentences comparing the sand in the two deserts.

Assess

1. **Recall Which kind of soil is likely to contain a lot of humus—desert soil or garden soil?** (garden soil)
2. **Explain Wind can easily erode dry, sandy soil. Are some types of desert soil more protected from erosion? Explain your answer.** (Yes, some desert soils have a crust that helps keep the soil from blowing away.)

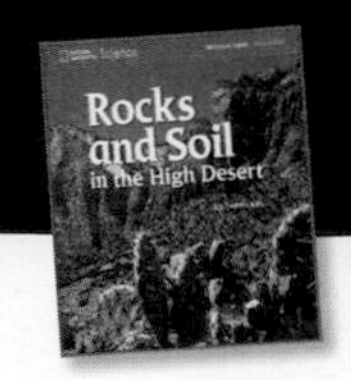

Conclusion

The high desert has rocks and soil. Rocks in some deserts are red. Soil in the desert is dry. Weathering and erosion can change rocks. Bits of rock become part of soil. Gravity can pull rock arches down.

Think About the Big Ideas

1. What can you observe about rocks in the high desert?
2. How do rocks change?
3. What can you observe about soil?

28

Following the ***Conclusion*** page of the *Become an Expert* book, rearrange groups to begin the ***Share and Compare*** section on page T89.

Conclusion

Sum Up

Tell students that a conclusion helps sum up the big ideas in a book. Have students restate the conclusion in their own words.

Answer the Big Idea Questions

Encourage students to sum up what they learned in the book and then share responses to the questions aloud.

1. **What can you observe about rocks in the high desert?** (You see arches and mountains. Many rocks are red and layered. They contain minerals.)
2. **How do rocks change?** (As rocks weather, bits break off or dissolve. Wind and water erode loose rock. Gravity pulls rocks down.)
3. **What can you observe about soil?** (Soil can be dry and sandy or it can have a crusty surface. A lot of the soil is red.)

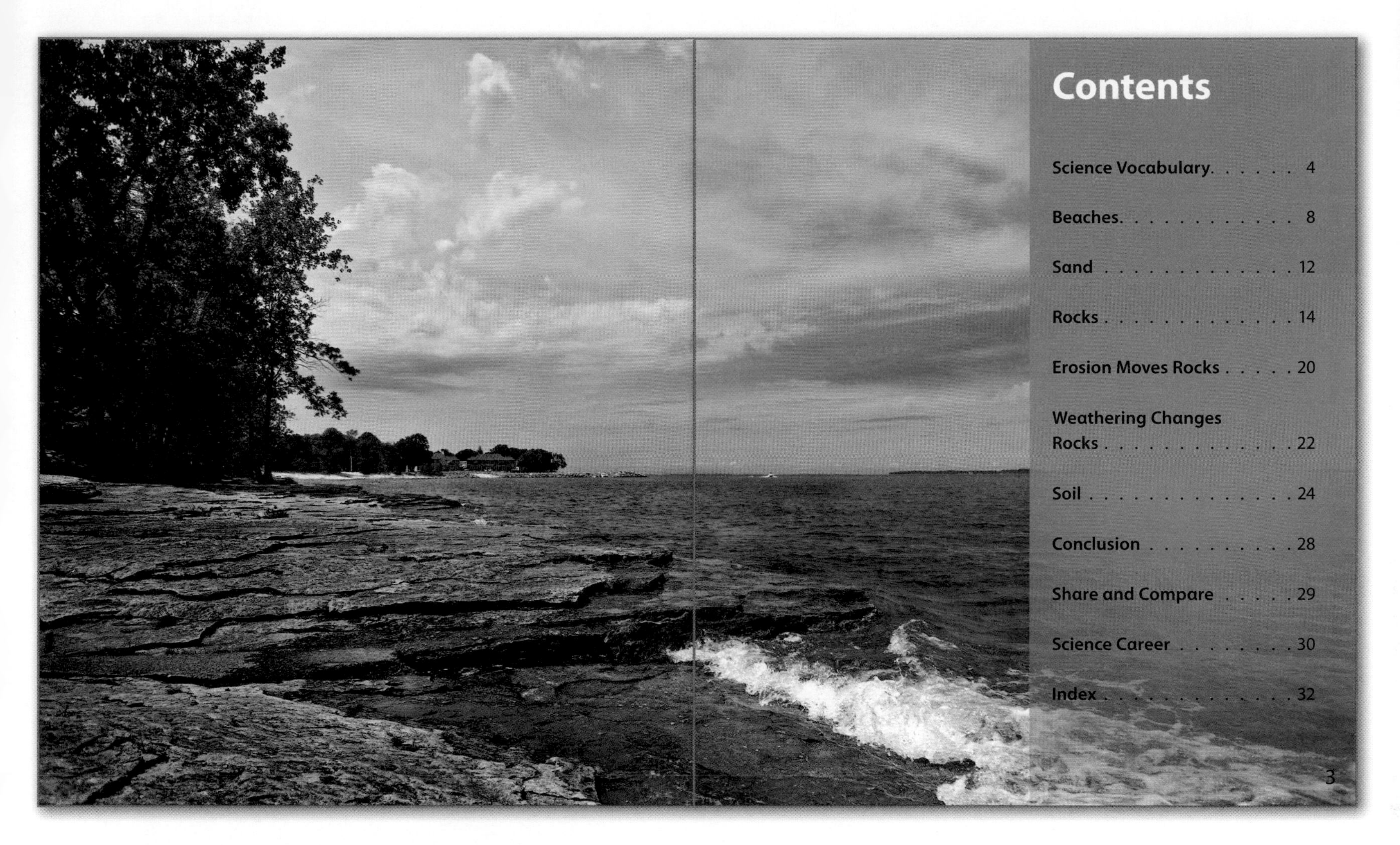

Use the Table of Contents

Preview

Ask students to preview the book by looking at the Table of Contents. Discuss how the book is organized. You may also want to look through the book with them.

Point to the word *Contents* on page 3.

- Say: **The Table of Contents shows what's inside a book. Use it to learn what is in a book and to find where parts of the book start.**
- Draw attention to the entries listed in the Table of Contents.
- Model looking for an entry on a particular topic and then turning to a page where an entry begins.
- Then have pairs work together; one partner identifies a topic he or she would like to read about, and the other tells the page number where it begins.
- Circulate and help students who are having difficulty.

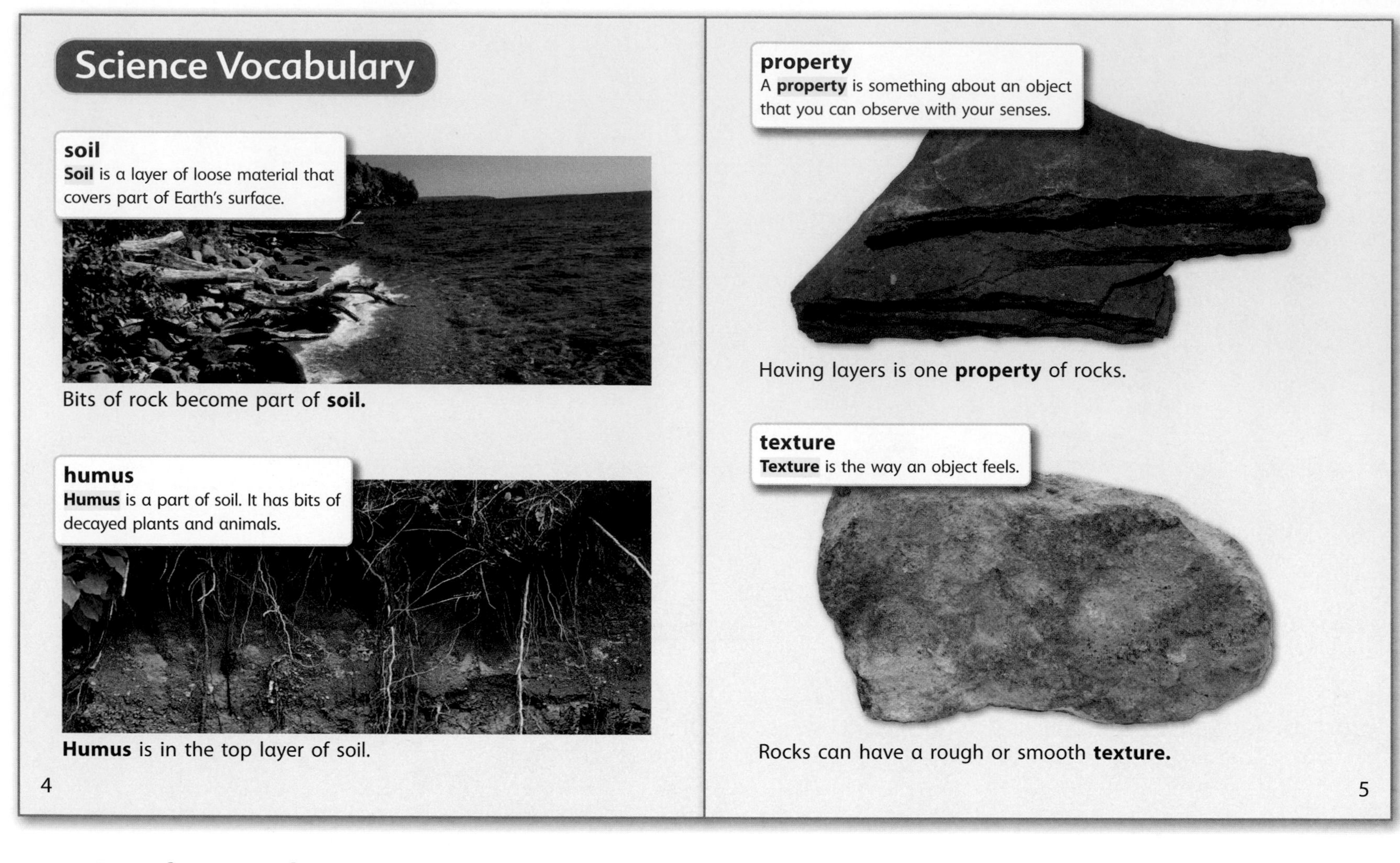

Review Science Vocabulary

Review the vocabulary that was introduced in the Big Ideas Big Book. Then use the following suggestions to relate the words to key science concepts:

- **soil** Say: **Soil can vary. It can contain dark brown material, bits of rock, or a combination of materials.** Have students point out areas covered with **soil** in the first photo on page 4.
- **humus** Read aloud the definition for **humus.** Have students study the photo at the bottom of page 4. Ask: **Which layer of this soil contains the most humus?** (top layer)
- **property** Say: **When we study rocks, we can observe properties such as layering.** Have students point out other **properties** of the rocks on page 5, such as size, color, texture, and shape.
- **texture** Point to the rock at the bottom of page 5. Say: **Imagine how this rock would feel if you rubbed it.** Ask: **How would you describe the texture?** (rough)

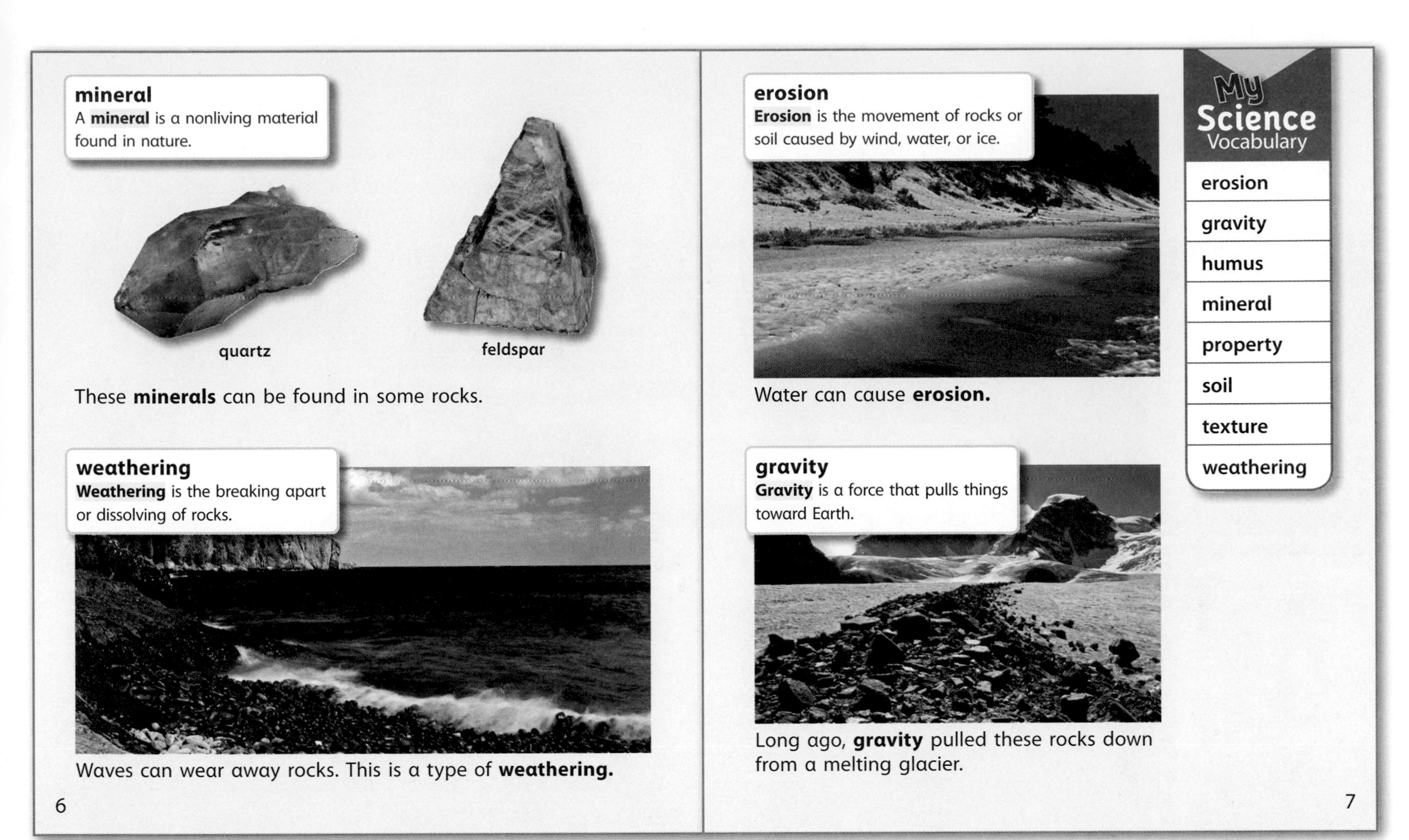

- **mineral** Read aloud the labels under the **minerals** pictured on page 6. Ask: **What do we call nonliving materials such as quartz and feldspar?** (minerals)
- **weathering** Point to the smooth rocks on the beach on page 6. Say: **Over time, bits of these rocks have worn away, making the rocks smooth.** Ask: **What has weathered these rocks?** (waves)
- **erosion** Read aloud the definition of **erosion**. Point to the photo at the top of page 7 and ask: **How can waves cause erosion?** (They move the sand as they go in and out.)
- **gravity** Ask: **When you drop a rock, what force pulls it downward?** (gravity) Have students look at the photo at the bottom of page 7. Explain: **These rocks were once on top of a glacier. When the glacier melted, gravity pulled the rocks downward.**

My Science Vocabulary

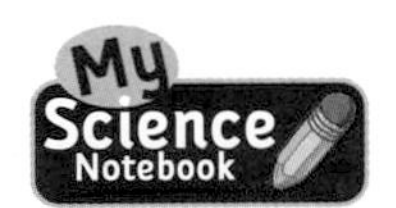

Have students copy the word list into their science notebook. Have students illustrate or explain in their own words their understanding of each new word.

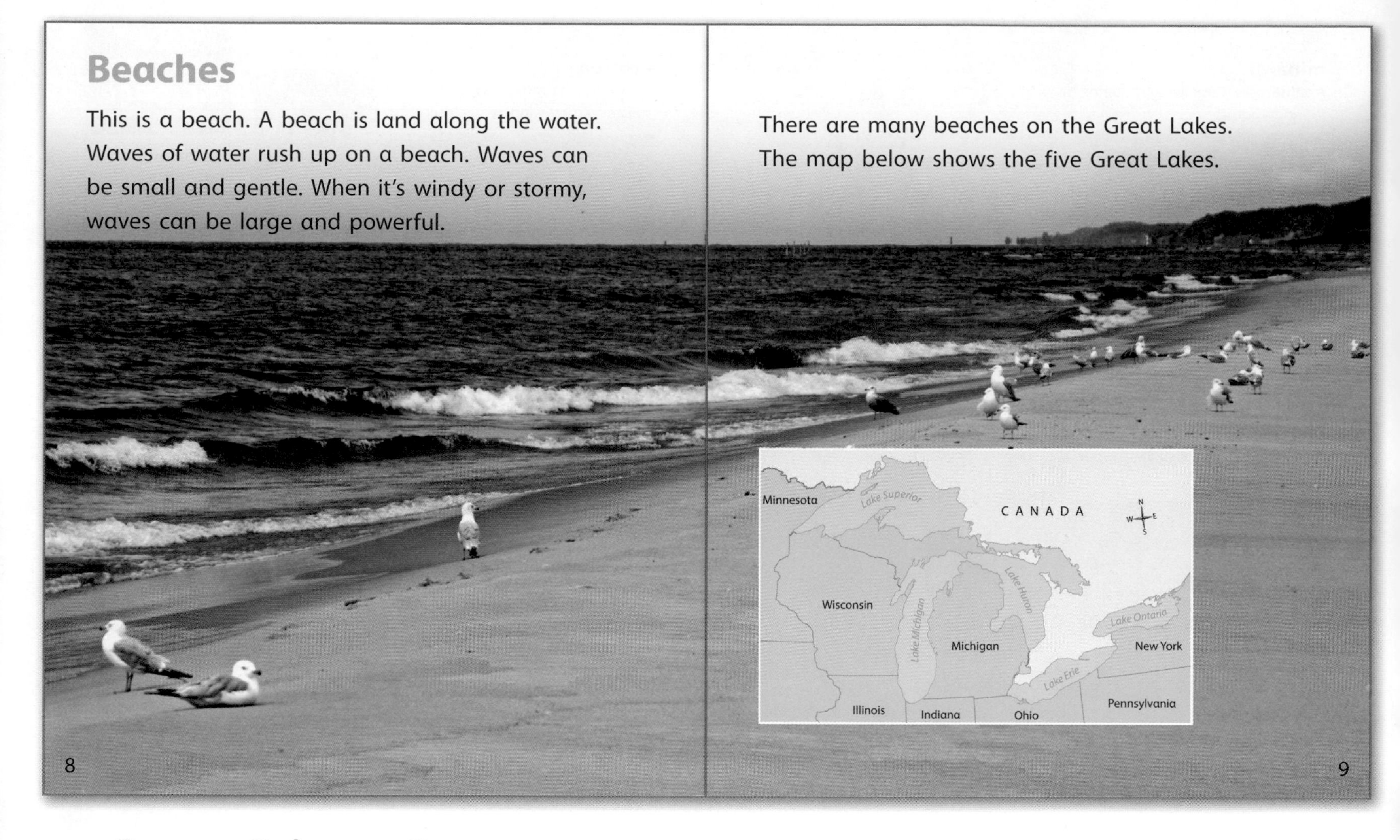

Access Science Content

Describe a Beach

To provide background, locate the Great Lakes on a large map of North America. Explain that these freshwater lakes are used for shipping and recreation. Have students trace a route from Lake Superior to the Atlantic Ocean.

- Ask students to describe how the water in the Great Lakes is different from ocean water. (It is fresh, not salty.) Then give students this tip for remembering the names of the lakes. Say: **The first letters of Huron, Ontario, Michigan, Erie, and Superior spell the word *homes*.** Have students locate each lake on the inset map on page 9.
- Point to the compass rose in the upper right part of the map. Ask: **Which way is north on this map?** (toward the top) Demonstrate how knowing one direction tells you the other three.
- Point to the photo on pages 8–9. Say: **Land that lies along water is called a beach. How would you describe this beach?** (sandy, washed by waves)
- Ask: **What happens to the water after it rushes up the beach?** (Some of it soaks into the sand; some of it flows back toward the lake.)

Text Features: Maps

Work with students to find and use the map features, including the compass rose, colors that represent water and states, and state borders.

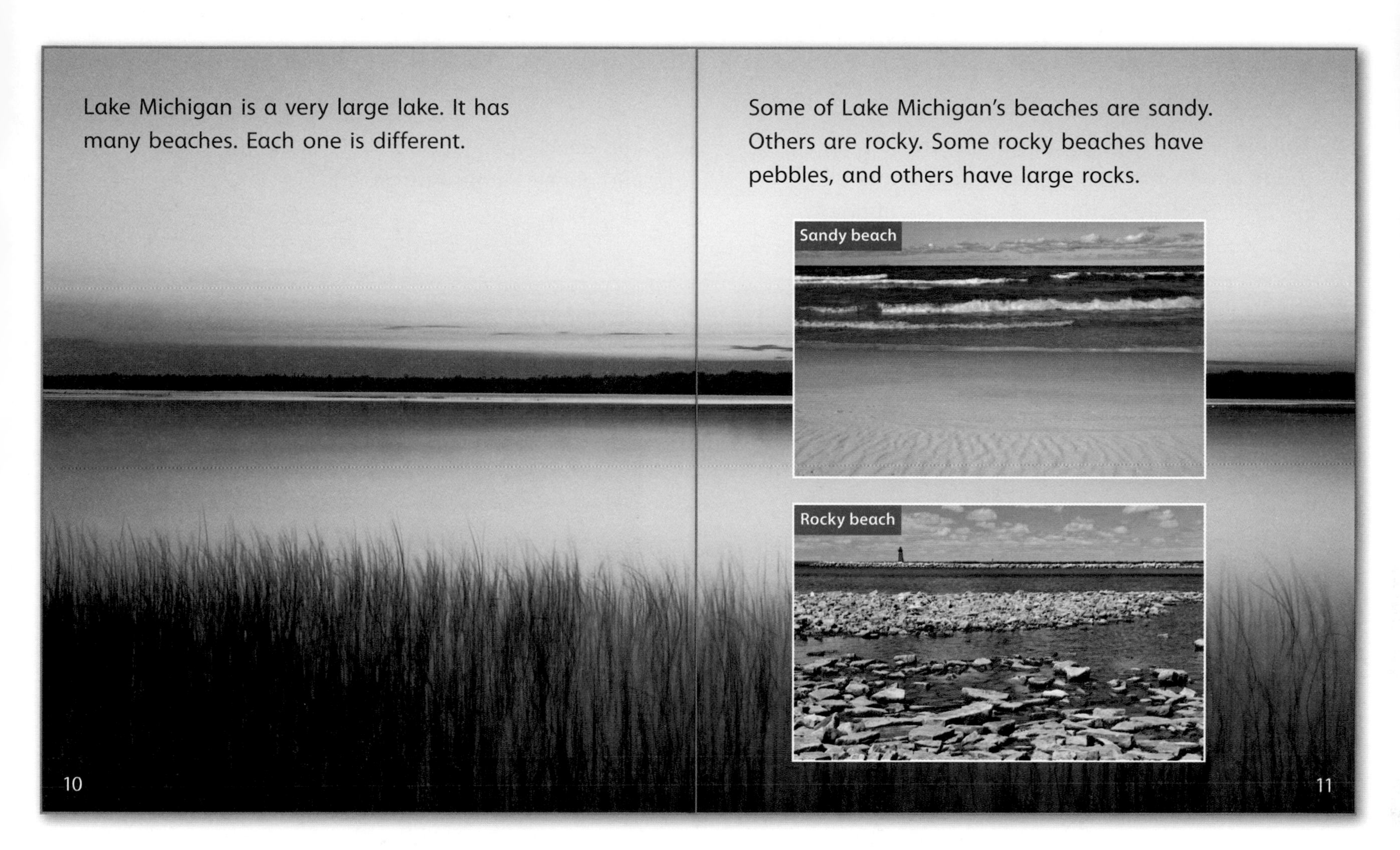

Access Science Content

Identify Different Types of Beaches

Students can study photos to learn about different kinds of beaches on Lake Michigan.

- Point to the photo that spans pages 10–11. Say: **This is Lake Michigan. Sometimes the water looks still as it does in this photo, but sometimes Lake Michigan has huge waves. The lake can look different at different times of day.** Ask: **At what time of day do you think this photo was taken?** (sunrise or sunset)
- Say: **The beaches on Lake Michigan vary, too.** Ask: **What kind of beach does the first small photo on page 11 show?** (a sandy beach) **How would you describe this beach?** (wide, covered with light-colored sand)
- Ask: **What kind of beach does the second small photo show?** (a rocky beach) **How would you describe this beach?** (jagged shoreline, covered with flat, sharp rocks)

Text Features: Photos

Ask: **What do the two small photos on page 11 show?** (a rocky beach and a sandy beach) **Why do you think the author included these photos?** (Possible answers: to compare rocky and sandy beaches; to show there are different kinds of beaches)

Assess

1. **Define What is a beach?** (land along water)
2. **Classify What two types of beaches would you find if you circled Lake Michigan?** (sandy and rocky beaches)

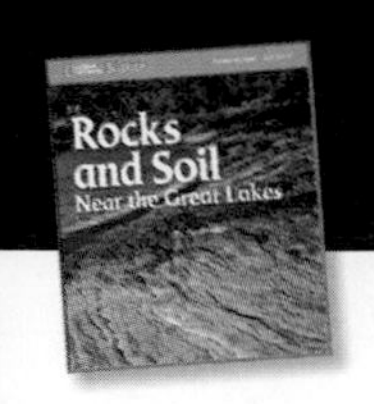

Sand

This beach is covered with sand. Sand can be made of different things. Some sand is made of tiny bits of shells. This sand is made of tiny bits of rock.

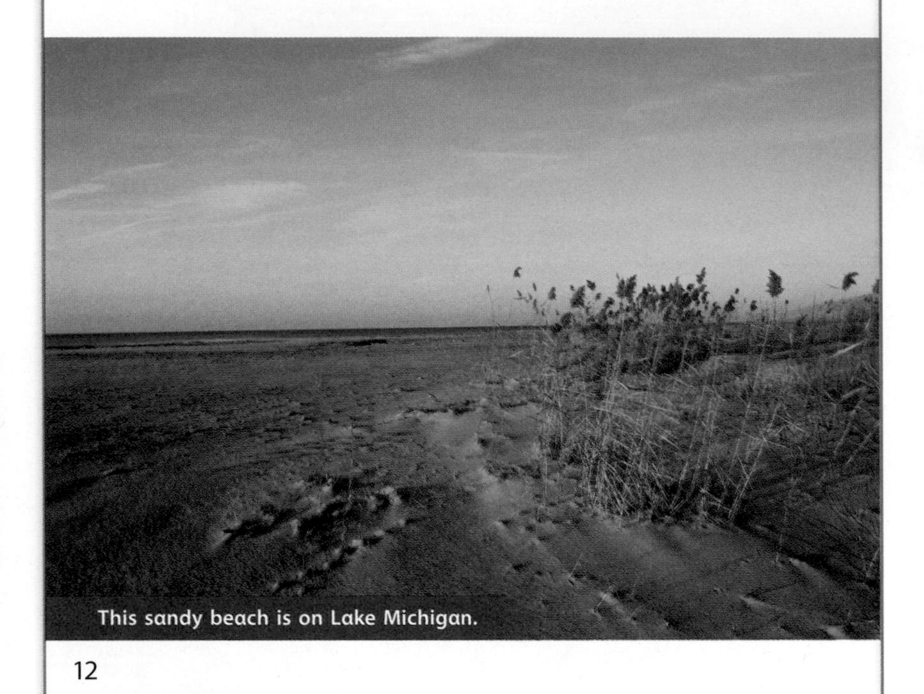

This sandy beach is on Lake Michigan.

12

This beach is sandy, too. Wind blows the sand into dunes. Plants may grow in the sandy soil of a dune.

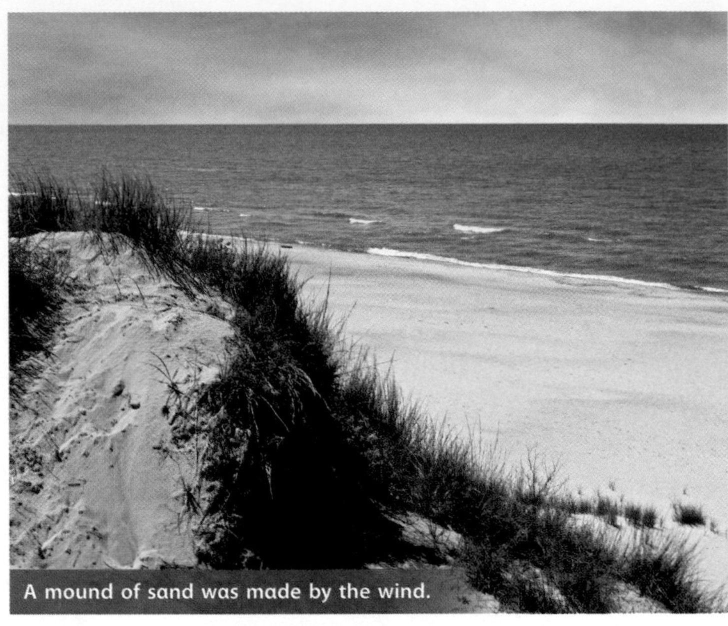

A mound of sand was made by the wind.

13

Access Science Content

Observe Sand on Lake Michigan Beaches

Students can observe photos of sand and sand dunes by Lake Michigan.

- Say: **Over time, tiny bits break off the rocks around Lake Michigan. These bits of rock collect.** Point to the beach on page 12. Ask: **What do you think this sand is made of?** (bits of rock)
- Say: **Wind blows loose sand into mounds called dunes.** Have students find and point to the dune in the photo on page 13.

Differentiated Instruction

ELL Language Support for Observing Sand on a Beach

BEGINNING	INTERMEDIATE	ADVANCED
Ask either/or questions about the photos on pages 12–13: **Is the beach rocky or sandy?**	Have students use Academic Language Frames to describe the photos on pages 12–13: *This beach is ____.* *A dune is a mound of ____.*	Have students use Academic Language Frames to elaborate: *This is a ____. It is made of ____. The ____ blows the ____.*

Assess

1. **Define** **What is a dune?** (sand blown into a mound)
2. **Classify** **Is the sand on Lake Michigan beaches made of tiny bits of shells or tiny bits of rock?** (tiny bits of rock)

Rocks

Some beaches are rocky. Rocks have different **properties.** Having layers is a property. Some rocks have layers. Other rocks do not have layers.

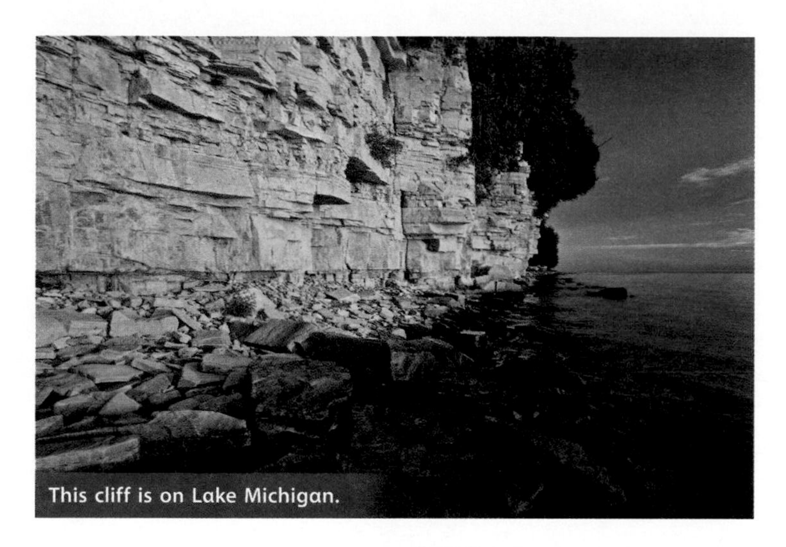

This cliff is on Lake Michigan.

property
A **property** is something about an object that you can observe with your senses.

Color and **texture** are properties, too. Some rocks have a rough texture. Some have a smooth texture. Texture is how an object feels when you touch it.

Properties	Words That Describe Properties
color	orange, brown, black
layers	layered, not layered
texture	rough, smooth

black color

some layers

rough texture

texture
Texture is the way an object feels.

Access Science Content

Identify Properties of Rocks

Help students use a chart and photos to identify **properties** of rocks.

- Read the definition of **properties.** Then point to the photo on page 14. Say: **One property of these rocks is layers.** Ask: **Which direction do the layers go?** (Some go across and some go up and down.) Ask students to use a finger to trace the horizontal and vertical layers in the rock cliff.
- Have students view the first column of the chart on page 15. Ask: **What properties are listed on the chart?** (color, layers, texture) Read aloud the definition of **texture** at the bottom of page 15. Ask: **Which words on the chart describe texture?** (rough, smooth)
- Point to the rock on the left on page 15 and ask students to describe its **properties.** Repeat with the pictures of the other rocks.

Real-World Connections

Place four or five rocks in a tub or paper bag. Let students feel the rocks (without looking at them) to determine which ones are rough in **texture** and which ones are smooth.

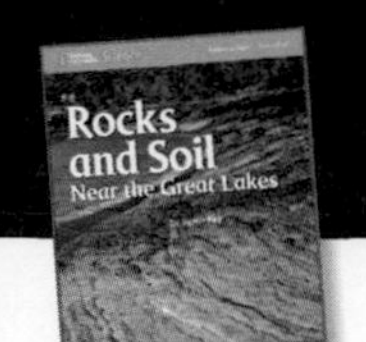

Most of the sand in the beaches around the Great Lakes is made of quartz. Quartz is a **mineral.** Minerals can be found in some rocks.

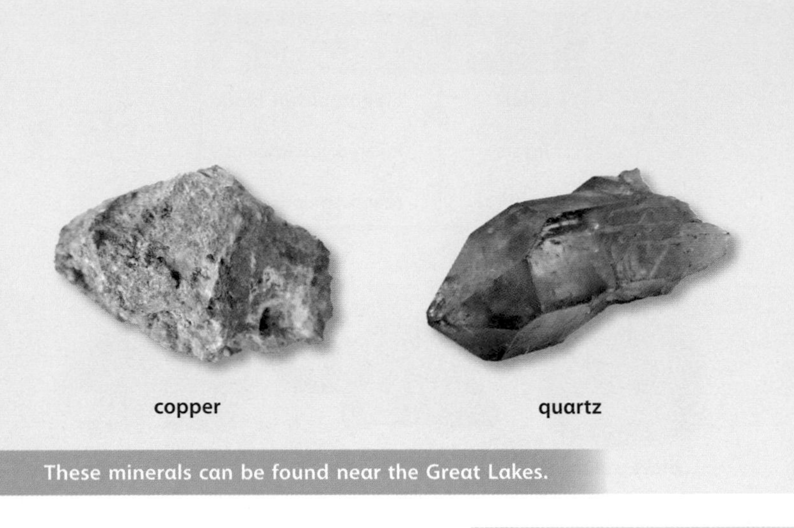

copper

quartz

These minerals can be found near the Great Lakes.

mineral
A **mineral** is a nonliving material found in nature.

16

Minerals have properties, too. Strength, or softness and hardness, is one property. How would you describe these minerals?

dolomite

feldspar

17

Access Science Content

Recognize that Minerals Have Properties

Help students realize that **minerals** are found in rocks and have properties.

- Read aloud the definition of **mineral.** Then point to the quartz specimen. Say: **Quartz is a mineral found in rocks and sand near the Great Lakes.**
- Say: **Minerals have properties, such as color and strength. Scientists measure strength on a scale of 1 to 10, from softest to hardest.** Have students find the copper specimen on page 16. Say: **Copper is about 3 on the scale. It is soft. Dolomite is between 3.5 and 4. It is a little harder than copper. Feldspar is 6. Quartz is 7. Is quartz soft or hard?** (hard)
- Tell students that a **mineral** that has a hardness of about 1 can be scratched with a fingernail.

Recording Observations

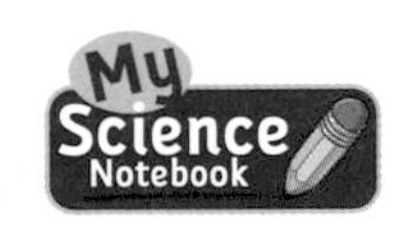

Work with students to position the **minerals** on pages 16–17 on a hardness scale. Explain that dolomite is between copper and feldspar in hardness. (copper, dolomite, feldspar, quartz)

There is a special type of rock on this beach in Michigan. It is called Petoskey stone. Petoskey stones have fossils of coral inside them.

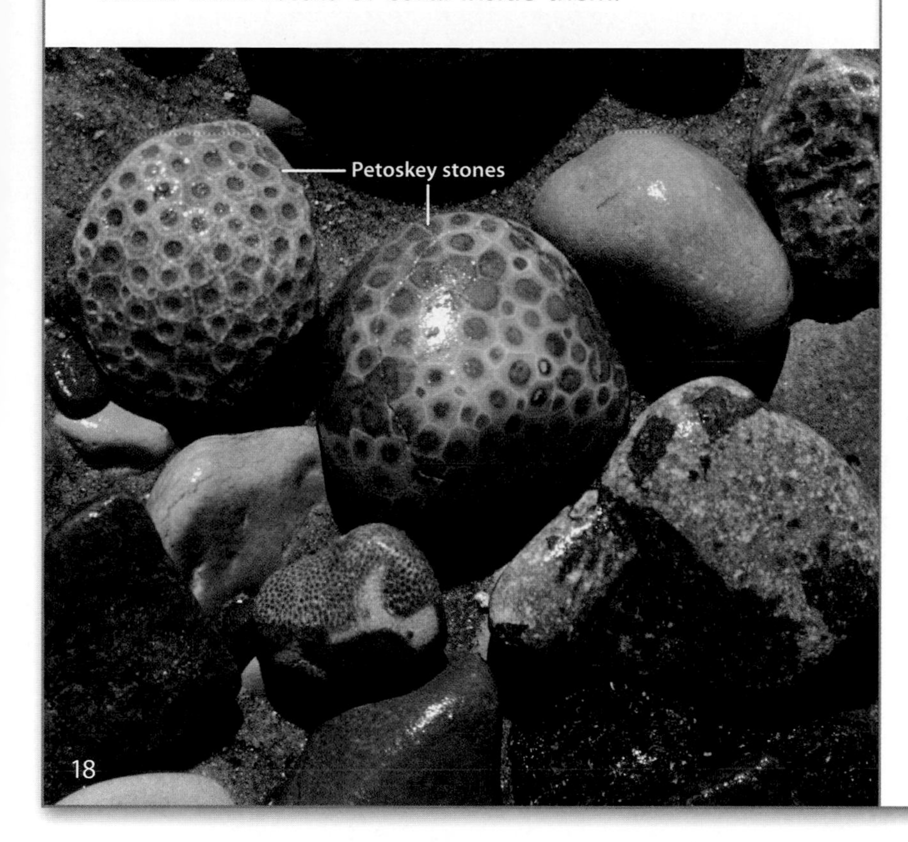

18

Water from the lake flows over the rocks and makes them smooth. Look at this polished Petoskey stone. What properties do you see?

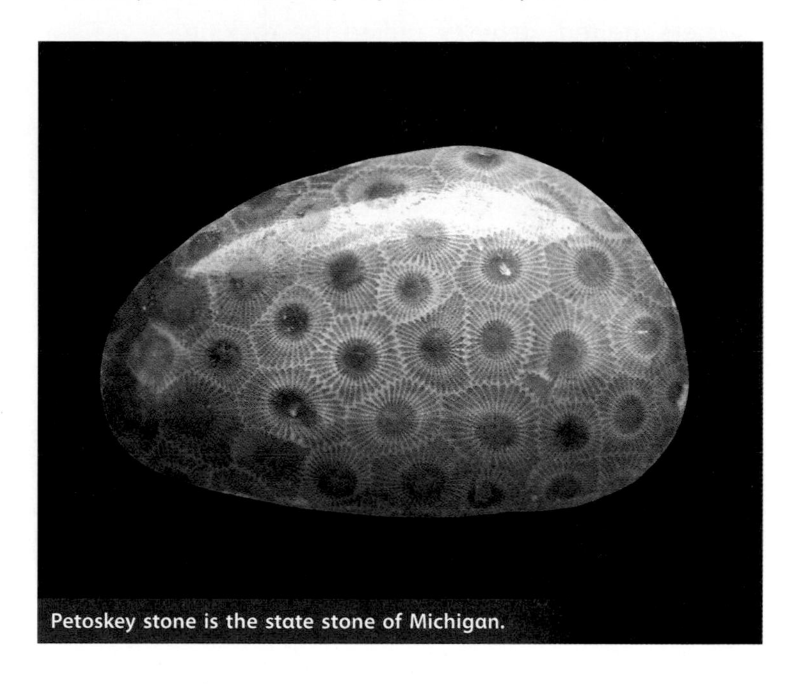

Petoskey stone is the state stone of Michigan.

19

Access Science Content

Observe Petoskey Stones

Students can use photos to observe the properties of Petoskey stones.

- Read aloud the label on page 18. Say: **Petoskey stones are often found near Petoskey, Michigan. They contain fossils of corals. Corals are tiny animals that make a hard skeleton outside their bodies. Over time, these skeletons become even harder, rock fossils.**
- Refer to the photo on page 18 as you ask: **How do the Petoskey stones look different from the other stones?** (The Petoskey stones have lines that form patterns.) Have students describe the pattern in the polished Petoskey stone on page 19. (dark centers, lines going outward, multi-sided borders)

Assess

1. **Recall What mineral is found in most of the sand around the Great Lakes?** (quartz)
2. **Cause and Effect What caused the pattern in a Petoskey stone?** (corals that became fossils)

Erosion Moves Rocks

There were once glaciers in Michigan. Glaciers moved rocks. This is called **erosion.** As the glaciers melted, **gravity** pulled the rocks to the ground from the ice.

Glaciers like this one once moved across Michigan. Glaciers are large sheets of moving ice.

erosion
Erosion is the movement of rocks or soil caused by wind, water, or ice.

gravity
Gravity is a force that pulls things toward Earth.

20

Water and wind cause erosion, too.

Waves drag sand from the beach. Waves also add sand to the beach.

Wind carries away sand. It also brings new sand to the beach.

21

Access Science Content

Recognize Ways that Rock Moves

Help students learn the role of glaciers, **gravity,** water, and wind in **erosion.**

- Read aloud the definitions and caption on page 20. Say: **Michigan's glaciers melted long ago. Gravity pulled the rocks they carried to the ground.**
- Ask students who have visited beaches: **When you stand in the waves on the beach, what happens to the sand around your feet?** (It moves.) Read aloud the caption under the first photo on page 21. Say: **Wind erodes beaches, too.** Have students point to the photo that shows blowing sand.

Make Inferences

Ask: **What new understanding can you gain from these pages?** (Possible answer: The book says waves and wind cause erosion to the beaches. I know Lake Michigan has many beaches. So I can tell that sometimes parts of beaches are lost, and sometimes parts are gained.)

Assess

1. **Recall What is a glacier?** (a large sheet of moving ice)
2. **Explain What happens to a sandy beach during the erosion process?** (Sand is carried away from the beach, or it is brought to the beach.)

Weathering Changes Rocks

Water and wind also cause **weathering.** Weathering can happen when rocks tumble in waves. It also happens when wind blows sand against rocks. Over time, the rocks wear down and become smooth.

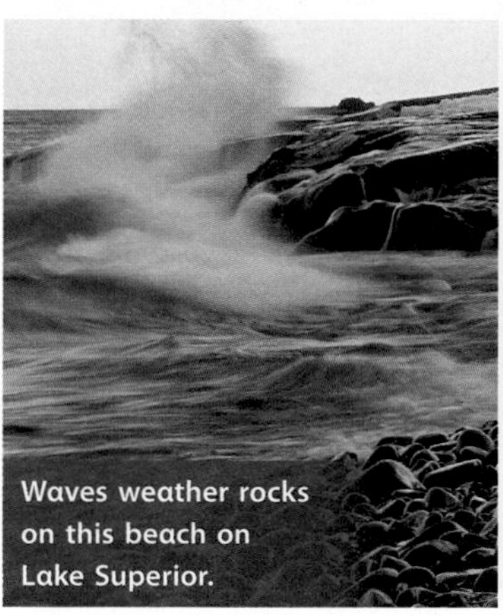
Waves weather rocks on this beach on Lake Superior.

Trees grow on these rocks that have been weathered by wind and water.

weathering
Weathering is the breaking apart or dissolving of rocks.

22

Weathering can happen when waves crash into rocks, too. Bits of rock break off. They become part of the beach. Water can also dissolve parts of rocks.

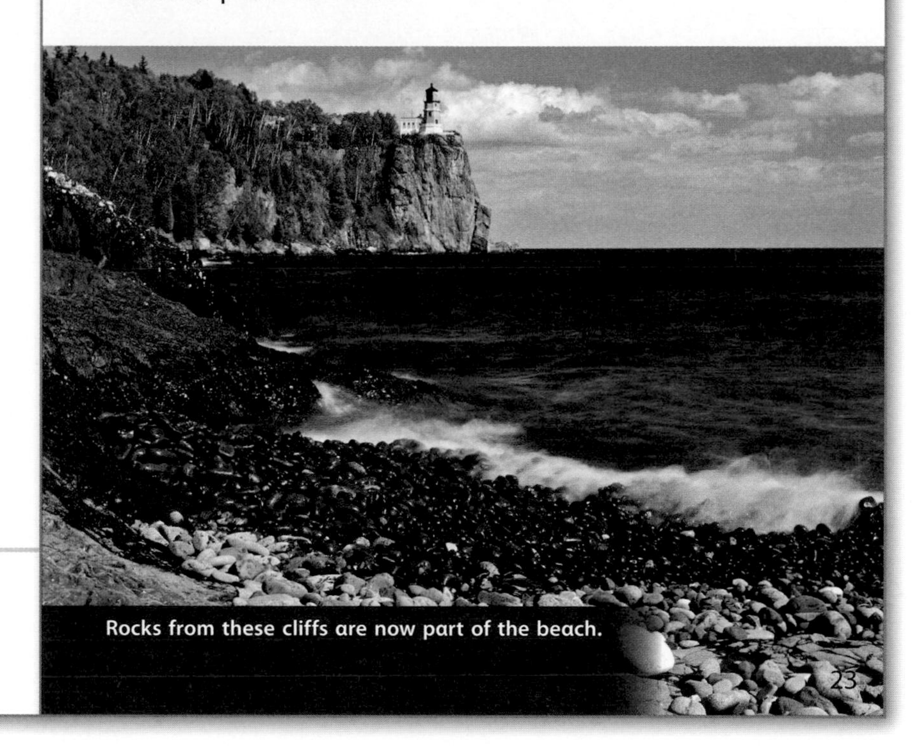
Rocks from these cliffs are now part of the beach.

23

Access Science Content

Observe Changes Caused by Weathering

Help students use photos to discover how **weathering** changes rocks.

- Read aloud the definition of **weathering.** Point to the first photo on page 22. Ask: **What is causing these rocks to become smooth?** (waves) **What have wind and water done to the rocks in the second photo?** (worn away parts, made a hole)
- Read aloud the caption on page 23. Ask: **How did the rocks break off?** (weathering by waves)

Make Inferences

Ask students what they can infer from the photo on page 23. You might ask students why they think many of the rocks are smooth. (Waves weathered and smoothed the rocks.)

Assess

1. **Name Sometimes crashing waves break rocks apart. What do we call this process?** (weathering)
2. **Cause and Effect If rocks on a beach are washed by the waves, how are they likely to change over time?** (They are likely to wear down and become smoother.)

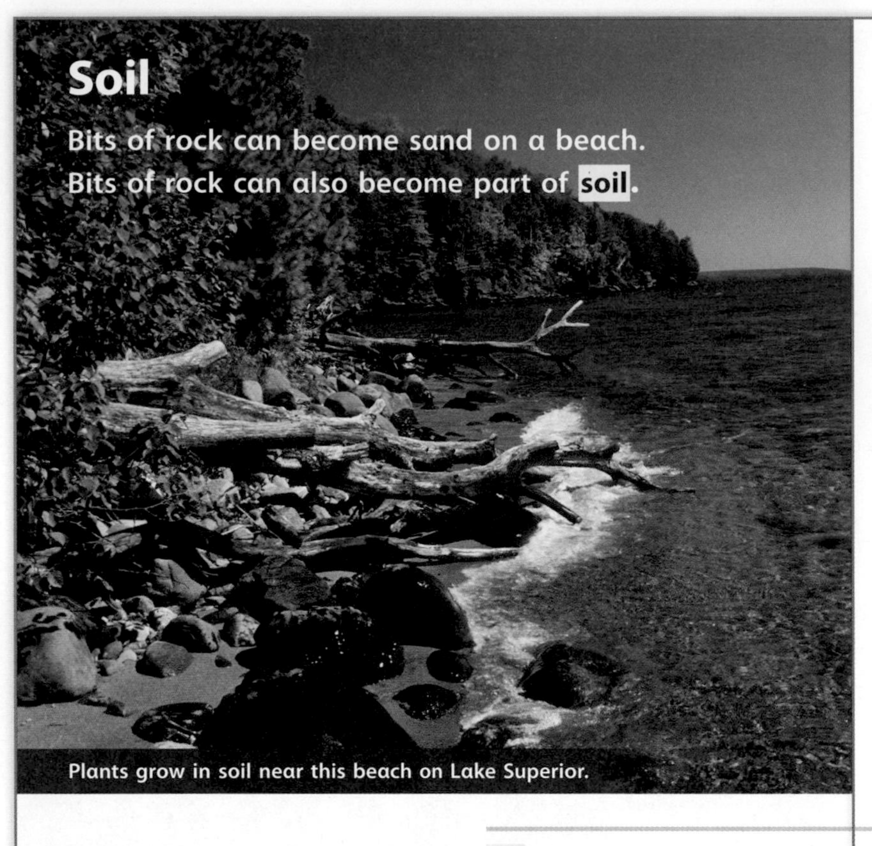

Plants grow in soil near this beach on Lake Superior.

Some soil has **humus** in it. Humus is bits of dead plants and animals. There are layers of soil near Lake Michigan. The dark layer on top has a lot of humus in it.

Plant roots hang from a dark layer of humus.

soil
Soil is a layer of loose material that covers part of Earth's surface.

humus
Humus is a part of soil. It has bits of decayed plants and animals.

24

25

Access Science Content

Describe Soil

Students can use photos and definitions to describe **soil** and its components.

- Have students look at the photo on page 24. Ask: **What in the photo is made of bits of rock?** (sand) Explain: **Soil also contains bits of rock.** Have students point out the plants that are growing in **soil** along the beach.
- Point to the photo on page 25. Say: **This soil is in layers. How do the colors of the two layers differ?** (The bottom layer is light in color and the top layer is dark.)
- Read aloud the definition at the bottom of page 25. Elaborate: **Humus gives soil a dark brown color. Humus holds water. Most plants grow well in soil that contains a lot of humus.** Have students study the photo. Ask: **Which layer contains the most humus?** (top layer)

Real-World Connections

Let students use zip bags to collect small samples of local **soil.** Have students use a hand lens to examine the samples for evidence of **humus.** Students should look for a dark brown color and for bits of partly decayed matter.

You can observe the properties of soil. Color and texture are properties of soil.

Soil in most gardens is dark brown. It feels soft.

26

Soil near most beaches has a light color. Soil made of very small bits of rocks feels smooth. Soil made of larger bits of rocks feels rough.

27

Access Science Content

Observe Properties of Different Soils

Students can view photos of soils to observe and compare their properties.

- On pages 26–27, point out the garden soil and the soil near a beach. Read the caption on page 26.
- Ask students to study the soils and compare their properties. Ask: **Which soil is darkest?** (garden soil) **Which soil would feel rough?** (soil near a beach) **Which soil is composed mainly of tiny bits of rock?** (soil near a beach) **Which soil likely contains the most moisture?** (garden soil)

Recording Observations

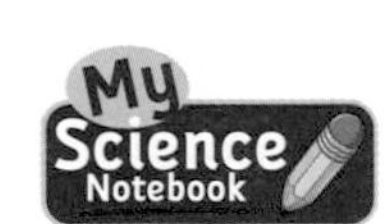

Have students suggest words to describe the soils on pages 25–27. Record the words in a three-column chart.

Assess

1. **Define What is soil?** (layer of loose material that covers part of Earth's surface)
2. **Infer Why do you think humus is mainly in the top layer of the soils near Lake Michigan?** (Many plants and animals live on or near the surface. When they die and decay, humus builds up in the top layer.)

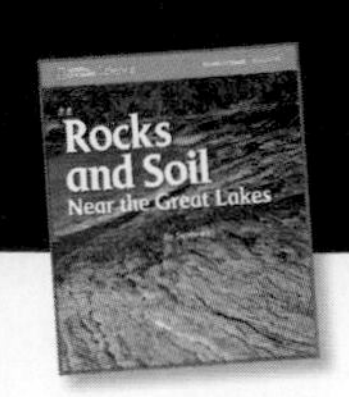

Conclusion

There are many beaches on the Great Lakes. Beaches can have rocks and sandy soil. Rocks and soil have properties, such as texture and color. Weathering and erosion can change rocks to soil over time.

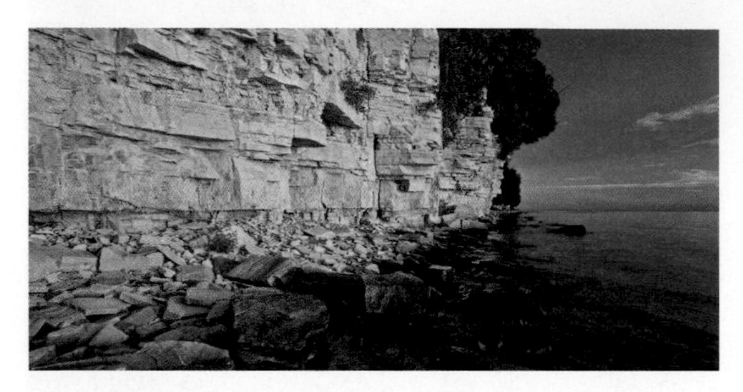

Think About the Big Ideas

1. What can you observe about rocks near the Great Lakes?
2. How do rocks change?
3. What can you observe about soil?

28

Following the ***Conclusion*** page of the *Become an Expert* book, rearrange groups to begin the ***Share and Compare*** section on page T89.

Conclusion

Sum Up

Tell students that a conclusion helps sum up the big ideas in a book. Have students restate the conclusion in their own words.

Answer the Big Idea Questions

Encourage students to sum up what they learned in the book and then share responses to the questions aloud.

1. **What can you observe about rocks near the Great Lakes?** (Some are layered. Some contain quartz. Petoskey stones contain fossilized coral.)
2. **How do rocks change?** (Water, wind, and glaciers move rock from place to place. Gravity pulls rocks down. Wind and waves can smooth rocks.)
3. **What can you observe about soil?** (The soil contains bits of rock. It may have layers, with humus in the top layer.)

Share and Compare

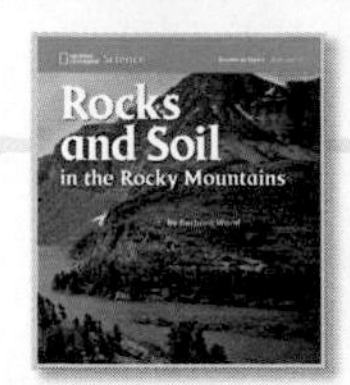

Turn and Talk

Compare rocks and soil in your books. How are they different? How are they alike?

Read

Find your favorite part of the book and read it to a classmate.

Write

Bring a rock to class. Write about its properties. Share your writing with a classmate.

Draw

Draw a picture that shows weathering or erosion. Talk about your drawing with a classmate.

29

Program Resources

Become an Expert Books

- *Rocks and Soil in the Rocky Mountains*
- *Rocks and Soil in the High Desert*
- *Rocks and Soil Near the Great Lakes*

eEdition at myNGconnect.com

Turn and Talk

Ask students to turn to a classmate and compare the rocks and soil they learned about in their Become an Expert books. Prompt students by asking:

- **How are the rocks you learned about alike and different?**
- **What are the different kinds of soil you learned about?**

Read

After students have read their favorite excerpts from each book, invite them to discuss the rocks and soils that they studied.

Write

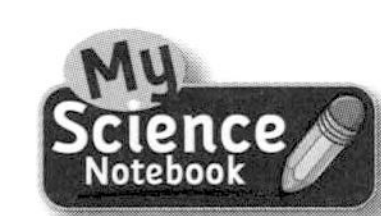

Have students bring in a rock. In their science notebook, have them write a few sentences describing its properties, such as color, texture, hardness, and whether it has layers. Students can share what they wrote with a classmate.

Draw

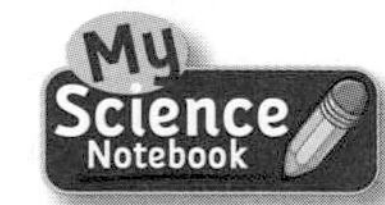

In their science notebook, have students draw an example of weathering or erosion. Have them label their pictures with the name of the process that they drew. Ask students to share their drawings.

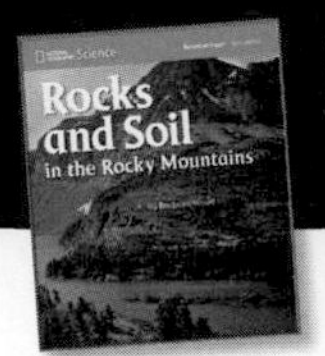

Meet Beverly Goodman

Scientists try to answer questions. They explore nature and make observations. Then they tell people what they find.

Beverly Goodman is a scientist. She studies rocks and soil on coasts, or land by water.

Beverly's team found a thick layer of shells underwater near Israel. Beverly wanted to find out why so many shells were there. By exploring, she and her team found that the layer of shells had pieces of pottery and rounded beach pebbles mixed together. These clues showed that a tsunami must have taken place. A tsunami is a huge wave. It can wash away rocks and soil, and even shells, and carry them to new places.

30

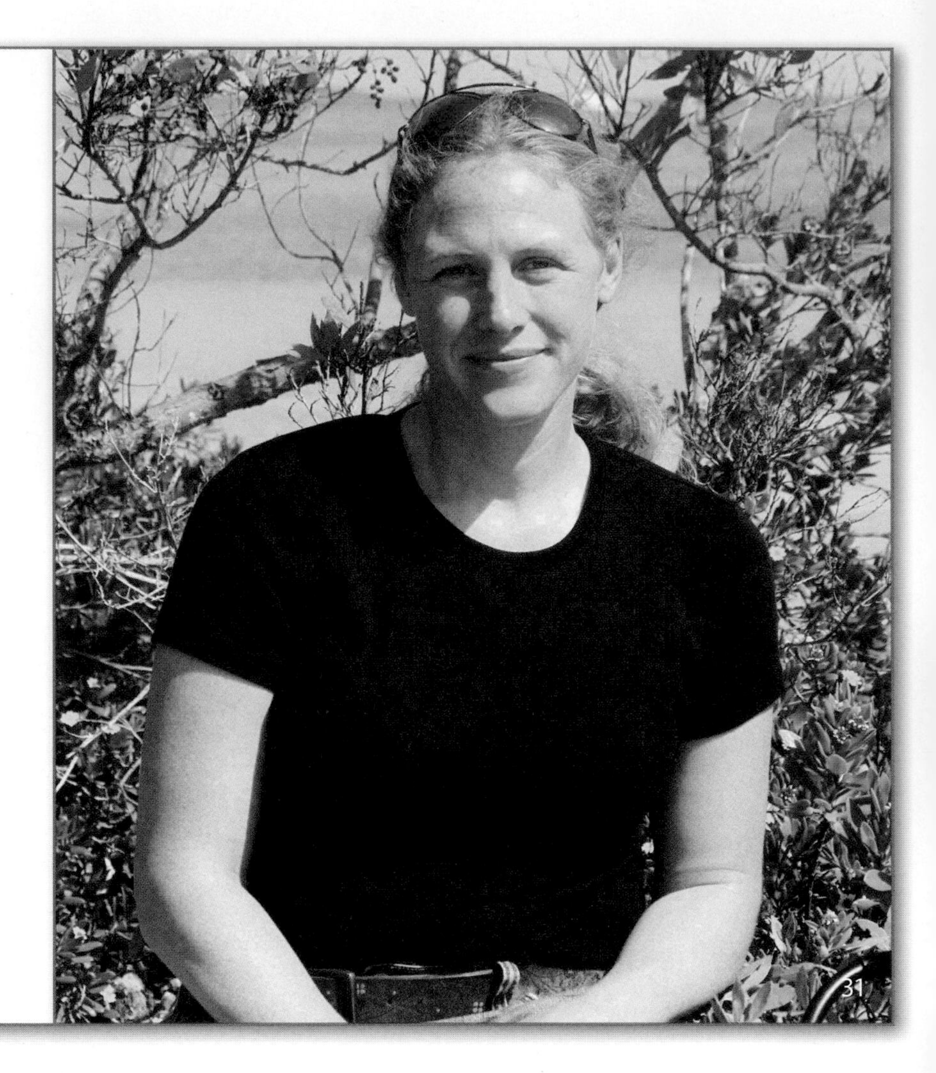

31

Science Career

Invite students to share what they learned about Beverly Goodman and the places where she does her work when they watched the *Rocks and Soil* video at the beginning of the unit. Ask students what they find interesting about Beverly Goodman's science career.

Technology in Earth Science

Discuss how scientists often use technology in scientific studies. Mention some of the technology that scientists use, such as cameras, video equipment, compasses, magnifying tools, or computers.

Find Out More

Help students research other science careers such as meteorology, oceanography, and geology.

5 Independently Use Multiple Strategies

Read Informational Text

Explore on Your Own books provide additional opportunities for your students to

- deepen their science content knowledge even more as they focus on one Big Idea
- independently apply multiple reading comprehension strategies as they read.

After applying the strategies in the Become an Expert books, students will independently read Explore on Your Own books. Facsimiles of the Explore on Your Own pages are shown on pages T92–T94.

Remind students to use multiple strategies on their own. Good readers

- use different strategies throughout a single text
- choose which strategies to use and when to use them.

In your classroom, post the Four Key Reading Comprehension Strategies so students can refer to them as they read on their own.

Preview and Predict

- Look over the text.
- Form ideas about how the text is organized and what it says.
- Confirm ideas about how the text is organized and what it says.

Monitor and Fix Up

- Think about whether the text is making sense and how it relates to what you know.
- Identify comprehension problems and clear up the problems.

Make Inferences

- Use what you know to figure out what is not said or shown directly.

Sum Up

- Pull together the text's big ideas.

EXPLORE ON YOUR OWN BOOKS ▫ *Independent*

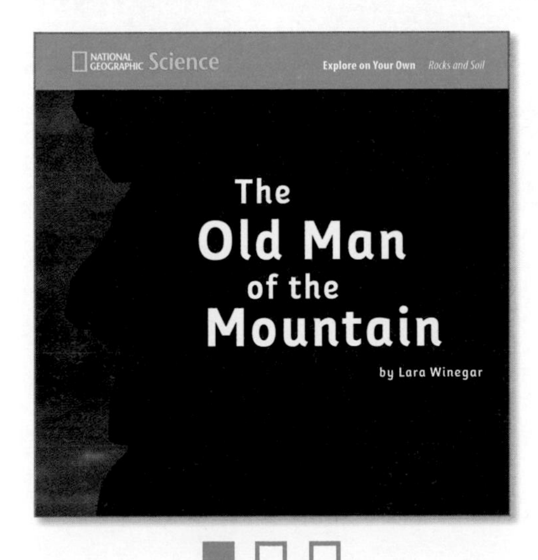

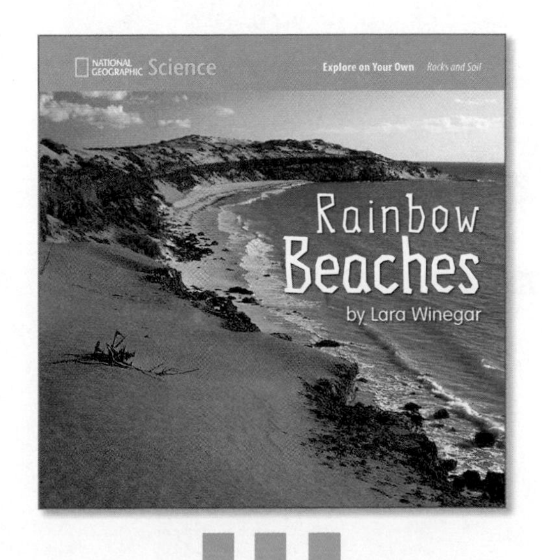

eEdition at myNGconnect.com

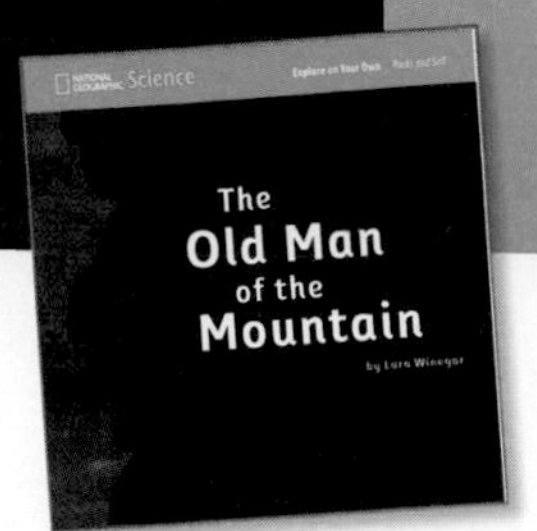

EXPLORE ON YOUR OWN ▫ *The Old Man of the Mountain*

Big Idea Question **How do rocks change?**

Unit Vocabulary *weathering, gravity*

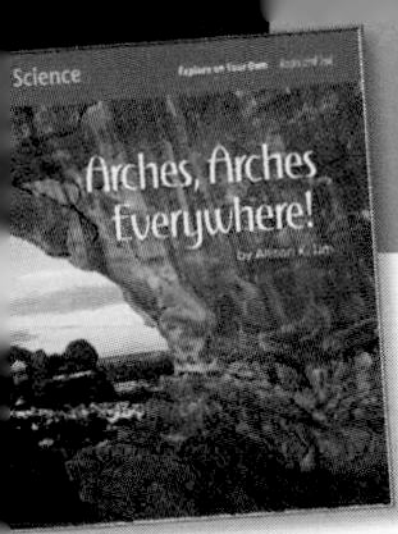

EXPLORE ON YOUR OWN ▫ *Arches, Arches Everywhere!*

Big Idea Question **How do rocks change?**

Unit Vocabulary *weathering, erosion*

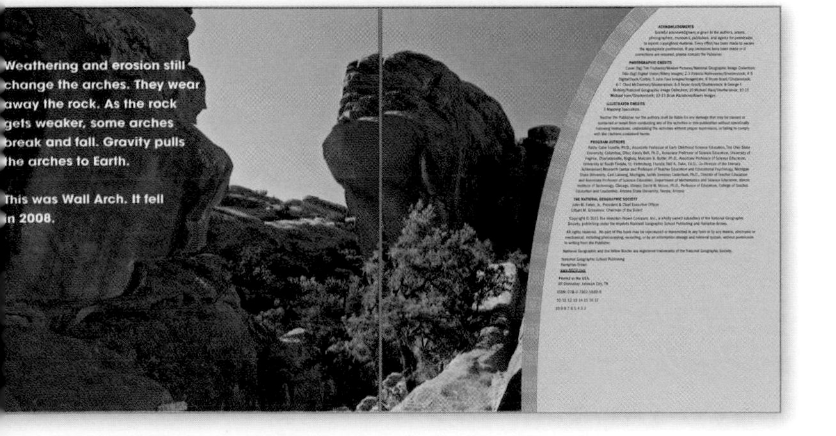

Big Idea Question **How do rocks change?**

Unit Vocabulary *weathering, mineral*

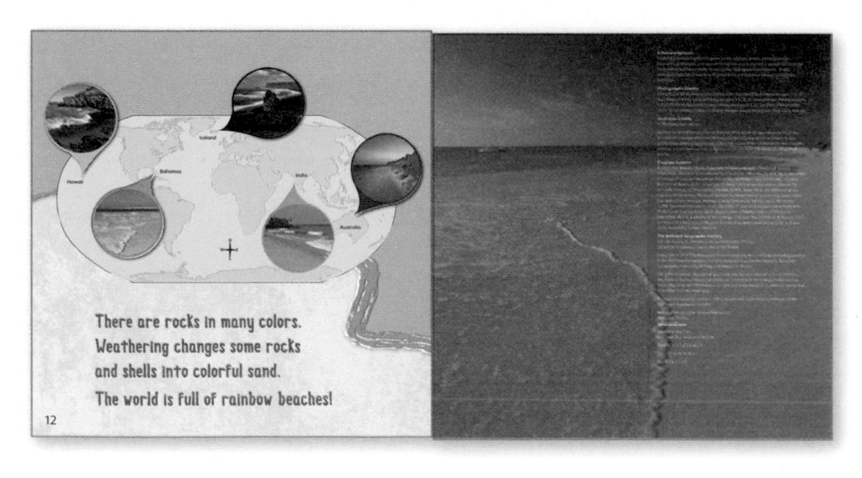

Write and Wrap up

Contents

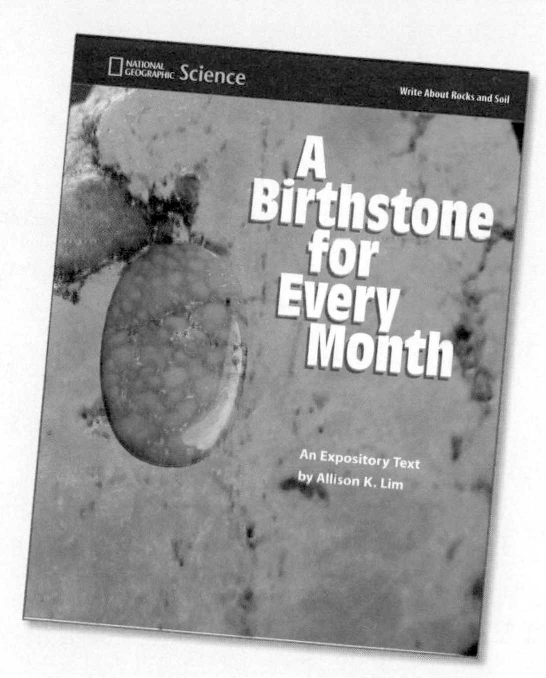
NATIONAL GEOGRAPHIC Science
Write About Rocks and Soil
A Birthstone for Every Month
An Expository Text
by Allison K. Lim

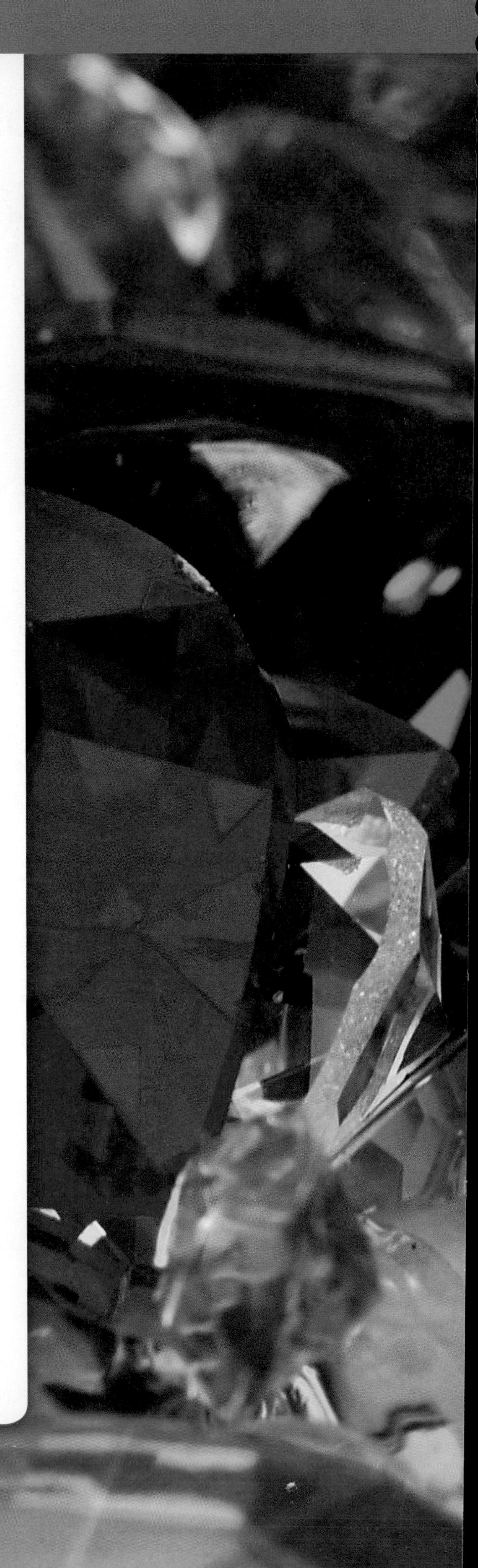

Teach the Genre

Nonfiction Narrative
Expository Text
Persuasive Text
Procedural Text

A genre has specific characteristics.

A Birthstone for Every Month includes several characteristics of an expository text.

AUTHOR'S PURPOSE ▫ Convey Information

- Expository texts report what is known about a particular topic in the natural world. The author gives information learned from experience and research.
- This book is about birthstones, which are found in nature.

TEXT STRUCTURE ▫ Opening Statement

- Expository texts often have an opening statement or general classification about the topic being presented.
- The beginning of this text includes, "Today, every month has a gemstone. They are called birthstones."

TEXT STRUCTURE ▫ Description of Characteristics

- Expository texts often describe the characteristics of living things, objects, or events.
- This text describes the characteristics of each birthstone. For example, the birthstone for January is a garnet. Most garnets are red.

GARNET	
Birthstone month	January
Color	red; different color
Uses	in sandpaper; glass polisher

TEXT FEATURES ▫ Photographs

- Expository texts often have photographs.
- This text includes photographs of birthstones in the rough and photographs after the birthstones are cut and polished.

TEXT FEATURES ▫ Specialized Vocabulary

- Expository texts often include some specialized vocabulary.
- This text uses specialized vocabulary, such as *crystals* and *minerals*.

Read Aloud

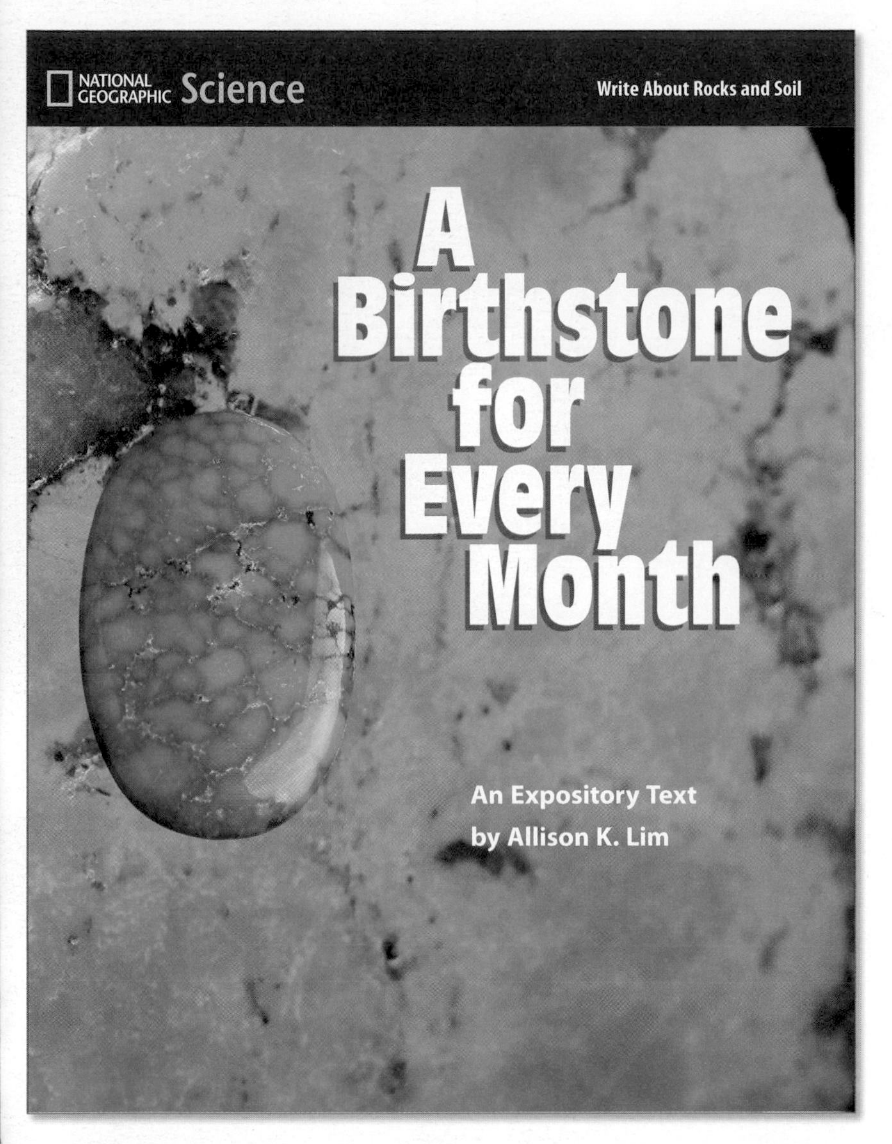

Introduce *A Birthstone for Every Month*

Display the cover and read the title, genre, and author's name. Tell students that they will learn information about the natural world—in this case, birthstones.

Tap Prior Knowledge

Tell students that they will read a book about birthstones. Engage students in a discussion about birthstones.

You might ask:

- **What do you know about birthstones?**
- **Do you know what your birthstone is?**
- **In nature, where do you think birthstones come from?**

Read for Different Purposes

You may want to read this book aloud to students twice. Read the first time for **science content,** finding places to draw attention to the unit's Big Ideas. Read the second time for **genre and writer's craft,** pointing out characteristics of expository writing and highlighting writer's craft. See pages T98–T100 for suggestions.

Read Aloud, continued

Read for Science Content

Read aloud the first paragraph on page 4. Point out that most birthstones are made of minerals. Ask: **Are minerals living or nonliving?** (nonliving)

Ask students to recall other nonliving things they have learned about, such as rocks and soil. Ask: **Are these things made by people or are they part of nature?** (They are part of nature.) Point out the photos on pages 4–5. Tell students that the rough birthstones found in nature are cut and then polished to make them smooth and shiny.

Have students discuss how people find birthstones. Remind students that many useful rocks are mined from the ground. Help them realize that birthstones can also be found underground.

Read for Genre and Writer's Craft

Tell students that expository texts sometimes have a Contents page. Display page 3. Point out that the Contents page includes an introduction and headings that list the birthstones for each month. The Contents page also includes page numbers that show where each topic is found.

Model how to read the Contents page by moving your finger from the heading *Introduction* to the page number on which the Introduction is found. Ask: **On what page would you find the Introduction?** (page 4) Have students find the page that includes information about their birthstone.

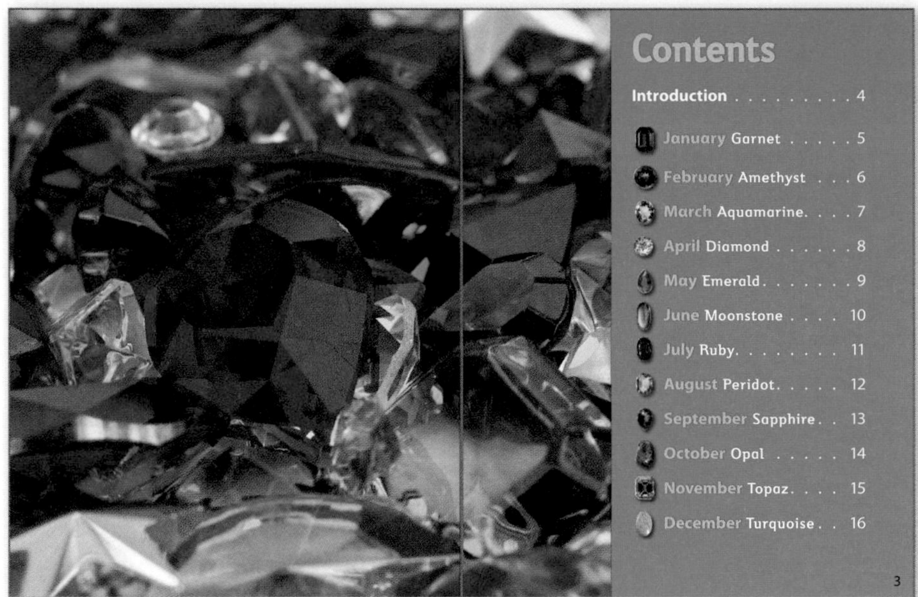

Contents

3

Introduction

Most gemstones are made of minerals. Long ago, people thought these colorful stones were magical. Today, every month has a gemstone. They are called birthstones.

Cut gemstones can be polished and made smooth. Uncut gemstones are called rough gemstones.

4

January
Garnet

The birthstone for January is garnet. Most garnets are red. But they can be many other colors as well. Garnets are used to make sandpaper and to polish glass.

5

February
Amethyst

The birthstone for February is amethyst. Amethysts are purple. Many amethysts form into crystals. The crystals have pointed tops and six sides.

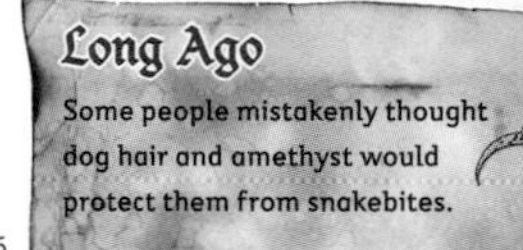

6

March
Aquamarine

The birthstone for March is aquamarine. Aquamarines are blue. *Aquamarine* means "water" and "sea." Some say people made eyeglasses with aquamarine 2,000 years ago!

7

April
Diamond

The birthstone for April is diamond. Most diamonds are clear. Diamonds are the hardest stones. Tools with diamond blades can cut through rock, concrete, and metal!

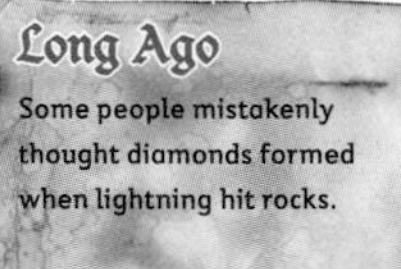

8

May
Emerald

The birthstone for May is emerald. Emeralds are green. People mined emeralds in Egypt thousands of years ago.

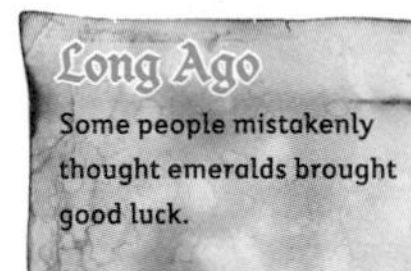

9

June
Moonstone

The birthstone for June is moonstone. Some moonstones are a shimmery pale blue. When light changes, moonstones may look different and appear to be another color.

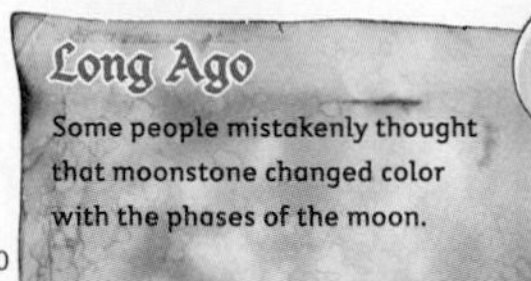

10

July
Ruby

The birthstone for July is ruby. Rubies are usually red. Some rubies look like they have a star inside.

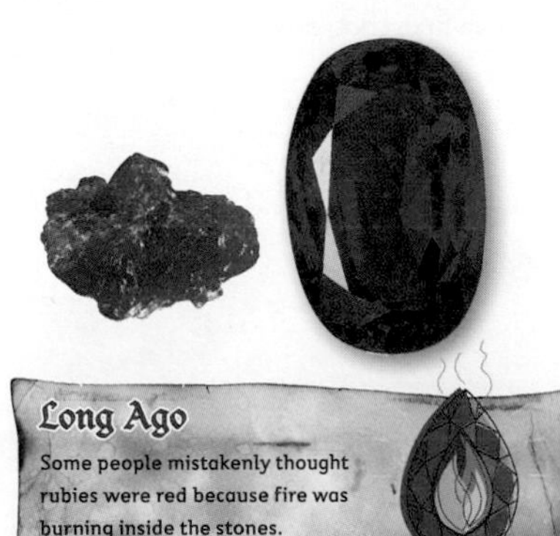

11

Read for Science Content

Remind students that a *property* is something about an object that you can observe with your senses. Ask students to give some examples of properties of rocks or stones, such as color, having layers, and strength. List their answers. Note that strength is whether a rock is crumbly or strong. It's how easily a rock breaks.

Have students look at the photos on page 6. Ask them to compare the color of the cut and the uncut amethyst. (The color is the same.) Ask: **How is the uncut amethyst different from the polished amethyst?** (This uncut amethyst has points and prongs. The polished amethyst has been cut into a perfect shape.)

Point out the diamonds on page 8. Tell students that diamonds are minerals. Ask: **Why do people use diamonds to make blades?** (Diamonds are hard.) Explain that one of the properties of diamonds is that they are harder than other minerals, concrete, or even metal. Because of this, saw blades that include bits of diamonds can cut through these materials. Hardness is a property of minerals only.

Read for Genre and Writer's Craft

Explain that expository texts often present ways that things are alike and different. Have students look at the set of photos on different pages. Ask: **What is the difference between the two photos of a birthstone on each page?** (One shows how the birthstone looks when it is uncut and the other shows how the birthstone looks when it is cut and polished.)

Tell students that expository texts often include headings. Read the headings *March* and *Aquamarine* on page 7. Ask: **What do the headings tell you?** (They tell you what month and what birthstone is being discussed.)

Read Aloud, continued

Read for Science Content

Remind students that people use earth materials, such as rocks and minerals, for different purposes. Ask: **What are many of the birthstones in this book used for?** (jewelry)

Remind students that earth materials are often mixtures of different things. Soil, for example, is a mixture of air, water, humus, and weathered rock. The color of a soil depends on its makeup. Ask students to look at the photo of an opal on page 14 and read the text. Point out that opals can have slightly different colors. Ask: **Why aren't all opals the same color?** (Opals may be made of different mixtures of minerals and other materials.)

Read for Genre and Writer's Craft

Point out to students the Author's Note on the inside back cover of the book. Ask students if the author knew all about birthstones before she began writing the book. Lead them to understand that the author did research to find out the information in the book. Tell them that authors of expository texts often do research before writing and want to share what they have learned with others.

August
Peridot

The birthstone for August is peridot. Peridots are green. Peridots are formed in volcanic rocks.

12

September
Sapphire

The birthstone for September is sapphire. Most sapphires are blue. They can be any color but red. Some sapphires look blue outdoors and purple indoors.

13

October
Opal

The birthstone for October is opal. Opals are colorful. Each one is different. Opals have water trapped inside them. Most opals formed when dinosaurs were alive!

14

November
Topaz

The birthstone for November is yellow or gold topaz. Some topaz is transparent. You can see through it!

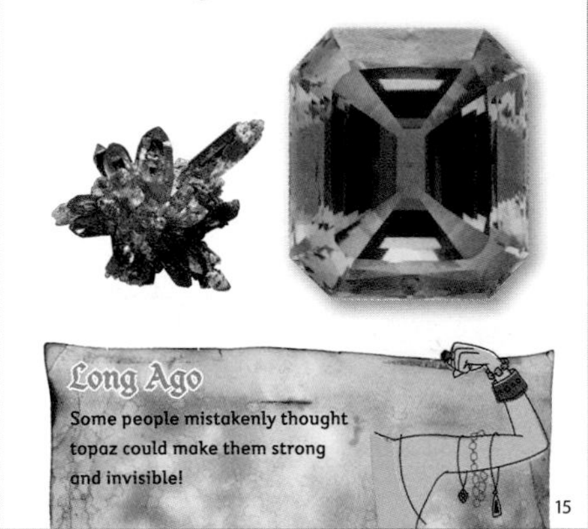

15

December
Turquoise

The birthstone for December is turquoise. Turquoise is greenish blue. Different minerals give turquoise its color. Turquoise can have lines that look like a web.

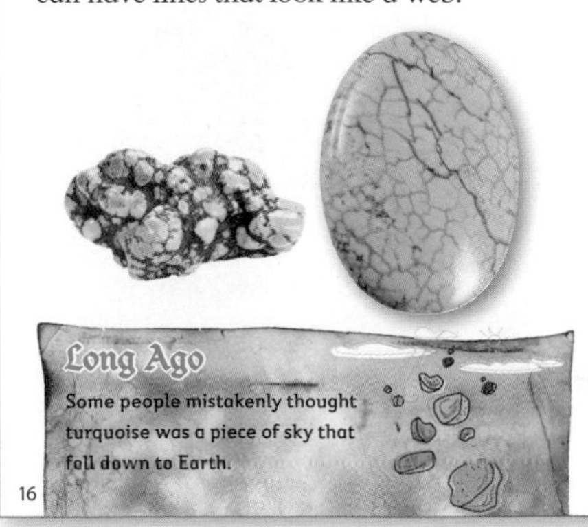

16

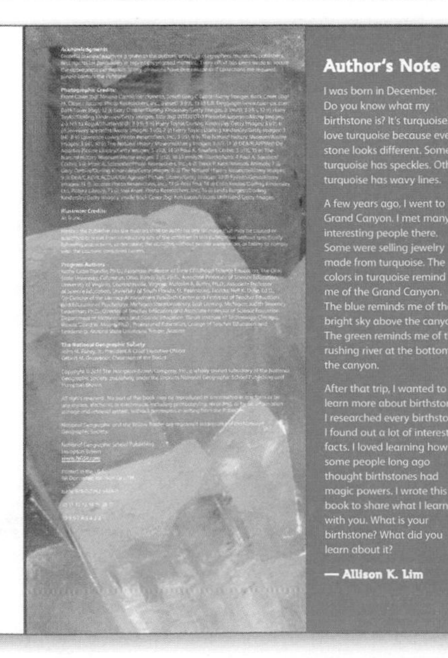
Author's Note

I was born in December. Do you know what my birthstone is? It's turquoise! I love turquoise because every stone looks different. Some turquoise has speckles. Other turquoise has wavy lines.

A few years ago, I went to the Grand Canyon. I met many interesting people there. Some were selling jewelry made from turquoise. The colors in turquoise remind me of the Grand Canyon. The blue reminds me of the bright sky above the canyon. The green reminds me of the rushing river at the bottom of the canyon.

After that trip, I wanted to learn more about birthstones. I researched every birthstone. I found out a lot of interesting facts. I loved learning how some people long ago thought birthstones had magic powers. I wrote this book to share what I learned with you. What is your birthstone? What did you learn about it?

— Allison K. Lim

Writing Projects

Dear Patty,

Today I learned about birthstones. Birthstones are gemstones. My birthday is in May. So my birthstone is emerald. Emeralds are green and are used in rings and other jewelry. People used to think that emeralds brought good luck.

What is your birthstone? Write and tell me about it.

Take care,

Sue

Writing Projects

After reading *A Birthstone for Every Month,* students can respond through writing. Here are some different writing projects to choose from.

For each project, provide models for students so they can incorporate common informational text features, such as a Contents page, opening statements, headings, descriptions of characteristics, or photos.

Provide a time for students to share their work with one another in small groups.

Write a Letter

- Have students write a letter to a friend or relative about birthstones. Explain that letters to friends or relatives usually have a friendly tone. Tell students to think of them as written chats with a friend.
- Help students learn to structure a letter if they do not already know how to do so.
- In the body of the letter, have students share what they have learned about birthstones. They might tell about their own birthstone, and also ask about the pen pal's birthstone.
- Encourage students to use some expository text features, such as description of characteristics or specialized vocabulary.
- Have students send their letters.

Make a Table

- Have students work in small groups to make tables about birthstones. Assign each group three to four birthstones.
- Each table should have a title, columns, and rows. As a group, students should decide what they would like to include in their tables. For example, the tables could include interesting facts about the birthstones, as well as physical properties.
- Have students compile their data into a poster-sized class table. This table can be displayed for other classes or posted in the library or in a local nature center. Invite students to use the table to teach others about birthstones.

Writing Projects, continued

Write a Field Guide

- Have students work as a class to write a field guide about birthstones.
- Before students begin writing, show them examples of field guides. Point out that field guides are used to identify birds, trees, minerals, and other things found in nature. Field guides include photos or illustrations, captions, and labels. They also include information about properties and uses of the things found in nature.
- Have small groups of students focus on different birthstones. If the field guide is prepared on the computer, tell students to use the **Digital Library** at **myNGconnect.com** to find photos of their birthstones. They can also look for photos that show how the birthstones are used.
- If students are working on paper, suggest that students place a photo, picture, or illustration and a label of each birthstone on a sheet of paper. They can write captions or labels that describe the stone's properties, uses, and other information.
- Have students organize the pages in alphabetical order, based on the names of the birthstones. If students are working on paper, have them work cooperatively to bind the pages together into a book. Place the book in the school office or library to share it with other classes to help them identify birthstones.

Build a Rock Collection

SMALL GROUP

Steps

1. Have students work outside in small groups to gather rocks. Suggest that they look for rocks that they find interesting or unusual, such as rocks with fossils.
2. If time permits, give students an extra day or two to bring in rocks from home.
3. Place a limit on the number of rocks each group contributes to the collection, such as five rocks. Have students work together in their groups to select the rocks to include in the class collection.
4. Tell students to assign a number to each rock. They should write labels and captions that describe the properties of the rocks. Have them use a table to organize the information.

ROCK PROPERTIES

	Color	Layers	Strength	Fossils
Rock 1	brown	layers	crumbly	no
Rock 2	white	no layers	strong	no

5. Have students refer to photos in the Digital Library at myNGconnect.com to try to identify the rocks in their collection.
6. Have each group present their rock collection to the class. Students should explain why they included certain rocks in the collection and sum up the properties of their rocks.
7. Help students create a class rock collection by combining the small groups' collections. Afterward, set up the rock collection in the school's display case. Invite students to present their collection to other classes.

Present the Big Ideas

After students present their work, lead them in a discussion to talk through the Big Ideas of the unit, helping them see in what ways their rock collection features the unit's Big Ideas.

- What can you observe about rocks?
- How do rocks change?
- What can you observe about soil?

NATIONAL GEOGRAPHIC

Science

	Kindergarten
LIFE SCIENCE	Plants **How Are Plants Alike and Different?**
	Animals **How Are Animals Alike and Different?**
EARTH SCIENCE	Day and Night **How Are Day and Night Different?**
	Weather and Seasons **What Can You Observe About the Weather?**
PHYSICAL SCIENCE	Observing Objects **What Can You Observe About Objects?**
	How Things Move **How Do Things Move?**

K–2 Scope and Sequence

Grades 1–2

Living Things
Chapter 1 **How Are Living and Nonliving Things Different?**
Chapter 2 **What Are the Basic Needs of Plants?**
Chapter 3 **What Are the Basic Needs of Humans and Animals?**

Habitats
Chapter 1 **Where Do Plants and Animals Live?**
Chapter 2 **What Do Plants and Animals Need to Survive?**
Chapter 3 **How Do Plants and Animals Depend on Each Other?**

Plants and Animals
Chapter 1 **How Are Plants Alike and Different?**
Chapter 2 **How Are Animals Alike and Different?**
Chapter 3 **How Do Plants and Animals Change?**

Life Cycles
Chapter 1 **How Do Plants Grow and Change?**
Chapter 2 **How Do Humans and Animals Grow and Change?**
Chapter 3 **How Did Some Plants and Animals Become Extinct?**

Land and Water
Chapter 1 **How Do People Use Earth's Land?**
Chapter 2 **How Do People Use Earth's Water?**
Chapter 3 **How Does Earth's Land Change?**

Rocks and Soil
Chapter 1 **What Can You Observe About Rocks?**
Chapter 2 **How Do Rocks Change?**
Chapter 3 **What Can You Observe About Soil?**

Sun, Moon, and Stars
Chapter 1 **What Can You See in the Sky?**
Chapter 2 **What Can You Observe About the Sun?**
Chapter 3 **What Can You Observe About the Moon?**

Weather
Chapter 1 **How Does the Sun Affect Earth?**
Chapter 2 **How Does Weather Change?**
Chapter 3 **How Is Weather Measured?**

Properties
Chapter 1 **How Can You Describe Objects?**
Chapter 2 **How Can You Compare Objects?**
Chapter 3 **What Are Solids and Liquids?**

Solids, Liquids, and Gases
Chapter 1 **What Are Solids, Liquids, and Gases?**
Chapter 2 **How Can You Observe and Measure Properties?**
Chapter 3 **How Do Liquids and Solids Change?**

Pushes and Pulls
Chapter 1 **What Are Pushes and Pulls?**
Chapter 2 **What Ways Do Objects Move?**
Chapter 3 **How Do Magnets Pull Objects?**

Forces and Motion
Chapter 1 **What Is a Force?**
Chapter 2 **What Is Gravity?**
Chapter 3 **What Are Magnets?**

NATIONAL GEOGRAPHIC

Science

Grade 3

LIFE SCIENCE

Chapter 1 **How Do Plants Live and Grow?**
Chapter 2 **How Are Animals Alike and Different?**
Chapter 3 **How Do Plants and Animals Live in Their Environment?**
Chapter 4 **How Do Plants and Animals Survive?**
Chapter 5 **How Do Plants and Animals Respond to Seasons?**

EARTH SCIENCE

Chapter 1 **How Are the Sun, Earth, and Moon Connected?**
Chapter 2 **What Properties Can You Observe About the Sun?**
Chapter 3 **What Can You Observe About Stars?**
Chapter 4 **What Can You Observe About Earth's Materials?**
Chapter 5 **What Are Earth's Resources?**
Chapter 6 **How Does Weathering and Erosion Change the Land?**
Chapter 7 **How Does Earth's Surface Change Quickly?**
Chapter 8 **How Does Earth's Water Move and Change?**

PHYSICAL SCIENCE

Chapter 1 **How Can You Describe and Measure Matter?**
Chapter 2 **What Are States of Matter?**
Chapter 3 **How Does Force Change Motion?**
Chapter 4 **What Is Energy?**
Chapter 5 **What Is Light?**

3–5 Scope and Sequence

Grade 4	Grade 5
Chapter 1 How Do Plants Grow and Reproduce? Chapter 2 How Do Animals Grow and Change? Chapter 3 How Do Living Things Depend on Their Environment? Chapter 4 How Do Adaptations Help Living Things Survive? Chapter 5 How Do Living Things Interact with Their Environment? Chapter 6 How Do the Parts of an Organism Work Together?	Chapter 1 How Do Scientists Classify Living Things? Chapter 2 What Are the Interactions in Ecosystems? Chapter 3 How Does Energy Move in an Ecosystem? Chapter 4 How Do Living Things Survive and Change? Chapter 5 How Do Parts of Living Things Work Together?
Chapter 1 How Do Earth and Its Moon Move? Chapter 2 How Are Rocks Alike and Different? Chapter 3 What Are Renewable and Nonrenewable Resources? Chapter 4 How Do Slow Processes Change Earth's Surface? Chapter 5 What Changes Do Volcanoes and Earthquakes Cause? Chapter 6 What Can We Observe About Weather?	Chapter 1 How Do Earth and Its Moon Create Cycles? Chapter 2 What Makes Up the Solar System? Chapter 3 How Are Rocks and Minerals Identified? Chapter 4 How Can We Protect Earth's Resources? Chapter 5 How Are Weather and the Water Cycle Connected?
Chapter 1 How Can You Describe and Measure Properties of Matter? Chapter 2 What Are Physical and Chemical Changes? Chapter 3 How Do Forces Act? Chapter 4 What Is Magnetism? Chapter 5 What Are Some Forms of Energy? Chapter 6 What Is Sound? Chapter 7 What Is Electricity?	Chapter 1 How Can You Describe Matter, Mixtures, and Solutions? Chapter 2 How Can Matter Change? Chapter 3 How Do You Describe Force and the Laws of Motion? Chapter 4 What Are Simple Machines? Chapter 5 How Do You Describe Different Forms of Energy? Chapter 6 How Does Electrical Energy Flow and Transform?

Metric and SI Units

The metric system is also called the International System of Units, or SI. Scientists, as well as most countries throughout the world, use the metric system. The United States uses customary units. The chart below will help you convert units between metric measurements and customary measurements.

	METRIC/SI	CUSTOMARY	CONVERSION	
Distance	centimeter	inch	1 cm = .39 in	1 in = 2.54 cm
	meter	foot	1 m = 3.28 ft	1 ft = .30 m
	kilometer	mile	1 km = .62 mi	1 mi = 1.61 km
Volume	milliliter	teaspoon	1 mL = .20 tsp	1 tsp = 4.93 mL
	liter	pint	1 L = 2.12 pt	1 pt = .47 L
	liter	quart	1 L = 1.06 qt	1 qt = .95 L
	liter	gallon	1 L = .26 gal	1 gal = 3.79 L
Mass	gram	ounce	1 g = .035 oz	1 oz = 28.35 g
	kilogram	pound	1 kg = 2.2 lbs	1 lb = .45 kg
Temperature	Celsius	Fahrenheit		
	0° water freezes	32° water freezes	°C = 5/9 (°F – 32)	
	100° water boils	212° water boils	°F = 9/5 °C + 32	

CONVERTING AMONG CUSTOMARY UNITS	
Distance	12 inches = 1 foot; 3 feet = 1 yard; 5280 feet = 1 mile
Volume	1 pint = 16 ounces; 1 quart = 32 ounces; 1 gallon = 128 ounces
Mass	1 pound = 16 ounces; 1 ton = 2000 pounds

CONVERTING AMONG METRIC UNITS	
Distance	1 centimeter = .01 meter; 1 kilometer = 1000 meters
Volume	1 milliliter = .001 liter
Mass	1 milligram = .001 gram; 1 kilogram = 1000 grams

Materials List

	INQUIRY	KIT MATERIALS	SCHOOL-SUPPLIED MATERIALS
CHAPTER 1 **What Can You Observe About Rocks?**	**Explore Activity** *Investigate Properties of Rocks* What are some properties of rocks you can observe? p. T1e	3 rocks hand lens metric ruler	crayons
	Directed Inquiry *Investigate More Properties of Rocks* How can you use properties to sort rocks? p. T15a	6 rocks hand lens	
CHAPTER 2 **How Do Rocks Change?**	**Directed Inquiry** *Investigate How Rocks Wear Away* What happens to sandstone when it is shaken in a jar with water? p. T15g	hand lens paper plate plastic jar with lid plastic spoon sandstone rock stopwatch	safety goggles water
	Guided Inquiry *Investigate How Water Affects Soil* What happens when you pour water slowly and quickly onto a hill of soil? p. T25e	clear plastic cup measuring cup paper cup plastic tub sandy soil spray bottle	2 books safety goggles water
CHAPTER 3 **What Can You Observe About Soil?**	**Guided Inquiry** *Investigate Soil Properties* Which kind of soil can hold the most water—sandy soil, humus, or clay soil? p. T25k	3 paper plates clay soil, humus, sandy soil clear plastic cup funnel hand lens measuring cup plastic spoon soil property card (Learning Master 26)	marker (for teacher use) newspapers (for teacher use) paper towel safety goggles water (100 mL)
UNIT INQUIRY	**Open Inquiry** *Do Your Own Investigation* Investigation Model: What happens if you grow some lima bean seedlings in sandy soil and some lima bean seedlings in humus soil? p. T37a	cup hand lens humus metric ruler plastic cups plastic spoon sandy soil	water

Glossary

compare

When you **compare,** you tell how objects or events are alike and different.

erosion

Erosion is the movement of rocks or soil caused by wind, water, or ice.

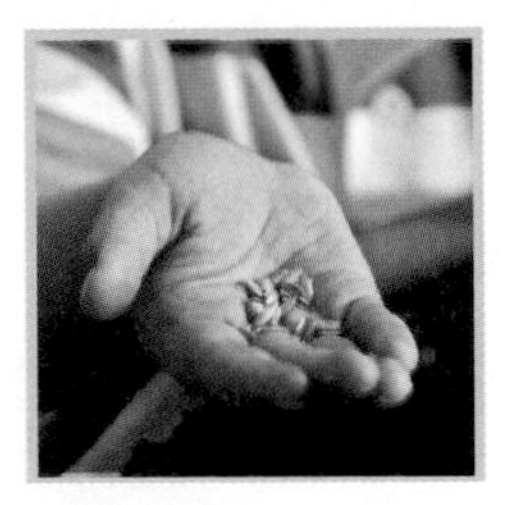

fair test

A **fair test** is when you change only one thing in an investigation and keep everything else the same.

gravity

Gravity is a force that pulls things toward Earth.

humus

Humus is a part of soil. It has bits of decayed plants and animals.

infer

When you **infer,** you use what you know and what you observe to draw a conclusion.

investigate

You **investigate** when you make a plan and carry out the plan to answer a question.

measure

When you **measure,** you find how much or how many.

mineral

A **mineral** is a nonliving material found in nature.

observe

When you **observe,** you use your senses to learn about an object or event.

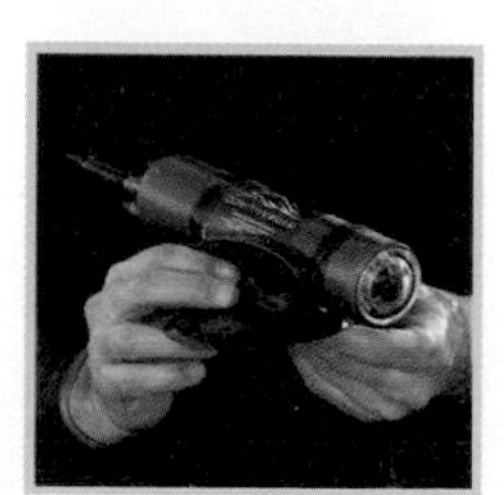

plan

When you make a **plan** to answer a question, you list the materials and steps you need to take.

Glossary

property

A **property** is something about an object that you can observe with your senses.

predict

When you **predict,** you tell what you think will happen.

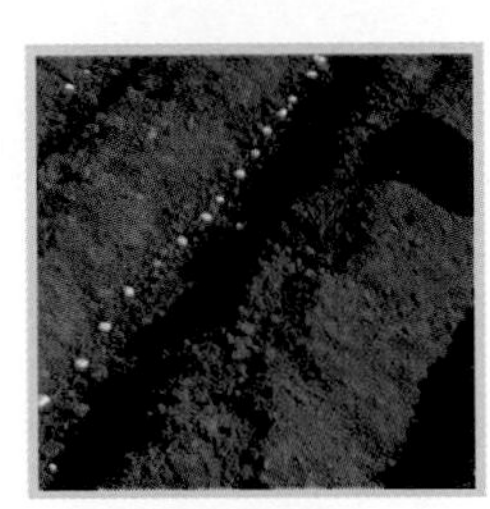

soil

Soil is a layer of loose material that covers part of Earth's surface.

sort

When you **sort,** you put things in groups.

texture

Texture is the way an object feels.

weathering

Weathering is the breaking apart or dissolving of rocks.

Notes

Index

Note: *p* signifies a photograph or drawing; SN refers to the Science Notebook.

S

T

U

V

W

Credits

Acknowledgments

Grateful acknowledgment is given to the authors, artists, photographers, museums, publishers, and agents for permission to reprint copyrighted material. Every effort has been made to secure the appropriate permission. If any omissions have been made or if corrections are required, please contact the Publisher.

Photographic Credits

Teacher's Edition: Cover (t) Taylor S. Kennedy/National Geographic Image Collection, (b) Stefan Auth/imagebroker/Alamy Images; ii–iii (bg) PhotoDisc/Getty Images; iv–v (bg) Radius Images/Photolibrary; vi (t) Albert Moldvay/National Geographic Image Collection, (bl) Taylor S. Kennedy/National Geographic Image Collection, (br) Gordon Wiltsie/National Geographic Image Collection; vii (tl) Paul Nicklen/National Geographic Image Collection, (tr) Bill Hatcher/National Geographic Image Collection, (b) Michael S. Lewis/National Geographic Image Collection; viii–xiv, tabs (bg) Taylor S. Kennedy/National Geographic Image Collection; T1a Mark Mallchok/Brella Productions; T1b (bg, inset) DigitalStock/Corbis; T3 Andrew Henderson/National Geographic Image Collection; T8 Maria Stenzel/National Geographic Image Collection; T15n George F. Mobley/National Geographic Image Collection; T25r Robert S. Patton/National Geographic Image Collection; T40–T41 John Foxx Images/Imagestate.

Big Idea and Vocabulary Cards: Card 1, Front: David Brimm/Alamy Images, Back: (l) Wally Eberhart/Visuals Unlimited, (c) John R. Foster/Photo Researchers, Inc., (r) Visuals Unlimited/Corbis; Card 2, Front: John Foxx Images/Imagestate, Back: (tl) John Foxx Images/Imagestate, (tr) James L. Stanfield/National Geographic Image Collection, (bl) Simon Price/Alamy Images, (br) Anatoly Maltsev/epa/Corbis; Card 3, Front: James L. Stanfield/National Geographic Image Collection, Back: Marvin Dembinsky Photo Associates/Alamy Images; Song Card, Front: Solstice Photography/Brand X Pictures/Jupiterimages, Back: (t) Comstock Images/Jupiterimages/Alamy Images, (c) Pixland/Jupiterimages/Alamy Images, (r) Photoroller/Shutterstock.

Program Authors

Kathy Cabe Trundle, Ph.D., Associate Professor of Early Childhood Science Education, The Ohio State University, Columbus, Ohio; Randy Bell, Ph.D., Associate Professor of Science Education, University of Virginia, Charlottesville, Virginia; Malcolm B. Butler, Ph.D., Associate Professor of Science Education, University of South Florida, St. Petersburg, Florida; Nell K. Duke, Ed.D., Co-Director of the Literacy Achievement Research Center and Professor of Teacher Education and Educational Psychology, Michigan State University, East Lansing, Michigan; Judith Sweeney Lederman, Ph.D., Director of Teacher Education and Associate Professor of Science Education, Department of Mathematics and Science Education, Illinois Institute of Technology, Chicago, Illinois; David W. Moore, Ph.D., Professor of Education, College of Teacher Education and Leadership, Arizona State University, Tempe, Arizona

National Geographic School Publishing
Hampton-Brown
www.NGSP.com

Printed in the USA.
RR Donnelley, Menasha, WI

ISBN: 978-0-7362-6388-7

11 12 13 14 15 16 17

10 9 8 7 6 5 4 3